Kings and Clans

David Newbury

Kings and Clans
Ijwi Island and the
Lake Kivu Rift,
1780–1840

The University of Wisconsin Press

The University of Wisconsin Press
114 North Murray Street
Madison, Wisconsin 53715

3 Henrietta Street
London WC2E 8LU, England

5   4   3   2   1

Printed in the United States of America

Library of Congress Cataloging-in-Publication Data
Newbury, David S.
    Kings and clans: Ijwi Island and the Lake Kivu Rift, 1780-1840 /
David Newbury.
    384 pp.   cm.
    Includes bibliographical references and index.
    ISBN 0-299-12890-3   ISBN 0-299-12894-6 (pbk.)
    1. Havu (African people)—Kings and rulers.   2. Havu (African people)—
Kinship.   3. Havu (African people)—History.   4. Migration, Internal—
Kivu, Lake (Rwanda and Zaire)   5. Clans—Zaire—Ijwi Island—History.
6. Ijwi Island (Zaire)—Politics and government.   7. Ijwi Island (Zaire)—History.
8. Kivu, Lake (Rwanda and Zaire)—History.   I. Title.
DT650.H38N48   1992
967.51'7—dc20   91-28932

Contents

List of Maps, Figures, and Tables

Preface

I first met Ntambuka, the *mwami* of Ijwi, in December of 1970. He was a man in his seventies then, but still extremely active in the affairs of his kingdom. His compound at Rambo, despite its somnolent outward appearance, was a fascinating center of constant visiting, discussion, court cases, and hospitality. But it was only as I came to know the various individuals involved at the court and to perceive even the rough outlines of the cases presented there that I began to appreciate this lively diversity and complexity.

From the very beginning of my research Ntambuka was receptive and helpful. His hospitality went far beyond simply providing lodging to this ignorant stranger who could barely speak the language and knew nothing of the island people among whom he was to live over the next five years. He entertained my questions with a patience, and even an interest, far beyond what his earlier experience with Europeans would have warranted; often he encouraged me to go further in my thinking, correcting my questions and providing intriguing new lines of inquiry to follow up.

And he wanted to be sure I got the record straight; on several occasions while I stayed at the court, he came into my room at Rambo at the first light of day in order to clarify or "correct" a point he felt had been poorly made or left unclear during the previous evening's discussion. He gave me total access to his conversations with his visitors and councillors during these evening séances, and on all other occasions as well. I was free to come and go as my own schedule and interest dictated. Many evenings were spent in this way, with the conversation ranging widely among the five or ten *barhunyi,* and the long shadows thrown up on the wall enhancing the dramatic gestures and consummate turns of phrase; these evening sessions remain some of the most vivid and cherished images for me still.

All members of the court were equally hospitable—as when, shortly after my arrival on the island, the king's wife MwaBisangwa took me to the kitchen to introduce me to the different varieties of newly harvested beans, explaining the growing conditions and preparation of each. Others at the court shared many aspects of their life with me, from children's games and musical instruments to hut construction and court politics.

This could be seen as simply an obvious form of co-optation, and indeed could well have led to my intellectual dependence on the court perspective. I was fully—painfully—aware of this possibility at the beginning, and through the initial stages of contact I remained skeptical of, as well as grateful for, their hospitality. But several factors, over and beyond my own skepticism, transpired to counter that development. One was time: in the end this "original" contact with Ijwi came to span several years (indeed in some respects it continues today), and eventually I became familiar with the island beyond the confines of the court. Another factor was the people of Ijwi themselves. Over time I got to know many of them well. They saw things through their own lenses, very much independently of the court vision. Once they got to know me better—for they were at first skeptical of me, too—many among them were not in the least reluctant to share their views with me. It can be unsettling to a young researcher, set to inquire into "Ijwi's history," to find that there is no such thing: many perceptions of the past were to emerge among Ijwi's polyvariant population. All too quickly it became apparent that there were precious few "traditions" on Ijwi's past, only perspectives, and that the most stimulating observations came not from "encyclopedic informants" but from true historians, reflective people responding thoughtfully to their past and present, on however modest a scale. The analysis to follow derives in great part from my efforts to accept and fully to account for, rather than to deny, the tensions between these different—and often apparently irreconcilable—perspectives.

A further factor which worked against my simply becoming the tool of the court's vision of the past was the king himself. Although I was fully welcomed at the court, the *mwami* made no attempt to impede my research in the hills. As soon as I had even a rudimentary grasp of the language, and had made some acquaintances and obtained an outline of the court's view of Ijwi history, I sought to leave the court milieu and live in the hills. Ntambuka was surprised, but helpful, and finally encouraging. His exile of over 26 years off Ijwi during the colonial period made him quick to realize there were others who had much to add. He always welcomed me at the court after that, but also did whatever he could to facilitate my work outside; and on several occasions, both in public and in private, I heard him strongly defend the work to others. What follows here is not the history of Ijwi as he saw it; but the work could not have been done as it was without his assistance and interest. He was not only a source of aid, encouragement and entertainment; he was also a symbol of why the work should be done at all: an old man quietly loyal to the internal politics and integrity of an island kingdom. Most of all, he was a very good friend, and it is to his memory, and to that of his late wife MwaBisangwa Tegesi, that I dedicate this work.

Many others contributed to this work in important ways; they are far too numerous to name individually here. Some have been noted in the list of persons interviewed, but many others contributed too—younger people and women whom I did not formally interview. I am indebted to all of them. Ntambuka's son Sibula was the first to encourage me to undertake the project, and it was he who introduced me to the island. Since then he has been invariably supportive and helpful, as has his entire family. Projet Ntaganda and Léocadie have aided the project in many ways; my wife and daughter and I, each in various ways, are grateful to them for friendship that is quiet and sure. On Ijwi I especially appreciated the help of Citoyens Sibula, Mudahama, Ntawiniga, Kalegamire, Sangara, Biryasi, Balegamire, Muhamiriza, and Rutega. Among those interviewed whose assistance was particularly helpful were Mugenzi, Ndwanyi, Ciringwe, Ngwasi, Nyamuheshera, Nyenyezi, Rubambiza, Kalwiira, Rwesi, Ndongozi, and Bahiga; it is not just a cliché to say that this is very much their history.

There was another group of young Bany'Iju who took a particular interest in the work and to whom I owe my thanks for help in many ways; they include Citoyens Bavugarije, Byakazi, Bafakolero, and Birora (who, though not himself from Ijwi, was intimately tied to the project). Especially important were those who worked with me for varying lengths of time. Citoyens Miderho, Baderha, and Mbarabukeye participated with intelligence, perseverance, and skill through much of the work; they were most enjoyable colleagues, and I owe them my deepest gratitude. Their interest in the project and personal friendship often sustained me through the difficult periods; the research could not have been done without them. Citoyen (now Abbé) Koko Balegamire also provided assistance and intelligent advice, both in helping with the translations and in many conversations, as did Abbé Cenyange Lubula.

I benefitted also from the intimate knowledge of Ijwi culture and language—as well as from the genial hospitality—of the priests on the island during my time there: Père René van Gansbeke, Père Pierre Croteau, Père Francis duPont, and Père Godefroid Trypsteen. The personnel of CEMUBAC (the Centre d'Etudes Médicales de l'Université de Bruxelles en Afrique Centrale) were invariably helpful and kind. I would particularly like to thank Mlle. G. Willems, Dr. H. Vis, Dr. J. Stanbury, Drs. P. Hennart, P. van Overscheldt, and A. Wayitu, as well as M. M. Caraël for their willing assistance with boat transport and for many other kindnesses.

Off Ijwi, many others were helpful was well. I can name only a few, but I hope others will find here an expression of my thanks. Citoyens Aramazani, Wufela, Birora, Ruzimbuka, and Citoyennes Ntawiniga and Mikekemo helped in many ways. Citoyens Tshimanga, Bishikwabo, and Bucyalimwe of the Institut Supérieur Pédagogique and M. Joseph Rwabukumba provided valuable advice in many discussions. Dr. Peter Kunkel, the former Directeur Général of the Institut pour la Recherche Scientifique en Afrique Centrale (IRSAC), was extremely helpful in the initial stages of the work and his successor, Citoyen Ntika-Nkumu, also allowed me the use of many facilities of IRSAC. In Rwanda as in Belgium, Marcel d'Hertefelt, the acting director of the Institut National de Recherche Scientifique, provided valuable assistance in all stages of this project; I enjoyed many stimulating and challenging discussions with him, and am grateful for his hospitality on many occasions. Professor André Coupez willingly answered my questions on linguistic matters. In Brussels, Jeanine Ntawiniga and the late Dr. André Aramazani, whose death has been a sad loss to Zairean (and particularly to Ijwi) scholarship, provided warm fellowship, intelligent companionship, and many happy moments. Ola Pawlowska has shown a steadfast interest in the project and provided thoughtful assistance in many ways over the years.

During the research I also benefitted from the intellectual stimulation and guidance of many others. I shared many enjoyable and enlightening conversations with Jacques Depelchin, Pauline Depelchin, Elinor Sosne, Richard Sigwalt, and Randall Packard. Mr. Robert Depelchin lodged my wife and me at Uvira while we undertook archival research there; our warmest thanks for his exuberant hospitality. At Makerere University in Kampala, Bertin Webster, Donald Denoon, and Keith Rennie were always kind hosts. I am particularly grateful to Dr. Rennie for his interest and encouragement and for many valuable insights during the early stages of the project. Conversations with David Cohen and Jim Freedman proved very valuable, also, during the later stages of sorting out my ideas on Ijwi history. Valentin Mudimbe, Elizabeth Boyi, Bogumil Jewsiewicki, Jean-Luc Vellut, David Henige, Tim Shaw, and Marcia Wright all lent friendship and support along the way, in ways they may not even be aware of—but then again, they may.

At the University of Wisconsin, the comments and advice of Professors Steven Feierman and Jan Vansina have also been very helpful. Professor Feierman's breadth of scholarship and incisive commentary have helped sharpen my own conceptual framework in many ways; I am grateful for his guidance. But my primary intellectual debt is to Jan Vansina, whose continuing enthusiasm and vast knowledge have been a source of inspiration throughout the project. I owe him my deepest thanks for his roles as scholar, teacher, and friend—and to Claudine for her deep appreciation of Africa and her calm strength in seeing so many students through a turbulent time of their lives. Rich Sigwalt, Tom Spear, Randall Packard, Bob Harms and others have also provided supportive criticism and critical support along the way. Their comments on the work at various stages have been most helpful.

There is one other person whose encouragement, support, ideas, and criticism have sustained this work from its inception. Despite the pressures of her own career and the demands of her own research, my wife, Catharine, has always lent a willing ear and a ready critique. On several occasions she took time from her own writing to join me in the fieldwork. Even in the writing stage, though we were often far removed from each other by the vagaries of separate teaching commitments, she has shared in the challenge and growth of a study taking shape. In its final form, it is not the way she would have written it; but it is not the way I would have written it, either, without her interest in it. To her, and to our daughter Elizabeth, go my deepest affection and respect.

Kings and Clans

Introduction

The Issues

Early in the nineteenth century, a man named Mwendanga arrived on Ijwi Island in Lake Kivu. He became the first of the Basibula dynasty of kings on the island. He came with ritualists of several clans—Baziralo, Bashaho, Banyambiriri, and others. Together, they established a kingdom.

This is the way kingship is commonly explained on Ijwi Island today. In such form, the origin of kingship on Ijwi appears as a cliché common to many societies of Africa—the state was created whole by the arrival of a king and his ritualists from outside. The focus is on the royal family; the history of others as active participants in the establishment of kingship is unimportant.

But this is more an assumption than a history; even the royal family lacks any comprehensive tradition on the establishment of kingship on Ijwi. In fact, there were many important alterations within Ijwi society associated with—and essential to—the transition to kingship, and these alterations preceded as well as followed the arrival of the royal family. Therefore an explanation of the nature of kingship on Ijwi need account for the changing social context which gave rise to the institutions of royalty on the island rather than focus exclusively on how the royal family integrated various pre-existing groups into the structures of kingship imported from outside.

This book seeks to understand how the changes that occurred in the area of Lake Kivu during the late eighteenth and early nineteenth centuries affected political developments on Ijwi. It examines two problems in particular: the integration of kingship norms into a changing society, and the relationship of changing clan identities to the process of political centralization. While governmental institutions such as those of kingship can be antagonistic to strong clan identifications, few studies of pre-colonial East Africa have considered the dynamic nature of the interactions between kingship and clanship. Data from the Lake Kivu Rift Valley, however, suggest that when examined historically the relationship between political power and social identity is more fluid, complex, and ambiguous than is often acknowledged—and that clan identities are more contextual than is often recognized.

Conventionally, the two concepts of kingship and clanship have been treated as distinct from each other, both in organization and in importance.

3

Kingship involves centralized and sovereign authority and usually includes delegated political powers within a hierarchical framework. Clan membership, on the other hand, is usually thought to be determined by internal criteria independent of the larger social context: ascribed status based on putative descent from a common ancestor, common exogamous functions, shared totems, and other ritual or social functions which concern the group as a whole. Because clans are often seen as unchanging structures, present-day clans are sometimes portrayed as having served as pre-dynastic political units, formerly exercising many of the political functions now performed by state structures. Therefore kingship and clanship are presumed to succeed each other in time, more or less as they supersede each other structurally. In this view, current clan structures are seen as the anachronistic residue of earlier political units, and recourse to clan identities is assumed to be only an atavistic response to political pressures.

The present work adopts a different perspective. On Ijwi there are many differences between clans in their organizational structures today, and even within any one clan there has been significant variation over time. Part of the purpose of this study will be to inquire into how this variation occurred, and to identify the historical factors which affected the changing clan identities within which people on Ijwi interacted. In the process we will re-examine the concepts by which clans are assumed to be everywhere identical in their internal composition, and consistent and unchanging through time.

Historically, clans do not appear as obstacles to the growth of wider political structures and ideologies on Ijwi, but as products of that growth. New clan identities coalesced at precisely that time when political competition was most intense; in fact, such cohesion may well have provided assured support (based on ascribed status) for competing factions in the emergent political arena. Therefore in this study kingship and clanship will be seen as different aspects of a single larger process, that is, as complementary as well as opposed concepts. On Ijwi each has been defined historically by the presence of the other: current clan identities were consolidated within the context of kingship, but kingship in turn (defined, as it is, predominantly in ritual terms) has meaning only within the broader clan structure of the island.

Historically and conceptually, therefore, kingship and clanship are dialectically related to each other; each is defined by the other and stands in opposition to the other, but together they form a single social field. To delineate the dynamic processes of this relationship, the analysis will focus on four inter-related themes: the changing nature of group identity on Ijwi; the changing contours of regional and local social processes which influenced institutional development; the specific political changes associated with the emergence of kingship on the island; and the cultural construction of clan identities and ritual forms as these evolved in the context of other transformations.

The Argument

There is no agreed definition of "clan" today in the anthropological literature. Nor has there ever been.[1] In the past, three intellectual problems proved to be serious obstacles to understanding this phenomenon. One was a tendency to equate definition with understanding. If defining an institution means understanding it, the search for a clear and consistent definition becomes the object of study. But no such clear and consistent definition of clan is possible, even within the Ijwi context alone. A second obstacle was the presumption of "internal tribal homogeneity"—the assumption that within a "tribal" category all social organization of a given type must be identical, ordered from above along the formal lines of a bureaucratic model. But cultural units are historical constructions, not "logical" designs; internal homogeneity among such units is rare.[2] The third obstacle was the assumption of institutional stasis—that these social institutions did not change over time; this assumption has never been adequately tested against the data.[3]

This work eschews the definitional approach to understanding social phenomena and illustrates the fallacy of presumed internal cultural homogeneity. It focusses on the third problem noted above: instead of searching for a static and consistent definition of clans, it seeks to understand the dynamics of social identities. It views clan identities and the actions based on them as individual social constructs, each formed under its own specific conditions and fully capable of changing, rather than as primordial givens. By situating clan identities within a wider historical framework than is normally the case, this study underscores both the cultural and temporal relativity of such social identities.

Within the present context of kingship on Ijwi, the largest social identity group is the "clan," *ishanja* (pl. *mashanja*) in Kihavu. The term *"ishanja,"* however, can refer to different levels of social identity and to different types of groups when judged by internal criteria. Even within any given clan there are sometimes important differences. The Balega, for example, currently form one of the largest clans on the island and include several clearly identifiable subgroups, distinguished from each other by distinct regional or historical criteria. Some of these subgroups (such as the Booze or the Babambo) have a strong sense of historical identity and form coherent social groups with recognized leadership; they also have defined territorial interests and certain religious or ritual functions. In these respects they differ from other Balega: The great majority of Balega have no local territorial focus; they have no claims to a common historical origin or to common migration patterns;

they acknowledge no clan head, no corporate functions, and no common totems; they participate in no common religious ceremonies; they do not claim to be descendants of a single common ancestor; they do not form an exogamous unit; they have no internal political functions (such as assigning land rights or assuming juridical functions in minor disputes); they do not share a common relationship to other clan units. They share only a common clan name. Thus neither internal coherence nor structural regularities are to be found among the different clan categories on Ijwi; in these respects they are similar to most other clans of the region.

Historically, too, these *ishanja* units show important variations in terms of both external identity (relations with others) and internal features. Such changes over time provide the principal thread of analysis in this book. In this analysis, the external components of clan identity, or the identity of one group relative to other similar groups, will be given more attention than internal constituents of identity (genealogies, land use, religious functions), both because they are seen as ultimately more important and because it is impossible to ascertain with any precision just what were these internal components of clan identity (or, indeed, if they held any signficance at all) at a time remove of 150–200 years.

But the focus here is not on clan categories for their own sake. Rather, these changing constituents are important for the role they play within the larger process of a changing political field on Ijwi. Thus in reassessing the relationship of political centralization to increasing social differentiation, this study will re-examine the arbitrary division between the social and the political domains. It will look at both as complementary and interwoven aspects of a single historical process. Such an approach is based on the premise that social identities are the essence of political action, and that political perceptions are fundamental to social identities.

The nature of political changes associated with the emergence of kingship on Ijwi Island, in Lake Kivu, therefore forms a second major concern of the book. Members of the present dynasty arrived on Ijwi in the early nineteenth century. They came essentially as political refugees, with no evident direct political support on the island. Although other people appear to have arrived from the mainland at roughly the same time, there is no indication that this royal family conquered Ijwi by military might or weight of numbers. Instead, a more plausible hypothesis on the formation of royalty emerges from the patterns of change occurring as Ijwi society restructured itself to meet new demands from an influx of immigrants. A new kingdom emerged on Ijwi not because institutions were imposed from outside and not from some collective need to bring "order out of chaos"; receptivity to royalty on Ijwi resulted from the nature of changing social relations on the island.

Accordingly, this work is not a conventional study of state formation, just as it is not a study of clan organization abstracted from social process. In a sense it transcends, and thus to some degree brings into question, the state formation hypotheses of earlier studies. Rather than focusing on the expansion of the power of the central court on Ijwi, this study explores a new approach to understanding the process of political consolidation: it re-examines the social transformations that preceded (and made possible) the establishment of the institutions of royalty.

Earlier works on state formation in Africa tended to privilege one aspect of the process: conquest by external actors or social alliances forged among clan units. This analysis denies neither external influences nor internal alliances. Instead, it seeks to place each in a wider historical frame of reference: rather than treat military power and social alliance as autonomous phenomena, it seeks to explain such political resources and alliances within an analytic context which accounts for a broader range of population segments. In such a perspective the study of state formation dissolves into social history; understanding institutional change requires an explanation of social process on a broader scale than is usually undertaken.

I have tried neither to neglect the reality of royal power nor to glorify it by presenting it as an isolated field of study in itself. To do so would not be conceptually justified or empirically valid, for many factors enter into the process of institutional consolidation. More important than royal power alone were the relationships forged among different kinds of power and the limitations which each placed on the other in the course of their interaction. Ultimately it was the relations among these different kinds of power—material, ritual, social, ethical, and conceptual—which carved out the essential parameters of the social context of the day. It is worth inquiring into the nature of these relationships; that is what I have tried to do here.

This concept of social context is something very different from a static ethnographic background to "real" political action. Indeed these changing relationships—the changing social context—not only "created" the kingdom by making royal power appear logical to the people of the culture; it also constrained the growth of the kingdom, channelling royal power along the lines of hegemony forged by the conjunction of institutions of royalty and social constructs. An analysis of clan roles in promoting this receptivity to royalty on the island, an exploration of clan participation in the public rituals of royalty (along with their implicit threat to withhold such participation), and an examination of succession struggles (especially the importance of local factors in influencing the outcome of such struggles) all illustrate the potential of channelling state power.

From this perspective, kingship was a product of many independent initiatives taken by the inhabitants of the island; it was not simply a product of the individual guile or collective force of new arrivals from the outside. Neither force nor guile was absent, of course; but they alone do not adequately explain what happened. This book examines the various ways by which the people of Ijwi integrated kingship within the emerging concepts of a widening social field and made the royal court a focal point of social interaction for the island as a whole. Nonetheless the court did not simply replace earlier forms of interaction. It altered these patterns of interaction in some ways, but it also strengthened and reinforced them. In so doing, it redefined—and in some cases, created—clan identities, by making them significant in the contemporary terms of ongoing social interaction, as well as in historical terms.

Change of this type, however, was neither ordered nor homogeneous. Kingship was created by societal changes, but it did not benefit all social groups equally. What happened on Ijwi, therefore, was not simply a process of "enlargement of scale." It also included structural transformations within Ijwi society, and thus re-created or redefined the nature of society on Ijwi. It is this structural transformation and the ways in which the new concepts of identity affected the island's eventual receptivity to royalty which will serve as the focus of this book.

Although this study is phrased in the idiom of historical inquiry, with a focus on the analysis of specific social change, there are two aspects of the Ijwi experience I wish to address at a more general level. One of those deals with the way in which a fundamental category of social identity—that of clan definition—is reconceptualized; this concern is considered at greater length in the Conclusion. The second theoretical issue pursued in this work concerns the role of ritual in understanding historical process. As with the perception of clans, the analysis of ritual performance has too often excised this form of collective expression from the specific historical conditions which give it meaning. Functionalist analysis reduces ritual to a surrogate for scientific reasoning. Some forms of structuralist analysis treat ritual only as the expression of primordial logical categories, as largely autonomous of social context and historical specificity. Both approaches have contributed in important ways to our understanding of certain features of ritual. But taken alone, each impoverishes our understanding by removing ritual performance from the specific conditions and context that make it meaningful to the participants. Although this analysis draws on insights from both traditions, it defines the contours of ritual understanding differently, placing greater emphasis on understanding the particular historical context within which ritual is performed. Specifically, it treats the royal ritual of Muganuro—the First Fruits ceremony on Ijwi Island—as both a product of history and an expression of that history.

Thus this work attempts not simply to reconstruct political events, not

simply to identify the contours of social process, but also to explore an important dimension of cultural dynamics over this vast region. Kingship is defined by the local population on Ijwi largely in ritual terms. Therefore to
understand the nature of kingship on Ijwi one must explore the meaning of
the rituals. The Muganuro ceremony is the most important annual ritual of
kingship on the island, held at the time of the first sorghum harvest, in late
February or early March. The performance of this ritual defines not just
kingship in the abstract but also, more specifically, the relationship of the
court to the population at large. At the same time it reinforces the meaning of
clan functions and identities within the context of kingship. Legitimate kingship exists only because clan leaders perform the prescribed ritual functions
which make kingship possible. But clans exist as coherent entities only because they participate in certain ways to validate kingship. Thus the Muganuro
ceremony illustrates the symbiotic relationship between kingship and clanship—both at a single moment and historically over time.

However, the analysis of the Muganuro ceremony does more, for it also
reflects the regional contours that have influenced Ijwi history. It is a ceremony which draws not only on local practices and beliefs but also on cultural
traditions shared with many societies in the region, both east and west of
Lake Kivu. Muganuro therefore defines Ijwi kingship as sovereign, but also
validates Ijwi kingship as a full participant in the structures of kingship
throughout the region. It thus illustrates one of the more ambiguous aspects
of sovereignty: acceptance within the wider political community beyond the
kingdom. Comparing regional variants of this ritual, as I have tried to do
here, reconfirms the importance of viewing kingship and social process on
Ijwi within a historical arena which encompasses the region as a whole.
Hence this analysis seeks to reinstate a cultural dimension to understanding
social process and to historical method.

The Intellectual Foundations

This book is a study in social change. But social change of course does not
happen in a vacuum. It can be understood only by situating social process
within the wider cultural and historical context, with history and culture seen
not as abstract forces guiding people's actions but as universes of action—the
domains within which such actions take place—as well as products of social
change. It is this cultural inheritance that gives meaning to people's actions;
therefore it is necessary to understand the wider cultural context if we are also
to understand the patterns, actions, and ideas that together constitute "history." As Sahlins notes: "History is culturally ordered, differently so in different societies, according to meaningful schemes of things."[4]

Recent research on Africa has been dominated by analytic paradigms associated with social history, and with good reason. We have sought to avoid the tendency to reify institutions or to equate ideology with action. We have sought to understand the effect of the decisions of outsiders on the lives of African people, and to distinguish the social reality of colonial power—or any centralized power imposed from above—from the conscious (but more often "rationalized") intentions of those in power. We have sought to understand how different people—of different genders, different classes, different communities, different cultural categories—actually live their lives. And we have sought to apply the understanding of social process produced by such an approach to the lives of people who are otherwise not given voice—those whom Wolf refers to as "the people without history," recalling both anthropologists' lack of historical sensitivity and historians' conventional neglect of cultures and classes of people without written traditions.[5]

But social history itself is not sufficient to explain, or even to understand, people's actions. To account for the perceptions, goals, and resources by which lived history was produced, we need to understand how it was that such actions seemed reasonable, desirable, and possible to the actors themselves. In its interpretation, therefore, social history often of necessity becomes cultural history, and increasingly, not just in Africa but in many areas of the world, social history is being studied within the larger context of cultural understanding.[6] The works of Emmanuel Le Roy Ladurie and Natalie Zemon Davis provide well-known examples of this trend for French history. In the United States, studies of the local community have considered a wide range of factors—changes in ecology, religion, marriage strategies, land ownership and farming techniques, family structures, witchcraft beliefs, and many other aspects of cultural experience—which together help define social differences.[7]

In other areas of the world, too, similar patterns of inquiry have been fruitful. In Latin America, for example, Michael Taussig's work focusses on workers of two quite different social formations, one in Colombia, one in Bolivia. Their perceptions of their own changing social conditions, Taussig suggests, derived from the way these people were situated within the larger structures of emergent capitalist relations and capitalist forms of production. But to understand their characterizations of their own history required understanding the basic principles of their moral economy outside the domain of "commodity fetishism" characteristic of mature capitalism. "No matter how painstaking we are in charting the chronology of history's great events . . . we will remain blind to history's great lesson both for society and for the future unless we include the imagination of power [the way in which the actors perceived power] as well as the power of the collective imagination."[8]

In southern Africa, Jean Comaroff's study of the Baralong-Tshidi draws on a variety of theoretical works to illuminate the ambiguities of Tshidi forms of cultural expression, focussing particularly on the proliferation of locally based, independent Christian churches among these people caught in the contradictions and paradoxes of capitalist development within an apartheid state.

> The process of articulation [between the Tshidi world and the colonial order] involved neither a mechanical supersession of the institutions of the industrial world nor the obliteration of indigenous forms; and it cannot be represented as a neat transition from precapitalist to capitalist modes. Rather, it operated within the logic of existing peripheral structures to transform them, ordering relations between their component elements and undermining prevailing arrangements. In so doing, it also reproduced and elaborated certain internal relations, changing their role within the social system itself. In this way, novel formations which were neither "traditional" nor "capitalist" . . . developed within the colonial arena. . . ."[9]

In a very suggestive fashion, she proceeds to discuss the "simultaneous reproduction and transformation of precolonial forms, giving rise to novel structures which challenge the dualist categories of conventional social science.[10]

This study of historical process in the Kivu Rift Valley retains Comaroff's skepticism towards conventional "dualist categories" and inquires into analogous processes of "reproduction and transformation" of cultural forms ("the process through which persons, acting upon an external environment, construct themselves as social beings"[11]), though it draws on a wider geographical range and seeks to analyze these processes at a much greater time depth. To do so is to risk losing some of the specificity and detail of the Tshidi study; but the similarity of interpretative approach, independently arrived at and applied to such different contexts, is nonetheless suggestive. Indeed, the similarities apply not only to general cultural interests but to specific cultural phenomena as well. Comaroff portrays the simultaneous ambiguity and conceptual coherence in the Zionist movements among the Tshidi in a fashion analogous to the way I understand the royal rituals of an emergent political order: "This religious movement, then, must be understood as a unique socio-cultural phenomenon, a dynamic construction wrought by the universal process of symbolic mediation working itself out in a specific historical context; as such it is simultaneously unique and yet an instance of a very general class of social movements."[12]

Elsewhere, too, recent studies have privileged the cultural foundations to social action. Elizabeth Traube's elegant study of ritual exchange among the Mambai of East Timor, for example, provides not only an intriguing introduction to the Mambai—written, as it is, in a very personal mode—but equally, a thoughtful assessment of the conceptual framework by which these cultural foundations are made accessible. In this case those cultural foundations consist of ritual performance; in fact, the Mambai consider themselves the guardians of the essential ritual of origins for all humanity. And once again, Traube's interests parallel the interests of a portion of this work:

> The fundamental problem [investigated here] is the relationship of symbolic categories to social action. . . . When symbolic schemes are insubstantiated in the unfolding of ritual processes, participants renew their understanding of the ties that bind them to others. In short, what are reproduced and strengthened in ritual performances are meaningful relations.[13]

In his work on Hawaii, Sahlins, too, concludes that cultural categories are essential for understanding specific social phenomena:

> The event (any event) unfolds simultaneously on two levels: as individual action and as collective representation; or better, as the *relation* between certain life histories and a history that is, over and above these, the existence of societies. To paraphrase Clifford Geertz, the event is a unique actualization of a general phenomenon.[14]

Finally, in a study that (among those mentioned here) most closely approaches the present work in structure and focus, Maurice Bloch discusses the circumcision rituals among the Imerina of Madagascar, describing them as he saw them performed, locating them within Imerina historical process, and tracing their evolution in the changing context of state power. What is remarkable about Bloch's study is that it draws on data dating from almost 200 years ago—and certainly from over 150 years distant—which relate directly to the circumcision ritual and which strongly suggest that there has been little substantive change in the internal components of this ritual performance over that time. The episodes, materiel, and instruments of the performance, the symbolism drawn on, the actors, and the social relations salient to these ritual structures—Bloch suggests that as far as can be determined none has shown any significant change over the last 200 years or so, despite the fact that this period witnessed dramatic and important transformations in other aspects of Imerina society.[15]

Many others of course have postulated ritual conservatism before. But Bloch advances an argument on the historicity of ritual based, not on assumptions of ritual atavism, but on contextual adaptability: that the external "functional" role of this ritual in Imerina culture was transformed several times over during that period, from a modest family ritual, to an elaborate royal ceremony—used by royalty for very specific political ends—to a reduced but still "national" observation, to a small-scale, semi-secret, local-level rite (during the height of colonial rule), to a renewed and revived public festivity with anti-Christian, anti-colonial, and anti-elite overtones. Bloch thus argues for examining the history of the ritual (at least in this case) not in terms of its internal content but in terms of its role in defining and articulating external, contextual relations: in assessing the meaning of ritual in former periods, "it is not . . . a question of trying to grasp the nature of the phenomenon by searching for what it means for the participants but by analysing how the ritual is manifested in history."[16]

Similarly on Ijwi, the cultural materials, the basic units of meaning from which these people forged their own society and carved their own patterns of historical change, were units shared widely in the region. What distinguished Ijwi from other areas—and set out the themes of Ijwi social change—was how those elements were combined and recombined to construct and reconstruct, to produce and reproduce, a social and ritual universe specific to Ijwi. As Bloch notes for the Imerina: "What we are seeking therefore when we try to understand how events construct culture are not rules of formation from a zero-point but rules of transformation of an already existing system. . . . History has no beginning: people always act in a world constructed by previous generations."[17] And as it was with Imerina ritual, so it was too with Ijwi royalty.

The Objectives

These works—and they are but representative of a wider genre—carry important theoretical implications. They illustrate how cultural history can illuminate social process and enhance the study of social history. But in all of them, the focus is on a central cultural phenomenon; social process and historical context are used to explain this phenomenon. Again, as Sahlins notes: "History is culturally ordered. . . . [But] the converse is also true: cultural schemes are historically ordered, since to a greater or lesser extent the meanings are reworked as they are practically enacted."[18]

This study differs in its emphasis. The focus here is not on the general analysis of ritual performance, but on the understanding of historical process in the Kivu Rift Valley during the early nineteenth century. I draw on a specific form of ritual performance—on an analysis of the public ceremony and the social categories associated with it—as both expression of and product of that changing historical field, and on the evolving perceptions of social identity. Because my central concern is to identify broader patterns of historical change, this book differs in its organization from other recent books on cultural history, noted above. It addresses directly the analysis of social process, not as background to some other objective, but as subject in itself; the discussion of ritual in chapter 12 is used to comment on, not to provide a rationale for, the discussion of historical process. Secondly, this is not a study of "culture without politics," nor does it treat culture as a sanitized surrogate for understanding political confrontation and the flow of power in society.[19] Instead, the analysis presented here seeks to situate changing cultural concepts of self-identity within a larger social field which includes political power, alliance, and ambiguity. Finally, the book ends, rather than opens, with a discussion of the theoretical implications of the study. In the course of this discussion I seek to locate this work and the nature of Ijwi social process within the current understanding of social phenomena, but the major objective is not to comment on a body of theoretical work as such, nor to develop a theory of social change abstracted from political context.

Instead, the analytic approach adopted here has three major objectives. At one level, the book presents a body of empirical data drawn from an area where little scholarly research had previously been undertaken. But this is more than simply "filling in the map" of African history; it is not the presentation of data alone which guides this work. At a second level, the analytic forms brought to bear on these data suggest new ways of interpreting and analyzing existing bodies of data from neighboring areas, both in Rwanda and Zaire—and perhaps for areas elsewhere as well. Such an approach requires accounting for (as opposed to synthesizing) variants within the data; confrontation and differentiation—but not necessarily resistance—are seen here as integral to the process of centralization. The approach also requires engaging in broad regional comparisons within a historical framework; this is intended as very much a regional study, but one which, at the same time, accounts for the specific local social determinants of oral data. Finally, this book argues for the need to consider a broader spectrum of the total cultural universe experienced by the actors of the day than is usually the case, for articulating history is not carried out in verbal (or written) forms of expression alone. Simply by virtue of being products of past social process, many cultural forms of expression encapsulate the legacy of social process and thus serve as "historical evidence in spite of themselves," in Marc Bloc's famous dictum. To limit ourselves to verbal forms of expression is in effect to limit ourselves only to conscious forms of historical process—forms which are readily susceptible to hegemonic perceptions and elite views of history.

The analytic dimension of this study has a more specific application as well. In the past, the Kivu Rift Valley has generally been dismissed as simply peripheral to powerful political centers nearby—Bushi to the southwest and Rwanda to the east, centers accepted as more "important" in the colonial context.[20] The domination of such political formations in the colonial and post-colonial periods, and their consequent domination of research perspectives, has led to the assumption that all major historical action has derived from these areas—that "history" is a concrete, quasi-physical characteristic, a specific cultural trait diffused from certain generating points. To be sure, the view from the periphery may not provide a total image of history in the dominant centers. But it is nonetheless a necessary element in understanding the history of more powerful units, not least as a means of circumventing the intellectual hegemony associated with the reproduction of social stratification in such highly centralized polities.[21]

But the most important dimensions of this work are in the arguments advanced at a conceptual level: this study seeks to reassess our perception of certain basic categories of African social organization—clan identities—as these have been accepted in the literature, past and current, in scholarly as well as in popular work. The data from Ijwi challenge three interpretations which are prevalent but largely unexplored. First, it is clear that clan formations were not primordial units; instead they evolved markedly over time. Second, clan structures were not opposed in any simplistic fashion to the establishment of a dynamic political order; instead they contributed directly to political change. Third, increasing clan differentiation, at one level, accompanied and facilitated the process of increased political centralization at another level; on Ijwi, at least, these two forms of hegemony reinforced each other.[22]

The Methods

The historical data on which this book is based are drawn primarily from oral interviews conducted in all parts of the island over various periods totalling about 10 months, during the years 1972–1975. Interviews on Ijwi were conducted in the Kihavu language and were carried out mostly with older men, from all clans and in all regions of the island. I tried to interview at least one member of each clan from each of the administrative villages on the island, but did not limit myself to them alone. For each interview an attempt was made to tailor questions to the particular locale, clan, or historical background, varying with each person. Interviews were also carried out on the mainland, both in Zaire (especially in the Havu and Tembo areas, but among Hunde and Shi as well) and in Rwanda.[23]

In addition to the historical interviews, I tried to inform myself through a variety of other techniques, including some structured interviews. Linguistic data were collected through Swadesh word lists, and clan statistics were compiled for every village. On Ijwi, village surveys were carried out with 100 percent male samples in three villages selected on specially determined contrasting criteria—age, clan homogeneity, size, and region. These surveys included questions on family composition, marriages, land, cattle, commerce, and religion. Special interviews were also conducted among a 40 percent sample of village capitas. One of the most valuable aspects of the research was the time spent at the royal court and living in the compounds of non-royals in all parts of the island. But in addition, I consulted materials in governmental archives in Zaire at every level—*collectivité, zone, sous-région,* and *région*—and among a variety of missionary archives of the area. Colonial archives were also consulted in Brussels.

The Organization of the Book

Kings and Clans reconstructs the history of the Kivu Rift Valley, now the border between Rwanda and Zaire, for the late eighteenth and early nineteenth centuries. This was a critical time, during which the intersection of many factors set the social contours which characterized the region at the time of European arrival; it was a time which produced the basic constructs of what became known as traditional society. Ecological transformations, the expansion of the Rwandan state structures into the Kivu Rift from the east, influences from the south (from the areas around Lake Tanganyika and from Burundi), the establishment of new political units west of Lake Kivu (in what is now Zaire), and the movement of many population groups all intersected in the development of these new forms of social relations. But the important transformation in the creation of "traditional society" on Ijwi Island was the formation of new social identities and new forms of political relations which led to the emergence of the new kingdom. This study explains how these and other social processes converged to that end.

The Kivu Rift today (and its immediate western hinterland) forms a divide between two of Africa's major culture zones. The mountains just west of the lake delineate the approximate western edge of the vast Interlacustrine culture zone stretching east to the Nile and south to Lake Tanganyika. Though there are significant variations included within the region, this zone is characterized by highly centralized polities, a marked degree of social stratification, and mixed economies (based on raising cattle as well as on agricultural production). This vast culture complex included a series of powerful states (among them Buganda, Bunyoro, Nkore, Karagwe, Rwanda, and Burundi), as a well as a plethora of smaller political units scattered throughout the region. To the west of the Rift today, the Mitumba Mountains define the eastern ramparts of an equally vast ecological zone associated with the forest areas of the Zaire River Basin. Although a wide range of social forms are found there, in the past most were marked by a relatively egalitarian political order, low levels of social hierarchy, a relatively high degree of mobility (both geographic and social), and economies based predominantly on gathering, trapping, fishing, and hunting.

Over the course of the eighteenth and nineteenth centuries the defining limits to these two vast culture zones shifted from east of Lake Kivu (200 years ago, what is now western Rwanda was clearly part of the forest culture zone) to west of the lake. Ijwi Island, in Lake Kivu, was within this transition zone; in fact the social changes on Ijwi discussed here were related to this broader ecological shift. Rather than a periphery, therefore, this area can be seen in historical terms as an important transition zone—and the people as significant mediators between the two major culture zones of central Africa. Tracing the historical outlines of interchange across this cultural divide provides an important rationale for this study.

Nonetheless, although the analysis as a whole makes sense only as a regional study, for clarity I concentrate on one particular locale. Ijwi Island, which included a population of about 50,000 at the time of the research, provided a clearly defined unit both geographically and socially, representative of political structures formerly more widely spread in the region. In the early 1970s, it was one of the few functioning kingdoms remaining in the area with any significant degree of internal coherence; the king on the island was young enough to be interested still in the affairs of his kingdom, but too old to participate actively in the politics of the larger Zairean state. He was simply the *mwami* of Ijwi.

The analysis is presented in three parts, each dealing with a different context within which Ijwi history evolved: the wider region, the island as a unit, and the Ijwi royal court. Each part also considers a different historical issue: the regional components of Ijwi history, the social transformations on the island just before the arrival of the royal family, and the political mechanisms by which the kingdom was established (among them the use of force, the creation of alliances, the co-optation of pre-existing ritual traditions, and the control of ritual hegemony). Although presented separately here, it is obvious that the factors present at one level of analysis were always at work in the others as well; there is a constant interplay in Ijwi history, as in all history, between wider regional trends, structural influences from within society, and short-term events.

Chapter 1 situates Ijwi Island within the wider region and provides a descriptive introduction to the basic features of life on the island at the time of the research. The second chapter identifies some of the forest-culture features present in Kivu Rift societies of the mid-eighteenth century. For this time remove, the data do not permit any precise historical reconstruction. Nonetheless, the Kivu Rift Valley formed a coherent cultural field at that time, and many of the elements more recently associated with "forest cultures" were also present in the social organization on Ijwi and widely throughout the region 200 years ago. By reaching back as far as ethnographic and oral sources allow, chapter 2 explores the common elements of this Rift Valley "prototype society" and establishes its range both east and west of the lake.

The model of this reconstructed Kivu Prototype Society both serves as a cultural baseline for the analysis to follow and provides a framework for understanding the sparse oral sources relating to this period on Ijwi Island discussed in chapter 3. After tracing out the mid-eighteenth-century patterns of social identity on Ijwi, chapter 3 concludes by considering the essential processes by which new identities were forged.

The next four chapters discuss the evolution of Ijwi society before the arrival of the royal family. Chapter 4 focusses on the area immediately east of Lake Kivu; it considers changes that occurred in the Kivu Prototype Society there, and examines the conditions which led some groups to settle on Ijwi from the east. It traces the intrusion of Rwandan state power into the area west of the mountainous Nile-Zaire Divide, and considers the effect of this political realignment on the people living east of the lake. The early histories of two Ijwi clans, the Banyakabwa and the Beshaza, are drawn on as illustrative of this process in chapter 5.

Chapters 6 and 7 examine the significance of these developments for the emergence of kingship on Ijwi. Each chapter focusses on a particular immigrant group (the Banyambiriri in chapter 6 and the Baziralo in chapter 7), illustrating their patterns of settlement and their relations with other groups on the island, and analyzing the historical construction of the ritual roles they assumed within Ijwi royalty. By focussing on these two groups, the two chapters also explore the cultural legacy of continuing social ties between Ijwi and areas east of the lake into the nineteenth century, ties which were instrumental in defining the later participatory roles of such groups within the changing political context on the island. These two chapters also illustrate the essential "puzzle" regarding relations between clan groups and royal power: that the most important ritual clans on Ijwi were neither the oldest nor the largest, nor did they hold the strongest historical claims to royal status off the island.

Chapters 8–12 consider the arrival of the Basibula family and their establishment as royalty on Ijwi. The earliest direct traditions available on the Basibula locate them at the southern end of Lake Kivu. But other indications emphasize linkages of Kivu Rift history at this time with areas farther south still. So once again regional considerations—this time with the area between Lakes Kivu and Tanganyika—are brought into play to understand later transformations occurring on Ijwi Island.

But the establishment of kingship is not the same as the arrival of the royal family. Part 3 considers the manner in which a new kingdom was established in a social context independent of earlier traditions of kingship. The argument, of course, draws on the material presented in earlier chapters, but the analysis in this section of the work focusses on the specific policies and processes by which a new political order was forged. Taken together these chapters assess four principal mechanisms by which the Basibula came to be accepted as royalty on Ijwi: their relations to recent arrivals on the island (chapter 9), their alliances, particularly marriage alliances, with those already there (chapter 10), their ties off the island and the significance of those ties for understanding the material basis of royal establishment (chapter 11), and—particularly important—the manner in which royal ritual facilitated the integration of kingship into the social structures of the island as a whole (chapter 12).

Although Muganuro, the First Fruits ceremony on Ijwi, helped to redefine the pattern of social identity on the island, and thus to legitimate the concept of royalty on Ijwi, the ritual field also defined the limits on royalty; public rituals were both the creators and guarantors of the identity patterns which resulted from the social evolution of Ijwi discussed in the earlier chapters. By drawing on ritual traditions from across a wider region, assessing the nature of the new forms of social differentiation on Ijwi, and accounting for the effects of specific policies of the royal line and their allies, chapter 12 recombines the three levels of analysis noted above—the evolving regional context, the changing structural patterns of social identity, and the specific strategies and conflicts which characterized court politics—within a single field of analysis.

The Conclusion relates these concepts—and the specific lessons of Ijwi historical experience—to broader theoretical perspectives on the nature of pre-colonial social change in Africa. It surveys recent writings on ethnicity and ethnic change, and suggests that the general processes currently associated with ethnic identities, as these coalesced and were reproduced during the colonial era, are also useful in understanding identity transformations at other social levels and at other times.[24] But even though such processes can be generalized across time and space, they are too general, too abstract, to serve as a theoretical formulation of great power. Changes in patterns of social identity are multivariant; they cannot be reduced to a few elements alone. Understanding them requires sensitivity to historical conjuncture and social context rather than dependence on some universal explanatory framework. So in this case, as in many others, theoretical insights are more valuable for providing the questions, the analytic lens through which to understand historical process, than they are for providing satisfactory answers in and of themselves—though they are nonetheless indispensable for that role. Understanding social change and political centralization 200 years ago on Ijwi still requires familiarity with the people there—the historical actors—and acquaintance with their world; it still needs to account for the social, intellectual, and material resources available to those people; and it still seeks an explanation of how the individual actors related to the cultural world within which they operated. To do so requires addressing the tension between the personal and cultural domains, just as it wrestles with the tension between examining the particular experience of Ijwi and understanding the general processes at work in the wider region.

1
Ijwi Island Today

The Havu are located on the rugged western shores and on the islands of Lake Kivu; it is as lakeshore peoples that they are culturally and historically one. In much of the area they inhabit, the mountains defining the western edge of the western Rift Valley rise steeply from the lake; therefore even the mainland Havu are oriented to the lake for communication and livelihood. Social and economic interactions among these lacustrine peoples have been reinforced by (but not limited to) a common political heritage provided by shared segments of a single royal dynasty, the Basibula. The peoples of the lake distinguish themselves from others irrespective of political affiliations and boundaries, but it is as subjects (or former subjects) of Basibula kings that they are defined as "Havu." Although they also share a language and other cultural features, it is the geographical and the political elements which most sharply distinguish the Havu from other peoples of the region.

There have, however, been important changes in the composition of the Havu peoples and in the location of the Basibula centers. Over the last two centuries these centers have shifted several times along the western shores of Lake Kivu. In the course of these dynastic shifts, some people have remained behind, some have moved on with the dynastic line, and still others have been newly incorporated into a reconstructed kingdom.

Dynastic schism has also extended Basibula norms and personnel into new areas, thus incorporating additional population elements into the Havu kingdoms and tying them to Havu identity. The effect of all these changes in place and personnel has been to encourage mobility and interaction among lakeshore areas, independent of recent political affiliations. This tradition of lacustrine mobility, like the movement and segmentation of the royal line itself, has contributed to the diversity of the population included within the Havu kingdoms.

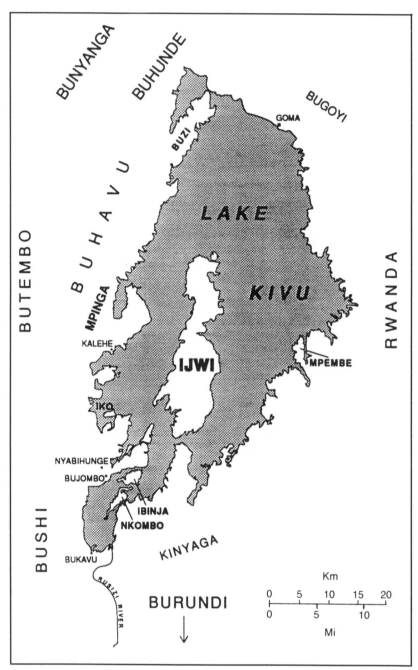

Map 1. Ijwi Island and neighboring areas

The Geography of Havu Settlement

The western Rift Valley constitutes one of the principal geological features of the African continent. In effect, it forms a great scar on the continental land mass, running north-south from the Nile Valley to the Zambezi, and is clearly delineated on the map of Africa by the long chain of Great Lakes with a characteristic north-south orientation. Lake Kivu (c. 75 miles long), one of those Great Lakes, lies at the highest point of the Rift Valley, some 5,000 feet above sea level.

In this area the Rift Valley serves as a cultural divide as well as a topographical and climatological divide. To the east, in the open savanna country of the East African plateau, the Interlacustrine kingdoms had in most cases developed a high degree of political centralization by the nineteenth century, with clearly defined patterns of social stratification, and a productive base which included both agricultural and pastoral activities. To the west were the forest cultures of the Zaire River Basin, characterized by relatively small-scale political units. Despite great cultural diversity, these societies were marked by a high degree of personal mobility and minimal administrative hierarchy, fundamentally egalitarian social structures with individual status determined more by achievement than ascription, and economies based on trapping, gathering, hunting, and fishing pursuits as well as on agriculture.[1] Today the topographical features of the Rift Valley serve as a clear divide between these two broad culture zones; historically, however, the Rift Valley societies have served more as intermediaries between the two zones.

The western Rift Valley narrows at Lake Kivu, so that the mountains defining the Rift, rising to over 10,000 feet, press in sharply on both sides of the lake. Therefore the topographical features surrounding the lake help shape a natural geographical community of shoreline peoples. With movement east and west away from the lake no easier than movement across the lake, Ijwi Island has come to serve as a focal point for the wide network of highly mobile lakeshore populations. Interaction is especially intense on the southern portion of the lake, where the straits separating Ijwi from the Nyamirundi Peninsula (now part of Rwanda) narrow to less than a mile, and the peninsulas of the present-day Zairean mainland, to the west, are not much farther distant from the island. But if proximity to these areas has been important to Ijwi's recent history, so has separation from them. While the island location offers its inhabitants access to mainland populations, it also defines them as different.

The geographical features characteristic of the region as a whole are particularly important for Ijwi Island. Its mid-lake location assures the island of a favored agricultural climate as well as an extensive field of social contacts. The Ijwi climate provides a longer and more reliable growing season

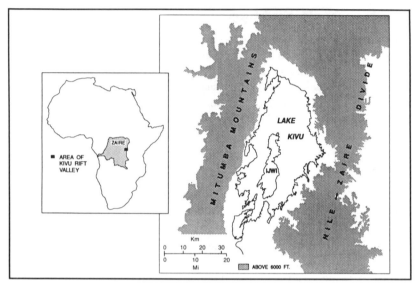

Map 2. Lake Kivu Rift Valley topography

than that of neighboring mainland areas, especially those to the east. The mountainous areas of the island itself, rising to 1,700 feet above the level of the lake and stretching east and west right across the center of the island, help preserve a productive climate for an agricultural community and serve as water catchment areas as well. Almost daily during the rainy season one can see from a distance the dense clouds building up and, by mid-afternoon, towering over the forested highlands of the island; many of Ijwi's rivers flow from these central highlands.

Benefitting from a wide variety of potential food crops and several cropping seasons, as well as seasons slightly different from those of mainland areas, the island has attracted immigrants from many different directions. From this there has developed a dense network of enduring contacts with the mainland areas around the lake; Ijwi's present population of more than 80,000 serves as the focal point for the Kivu lakeshore community, with continuing contacts both east and west. The very shape of the island contributes to its people's lacustrine focus. Ijwi is roughly 25 miles long and 6 miles wide at its widest, but narrows to less than 2 miles in some places; its long shoreline relative to area and its rugged terrain mean that much travel, even between communities on the island itself, is done by water.

But geographical features have helped determine regional history more precisely still, not just by encouraging general mobility, but more specifically by shaping the flow of social interactions and the nature of Ijwi's external

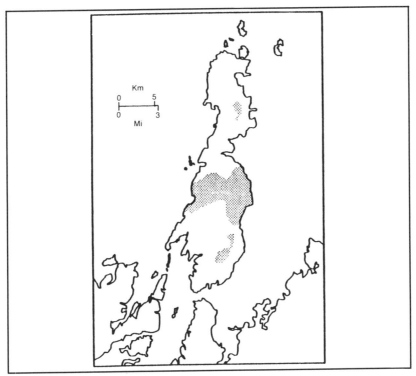

Map 3. Ijwi Island mountain culture

contacts. On the western mainland, the areas most suitable for dense settlement are found on the lacustrine plain and neighboring plateau, widest at the
extreme southwestern corner of the lake. Farther north, the plateau and the
plain both narrow until, mid-way along the lakeshore they are virtually non-
existent; directly west of Ijwi, in Mpinga, for example, the plain narrows
until in some places it is no more than 50 yards wide. This pattern continues
for the northern half of the western shoreline. There the mountains sometimes rise directly from the lake itself to 4,000 feet and more above the lake
level. The rugged terrain in such areas is much less suitable to dense settlement than are the southwestern shores, with their wide plain and broad
plateau hinterland. Therefore when, during the nineteenth century, the parent line of the Ijwi royal dynasty moved progressively north along the western
lakeshore, it moved into areas of decreasing population density, and this
reduced the political significance of the new Havu centers on the western
mainland. In part because of the sparse lakeshore population in Mpinga,
and the increasing distance between Ijwi and the mainland dynasty as the

mainland line moved north, there has been little interaction between these two Basibula families since their separation.

To the east, by contrast, reduced contact between Ijwi and the mainland resulted not from the remoteness of Ijwi from other political centers, but from the very expansion of Rwandan political power into lakeshore areas. In the eighteenth century the areas closest to Ijwi on the eastern shore of the lake were relatively removed from the political centers of Rwanda. From the late eighteenth century, however, Rwanda's political expansion towards the lake tended to reduce this political distance. With their gradual incorporation into the Rwandan political and economic network, the eastern mainland areas geographically closest to the island became increasingly separated from Ijwi politically. During much of this period, a similar (though less intensive) pro-cess was occurring in areas to the southwest of the lake as the Shi kingdoms moved north, gradually extending their power to the lakeshore. In these ways, political space in the Kivu Rift was restructured. Though Ijwi ties with the mainland areas were never entirely severed, the political geography of the region tended increasingly to emphasize the separation of the Ijwi royal dynasty from the mainland peoples and kingdoms, and thus indirectly to reinforce Ijwi's internal political and social focus.

Residence on Ijwi

The lacustrine orientation of the Havu peoples has been accentuated by the lakeshore contours, for the southwestern sector of Lake Kivu is punctuated by many islands of various sizes and indented with innumerable peninsulas forming long inlets and broad bays. In the rainy season when the fields are cultivated and the air is clear, an intricate mosaic of browns, reds, and greens extends right to the water's edge; in the lakeshore areas the soil is rich and intensively cultivated. Most important among the wide variety of agricul-tural crops cultivated today are beans (the staple), bananas, sweet potatoes, maize, sorghum, plantains, groundnuts, yams, and, increasingly, manioc. Although their economic orientations are primarily to crop production, the Havu also raise cattle, goats, sheep, pigs, and chickens. Fishing is important for some segments of the population; in the past, hunting, too, was pursued, though today there are few areas of Buhavu where this is continued on any significant scale.

Residence on Ijwi is characterized by a variety of patterns. An indi-vidual homestead is usually formed around a nuclear family—a man, his wife, and children. (Polygyny occurs rarely, and even then the wives indi-vidually tend to have homesteads in different parts of the island, forming their own nuclear households.) Sometimes younger brothers of the homestead head, or his divorced or widowed sisters, will join the homestead as well. In general, these homesteads are dispersed, each one surrounded by its banana grove and, ideally, by its fields. But often, too, the nature of the terrain encourages a tighter clustering of several homesteads, frequently related by kinship or marriage; in this way, grown children, brothers, mothers, or grandparents of a homestead head often live close to each other. Such clustering is particularly evident in the older areas of settlement, and in the more mountainous regions of the east. In some of these areas, therefore, a family is separated from its fields by some distance. This pattern is increasingly common today; the lack of available land for cultivation results in increasing residential concentrations, as people attempt to preserve the best land for cultivation.

Usually the residence consists of a single, semi-spherical hut, thatched with straw. These graceful and utilitarian structures serve many purposes: the various reed partitions and several layers of vertical shelving define spaces for socializing, cooking, sheltering livestock, storage, and sleeping. The earth floors were in the past polished and covered with sweet grass, but this is less common today. The hut can accommodate all purposes, but most activities take place in the courtyard in front of the hut. Although usually without the reed enclosure found in neighboring cultures (Rwanda and Bushi), homesteads in most areas of the island are partially shielded by banana groves or forest growth. In some areas, especially in the eastern highlands and near the forest, houses of a circular clay construction with a conical thatch roof are common. Often several of these constitute a homestead, and the clustering of several homesteads together is particularly apparent in such communities. In earlier days, community interaction everywhere was fostered by the fact that paths led directly from one homestead to another, and all movement therefore passed through one another's residence. However, with the construction of roads, this form of interaction has decreased; today paths tend to converge on the roads, bypassing the homesteads and therefore dissolving the web of interaction and intimacy that earlier defined the neighborhood communities.

The seasonal requirements of an agricultural community form the principal activities of the people on Ijwi. For some crops, especially beans and sorghum, planting begins in late August and continues intensively through September, with cultivation and weeding carried out by both men and women. The first harvest of beans occurs in December, and those for groundnuts and sorghum occur in January and February. The sorghum harvest is concurrent with a second crop planting, which is most intensive for beans and vegetables, in February and March. From late December to January there is a short dry season, during which the rains fall with less regularity, but seldom entirely cease. Usually this is neither severe enough nor long enough to alter the activities of cultivation, and in the more mountainous areas the only indication of this "dry season" is the haze that hovers over the lake.

The rains taper off in June, and the months of July and August are virtually devoid of precipitation. As is common elsewhere, the long dry season, with food and time available, constitutes the period of most intensive social and domestic activity; it is a time for marriages, travel, trade, visiting, dancing, religious ceremonies, and upkeep of the home, boats, tools, nets, and other implements of daily life. During this season the haze gathers over the mainland, the browns predominate on the hillsides, and a steady dry wind, the most characteristic feature of the long dry season, sets in from the southwest.

For some sections of the population, especially the young men, fishing is an important activity. Much of this is for smaller fish (*ndagala* and *ndugu*— about two inches in length) and is done from the shoreline. In this fishing, nets are set in a wide arc offshore and gradually drawn in to the beaches. Other fishermen set out nets from boats, and some fishing by hook and line is carried out by very young boys, who perch themselves precariously on rafts built of banana tree trunks and slide through lakeside reeds in search of prey and excitement.

In the past, some fishermen specialized in spearing fish with long metal rods *(imigera)* while swimming under water. Nets, made either with light nylon thread or fibers obtained from banana leaves and trunks, are also used from boats in mid-lake to catch larger types of fish (*nfi*, "tilapia"); today these fish are mostly sold in urban centers on the mainland. Because of the methane content of the lake and its extreme depth, fishing is not a particularly productive occupation; nonetheless, fish are a valued and appreciated food item, even at the royal court, and the consumption of fish is an important element in rituals such as the annual First Fruits ceremony and (less formally) in the festivities celebrating the birth of a child.[2]

Although not a primary source of food, the lake is extremely important to the people of Ijwi. Bany'Iju are known as excellent boatsmen, and their reputation is well deserved. For although the lake is often calm, dangerous storms can blow up quickly and move with speed across the lake. Long voyages are always hazardous, particularly during the rainy season; every year the lake takes its toll. Still, for skill, speed, endurance, and general boating knowledge, many of Ijwi's youth are outstanding; both sexes and all ages travel frequently and fearlessly over long distances on the lake.

Despite this, boatbuilding is today an important occupation for only a few. Trees of the right type and size are scarce on Ijwi; many boats are obtained from Buhavu on the western mainland, where larger trees are still available. Moreover, modern boat transport is regularly available to Goma (at the northern end of the lake) and Bukavu (at the southern end). Canoes are still made by some older men, however, those with time on their hands, and by some families (called Abeeja—specialists in canoe-making) who live far up in the forest.

Launching a boat involves dragging it sometimes for several miles over mountainous terrain, and therefore brings together many people from the neighborhood; it is an occasion of some festivity, and much beer is provided by the boatbuilders for those who come to help haul the boat to water. Each canoe is carved from the trunk of a carefully selected tree, by both burning out the interior and hewing with axes and adzes. The best boats are hewn to have very thin sides, but they are nonetheless strong and flexible. Length and size vary a great deal; most today would carry a dozen people and cargo. Some, however, are much larger, and many people told me that most boats of the past were enormous by today's standards, carrying easily 20–30 people and a full cargo.[3]

The size of a boat is generally measured by the number of goats it is capable of carrying, and some hold up to 30 or 40. Today the largest boats are used for commerce, usually taking bananas, banana beer (for which Ijwi is famous), and other agricultural goods to mainland outlets, especially those at the southern end of the lake—both in Zaire (to the city of Bukavu) and, equally frequently, to Rwanda (the region of Kinyaga).[4] From the northern parts of the island such trips can require up to 16 hours on the lake. A trip from northern Ijwi to the northern end of the lake, however, will sometimes take more than a day, and frequently the rowers on these voyages will stop at islands along the way.

Because of their boating skill, the Bany'Iju frequently take their goods for trade and friendship off the island, rather than depend on traders from outside travelling to Ijwi. Until recently, relatively few mainlanders came to Ijwi. This resulted from, and perpetuated, the reputation of Ijwi as being a distant and somewhat anti-social area, a land of smugglers and sorcerers; even today for Zairean officials, as formerly for the poets of the Rwandan central court, Ijwi is considered "the land beyond the mists." Such a reputation has placed the initiative for interaction with the mainland in the hands of the Bany'Iju, a fact which they have been quick to capitalize on. Earlier cattle contracts in Rwanda, for example, were seen by Rwandans as reciprocal agreements, symbolizing an ongoing relationship of subordination. The Bany'Iju, on the other hand, saw these as terminal exchanges, and this perspective was confirmed by their isolation and reputation; rarely would a Rwandan venture to Ijwi to claim the offspring "owed."

Another important activity which is not affected by the seasons is that of brewing beer. Banana beer[5] is used for all formal social interaction (and a good deal of informal social interaction as well). Beer is the social good *par excellence*. It is a required element of all formal visits—by those seeking land, cattle, wives, or reconciliation, or to express thanks, pleasure, or social bonding. Beer is also used to introduce oneself to the court, and it is distributed widely at the court and among friends. To deny beer when it is available, no matter what the status of those present, is the gravest of insults. All socially prescribed gift exchanges are accompanied by beer: it is consumed by those who accompany the gifts as well as by the recipients, and it need be offered to certain relations of the donor (e.g., to the maternal uncle in marriage exchanges) and distributed by the recipient to certain of his kin as well. Beer is thus the great lubricant of the Ijwi social system. The Bany'Iju pride themselves, and justifiably so, on the high quality of their beer.[6]

Although beer-making is not a specialized function limited to only a few, certain areas on Ijwi are favored in banana production and in water quality, and these areas today enjoy a reputation for superior beer. Those with contacts with such areas possess a major resource in attracting a social clientele; Ijwi beer is a treasured good easily recognized even in Bukavu.[7] There are two aspects to the social relations of beer: while the distribution and consumption of beer are the primary links in creating and preserving ties outside the kin group, its preparation is a major activity which involves the whole family. All ages of both sexes participate in its preparation at some stage, whether in harvesting or peeling the bananas, in gathering the grasses used to mash the banana pulp for its juice, in siphoning the beer through the funnels made of gourd-necks, or in roasting sorghum used for fermentation of the beer.

Banana cultivation is a year-round preoccupation, and one of the few agricultural pursuits restricted to males. But the products from this are not restricted to the social role of beer exchange: banana plants provide a wide range of products with a utilitarian value. As food, many types of bananas are prepared in a variety of ways. In addition, the banana plant provides material for many non-alimentary uses: as cord, benches (used particularly as thwarts in boats), gutters on huts to catch rainwater, conduits for water from springs, umbrellas, wrapping (especially for food and tobacco), roofing for huts, "tablecloths" on which to prepare food, and many toys for children (e.g., young girls carry the flowers on their backs as "dolls," and other children make shoes, hats, skirts, belts, or epaulets with banana products). Finally, and not least important, the banana grove itself provides a cool moist atmosphere year round in the immediate vicinity of the homestead—a social parlor *par excellence*.[8]

The banana grove therefore provides the essential atmosphere of an established homestead; in a sense it *is* the homestead, and to plant a banana grove is to assert permanent claim to the land occupied or cultivated. This correlates with the fact (as the Bany'Iju insist) that banana groves flourish best when immediately adjacent to the homestead, where they can be enriched with ashes, garbage, and animal manure, and where they benefit, according to these people, from "household smoke"—a metaphor for being near human life. While banana groves are therefore a social good, creating and preserving ties among families, they are equally a cultural good, representing the complete and productive homestead.

Beer is today transported in large calabashes *(ndaha),* but the term used for beer-filled calabashes, especially on prescribed presentations, is *"kabindi"* (which normally refers to a large clay pot).[9] Today on Ijwi pot-making is a relatively restricted skill. There are some areas and some families, including Barhwa ("pygmies") but not exclusive to them, who are known for their pot-making skill *(ababumbi).* Making good pots *(nanga)* requires the selection of proper clays, the careful and skillful construction of the pot itself, and knowledge of the technique of firing. My own observation suggests that pot-making is most important in the eastern highland areas (Bukere, Bushake, Bwando), but I did not inquire about this systematically. All pots are made by the coil method, but certain variations within this method are noticeable: some pot-makers (e.g., at Bukere) start with the neck and finish by rounding off the bottom, while others (such as the Barhwa at Cisiiza) make the bowl first, and the neck and lip last—adding it on to the finished bowl. Firing is done very cursorily. Once dry, the pots are placed in a nest of dry grass, covered over with more grass, and fired. This provides only a partial firing, but because pots are used mainly for cooking, they tend to harden with use.

Market activity occurs throughout the year, and today markets are held daily in different parts of the island on a rotating basis. Most trading is done among Bany'Iju, although outsiders also frequent regular ("official") markets. These not only provide for the sale and exchange of agricultural goods but also include a myriad of imported products, many of them essentials for contemporary life on Ijwi: salt, sugar, soap, kerosene, nails, thread, utensils, cloth, cigarettes, blankets, batteries, clothes, and tin cooking pots. As elsewhere in contemporary Africa, markets are also colorful focal points of social activity and important arenas of administrative control. A certain amount of government regulation accompanies recognized markets, although it is not infrequent to find small ad hoc markets on paths anywhere on Ijwi.[10] In addition to collecting payments from traders for the right to have space at market, government authorities are also responsible for inspecting the meat sold. Frequently the market is an occasion for checking on delinquent taxpayers (or arranging not to pay taxes, as the case may be) and for conducting other business of various types. In addition, markets serve as exchanges for Rwandan currency, used for purchasing many essential goods (tin roofing, blankets, salt, building materials, radios); in Rwanda the prices of these and other imported goods are often only a fraction of what they are in Zaire.

External Institutions on Ijwi

Ijwi social life today is predominantly rural in character, but it is not isolated, nor has it ever been. Currently, in addition to the important role of canoe transport, large government-run boats call almost daily at one or another landing on the island on their runs between Bukavu and Goma (at the southern and northern ends of Lake Kivu). Improved contacts with the Zairean mainland are a major preoccupation of Ijwi's elites, especially those nurses, teachers, or administrative officials from outside Ijwi. Indeed, there are many linkages of Ijwi society and economy with urban centers on the mainland, and with the larger political and economic arena of contemporary Zaire.

Aside from the Zairean administrative cadre, the most important vehicle of external influence on contemporary Ijwi society is the Catholic church. (Seventh-Day Adventists from Rwanda established a station on Ijwi in the first decade of the century and Presbyterians from 1910; both withdrew after World War I. Although Catholic catechists were on Ijwi from shortly after World War I, the first Catholic mission on the island dates from 1936.) Most of the schools on Ijwi were originally run by the Catholic missions, and many of the most influential teachers are still tied to the parish network. Prior to the imposition of government restrictions, the church also organized several youth groups and women's organizations.

Several other Christian churches are represented on Ijwi—Adventist, Baptist, Kimbanguist, Anglican—and recently some of them have opened new schools of their own. The activities of these groups, especially that of the Catholic Sunday mass, continue to be a focus of social activity for many on the island. Another institutional contact outside Ijwi is the hospital, with its series of dispensaries. Although no doctor was resident on the island during the time I was there, doctors from the mainland visited the dispensaries on the western lakeshore frequently.[11] (From the early 1980s the hospital has been administered by the Catholic church, and there is now a resident doctor on the island.)

There were several primary schools on the island, and their number increased considerably during the early 1970s. In addition, there was one post-primary teacher-training institute, and the island authorities were enthusiastically preparing a full secondary school at the time of my departure. In addition to their roles as educational and socialization institutions, the schools are also very important in other ways, and schoolteachers, especially those who are from Ijwi themselves, often derive important local status from their positions. Many of today's elite on Ijwi are, or were, teachers.

One of the major institutions on the island is the plantation, formerly LINEA, growing mainly coffee and *Cinchona* for quinine.[12] This plantation constitutes approximately one-sixth of the island's land area, including some of the best agricultural land. The work force, consisting of people from Ijwi, varies by season and by the perceived financial and political health of the plantation. During the time I was on the island, ownership of the plantation was transferred from a Belgian to a Zairean; this had an impact on the personnel and influenced both hiring policies and agricultural practices (but not wage structure). But LINEA is only a small legacy of a much wider network of colonial enterprises in the region, and these were dependent on the availability of labor supplies. During the colonial period, almost all Bany'Iju men were conscripted to work for varying lengths of time on one or another colonial project. It is very rare indeed to find an older man who has never worked off the island, either on plantations or in mines, or in the urban centers as craftsman, laborer, or domestic help. Colonial penetration for labor conscription went very deep.

The time of this research corresponded with substantial changes in the local politics of eastern Kivu, and these, too, affected Ijwi's relationship with external institutions. In 1974 Ijwi was separated administratively from the Zone of Kalehe and provided with its own zone administration, thus linking Ijwi more directly with the regional political network.[13] This change evoked a good deal of interest and discussion on Ijwi, and provided administrative positions for some members of the Ijwi educated elite. Most of the senior officials at the zone level were not Bany'Iju, however, and their preoccupations, both personal and professional, were for the most part directed away from Ijwi society. New taxes (some legal, others improvised), forced labor, expropriation of small stock, administrative harassment, and outright brutality increased dramatically on Ijwi over the 1970s under the Mobutu regime, and for a while the island was under virtual military occupation. But state personnel, including the 50 or so armed soldiers, were not incorporated into the social networks of the island. Thus, although the administrative impact of the Zaire state apparatus remains wide-ranging and incessant on Ijwi, the presence of such authorities remains only superficial.

Internal Administrative Structures on Ijwi

The primary political structure of Ijwi society is today provided by the organization of the kingdom, an institution which overlaps, but is not congruent with, the official administration. In the southern part of the island at the time of my research the focal point of the kingdom was the *bwami*, the royal court at Rambo; this was the location of the tribunal dealing with disputes over land, divorce, bridewealth, cattle, witchcraft, inheritance, the transgression of taboos, and similar litigation. It was also the principal administrative center for the southern part of the island, where statistical data were recorded and kept, including reports on census, taxation, agriculture and livestock, as well as the register of births, deaths, marriages, changes in residence, and similar alterations in civil status.

But the *bwami* is more than simply an administrative center; it is the royal court, the major social focus of the kingdom, and the residence of the *mwami*. It is a place of continual visits by the *mwami*'s advisors, friends, ritualists, and clients, those petitioning a grievance, and those seeking status and recognition at the court. It is a place of the perpetual *mucuba* game (a board game similar to the game of chess in its complexity and subtlety).[14] It is equally the place of perpetual visits and hospitality, often till late into the evenings, when friends of the king gather to trade stories and discuss the affairs and people of the kingdom, to laugh, to gossip, to reflect on the present and the past, to speculate on the future, and especially to share friendship. It is a place where social etiquette is practiced and polished, and differs from social etiquette elsewhere on the island. It is, most of all, the place where oratory most becomes an art, and the long shadows thrown up on the walls during these evening séances are as dramatic as the oratory is theatrical.

The kingdom, however, does not exist only at Rambo; the principal residence of the present king is only one center of many. Other royal residences, those of his wives and his sons or other relatives, are scattered across the island. And the kingdom is more, of course, than just the royal family; it is, in an important way, the structure of relations on the island. Even in its imperfect institutional integration into Ijwi society, the kingdom is a way of looking at things, from land rights and social relations to social graces. It is also power, and the relations of kingship therefore spread to all corners of the island.

There is another administrative sector on Ijwi, on the northern part of the island; though headed also by a member of the royal family, this sector provides a very different ambiance. The administrative division of the island was a result of colonial rule, but it was based on an enduring cleavage within the royal family.[15] The *sultani* in the north has none of the ritual status and importance of the king in the south; social differences in the north, in some respects more pronounced than those in the south, result from the ties to the administrative framework of the Zairean state structures. Although the homes of the *sultani* in the north serve in some measure as social foci, the importance of this "kingship" derives almost exclusively from its administrative functions.

There are essentially three lines of administrative structure which reach out from the court; though the character of administrative relations in the north differ somewhat from those in the south, all three administrative forms are present throughout the island. In their operation, they are less important as administrative "structures" of the kingdom than as channels of communication. They are divisible very roughly into the conventional categories of legislative functions (using primarily political processes), executive functions (essentially administrative processes), and judicial functions (combining strong elements of both). On Ijwi these functions are nowhere clearly defined by separate personnel, but they nevertheless tend to concentrate in the various roles described below.

A *murhwali* (pl. *barhwali*) is a son (or direct descendant) of the king, formally recognized as a royal representative of the court in a given area. *Barhwali* serve as the eyes and ears of the king, and they oversee other appointees as well. But their most evident function is that of minor judiciaries, handling petty cases of theft, cattle or contract disputes, disagreements over land, marriage or domestic discord, and personal grievances dealing with social etiquette. In some ways, their homes serve as minor royal courts (but without the royal etiquette), regional centers for social congregation, and places to discuss agricultural work and division of labor, pending court cases and new policy, and local and foreign news. The informality of these centers makes them much more accessible than the central court for most Bany'Iju. Though these courts can try to smooth over difficulties, they cannot enforce judgment, and there are some cases they cannot adjudicate—witchcraft accusations, some divorce cases, and certain land disputes among them. But they can bring local pressure to bear on settling a dispute before it goes to the central court, and if it does, the local *murhwali* will likely have an influential say there.

A parallel but more direct line of communication to the central court is that of the *barhunyi* and *ngaligali*. *Barhunyi* are the court favorites, friends of the king, who spend virtually all their time at the court: advising the king, socializing with him, and sometimes representing him to others, they live in their own hut just outside the royal enclosure. They are also the principal judges at the court, and are among the very few who can publicly disagree with the king. Requests to the king often pass through one of them as intermediary, for they are among the most respected men of the kingdom, not only for their influence but for their intelligence as well. At the time I was on Ijwi there were four such *barhunyi,* although a fifth man was trying (without apparent success) to insert himself among their number.

Barhunyi are commoners and therefore valuable for representing commoner viewpoints at the court. But they are men of the court all the same, and their interest is the court's interest. *Ngaligali,* on the other hand, are also "friends of the king," but they live in the hills. These men are able to visit the court freely without formal introduction; they are expected to be there frequently but not continuously—for they are also expected to live in the countryside. *Ngaligali* are independent of the normal administrative channels. Instead of prestations to the "capitas" (village administrative officials), for example, they provide gifts directly to the court; instead of answering a capita's demands, they answer only to the court. In fact, they report on the capitas—and on the court itself—to the king. Although they are not formally judges, they can play an influential role in certain court cases. While they cannot contradict the king directly, they can (and are expected to) serve as the people's representatives at the court. But the position is determined by the court; it is thus a tenuous role at best, one in which the incumbent is likely to incur the resentment of the capitas, other neighbors in the hills, and even the court itself. Turnover is rapid, and rarely does the role pass from father to son.

Barhambo are those appointed by the court to oversee and carry out court policy. Today this position is fully integrated into the broader administrative system as "village capita,"[16] so the functions of these men mostly concern the conventional tasks of tax collection, labor recruitment for the continuing forms of forced labor for "public" works (for the official government, not the Ijwi court), occasional court prestations, and general peace and order in a given area. They also facilitate the tasks of other government workers, visiting political authorities, census takers, veterinarians, and the occasional itinerant historian-anthropologist.

There are several levels of *barhambo* appointments: in each half of the island there are three *banotabule* ("notables," more recently termed *chefs de localité*), each of whom oversee 10–15 *bakapita de village* (also referred to in most contexts as *barhambo,* meaning simply "appointees"). The *barhambo* are administrative intermediaries to the court; but the real administrative tasks are carried out by the village capitas. Capitas are appointed by the court and can be removed by the court, but they are usually retained only so long as they retain the good will of the population. In some areas (especially in the east) a capita is also the recognized village head, often the senior representative of the dominant clan of the village, and it is not uncommon to find a hereditary tendency to such appointments in these areas. *Bakapita* are frequently at the court, but their influence there is variable. Some are virtually ignored, whereas others have great status. Paradoxically, among those with the greatest respect are those who are representative of strong viable local constituencies, rather than those who are most completely the "King's Men." Those with strong constituencies seem almost to cumulate the roles of *barhunyi* and *ngaligali,* their influence at the court often supersedes that of their *barhambo* superiors, the *banotabule.*

Criteria for recruitment to these positions vary. During the 1930s the southern half of the island was ruled by a chief from the north; he replaced many capitas with his own men, either friends from the north or a type of "new men" of the colonial period—often literate, often with experience in dealing with Europeans (as former catechists, teachers, plantation workers, or domestics). (Indeed in the north the capitas and the "new men" were often one and the same, since the chief often selected capitas from among those with experience in colonial culture and because capitas there were encouraged to acquire the skills and characteristics associated with the superimposed colonial culture.) But such a policy of appointment from above resulted in constant friction at the village level, and there often developed strong antagonisms between the administrative cadre and the population. In many areas on Ijwi today, these appointees are remembered as particularly brutal in their desire to enforce colonial structures, and also in using colonial forms of coercion for their own benefit. Eventually the island was divided administratively, and new appointees in the south tended to be loyal supporters of the royal line or local representatives. In the north, the appointment of capitas is still characterized by qualities of "administrative efficiency." There, a capita is sometimes named from outside the village of his appointment, often from among the educated elite. Still, for the most part administration at the local level is closely intertwined with the structures of the kingdom, co-opting and often altering these royal structures in fundamental ways.

Kingship and Other Forms of Social Interaction

The major public festivity of kingship on Ijwi is the First Fruits ceremony known as Muganuro. But despite the efforts of the court, even this is declining in importance in the eyes of most Bany'Iju. This is a significant change, for Muganuro was formerly the most important expression of kingship on Ijwi: when the ritually enthroned king was exiled from the island during the colonial period, the ceremony was not held; and the *sultani* in the north does not participate in a Muganuro ceremony—neither in that of the kingdom nor in his own. Muganuro was also the single recurrent occasion when the general population of the island came into direct contact with kingship. Today, however, Muganuro is increasingly becoming a private affair between the king and his ritualists; for the population as a whole, kingship is increasingly intertwined with the state administration and is viewed in terms of political power rather than in terms of ritual proprieties.

This represents a major shift in the concept of kingship, away from the ritual, symbolic functions which kingship fulfilled for Ijwi society in the past. Whereas formerly kingship served as a focus of identity for the island as a whole, today identities are determined with regard to "outside" institutions or localized geographical influences. While the *mwami's* authority may remain important to some (although within a limited domain), his actual power is circumscribed: power lies in the hands of the administration. Even in the past, of course, most people were not directly affected by royalty. The court was not unimportant to Ijwi society, but it was simply not pre-eminent in the daily lives of most individuals; aside from succession disputes, Muganuro was virtually the only time when the court's activities served as a focus of interest for the whole island.

For most interaction, social horizons on Ijwi were much lower, and interlocking social networks were articulated independently of kingship. Residence and locality were probably the most important features in defining social ties. Marriages on Ijwi were generally unstable, and divorce relatively frequent.[17] The circulation of women (and men) created a changing field of social relations and personal ties for many individuals—but did not sever earlier networks. Bilateral ties independent of marital status were important for ritual and social purposes, even though descent was patrilineal. (Ritual norms, for example, required the joint participation of a man and a woman at ceremonies following the birth of a grandchild, regardless of their domestic status at the time.) Thus marriage created social bonds which outlasted any given marital bond; these became important alliance mechanisms outside a given locale, especially where women moved to other villages in this predominantly (but not exclusively) virilocal society. As a general rule, kingship played no direct role in these alliance patterns.

Individual bloodpacts *(cihango)* were another important means of creating social ties; in some respects bloodpact ties were more important than kinship in defining social behavior. Such ties were frequent on Ijwi in the recent past; many older men cited half a dozen or more such contracts. It was rare to find a man with no bloodpact ties at all. Because bloodpacts were especially important to commercial ties, they were also an important mechanism for creating enduring ties outside Ijwi, especially on the mainland east of the lake. Cattle clientship offered another way of cementing social ties, but this form of interaction apparently was rare on Ijwi until the mid-nineteenth century or so. Most of these were ties with the east, and they too tended to be very unstable. But epizootics, cattle raids, and diminished pastureland during the colonial period took a heavy toll on the herds of Ijwi, and today land clientship is much more important than cattle clientship in defining and extending social bonds.

Only among those close to the court does proximity to the court or king help to define status: kingship does not directly penetrate into the lives of most people in any important way. As will be discussed below, kingship was more important for organizing social determinants at a higher analytic level. Most people simply ignored kingship in their normal activities—and for the most part kingship ignored them. The fundamental strands of social organization and social interaction were found in the complex web of more local-level mechanisms: marriage, residence, bloodpacts, commercial ties, and (less so) clientship. But all these frequently tied individuals to others outside Ijwi as well as defined their status within Ijwi society. Thus the social network of the Bany'Iju was not determined by the geographical contours of Ijwi Island alone. Nor, initially, did political identities conform to those contours.

Clanship became an important social factor in determining joking relations (to be discussed below); it has also been important in claiming identity when moving into a new area. Immigrants to Ijwi seek the clan status of one of the Ijwi clans; likewise, those moving off Ijwi to the mainland find it useful to claim membership in a mainland clan (though often the same clans are found in both places). Aside from that, clanship is primarily important for its ritual role on Ijwi, a role most clearly expressed at Muganuro. Clearly it is in relations with the court that clanship achieves its most important "political" functions on Ijwi.

Thus Ijwi is not an isolated corner of African society, nor was it ever so during the previous 200 years, as far back as oral traditions can inform us. For there have always been multiple contacts with outside institutions, peoples, ideas, concepts, and power. In fact, Ijwi as a coherent social unit distinct from other areas is only a recent concept. Through most of the island's history, the various Ijwi communities are more properly seen as extensions of various social networks from the mainland. Only from the mid-nineteenth century did the island cohere as a distinct social unit; only then did political identities begin to coincide with the geographic realities of Ijwi's separation from the mainland. The following chapters attempt to identify these aspects of Ijwi's changing external social contacts and growing internal coherence (for the two were intimately related). Our goal will be to trace the evolution of these historical factors and processes, and assess their contribution to the transformation of Ijwi society.

Part 1
The Regional Context

2
An Overview of Kivu Culture, c. 1750

The previous chapter has sketched out some of the characteristic features of Ijwi society in the early 1970s. But Ijwi society was not always organized along these lines, nor did it exist in isolation. It has changed dramatically over the past 200 years, and in an important sense regional interaction served as a catalyst for the transformations which have occurred on the island. Later chapters will consider the regional influences acting on Ijwi history. This chapter has two objectives: to examine the broader historical context for understanding the social processes, political traditions, and ritual expressions which characterized the Rift Valley region; and to establish the geographical range of these cultural features some 200 years ago.

The data available do not permit the reconstruction of a narrative history for the region as a whole at this time remove; therefore the argument here takes on a special character. Relying mainly on published data, I will first draw on materials relating to present-day Nyanga society, northwest of Lake Kivu. My own fieldwork indicates that many features of Nyanga social structure are found in other societies in the forest areas west of the Mitumba Mountains (that is, west of the Kivu Rift).[1] But the data also indicate that the characteristics now most evident in the areas west of the Rift were not, in the past, limited to their present distribution: Ijwi, Rwandan, Shi, and Havu historical traditions suggest that many societies of the mid-eighteenth-century western Rift shared similarities with more recent Nyanga society (even though today these societies differ markedly from Nyanga norms). From this, I shall argue that societies which shared such cultural elements formerly were found at least as far east as the Nile-Zaire Divide (east of Lake Kivu) and north-south the length of Lake Kivu, an area which includes Ijwi Island. This prototype society will serve as a representative baseline from which to trace the evolution of Ijwi society from the late eighteenth century.[2]

I am not arguing, of course, that the societies west of Lake Kivu have not themselves changed. Instead, I am arguing only that the general features most clearly represented in these societies today were formerly more wide-

43

spread and thus represent an older structural layer to social action in the region. In Rwanda, for example, east of Lake Kivu, state power has restructured society along very different lines. Yet in some parts of Rwanda—those areas least effectively incorporated into the more recent Rwandan state structures—social forms of the type sketched out here endured well into this century. Indeed, within the Rwandan context alone, such features have been dismissed simply as anomalous culture traits. But examining these data within a broader regional framework and a deeper historical perspective helps clarify the logic behind them. Such an analysis thus simultaneously establishes the extent of earlier cultural features throughout the region and explains their apparent anomaly within Rwandan culture.

The Geographical Setting

The mountain ranges paralleling Lake Kivu to both the east and west reach over 10,000 feet, with a few isolated peaks in the north approaching 15,000 feet. (Lake Kivu is just under 5,000 feet above sea level.) Rising sharply from the Rift and separating ecological as well as cultural zones, these mountains have been as significant in influencing historical interactions in the area as they are imposing features of the topography. East of the Zaire-Nile Divide, just east of Lake Kivu, were the states of the East African Interlacustrine culture complex. For the Lake Kivu area of the later eighteenth and nineteenth centuries, the most influential of these states was the expanding power of Rwanda. West of the lake, beyond the Mitumba Mountains (in present-day Zaire), lived peoples who formed part of the vast cultural block extending, at one level of cultural abstraction, through the equatorial forest areas of the Zaire River Basin.

Between the two culture zones, the peoples of the Rift Valley shared elements with each, in a shifting balance through time as the ecology changed and as historical relations with new people developed. Today, the Rift Valley cultures—the Hunde, Havu, and Shi—are considered more closely associated with the Interlacustrine complex than the forest complex. But there are important indications (to be considered below) that in the early eighteenth century the type of culture now associated with the forest areas of the Zaire Basin was more widespread; it was shared with the peoples of the Rift Valley and beyond, into the mountainous Nile-Zaire Divide east of the lake.

The type of mobility characteristic of each of these areas was significant in determining the impact of interaction in the region. In the forest areas, widely scattered village settlements and a high degree of individual mobility meant that contacts among different groups were frequent but not enduring. Ideas and material items diffused widely, but their spread cannot be traced to any particular source, nor is it possible to identify established lines of com-

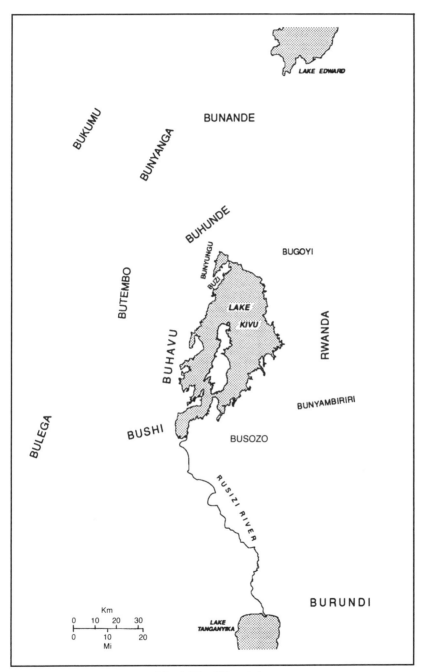

Map 4. Kivu Rift societies

45

munication which could be controlled by a single powerful group. In these areas there were no broad "migratory patterns" involving identifiable groups making permanent moves and taking with them specific cultural features. By contrast, in the more densely populated Interlacustrine areas east of the Rift a second type of mobility was more common. This involved permanent moves of discrete population segments leaving one place to settle in a new area. Because these moves were clearly defined, the diffusion of specific symbols and rituals within this mobility pattern came to be associated with specific population groups. Consequently this pattern was also often associated with specific concepts of power relationships.

Distinguishing between these two mobility patterns helps explain why it is difficult to trace specific "external inputs" to Ijwi culture simply by tracing population movements. The rituals which contributed to the formation of centralized kingship on the island, for example, were for the most part diffused according to the forest culture pattern of communication preceding the establishment of royalty. But later population groups arrived in a context more closely corresponding to the second mobility pattern noted above. Although the two forms overlapped, the relative importance of each and the significance of their impact became altered over time. To explain the diffusion of rituals contributing to royalty by recourse to a model of recent population movement, however, would be to misrepresent the historical processes at work.

Early historical influences around Lake Kivu were transmitted primarily along certain east-west axes, through the corridors of cultural interchange provided by breaks in the topographical features that define the Rift. The three most important such communication corridors in this area were the Lake Edward Plain (between the Ruwenzori and Virunga mountain massifs), the area around the northern end of Lake Kivu, and the Rusizi Plain at the northern end of Lake Tanganyika. Ijwi lay close to the second of these communication corridors, and thus experienced contacts with areas of relatively wide geographical spread. The location of the Nyanga peoples—just to the west of this interaction zone—makes them a valuable focus for understanding the prototype society stretching through the Kivu Rift.

The Kivu Prototype Society

The Nyanga live in the dense rainforest of the eastern Zaire Basin, and the dominating character of this forest environment is reflected in many aspects of their culture.[3] Still, some cultural elements appear to tie them historically to cultures now located east of the forest areas, in the savanna areas of the Interlacustrine zone east of the western Rift Valley: by some classifications, for example, the Nyanga form the western-most edge of the Interlacustrine language family. Certain aspects of Nyanga social organization also suggest considerable historical interaction with Interlacustrine peoples. It is these aspects of their social organization that will guide our inquiry here.

Nyanga Social Structure

The Nyanga lived characteristically in village communities of 75–100 residents each, scattered widely through the forest.[4] Much of their economic life was based on hunting and collecting the products of an environment which is rich and productive to those who know it well. This economic pattern both limited the size of the villages and encouraged the mobility of their individual residents. Therefore although the villages themselves were permanent, the mobility associated with Nyanga economic life meant that the composition of a village might change frequently. This in turn enhanced cooperation between villages, because members of one village were often well known (perhaps as earlier residents) in several other villages.

Interaction among the Nyanga occurred without a dense concentration of political power. The combination of high value placed on cooperation, high personal mobility, and the small size of settlement led to the development of a fine web of ritual, social, political, and economic ties throughout Bunyanga and beyond.[5] From this, many small politically autonomous groups were incorporated within a wide framework of intensive personal interaction and effective cooperation.[6] Therefore, although the individual polity formed a sovereign unit, it was not entirely an independent unit. The intense interaction between neighboring areas that was such an essential feature of Nyanga culture meant that each unit was effectively encapsulated within the dynamics of the larger region. Before the late eighteenth century the societies of the Lake Kivu Rift appear to have shared this pattern of an intense web of crosscutting ties among individuals, families, hunting groups, and residential units. Both oral references and current social patterns in some areas of the island confirm the models for Ijwi; but this aspect of political interaction was to change dramatically in the Interlacustrine areas with the emergence of increasingly formalized political structures and increasingly concentrated forms of political power.

Many Nyanga social institutions reflected the fluidity of such a system. A variety of forms were available as expressions of social cohesion, and most of these lacked clearly defined rules of exclusion. "Clans" in Bunyanga, for example, were little more than "fictive units"; they were dispersed, noncorporate, non-exogamous, and without juridical functions.[7] The lack of clearly defined internal functions of clans and the lack of established criteria determining clan membership among the Nyanga are also characteristic of clan organization among neighboring peoples, including those in the western Rift area.

Specific clan identities among the Nyanga were sometimes extended to neighboring societies; often they assumed different names.[8] This implies that common clan identity resulted at least in part from criteria external to the clan itself (such as shared perceived status relative to others, or relative to a ritual function), rather than exclusively from a process of historical diffusion or descent from a common original source. Among some peoples culturally related to the Nyanga, the concept of clan as a common group of people with clearly defined responsibilities to each other, or as a historically determined descent category, virtually disappeared.[9]

The differences between Bunyanga and areas farther east illustrate that clan organizations in those areas have been strongly influenced by the nature of the political structure within which they operated. To the east, the intensity of administrative hierarchy seems to have been particularly important in encouraging the formation of corporate groups.[10] With greater demands for a more clearly defined group membership, identities which had formerly been relatively fluid (such as clans) had a tendency to polarize and to become more exclusive of each other. With the flexibility of individual identities and the possibility of forming cross-cutting ties greatly reduced, the social distance between groups became more clearly defined. In such contexts greater importance was given to a single, dominant criterion of group membership. Therefore clan identities in the Interlacustrine areas came to be more exclusive and applicable in all contexts, whereas identities in the Nyanga type of society were multiple and selective, more likely to alter with each particular context.

Even at lower levels of Nyanga kinship identity, not all rules of belonging were based on internal criteria.[11] Lineage membership, for example, was a status that could be achieved in a variety of ways, although agnatic descent was viewed as the most important criterion. Potential lineage members included the descendants of female members of the lineage (or even of clients of female members), the children of "incorporated" members (often comprising "significant numbers of individuals"), or the children of "assimilated" members (who nonetheless retained the "flavor" of their foreign origins). One way that female members could "produce" children for the lineage was by marrying (or inheriting) other women as their own wives. The female "husband" then served as sociological father to the children of her wives, and these children were considered to belong to her lineage. The children of the sisters or daughters of the eponymous founder of a lineage were often considered members of that lineage (as were sometimes the children of the sisters or daughters of any agnatic descendant of that founder). In some cases, even the children of women related to wives of men belonging to a certain lineage came to be considered members of that lineage (e.g., their mother's sister's husband's lineage).

Lineage membership was therefore extremely heterogeneous, with recruitment in fact based on bilateral principles. Membership in such identity groups could be traced at least in part through female links as well as through male links; a high proportion of genealogies among the Nyanga included women's names. Many women among the Nyanga did not marry (or they were "married" to spirits); such a woman's children were considered members of their mother's lineage, and their mother's brother served as their sociological father. The children therefore considered their mother and father (*pater*, not *genitor*) to be of the same lineage, in a relationship paralleling the royal institution of the *mumbo*, to be discussed below.[12]

In other ways, too, maternal uncles in Nyanga society held important ritual and social roles in relation to their sororal nephews. "Un individu pauvre" was one who was not protected by powerful maternal uncles.[13] Thus a man "belonged" in some respects both to the descent group of his mother's brother and to that of his own father, and recruitment to a given lineage could be based on either descent line. The importance of the maternal uncle is a characteristic found widely throughout the region; strong reciprocal responsibilities often adhere between a maternal uncle and his sororal nephew, even if these are not always seen as specifically lineage ties. The Lega, for instance, recognize at least seven types of maternal uncles.[14] As do many other peoples, the people of Ijwi also recognize strong links between the maternal uncle and sororal nephew; matrilateral ties are today, for example, a favored form of marriage alliance.

In Nyanga society, matrilateral ties assumed special importance when disputes occurred within the patrilaterally defined family; in that case, the natural allies of the antagonists were the families of their respective maternal uncles. This common pattern of alliance will be discussed with reference to Ijwi royal history in chapter 10. The important point to note here is that bilateral ties were an integral part of the basic social organization of the smaller-scale societies such as the Nyanga; the strength of such a dense network of interlocking bilateral ties provided a great deal of flexibility to Nyanga society, tending to impede the formation of exclusive group membership. This pattern of bilateral political factions was also present in the more centralized states; insofar as it contradicted the ideology of male descent as the exclusive basis of group definition it reflected more flexible social identities in the past.

Because of the variety of recruitment mechanisms among the Nyanga and the lack of clearly defined rules of exclusion, the very concept of "lineage" itself was flexible. In Kinyanga, the language of the Nyanga, three different terms refer to different aspects of lineage conceptions: "*kisasa*" refers to the genealogical aspect; "*rushu*," to the socio-political aspect; and "*kihanga*," to the co-residential aspect. Residence within a local community was a particularly strong determinant of identity, because so many mechanisms could be used to incorporate non-kin into the local group. Often a kinship idiom was used to express this created bond, and therefore co-residence often led to the assumption of lineage identity with the agnatic "core." Bloodpacts, initiation societies, and the numerous ritual statuses within the polity were also used to strengthen the concept of a common identity within the community.[15] In some parts of Bunyanga elaborate circumcision ceremonies, derived from the Kumu, neighbors to the west, were also important.[16]

Membership in a village community was important to the individual, for the forest environment did not encourage scattered, individual homesteads. But the environment also limited the size of these communities; because the economic potential of the forest and the requirements of a trapping-gathering culture did not favor the emergence of large villages, young men and women continually moved out. They usually did so as individuals, not as groups, and therefore often sought to join established villages rather than set up new ones. Assimilation to a new village occurred on an individual basis; new members became gradually absorbed into the lineage and the children were accepted as fully part of the lineage. Over time, therefore, there was no continuing difference in their status distinguishing them from other lineage members. Nor did there develop an enduring system of "client lineages" as existed elsewhere in Africa, where lineage affiliation was more rigorously determined. The absence of clearly defined rules of exclusion relating to group membership among the Nyanga also meant that an individual was able to maintain ties with a former lineage even while being assimilated into a new one.

Men usually moved to villages where they would have access to land rights (for hunting and trapping as well as for agriculture). Thus they often moved to villages where they had some previous ties. But even among these villages the range of choice was still very wide. One important factor in attracting men to a particular village was the presence of women there; thus it was advantageous for an agnatic group which sought to increase its numbers to retain as many women as possible in the village. As noted above, one way of doing this was by "marrying" a woman of the village to a spirit: she thus stayed in the village; her children were considered members of her own agnatic group and were fully accepted as "agnates" within the village. Even where there were no unmarried men from outside the agnatic group in the village, women married to spirits could also choose as their lovers married men from outside the exogamous group. Thus it is that many women in Nyanga society did not marry, or at least did not marry young; their children were fully accepted within their mothers' lineages and identified with the agnatic core of the village.[17]

The distribution of economic rights presented no obstacle to this pattern. Married or unmarried, a woman had access to bananas from the groves of a wide range of cognatic and affinal relatives: those of her parents, her maternal uncles' wives, her brothers' wives, her husband's unmarried sisters, her husband's brothers' wives, and others. Similarly she could call on the assistance of a wide range of people to help her clear a new banana grove, and this could be done at any time of the year. Single women were also provided for economically in other ways. Hunting and trapping were the prerogatives of men, but within the village the distribution of game meat was the responsibility of the head of the agnatic core; all members shared in this distribution in some way.[18]

There were similar procedures at the level of the larger polity. For economic distribution, certain portions of game trapped by the village members were passed on to the representative of the royal family of the polity. But most important for the strength of the royal family was the control over the reproductive capacities of women within this lineage, for the size of the royal lineage was one of the principal sources of prestige and power in the polity. Size was determined in part by the number of non-agnates associated with the agnatic core. But more important to lineage size was the strong tendency for women of the royal family to be married to spirits or given as concubines to clients or associates of the royal family. Women who did not marry outside the lineage enabled the royal lineage to augment its numbers more rapidly than other groups, both by producing children for the lineage and by attracting clients. These men would return part of their produce, especially game meat, to the royal lineage; along with representatives of the ritualist families, they would also help clear banana groves.[19] Thus neither descent patterns nor economic necessity made conventional clan (or even lineage) identity essential.

Nyanga Political Organization

Political units within Bunyanga seldom exceeded 1,000 inhabitants; most numbered only a few hundred individuals.[20] The defining characteristic of the Nyanga polity and the central focus around which all else revolved was the titled position of *mubake*. The personage of the *mubake* provided a ritual and social focus for the political community, and represented its unity. At the same time competition over the position of *mubake* made this position the object of spirited political maneuverings, the goal of which was to place one or another candidate in that prestigious role. Therefore the role of *mubake* was simultaneously the source of continuity and instability within Nyanga society.

Politically, the *mubake* appears to have been little more than a symbolic figurehead.[21] Executive power was dispersed among many groups, individuals, factions, and families: the *batambo* (the heads of localized family segments), *barusi* (members of the dispersed royal family), *bakungu* (councillors), and *bandirabitambo* (ritual specialists), in addition to numerous other ritual or social dignitaries.[22] Each group defined by ritual function was divided into several subgroups by seniority and minor differences in functions. Nonetheless, in each case individuals sharing a common title often acted as a group: they arrived at decisions communally or performed their functions communally. So corporate status was defined more by ritual function and proximity to royal status than by descent.

The multiplicity of these roles and the small size of the polity imply that a very high proportion of families were directly tied to the ritual or executive complex of a Nyanga polity. Most men could hope to accede to at least one such title, or be closely tied to one through kin or client ties. With the accessibility of such a wide range of ties to royal status, mechanisms such as clan ties played a small role in individual identification with the Nyanga political unit. Putative kinship based on clan identities (serving as an intermediary mechanism linking an individual to court politics) was of little importance in these contexts where identity was defined directly in relation to other individuals. Clan identities therefore were more important for relations with people outside the polity than within it; it is in these contexts of external relations that the sources most frequently emphasize the saliency of clan concepts.[23]

In addition to the wide diffusion of decision-making power within the polity, there were other constraints imposed on the *mubake* which made him poorly qualified to exercise power. Ideally, he spent his youth secluded, thus symbolizing his separation from the rest of society. This policy was intended to protect him ritually as well as physically from potential danger. Nonetheless, because of the intensity of political conflict focussing on the status of *mubake*, individual reigns were often very short.[24] Consequently, a *mubake* was often very young at the time of his accession, and he often did not have the chance to develop his political skills even after acceding to the position. The ritual prescriptions surrounding his role also included prohibitions on meeting certain people and limitations on some types of travel (such as crossing certain rivers). In a highly mobile society where face-to-face contacts were essential to the political process, these requirements presented severe obstacles to effective political action on the part of the *mubake*. Finally, the *mubake* was considered a member of no particular clan.[25] At one level this reinforced his identity with the kingdom as a whole; at the same time it deprived him of a personal political base. Unable to draw on his own political resources, the Nyanga *mubake* was left in a position of considerable political insecurity.

Under these circumstances, political action was oriented more to preserving the continuity of the polity than to mobilizing power for other purposes. The most important role for assuring continuity was that of the *mumbo,* the designated mother of the successor to the *mubake*. Within the Nyanga context, where political competition focussed on the question of who was to succeed to *mubake* status, the presence of the *mumbo* was more important than that of the *mubake* himself, for the choice of *mumbo* (ideally) determined the choice of successor. Because the successor was defined as the son (real or adoptive) of a given woman, her presence was the ultimate guarantee for the kingdom's continuity. Therefore the designation of these wives was subject to even more complex rules than was the choice of the successor himself.[26]

The *mumbo* was both the ritual wife of the reigning *mubake* and the woman designated to provide the *mubake*'s eventual successor. But she was also, ideally, a (biological or classificatory) half-sister to the *mubake*. Each *mubake* therefore could theoretically claim maternal and paternal descent within the same lineage; in fact, by the logic of this model the *mubake*'s maternal and paternal grandfather would be the same person.[27] But in reality there were many obstacles to attaining the normative ideal.[28] First, the very nature of the *mumbo*'s relations with the *mubake* made it unlikely that the successor would have been the child of the reigning *mubake*. Although the enthronement rituals included ritual intercourse between the *mubake* and the *mumbo*, this was the only time they were permitted to have sexual relations with each other; after the enthronement the *mumbo* was secluded and carefully guarded from the *mubake*.[29] Yet the successor, ideally, was not the first-born child of the *mumbo*, but the first male born after a female. Furthermore, there were multiple mechanisms to assure that there was a recognized alternative policy for naming the heir, in case the *mumbo* did not herself give birth to a male heir.[30]

The presence of such complex mechanisms to assure a successor was eloquent testimony to the fact that very often the *mubake* was not the genitor of his successor. Often a successor was chosen from among the children born before a woman's accession to *mumbo* status, or during her exile away from the *mubake*, or even long after the *mubake*'s death. Other wives of the *mubake* (but only ritually prescribed wives) could produce a successor in case the *mumbo* failed to do so; so could an unmarried daughter of the *mumbo*, the *mumbo*'s father (as genitor), the *mumbo*'s sister, the servant (or even "wife") of the *mumbo*, or any candidate from outside adopted by the *mumbo*. According to Biebuyck, cases such as these occurred very frequently.[31]

To illustrate this complex process, Biebuyck cites the case of a *mumbo* without children, who then married another woman (from her own resources). The "wife" in turn gave birth to two sons, who were accepted as proper sons of the *mumbo* (the "husband" within this particular marriage context). These two sons were therefore capable of succeeding to the position of *mubake*. But the *mumbo* in question was the *mumbo* of a man who himself had succeeded as classificatory sororal nephew of the preceding *mubake* (who had died with no children of his own); in fact he was the son of the unmarried daughter of the unmarried consanguine sister of the former *mubake*. In other words, in this case the *mubake*'s sister was said to have produced the heir (through her own unmarried daughter), even though she had not officially been installed as *mumbo* of her brother. Because she was a member of the descent group headed by her brother, her grandson was able to accede to the perquisites of a son of the *mubake* himself—he was treated as the true son of the *mubake*.[32]

I have dwelled on this aspect of royalty here both because it was central to the political system of the Nyanga and because it serves as a useful indicator of the nature of Rift Valley societies of the past. As will be discussed below, the evidence suggests that both the *mubake*-figure itself, referred to as *mwami* (or *muhinza*) east of the lake, and the distinctive patterns of succession to the status of *mubake* were also present in societies east of Lake Kivu, prior to the consolidation of power in this area by the Abanyiginya dynasty of Rwanda during the eighteenth and nineteenth centuries. The traditions on this point are specific enough and the associated data on the wide geographical spread of more general ritual patterns in the region are strong enough to indicate that throughout the area the nature of former socio-political organization in many important respects resembled that found today among the Nyanga, as summarized here.[33]

The aspects of Nyanga politics discussed above also relate to more recent succession struggles in the Rift area. Although the succession practices in the two Havu kingdoms (Mpinga and Ijwi) and in Rwanda all differ from each other, in all three areas the real succession struggle did not take place after the king's death, but long before that. This was the struggle between the king's wives, each of whom sought to increase her political resources in order to place her own son on the throne. The queen mother was often selected not after the succession, as mother of the named successor, but on other grounds, independent of the prior choice of "legitimate" successor to the king. The politics of succession therefore essentially focussed on the choice of queen mother, because a person in this position was able to mobilize superior political resources to legitimate the succession of her son. Thus the arguments over the legitimacy of one or another candidate often focussed on the legitimacy of the candidate's mother to serve as queen mother and thus to produce the heir. As will be discussed in chapter 11, for Ijwi successions, those who worked outside this framework were seldom successful in mobilizing the population to their cause.[34]

In addition to the role of *mumbo*, the ritual and political role of women in Bunyanga was reflected in many other contexts. There were many types of prescribed royal marriages among the Nyanga, and each wife held a different title and fulfilled different ritual and social roles from those of her colleagues. In some cases, one woman married another woman; the children born to either woman in such a union then belonged to the descent group of the female "husband."[35] Women also served as pawns (*bikumi;* sing. *cikumi*) in debt payments and therefore as alliance mechanisms between two groups. (In some cases a single woman could pass through several such alliance formations in this fashion.) Although such a woman was not formally married, her children belonged to the host lineage rather than to their mother's natal lineage, as did the children of other unmarried women.[36] Finally, there were various types of marriages and other arrangements which women could enter into, including the role of village wife, or wife of one of several spirits.[37] The great variety of social roles open to women illustrates the heterogeneous nature of alliance ties in Bunyanga, ties to which descent-group affiliation was often a secondary concern.

Individual leadership roles among the Nyanga provide another indication of the earlier spread of common historical ties throughout the Rift Valley area; as noted in chapter 1 these positions (and even some of the terminology) are also present on Ijwi. Three of those roles will be discussed here: the *barusi* (sing. *murusi*), the *bakungu,* and the *bandirabitambo*. Barusi were male sons of the king. (But excluded from this status were the sons of the *mumbo* and those of one other wife referred to as *nyabana;* these males were the most likely successors to the position of *mubake*.) Although the status of *murusi* was ascribed by birth, it was not permanent: one could leave this status, as often happened, by leaving the polity of one's birth. *Barusi* lived scattered throughout the kingdom, and seldom acted as a corporate group, playing only a minor role in the decision-making powers of the polity.[38]

Most powers—the power to call public meetings, to decide on succession, to consult public oracles, or to set in motion certain rituals—were exercised by a group of men called *bakungu*. This was a hereditary status; *bakungu* appear to have served as representatives of local kinship and residential groups widely dispersed throughout the polity. Although no representative statistics are provided, Biebuyck notes that in the 1950s *bakungu* status comprised a large proportion of the men of the polities he studied. The *bakungu* themselves were subdivided into several recognizable segments with specific functions and various individual titled positions. Because they often had clients of their own, they served as one of the most important lines of communication ramifying widely throughout the polity; in addition they served as a potential class distinct from the royal *barusi*.[39]

Ritual functions were primarily the domain of the *bandirabitambo,* another hereditary position among the Nyanga. The rituals of royalty seem to have been similar throughout Bunyanga, but there was no regular association of a particular ritual function with a particular ritual status among the various polities. Therefore although the ritual functions were similar, the members of the *bandirabitambo* varied from one polity to another; the ritual functions were autonomous of any particular hereditary group.

One set of functions that does seem to have been regularly associated with a given title was that associated with Musao, a member of the Basao clan. Although present in all parts of Bunyanga, the Basao were most strongly associated with Buhunde to the east of Bunyanga, just northwest of Lake Kivu. Though Musao could not inhabit the same village as the *mubake,* his principal duties were directly linked to the person of the chief; he played particularly important roles at the enthronement ceremony and during life-cycle rituals. In addition to guarding much of the royal regalia, he served as "male wife" of the *mubake* at the enthronement, preparing the bed for ritual intercourse of the *mubake* and *mumbo,* and cooking ritual meals. In the life-cycle rituals, he replaced the *mubake* on some occasions, thus emphasizing the strong role identity of Musao with the king.[40] A similar ritual role is found in other kingdoms of the Kivu Rift today. On Ijwi the ritualist named Mushaho also has a prominent role in royal rituals; he also sometimes ritually replaces the king *(mwami)* in these ceremonies. Like his counterpart in Bunyanga, his duties do not end with the formal royal rituals; Mushaho is continuously in attendance at the *mwami*'s residence, performing duties associated with the domestic life of the court. (Mushaho's ritual role on Ijwi will be discussed in greater detail in chapter 12).

Bunyanga therefore clearly shares marked similarities, both in the rituals performed and in ritualists' titles, with other areas in the Rift region. But throughout this wider region there is no regular association of specific ritualists with a set of given ritual functions (Musao being an exception). Even where there are strong apparent similarities, these ritual functions can be subdivided among many ritualists or cumulated in the hands of a few; they are general structural similarities, not precise reconstructions. Therefore it is a hazardous exercise to try to trace the diffusion of rituals by tracing the movement of populations, or, to reverse the relationship, to try to trace population movements on the basis of ritual diffusion.

The *mubande* ceremonies, the central rites associated with kingship, provide another example of the strong ritual continuities found throughout the region. Although the rituals associated with this term are apparently most highly elaborated among the Nyanga, similar rites are also found among the Tembo, Hunde, Lega, Nande, Kapiri, and Kumu of the forest areas. In the immediate area of Lake Kivu the term *"mubande"* is found associated with slightly different objects and rites in the Shi states of Kaziba, Ngweshe, Kabare (as well as in other Shi states), in Mpinga (a Havu state), and on Ijwi. Despite their common central role in kingship, there are important variations in the form of these rituals. The Nyanga *mubande* rituals are particularly interesting, however, because although essential to kingship they are autonomous of it. The Nyanga forms will therefore be discussed briefly here; in their Ijwi context, these rituals will be considered at greater length in chapter 12.

Among Nyanga the term *"mubande"* refers both to certain types of quartz crystals and to an initiation society composed of married men who were responsible for organizing circumcision ceremonies.[41] The *mubande* society among the Nyanga included several grades; its ceremonies were held at various prescribed times, as well as occasionally at the time of epidemics. It was also important at the enthronement of a *mubake,* where the members of the *mubande* society affirmed the responsibilities of the *mubake,* to remind him of the proper behavior of the *mubake* towards his subjects and thus to incorporate the individual king within his public role as *mubake.* The *mubande* rites at enthronement therefore defined the relationship of a king to his people. But these royal rituals were only an extension of the larger field of rituals associated with the *mubande* society; their more important role was that of preparing youths for initiation as full adult members of society.

Among the Hunde, neighboring the Nyanga to the east, *mubande* is portrayed quite differently, as exclusively a part of the ritual of royal succession. In direct contrast to the Nyanga situation, *mubande* in Buhunde is said to have consisted solely of a rite whose object was to remind the population of their obligations and loyalty to the *mwami.* Every titleholder of the kingdom attended the ceremony, and each had to swear allegiance individually to the king, identified with the *mubande* crystals.

There are clearly significant differences in the way this ritual is portrayed in these two areas. The nature of the sources, however, makes it likely that these differences derive in large part from the sources themselves rather than represent historical and cultural transformations of the rituals and concepts behind the sources. The description of the Nyanga *mubande* ceremonies was written by a Nyanga priest on the basis of broad inquiry among the Nyanga. The section on the Hunde was written by a European priest on the basis of data obtained from a single gathering summoned and presided over by the colonially installed "grand chef de tout le Buhunde,"[42] a position created, imposed, and maintained by the colonial power. The strong centrist approach in the *mubande* data from Buhunde contrasts markedly with most other data on precolonial Hunde social organization; these data stress the similarities of Hunde and Nyanga cultures in the past, including their noncentralized political organization. Comparing the Hunde *mubande* description with that from Bunyanga, where *mubande* is much more in concert with other aspects of the society, suggests that the Hunde data result from a reinterpretation of the ritual within the colonial context, or rather within the context of colonial chiefship; the portrayal of the Nyanga form is probably a closer representation of an earlier form.[43]

Elsewhere in the region, the term *"mubande"* is applied to a substance composed of dried earth mixed with many types of herbs from different locales. On Ijwi Island this is used both as a common medicine considered particularly effective against leprosy (and thus important in treating cases of transgressing taboos) and as part of the royal ceremonies. In the latter context it is associated with enthronement and with the annual First Fruits ceremonies, where *mubande* is ground and added to beer; the mixture is drunk by the ritualists and others. A similar description of *mubande* as a ritual substance and as a medicine is provided for the kingdom of Kaziba, just south of Bushi, located between Lakes Kivu and Tanganyika.[44] Even in the context of these royal rituals, *mubande* is not exclusive to royalty or to the ritualists; it is eagerly sought by all the people. In this sense the use of *mubande* corresponds more closely to the Nyanga model than to the Hunde portrayal noted above.

In Buhavu (Mpinga; the mainland west of Lake Kivu) and in central Bushi (Buhaya and Ngweshe), however, the concept of *mubande* is rather different. There, the term *"mubande"* refers to the annual royal ceremony, and the performance of this ceremony is known as *okunyw'omubande* ("to drink the *mubande*"). This terminology would imply that the Shi traditions derive from the Kaziba-Ijwi form, and the spread of the different traditions would also conform to such a hypothesis. But the substance of *mubande,* as used on Ijwi and in Kaziba, is not present in the central Shi rites. Despite the name given to the ceremony as a whole, there is no particular ritual of drinking *mubande* as in fact there is on Ijwi. In central Bushi (Buhaya), nothing is known of *mubande* the substance; *"mubande"* is known only as the term for the ritual.[45] The *mubande* rituals thus serve as yet another example of a cultural tradition whose variations are spread widely in the region.

The Nyanga Prototype and Neighboring Societies

From the preceding remarks, it is clear that, despite current differences, Bunyanga and the cultures of the Kivu Rift share both specific contacts from more recent interaction and a common historical legacy of considerable time depth. Data from east of Lake Kivu and general observations from Ijwi Island confirm the suggestion that the general outlines of present-day Nyanga society are indicative of other societies, formerly widely spread in the Rift Valley region. On this basis the Nyanga system can be used as a prototype for the political features general to the Lake Kivu Rift Valley prior to the mid-eighteenth century.

The Hunde peoples neighbor the Nyanga directly to the east and share many aspects of their culture. The common features shared between the Hunde and the peoples to their west, however, have been neglected in most sources, because more recent changes in Hunde society have strengthened the similarities of Buhunde to the Interlacustrine areas.[46] Many Rwandans were settled in the area in the 1930s and 1940s, and many European plantations were located there; in addition the political structures of Buhunde were also reorganized into a single administrative framework under a single colonially imposed chief.[47] The present differences between the political systems of Bunyanga and Buhunde, therefore, seem to be largely products of the more recent period. However, there is considerable evidence that before the period of colonial rule the Hunde were organized into many small polities along the Nyanga model described above, and that they shared many other similarities with the Nyanga as well. Intensive historical interaction also occurred between the Nyanga and the Hunde populations, in population movements as well as in commercial and marriage ties.[48]

Farther east, historical ties between Buhunde and the Bugoyi region (in what is today northwestern Rwanda) were also strong. Population movements and commercial ties during the nineteenth century attest to what appears to have been a dense and enduring network of interaction across the northern end of Lake Kivu between Nyanga areas and northern Rwanda.[49] Linguistic evidence indicates that, in the past, the language spoken in Bugoyi was similar to Kihunde.[50] Ritual concepts common to the peoples around the northern end of Lake Kivu, and apparently relating to the distant past, also indicate that this northern Kivu corridor played an important role in cultural interaction in the area.[51]

Today, certain areas on Ijwi Island also show aspects of this type of culture. This is especially apparent in the religious spirits revered; two "Hunde" spirits, Muhima and Maheshe, though known throughout Ijwi, are especially prevalent in the northern parts of Ijwi and in the eastern highland areas.[52] Women in the north were sometimes exchanged in transactions involving fields, reflecting the *cikumi* pattern found farther west.[53] In addition, lexical items similar to Kihunde and Kitembo are found only in these areas on Ijwi.[54] Certain songs in eastern Ijwi are sung in dialects of Kitembo and Kihunde still today;[55] foods and material culture also distinguish this area from other areas of the island today and reflect forest culture items.[56] Even social behavior norms—large gatherings with open, very informal interaction—differ from the prevalent pattern elsewhere on the island, but they conform exactly to the model of the forest areas. Patterns of immigration and emigration tie these areas of Ijwi particularly to Buzi and Buhunde at the northwest corner of the lake; they therefore serve as a direct tie-in to the communication corridor at the north end of the lake.

Several factors indicate that this series of culture traits was not introduced recently; these traits represent retentions from earlier cultural norms, formerly more widely spread in the general area and on Ijwi. This portion of Ijwi is remote from royal centers, and distinguished from the rest of the island in terrain, livelihood, and outside contacts (which are less intensive and less continuous); settlement of the present groups there occurred predominantly in the eighteenth century, before the changes associated with royalty. In addition, data from elsewhere in the area indicate that at least some of these forest culture aspects (or associated aspects of culture) were widely diffused off the island as well, and therefore probably they are more representative of earlier cultural norms than of specific immigration patterns. These will be explored later; the next chapter will consider the likelihood that a culture similar to the Nyanga prototype was predominant on Ijwi during the eighteenth century. Here we shall examine some of the more specific regional manifestations of such a prototype society, drawing on archeological, ritual, and linguistic data.

The Historical Application of the Prototype Model

The argument that a prototype society such as that postulated here corresponds to social institutions formerly present throughout the region does not rest on selective comparisons from present-day societies alone. Archeological data suggest that the Rift Valley area shares a pattern of cultural continuity with areas to the west, distinct from that indicated by archeological traditions east of the Nile-Zaire Divide. Still other data suggest that a forest environment formerly spread throughout the region, providing an ecology similar to that of the Nyanga area today but different from that currently found in the Rift Valley. Finally, Rwandan oral traditions make it clear that the eighteenth-century polities east of Lake Kivu included many of the political features shown above to be essential to the political organization of the Nyanga polities.

Rift Valley Continuities and Archeological Findings

Although little archeological work has yet been carried out in the immediate area of Lake Kivu, what has been done lends support to the broad historical schema presented in this chapter. Tentative as they are, the results indicate that localized patterns of culture were stable over time and that in the past the Nile-Zaire Divide east of Lake Kivu formed a major cultural, as well as geographical, divide; sites immediately east and west of the lake were more similar to each other than either group was to sites east of the divide (see Map 5). This archeological evidence therefore implies that in the past the Lake Kivu region showed closer cultural continuities with the west than with the east—that the Rift Valley area shared a basic material culture substratum with the forest areas west of the Mitumba Mountains and was distinct from the Interlacustrine patterns east of the divide.

On the basis of a recent review of archeological research carried out in the area, F. Van Noten has dispensed with the earlier classification of the Urewe ware as applied to Rwanda, because in his opinion it is too broad a rubric to be useful for classifications of whole cultures.[57] His reclassification

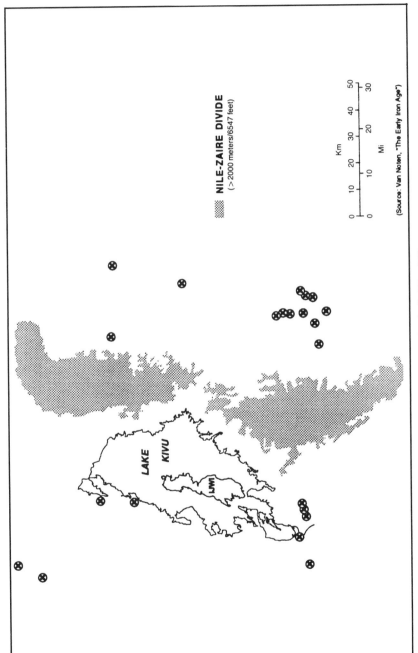

Map 5. Archeological sites in the Kivu Rift area

NILE-ZAIRE DIVIDE
(>2000 meters/6547 feet)

Km

Mi

(Source: Van Noten, "The Early Iron Age")

LAKE
KIVU

LWI

of sites and industries suggests that, in accounting for differences in material culture, at least in this area, regional or local variations should be considered more significant criteria of classification than temporal evolution taken alone. Such an analytic approach leads Van Noten to conclude that Late Stone Age–Early Iron Age industries were localized and more or less stabilized over relatively long periods of time. His assessment thus implicitly questions the common practice of generalizing temporal evolution over vast areas on the basis of evidence derived from sites which are widely separated geographically as well as chronologically.

Some of these archeological insights can be fruitfully transferred to more recent cultural patterns. Where material aspects of cultures were geographically stabilized over long periods of time and apparently remained distinct from other industries not far distant, it is probable that other aspects of culture followed similar patterns. On this basis it could also be hypothesized that despite the potential for interaction and interchange, the two important culture zones dealt with here—that of the forest cultures and that of the Interlacustrine cultures—remained relatively stable over long time periods.

Van Noten's reclassification of these sites within such a broad regional perspective also follows, in every case, the geographical division of the Nile-Zaire Divide—east of Lake Kivu, not west of the lake, where the cultural divide is presently located. In his presentation, all members of the same classificatory subsets, or "industries," are located on the same side of the divide, even where different sites within a given industry are separated by over 100 kilometers. The paucity of sites (and dates) west of the lake, and especially from the area around the northern end of Lake Kivu, presently precludes any definite conclusions on this point; sites in Buhunde and Bugoyi, the most important areas for our present interest, are especially rare. But Van Noten groups one site on the northwestern shore of Lake Kivu (that named Km. 150), for example, with industries south of the lake and east of the Rusizi but west of the divide. These industries, Van Noten notes, are clearly distinguished from industries east of the divide.[58]

These data—or rather Van Noten's interpretation of these data—argue strongly for past cultural similarities of areas west of Lake Kivu with areas just east of the lake, thus tying Ijwi culturally to the forest culture patterns. Other data drawn from the published historical traditions of Rwanda—a state that is today very different in political structure and social organization from those portrayed for the Kivu Prototype Societies sketched out here—suggest a similar conclusion. Indeed Rwandan sources reflect this pattern directly, referring to the people living west of the Nile-Zaire Divide (but still east of the lake) as "Banyabungo" or "Bashi," thus grouping them culturally with the population of the Rift Valley and those west of the lake.[59]

East of Lake Kivu

There exists an extraordinary corpus of historical traditions relating to Rwanda and focussing on the royal history of the Abanyiginya dynasties.[60] Where earlier polities are mentioned at all, these appear only as backdrops to—and victims of—the heroics of the Rwandan kings. Nonetheless, it is clear that many smaller polities, independent of the Abanyiginya regime, were formerly located in the mountainous Nile-Zaire Divide area of what is now western Rwanda. Some of these remained independent of the Rwandan state structures until well into the period of colonial rule, but most were absorbed into the Rwandan state structures in the eighteenth and nineteenth centuries.[61]

From fragmentary references, it appears that these societies were structured along lines very similar to those portrayed above for the Nyanga. The mobile way of life of these people, stressing the importance of hunting, was thoroughly compatible with the forest environment. They lived in small villages with their houses grouped together in a pattern distinct from that found elsewhere in Rwanda.[62] Although these areas served as refuge for some political fugitives from Rwanda, there were apparently few ties to the Rwandan social network until the imposition of Tutsi rule.

All sources mention the importance of the rituals associated with royalty in these polities; they give special attention to those which pertained directly to the person of the *mwami* (*umuhinza* in the Rwandan court sources), the social and ritual focus of the polity.[63] As with the *mubake* in Bunyanga, the *mwami* was withdrawn from society during his youth. During this time his mother exercised great influence not only over her son and royal successor but also on the broader politics of the domain. Even after his succession it seems the *mwami* was surrounded with ritual precautions: both his mobility and contact with others were restricted and, as elsewhere, many of the rituals associated with the well-being of the polity depended on him. One of the most important of these ritual functions was that of performing the First Fruits ceremonies for certain crops.[64]

These functions are similar to those of the Rwandan *mwami*, still, several features distinguish the polities of the divide from the Rwandan state and reflect similarities with the forest cultures as discussed above. All sources stress the collegial quality of political decision-making in these polities: the *mwami* "avait la sagesse de ne prendre aucune décision importante sans avoir d'abord consulté son conseil composé de quelques personnages plus influents des familles de son ressort. . . ."[65] Succession did not pass from father to son; instead, the *mwami* often designated a close relative, frequently his sororal nephew—the son of his sister. One observer notes that this type of succession was not arbitrary; it was a pattern apparently socially prescribed,

determined only after careful deliberation and public approval. The designated successor in Bushiru, for example,

> was not necessarily his [the *mwami*'s] eldest son, nor even one of his sons at
> all, but it was always a close relative. Thus [for example], Kidahiro, whom
> Nyamakwa [the *"muhinza"* of Bushiru; d. 1938] had certainly chosen to succeed
> him, was only one of his nephews. This choice was not determined carelessly,
> that is, not without having presented the case to his entourage.[66]

A different aspect of these succession practices is that described for
Busozo, another small polity, located in what is now the extreme southwestern corner of Rwanda. Here, the *mwami* could not appear in public
before he had fathered two children, one girl and one boy.[67] The order of
birth is not mentioned and the mother of these children is not noted. But it is
clear from the context that this custom was part of the process relating to the
succession; the implication is that, as in Bunyanga, the successor should
follow the birth of a sister. Prior to the birth of these two children the *mwami*
was secluded, and the political influence of the "queen mother" (her exact
relationship to the *mwami* is not stated) was at its apogee. Remarkably, this
institution, too, parallels the process of succession in Nyanga polities, where
the successor was, ideally, the first son born after a daughter—and born to
the (classificatory) sister of the *mubake.*[68]

These (and other) data suggest that in this area there existed a series of
small-scale polities, characterized by a mobile forest population and a strong
ritual focus on the sovereign. Despite the ritual pre-eminence of this role,
political power appears to have been widely diffused among a large number of
dignitaries, councillors, and ritual specialists. What is significant is not the
inadequacy of the data in the Rwandan sources but the fact that what little is
known of the social and ritual characteristics of these polities east of Lake Kivu
corresponds so well with the Nyanga data.[69] It is also remarkable that they
share this common set of political assumptions and structures even despite
their diverse "origins," the specific social antecedents so beloved by diffusionist
analysts.[70] Thus these diverse data all converge—ethnographic evidence from
west of Lake Kivu, archeological evidence from throughout the area, and oral
evidence from east of the lake. This lends support to the hypothesis that institutions similar to those presently found in the forested areas west of Lake Kivu
were formerly also present east of the lake and west of the Nile-Zaire Divide,
and thus their spread included the entire Rift Valley. Such data also help
establish the range and general characteristics of the Kivu Prototype Society
common throughout the Kivu Rift in the not-too-distant past. General as it is,
this model also serves as a serviceable baseline from which to assess the transformations that have occurred in the region since the late eighteenth century.

3

The Process of Social Transformation
on Ijwi Island

Ijwi Island traditions, too, include references to a Kivu Prototype Society as sketched out in chapter 2. But these traditions are of a particular character. They refer neither to discrete, particular events nor to specific, identifiable individuals. Instead they are fragmentary and composite traditions; they consist of only vague allusions to apparently timeless structural characteristics of a general culture type no longer represented on Ijwi. We cannot therefore reconstruct an internal narrative "history" of these groups as that term is understood today, for none is accessible at this time depth.

Nonetheless, it is useful to examine these widespread, if superficial, references still found on Ijwi, for two reasons. Even if they cannot be used to establish with any precision the nature of Ijwi culture and history of 200 years ago, they can be used to identify the means by which such groups of early inhabitants were incorporated into Ijwi society as it evolved over the mid- and late-eighteenth century. More important, understanding the manner by which these earlier groups are identified in current traditions is instrumental in understanding the process of emergent group identities on Ijwi. If it is clear that there was no single corporate group on Ijwi 200 years ago, it is equally clear that more recent arrivals tend to identify these various peoples as precisely that—a single social category. This form of group representation of the Other in the traditions both reflects and reinforces the wider social process of group identities emerging along new lines. The traditions which portray the early inhabitants as a single social category, therefore, are in part the effect of a slow process of consolidation and in part one of the very means by which such consolidation took place.

Consequently, rather than focus on the internal narrative history of these eighteenth-century inhabitants of Ijwi, this chapter will assess the character of the traditions relating to the groups forming the "prototype society" on Ijwi—traditions which speak more to the relations of such groups with others than to the internal histories of their members. After a brief look at the nature of oral traditions on Ijwi, we shall consider the content and prove-

65

nience of the specific sources relating to the early populations, suggesting the process by which such early groups were incorporated into the evolving Ijwi social universe. An immigrant group known as the Banyakabwa was particularly instrumental in the formation of wider new group identities on Ijwi; therefore this chapter gives special attention to the role of the Banyakabwa in the consolidation of such "clan" identities.

But the Banyakabwa were only one of several groups to arrive on Ijwi from east of the lake during the mid-eighteenth century. Subsequent chapters will explore the wider context and examine the pressures that brought the Banyakabwa and others to Ijwi; in so doing they will explore the broader external factors acting on the Kivu Rift Prototype Societies, both on Ijwi and elsewhere, during this period.

Social Identity in Ijwi Oral Traditions

Pre-Basibula clans on Ijwi can be divided into three categories according to the predominant type of historical traditions associated with them: those groups not present on Ijwi today, but mentioned in the traditions of others; those groups with a continuous presence on Ijwi, but which did not later develop close ties to the Basibula royal family; and those present on the island today which did develop ties to the royal family through ritual, social, or administrative mechanisms.

Oral traditions on the first group (called Group I traditions here) are entirely different from those relating to the others. At first glance they appear to refer to an indefinite historical past: they do not relate to any definite time period, nor do they refer to present groups on Ijwi, and hence they apparently lack continuity with the present. These are third-party traditions, expressed with references to "they," not "we." Therefore the groups referred to often appear extraneous to present categories of both time and society, an example of how social distancing and chronological remove intersect and reinforce each other: the people of Ijwi today do not accept these early cultures as part of present Ijwi society, only as part of a different social universe located in an allochronic world.

Today, Bany'Iju consider themselves distinct from this type of society in the conceptual sense of being in opposition to it, not in the temporal sense of having evolved from it. In fact, the traditions not only portray early groups on Ijwi, they also often ridicule them; thus these stories help reinforce contemporary Ijwi concepts of society by reference to an "anti-society." In this view, the culture (or cultures) portrayed in Group I traditions was not a "predecessor" society from which present Ijwi society grew; rather, it was a different society entirely, inhabited by different types of people. Neither the origins nor the current identity of the people mentioned in these traditions are of any interest to most people on Ijwi today; they were simply the characters of some interesting stories. Curiosity on Ijwi about these people as historical actors is analogous to Western curiosity about the origins or destiny of the Seven Dwarfs.

And yet, there is more to these traditions than such a perspective accounts for. There are ways in which these two opposed social models (the current and the allochronic) are linked, not only in their conceptual complementarity—as an anti-society that reinforces contemporary social norms on Ijwi—but also in their historical derivation. It is this relationship which provides the focus of inquiry in this chapter.

The second category of historical traditions on Ijwi, which I shall refer to as Group II traditions, includes the least standardized of all the historical traditions on Ijwi. The members of those clans associated with them (such as the Bahande and the Bakanga) have no common story of arrival, they perform no ritual functions at the level of the royal court today, and they do not share a strong corporate sentiment beyond the localized groups. Because they lack intensive interaction with the royal line, these clans are marginal to the current social arena. Because Group II traditions seldom refer to other groups and therefore do not "tie in" directly to the history of the island as a whole, they appear to consist of a set of episodes unrelated to wider currents of social change.

Traditions of this type also have a shallow time depth, usually referring only to living people (or their fathers). In their narrative form they tend to be fragmentary and discontinuous, as well as lacking historical depth; it is difficult to reconstruct patterns of change from them. In certain respects Group I and Group II traditions share similar characteristics; they frequently draw on mythical themes, for example, and they both show an allochronic relationship to other features of retained Ijwi history. Nonetheless, they differ from each other in the nature of this allochronic character. Traditions in Group I seem to refer to an indefinite past because they lack present social referents, whereas traditions in Group II refer to an indefinite past for lack of a concept of change within the group.

The third category of traditions on Ijwi (Group III traditions) is associated with clans which have developed linkages of various types with the royal family. Compared with other types of traditions, Group III traditions tend to be longer and fuller. They are especially concerned with people and events associated with the central court; they recount details of external conflicts or internal succession disputes, land claims, and alliances. In other words these traditions refer to socially constituted groups, acting in a context of relations with others. These traditions include detailed family histories, and by cross-references they can be supplemented with data from the royal histories or traditions of other clans. As a body, therefore, these are among the richest of the traditions, especially for the periods following the Basibula arrival; they add circumstantial detail to the royal narrative while considering a much wider range of interests than do the royal traditions. Group III traditions will therefore be discussed more fully in subsequent chapters.

This chapter focusses on Group I traditions. The analysis will identify the social referents of these traditions and show how these earlier identities have been lost to present Ijwi society. At a different level it will analyze an example of identity transformation on Ijwi, illustrating how changes in identities result from alterations in the larger social context. These alterations do not necessarily imply the introduction of specific new culture traits from outside. What changed was the pattern of social perceptions and behavior, the structure of social classifications.

Group I Traditions

Canoes from Clay and Lances from Plants

Traditions relating to groups no longer present on Ijwi all emphasize the differences between their way of life and that of Ijwi groups today. People on Ijwi today characterize these earlier people as lacking "intelligence"—lacking technical knowledge and general social behavior corresponding to present norms. One of the most widespread stories illustrating this concerns a people called the Binyalenge, who wanted to go to the mainland. They built a great canoe in clay, dried and fired it carefully, and set out for their destination. When well out on the lake, the clay canoe dissolved and all the occupants drowned.[1]

Another example of this type of story concerns the people called the BeneNyamuhiva, who fought against more recent arrivals, using as spears the stems of the *bifunu* plant, (a type of yam).[2] Today the people of Ijwi consider that image absurd; *bifunu* is considered suitable only as food for old people: the tubers take a very long time to prepare, and only the elderly, who spend most of their time at home in their compounds, have such time at their disposal. Although no longer considered acceptable as food for the general Ijwi population, *bifunu* are assumed to have served as a staple on Ijwi in the past.[3]

It is possible that these traditions are associated with earlier peoples because *bifunu,* so prominent in the traditions, are presently appreciated only by old people. But this association is not likely to be the origin of the tradition so much as the explanation for its retention. This type of plant is frequently used as food in the forest areas similar to those of the prototype society postulated in chapter 2; it is therefore likely that this was a former generalized food crop now in the process of being phased out. Other evidence also indicates that the *bifunu* tradition refers to earlier Ijwi cultural attributes now only vaguely apparent, rather than derives from present cultural differences alone. *Bifunu* differ from present root crops used as food (such as sweet potatoes) in the same ways that other former crops differ from more recent successors: both their period of maturation and their cooking time are longer. Postulating *bifunu* as an early food on Ijwi thus correlates with general patterns of the evolution of food crops on the island.

Although some elements of the traditions can be related to Ijwi's past, the historical value of these traditions is not to be found in their content but in their associations with particular places and clans today. The timeless quality of the clay canoe and *bifunu* traditions on Ijwi is reinforced by the fact that both these traditions are clichés with wide diffusion in the region. The clay canoe motif is found, for example, among the Bakonjo to the north and at least as far east as Lake Victoria.[4] The *bifunu* motif in various forms (other than their use as spears) is present in traditions of the Nyanga and Hunde to the west and north of Lake Kivu.[5] It is also closely associated on Ijwi with the traditions of the Bakanga, a clan whose present members claim ties to the southwest of Lake Kivu.[6] Obviously these stereotypical elements are important not only as self-contained historical reports, and not only as condensed clichés. Instead they have a further purpose, as statements defining the differences of present Ijwi culture from an earlier unidentified population—and disparaging statements at that, since clay canoes dissolve and *bifunu* make neither good spears nor (on Ijwi today) good food.

Nyamuhiva and the Binyalenge

The principal names found in these traditions are Nyamuhiva and the Binyalenge.[7] Sometimes a direct correlation is made between these two names: the Binyalenge (or Banyalenge) are often assumed to be the "children" of Nyamuhiva; conversely, Nyamuhiva is often seen as the *mukulu* (elder or leader) or *mwami* of the Binyalenge. But the two traditions are nonetheless distinct: "Nyamuhiva" frequently refers to an individual or title, whereas "Binyalenge" is more often used as a corporate name applied to a group.[8]

The internal differences between the two traditions are associated with distinct regional distributions on Ijwi—regions that correspond with identifiable cultural differences. Over three-quarters of the references to Nyamuhiva were from the south of the island, whereas over three-quarters of those to the Binyalenge were from the north.[9] In other contexts, people from the north of Ijwi generally cite traditions that contain more precise references to individual names and titles, and are less concerned with wider group identities than are those in the south. But in this particular case, the traditions from the north refer more frequently to a generalized group (the Binyalenge) than to specific individuals (such as Nyamuhiva). Because they differ from the gen-

eral pattern of regional characteristics, these distinctive but consistent references underscore the association of the Binyalenge traditions in the north
with particular social groups.

In the south of Ijwi, accounts about early peoples in general, and
Nyamuhiva in particular, are fullest and most frequent along the southern
rim of the present forest area or areas recently associated with forest.[10] These
traditions also make frequent mention of hunting activities, and often explicitly associate Nyamuhiva (and less frequently the Binyalenge) with the forest.
Where a locale is specified in the tradition, forest areas are cited in almost 80
percent of the cases; many claim that Nyamuhiva's former home was located
in what is today the uninhabited forest of Nyamusize.[11]

In the north, however, clan correlations were more important than milieu
in accounting for different forms of the traditions: references to the Binyalenge
(again, found mostly in the north) were more often derived from a single clan
than specifically from a forest area, whereas references to Nyamuhiva (especially frequent in the south) were derived from forest areas twice as frequently as from the clan most often citing them. Similar features differentiate
the Nyamuhiva and Binyalenge traditions in their content. There is a strong
association (by third parties) of the Binyalenge traditions with specific,
named clan groups (the Banyakabwa and the Booze), rather than with a
distinct area, as is the case for the traditions on Nyamuhiva.

These structural differences within the genre can be linked to specific
characteristics of settlement in the north and south of Ijwi. Settlement in the
north generally followed a pattern of individuals or single families moving
from elsewhere on Ijwi. In comparison to the south, new settlers were more
frequently assimilated into the northern social structure in small segments
than as large groups. Under these circumstances, classifications applied to a
pre-existing population (such as the "Binyalenge") may actually have been
strengthened rather than threatened or dissolved by immigration; traditions
of the earlier groups would have been altered less in the north than in the
south, where earlier inhabitants interacted with more numerous immigrant
groups, not with individual settlers.

Different external ties also help explain regional differences in the traditions relating to older populations. In the north, strong ties have been maintained with areas around the northern end of the lake: to Bubale and Buzi
(in present-day Buhavu), and Bunyungu (in Buhunde). In Ijwi perceptions,
these areas share a culture similar to that portrayed in the traditions of this
category; indeed, some of these cultural features persist in the north of Ijwi.
In the south, however, current settlement patterns, political norms, and outside ties all make the forest culture norms appear slightly archaic. Therefore
oral sources from the south associate the cultures portrayed in these traditions
with an individual (a king, or *mwami*, Nyamuhiva) living in the remote and

(to the people of the south) culturally "removed" forest, rather than with a group living in areas now densely populated. (It is also noteworthy that the south has always been the area of the island most closely associated with kingship, the north always having been somewhat peripheral to the "culture of kingship," though not immune from the exercise of royal power—hence the references in the south to Nyamuhiva as a *"mwami,"* to represent the corporate group.)

Finally, the north is today the primary settlement area of the Banya-kabwa, one of the oldest clans on Ijwi, and one that possesses a strong sense of corporate identity which continues into the present. It is members of this clan in the north who recount the most consistent traditions relating to the Binya-lenge; the Banyakabwa appear to have had early contacts with the Binya-lenge and to have best preserved the memory of this group. Binyalenge tra-ditions therefore seem to have been best remembered where these people were in contact with an early important clan, the Banyakabwa. This pattern reflects the general characteristics of contemporary traditions elsewhere on Ijwi, as noted above: historical traditions on Ijwi show greater time depth and precision when integrated with the traditions of an important and clearly defined clan group.

Identifying the Binyalenge

Despite their differences, the traditions of the Binyalenge and Nyamuhiva both conform to a regular pattern, which indicates that there is in fact a common historical quality to them. But to reconstruct patterns of change from these traditions, it is first necessary to explore the historical continuity of the groups which they describe. This section seeks to establish the current identity of the Binyalenge. The next section will inquire into the processes which resulted in the loss of earlier Binyalenge identity, and led instead to the formation of new group identities based on different criteria.

In the North: The Binyalenge and the Booze

Although the Binyalenge no longer exist as an identifiable group on Ijwi, some indications associate them with present groups. Traditions in the north (especially those of the Banyakabwa) commonly identify the Binyalenge with "Nankola," the representative of the village of Nkola; Nkola today is com-posed almost exclusively of members of a single subclan, the Booze, widely accepted as part of the larger Balega clan group. It would thus appear that, at least in the north of Ijwi, the Binyalenge can be identified with the present Booze clan.

However, the traditions relating to the Binyalenge are very different from the consistent and widespread historical traditions by which the Booze remember their past. In fact, more specific references from among the Booze themselves locate the Binyalenge descendants in Busobe, a village near Nkola, itself composed of a population that is 80 percent Booze.[12] The evidence from within the Booze traditions therefore contradicts the indications suggesting that the Binyalenge have simply "become" the Booze. The village of Nkola has a strong corporate identity deriving from its clan homogeneity, its claims to special ritual prerogatives, and its particular historical identity. Nkola is recognized as having been a place of refuge in the past—autonomous of the king's authority—and the representative of the corporate group, with the title of Nankola, is remembered as formerly having enjoyed the status of ritualist of the *mwami*. Although considered members of the Balega clan, the Booze form a subclan, distinct from other Balega on historical grounds; they claim to have received the name Booze for their role in having "saved" one of the most celebrated of Rwandan kings, Ruganzu Ndori, from his enemies near the lake.[13] This sense of common participation with a critical event in the historical past has provided the Booze with an extremely strong sense of cohesion, reinforced by a pattern of residential localization which distinguishes them sharply from most other groups within the Balega clan: the Booze live essentially in two large centers on Ijwi, of which Nkola-Busobe is the oldest. In many features, then, the Booze are distinct from the more general Balega clan identity with which they are universally associated.

Although Nkola and Busobe are apparently related villages, specific Booze historical traditions are not strongly held in Busobe; they are known, but not known well. Instead, despite the fact that the population there claims Booze clan identity, traditions in Busobe conform more to the "Binyalenge" pattern. Several Booze interviewed in Busobe identified with a certain "Kilembelembe" (or "Ciremberembe") as a distant ancestor,[14] but Kilembelembe is a personification of the term "Bilembelembe," a variant form of reference to the Binyalenge, or a historically associated group.[15] In fact, some Booze in Busobe refer to their ancestors directly as Binyalenge; this had no parallel in Nkola.[16]

Busobe appears to be an old settlement, because the inhabitants of the village deny ever having given tribute for their land.[17] Although this is not infrequent in the north of Ijwi, it is unusual for communities which are secondary (and more recent) settlements. Despite common Booze status, Busobe is not and apparently never has been seen as administratively one with Nkola by the inhabitants of the two communities; it is not simply an extension of the Nkola community under the jurisdiction of Nankola. Therefore, whereas Nkola's exemption from tribute is based on ritual considerations, Busobe's exemptions are based on different grounds—the duration of settlement. But because neither remains exempt from taxation today, the specific explanations are no longer articulated; only the memory of their former (similar) status is retained by most people outside the villages.

The inhabitants of Busobe are also explicit in identifying yams *(bifunu)* and sorghum, two very old crops on Ijwi, as their former food staples. Sorghum is still appreciated as food on Ijwi today, although it is seldom used directly as food in deference to its role in fermenting banana beer. Yams, by contrast, are disdained by most Bany'Iju, who refer to them as the food of old people. What is significant in this context is that yams, disdained as food elsewhere on the island but readily acknowledged as such in Busobe, are also notable in the historical traditions relating to the Binyalenge.

There is another important historical distinction between Busobe and Nkola, and it is one which confirms the status of the Busobe population as descendants of very old inhabitants of Ijwi. The Booze of Nkola (and elsewhere) have consistent traditions of their arrival from outside Ijwi. People of Busobe know of this Booze "tradition of genesis" but reject its application to themselves; instead, they assert their own claims to "indigenous" status, expressed through more indirect testimony. In Busobe they affirm that the former rituals for their ancestors were held at the time of the first sorghum harvest (in late February). This is the very time at which the present First Fruits rituals are celebrated by the Ijwi king and court; one particularly reliable member of the community even stated that it was because the people of Busobe formerly celebrated the First Fruits that the *bami* (the kings) celebrate Muganuro at that time.[18] The Busobe tradition therefore challenges the exclusive claim of the royal court to this ceremony and is at odds with the prevalent assertion elsewhere on the island of the "state created whole," that is, that state functions were imported with the Basibula. (No one, not even the king, took exception to this statement which might otherwise be seen as *lèse-majesté*.)

Finally, there has been recent out-migration from Busobe to Buzi, a peninsula in the northwestern corner of Lake Kivu, near Buhunde. Although such mobility is common to other clans in the north, this case is significant because the Booze and the Balega in general do not have a tradition of mobility. Despite this lack of movement (and especially despite the lack of traditions of immigration in general), one Mwooze from Busobe did note that the first Mwooze to come to Busobe was a man named Ciremberembe. He had come from "Rwanda, Buzi, and Buhunde," from "kwa Gashenda"—a country now under the *mwami* Kalinda (that is, within the colonially delimited jurisdiction of Buhunde).[19] This reference reinforces the perception of historical ties to the northwest, the region closest to Ijwi which is presently identified, in Ijwi terms, as a forest culture.[20] Thus this tradition seems to reinforce, once again, the association of the Binyalenge with the forest cultures to the west.

Therefore, despite the easy interaction and current conceptual confusion between Nkola and Busobe, it would seem in fact that these two communities represent distinct historical groups. Although proximate, the two are not identical; their composition clearly identifies the village of Nkola as historically Booze and Busobe as essentially Binyalenge. Consequently, the current association of the Binyalenge with Booze identity can be seen as resulting from two processes: the fusion of two historically distinct groups sharing a common Balega identity (in terms of categories placed on them by others); and, independent of this, their shared social status relative to other groups in the past, in this case especially to the Banyakabwa.

It is significant that the Binyalenge traditions (and the association of the Binyalenge with Nankola) are strongest among the Banyakabwa. The Banyakabwa were an important corporate group on their arrival on the island, as they are still today in the north. Thus it is likely that in defining themselves apart from all earlier inhabitants, they perceived the Binyalenge and Booze as a common group. The important historical status of the Banyakabwa meant that in time their perceptions of the Binyalenge were accepted by the later arrivals; Binyalenge identity was thus fused with that of the Booze and, beyond that, with the Balega. Since then, the social categorization of these two peoples has been defined on Ijwi by this early perception on the part of the Banyakabwa; for the immigrant groups, powerful as they were, the historical distinctions of the two earlier groups, if recognized at all, were unimportant.

Faced with the arrival of new corporate groups, the Binyalenge and Booze apparently came to accept others' definitions of their social identities, retaining their differences only in a few unrelated traditions and activities. Their identities relative to others came to be redefined in terms of their relationship with the wider (changing) social milieu on the island. Formerly the Binyalenge and Booze together constituted that milieu; after the arrival of the Banyakabwa (and others) they were only a part of it. They could no longer simply absorb newcomers. Instead they became absorbed into the new context, and their parameters of identity were redefined in the process.

This interpretation, that two distinct early groups have been socially "fused" in the perceptions of other groups, is reinforced by parallels from the south. There, the descendants of Nyamuhiva are generally associated with areas where Balega are numerous (such as the villages of Cassi, Kimomo, and Bunyama), just as the Binyalenge descendants in the north are associated with Booze areas. But it is likely that the assimilation to Balega clan status of groups associated with Nyamuhiva was a more recent and more conscious phenomenon in the south.[21] Some people there state directly that the descendants of Nyamuhiva are Balega:

All the Balega are his [Nyamuhiva's] children; they just mixed with other Balega.[22]

The Binyalenge are Balega; Nyamuhiva was their leader.[23]

Nyamuhiva was a pygmy; he was of the Lega clan.[24]

Thus the process of consolidating diverse groups into a single social classification by others was not unique to the Binyalenge. Although their history and settlement patterns distinguish them from other Balega groups, the Booze (the clan of Nankola) are universally accepted as a constituent group of the Balega. Just as the Binyalenge were subsumed within a more inclusive Booze classification in the north, the Booze themselves have become identified as Balega on an Ijwi-wide level. Although this process had occurred at two levels (Binyalenge-Booze and Booze-Balega), the result was that the Binyalenge became identified as Balega throughout Ijwi.

It is significant that Binyalenge identification as Booze is particularly marked in the far north. In fact, both Banyakabwa influence and Binyalenge traditions are strongest in the extreme north of Ijwi; in these communities the Booze are the only Balega groups present in any significant numbers. Therefore, in the traditions from northern Ijwi the Booze tend to serve as a focal point for the process elsewhere associated more generally with the broader identification of Balega. The differences between the north and the south (i.e., the identification of Binyalenge as Booze or Balega), therefore, can be seen as variants of a single process occurring over the island as a whole.

In the South: The Banyakabwa, the Binyalenge, and Nyamuhiva

In the course of their long common history on Ijwi, the Binyalenge and Banyakabwa have experienced considerable interaction with each other. If current traditions are a valid guide, historical contacts between them were particularly intense in the southern portion of the island. Whereas in the north the traditions portray the two groups as having been opposed, in the south they are fused, if not confused: "The Banyakabwa and Banyahiva [a generic term for all hunting/forest groups, and the corporate form of Nyamuhiva] were the same clan; Balimucabo [an early ancestor of the Banyakabwa] was the 'son' of Nyamuhiva."[25] Traditions in the south from non-Banyakabwa sources specifically note a common identity of Banyakabwa and the Binyalenge-Nyamuhiva, either directly or through common localization. Some traditions, for example, associate Nyamuhiva with areas in the south which were historically Banyakabwa centers: "Nyamuhiva is the same as Nyamuziga [a prominent patriarch of the Banyakabwa in the area]; he lived at Bushake," a hill identified as the former residence of an important family of Banyakabwa.[26] And even more imprecise associations abound for this area: "The Banyakabwa swam with Ruganzu" (Ruganzu Ndori, a famous Rwandan king).[27] (This associates the Banyakabwa traditions with the Booze traditions both on and off Ijwi. It is clearly etiological; it explains the association of these two clans on Ijwi today by reference to a common legacy of the distant past—their association with Rwandan kings.) Therefore, the historical interactions between Binyalenge and Banyakabwa, the frequent references that both groups provided "kings" before the arrival of the Basibula, and their common identification as hunters, all help reinforce and perpetuate the confusion of the two clans in the historical traditions on Ijwi when referring to the distant past (even though in today's terms the two clan identities are seen as clearly distinct).

This conflation apparently results from a process of categorization similar to that found in the northern traditions. In the north, the Binyalenge and Booze were so clearly distinguished from the Banyakabwa that their own differences were minimized. Socially and in their internal histories, the Banyakabwa and Binyalenge are clearly distinct from each other, in the south as in the north. But traditions about them from other clans in the south do not emphasize such differences; instead they privilege the contemporaneity of the Binyalenge and Banyakabwa and their common relation with other (probably later) social units. Moreover the Banyakabwa are less influential in the south than in the north, where the impact of other clans on extant traditions of this type has been very slight. Consequently traditions in the south define these two groups—Banyakabwa and Binyalenge—within a common category. In the eyes of others, therefore, the process of consolidation was similar in the two areas of Ijwi, but the effect was very different: in the south the Binyalenge are seen as autonomous predecessors to the Banyakabwa; in the north, they are associated with the Booze and, through them, with a wider Balega identity.

The progression of succeeding identities has to be seen within the cultural codes characteristic of the two regions. Traditions of the south show a clear historical progression of prestigious groups on Ijwi from the Binyalenge-Nyamuhiva to the Banyakabwa to the Basibula, the present royal family; group identities are often expressed through personal representations—Nyamuhiva for the Binyalenge, Nyamuziga for the Banyakabwa, Mwendanga for the Basibula. The Banyakabwa are often taken to have succeeded the Binyalenge in this status succession and therefore to be identified with them: structural equivalence becomes expressed as identity. This explains the confusion in time and perceived social position of these groups in the traditions. Furthermore, the identities of these two groups all privilege similar cultural assumptions: while traditions in the north describe the Binyalenge as merely forest dwellers, Binyalenge traditions in the south give prominence to Nyamuhiva, "the Hunter." So both the Binyalenge-Nyamuhiva (through their association with forest areas) and the Banyakabwa (largely because of their name)[28] are commonly associated with hunting cultures. In the north, by contrast, the Binyalenge are usually portrayed as distinct from the Banyakabwa, lacking even the common prestige as formerly an eminent group. There, Banyakabwa group coherence is strong, and their associations are not with hunting but with royalty (though obviously these may not be exclusive concepts).

The Process of Redefining Social Identities

In the south, people in the eastern areas and in areas bordering the southern edge of the forest all seem to have a general acquaintance with the "archaic" (Group I) traditions of the type considered here. The association of these traditions with the forest areas is explained by the nature of the traditions themselves, because they deal primarily with peoples of perceived forest culture.[29] But this does not explain their association with the Balega, since the Balega are not currently taken to be representative of forest cultures on Ijwi. Other more recent immigrants from the west, particularly those living near the forest still today, would serve as more suitable referents for these traditions. Therefore it is likely that the Binyalenge-Nyamuhiva traditions testify to a shared historical and cultural substratum among several Balega subgroups, whose common heritage of the distant past is no longer otherwise retained.

When all their subgroups are taken into account, the Balega are one of the two largest clans on Ijwi today; the clan is more than twice the size of the median clan population on Ijwi, and Balega account for 25 percent of the total Ijwi population. They are also the most widely dispersed clan. There is no major center recognized for all Balega, or (with one or two exceptions) subsidiary centers for localized subgroups, and this lack of a center of geographical dispersion contrasts strongly with the case of other large clans on the island. Taken together, these factors—the size, dispersal, and relative fragmentation of the Balega—indicate long residence on Ijwi.

But in addition to their length of time on Ijwi, the relative size of different groups can be affected by mobility (emigration/immigration), differential birth and death rates, and changes in clan identification through association and assimilation. Traditions of migration, however, are notably absent, at least among those Balega referred to here as Balega* groups.[30] This is especially significant because movement is so prominent in the traditions of other clans on Ijwi. Although the Balega* have been less affected by recent emigration than many other groups, all emigration on any significant scale is apparently a recent phenomenon, so this factor alone does not account for such a discrepancy in clan size; the Balega* are much more numerous than

the median clan size.[31] Therefore, since there is no tradition of recent migration among the Balega, in accounting for its size, the important aspect to
consider is the clan's growth rather than its lack of flight.

There is no indication of a higher birth rate among the Balega* than
among other groups. Their infrequent ties off Ijwi indicate that the Balega*
did not have access to a marriage pool different from those of other Ijwi
groups, nor as a group are they considered wealthy and thus able to provide
for a higher polygynous rate than others on Ijwi.[32] There also seem to have
been no factors differentiating Balega* death rates from those of other groups
on Ijwi. If indeed Balega numerical preponderance were a result of lower
death rates, this would indicate greater adaptation and hence longer residence on Ijwi, and thus support the hypothesis that Balega* identity has
absorbed Binyalenge-Nyamuhiva groups, the early inhabitants.

Finally, although it is clear that individuals have shifted identity groups,
there is no indication that this shift occurred from present groups on Ijwi
towards Balega* on a scale large enough to account for a markedly higher
population among the Balega*. It is more likely that this process occurred by
the incorporation of earlier groups in their entirety (i.e., by a shift in conceptual categories) rather than by more recent assimilation of individuals from
other clans. The incorporation of whole groups presumes a different social
process from the absorption of individuals. In the latter case, individuals
move between recognized groups, but the group boundaries are maintained.
In the former case, the classifications of group identity themselves alter.

If the Balega* are in fact an old population on Ijwi (or encapsulate
earlier populations) as well as one of the largest clans on the island, it is
interesting that this status is not recognized by significant recent participation in royal rituals, since these features are associated with the status of
"owners of the soil." (Elsewhere such groups often are prominent in societal
rituals. But on Ijwi there is no formal "owner-of-the-soil" prestige associated
with the Balega; though minimal today, the ritual functions associated with
such status are performed by Barhwa ["pygmies"].) And although one Balega center (Bushovu) is renowned for its ironworking, ritual authority in this
domain is vested not in the Balega but in the strongest of the ritual clans, the
Bashaho, a clan which otherwise has no general reputation as ironworkers.[33]
It would therefore seem reasonable that on the arrival of the present (Basibula) dynasty, the Balega* groups were dispersed and lacked corporate identity. Apparently they served neither as a threat nor as an important ally to the
newcomers, as did other pre-Basibula clans. Such weak corporate capacity in
the past suggests that their current common identity as Balega has in fact
strengthened over the last 150 years. Why that happened and what were the
repercussions of this process of reconstructing group identity are the subject
of this study.

The nature of Balega* internal organization, especially the apparent lack of any corporate identity among the different segments of the "clan," reinforces the conclusion that they were formed from formerly independent dispersed units. Balega* genealogies are neither consistent nor deep; frequently, they are much shallower than is common among other clans. It is also difficult to relate any given Balega* group genealogically to other Balega* groups. Therefore their present heterogeneity has probably not resulted from the fragmentation of a formerly more cohesive group into shallower segments. Instead the data indicate that the process involved more of a fusion of several culturally related but formerly distinct populations now classified under a common identity norm.

Viewing the Balega* in this way correlates with the persistent, if vague, association of early populations with Balega* traditions and areas. The structure of these Balega* groups corresponds with other indications that these early populations shared a culture similar to the forest culture, where groups were also dispersed in small localized segments with little internal cohesion or exclusive social definition. The small size of such early groups would correspond with other indications of association with forest cultures discussed in the preceding chapter. There was apparently little corporate identity distinguishing these groups from each other, because this would likely have resulted in stronger internal cohesion and hence continuity to the present. Eventually they were able to fuse their separate identities into a larger whole—the Balega—with few traces of their former localized autonomy. Thus the various groups which composed the early population on Ijwi, probably organized along the lines of those described in chapter 2, seem to have been subsumed within larger identity groups primarily as a result of the changing social context on Ijwi Island.

This chapter has explored the process of emergent social categories on Ijwi. Despite the common assumption of current clan structures as "primordial units" (even, or especially, among clan members themselves), the indications are that similar changing political environments resulted in the emergence of new social identities in Buganda, Rwanda, and in other Interlacustrine areas, as well as in the Kivu Rift.[34] But it is a process very difficult to trace with historical precision, for at least three reasons. First, it was associated not just with immigrant groups but more specifically with the consolidation of state power as well. Under these circumstances new clan identities were associated with the hegemony of cultural categories and even the definition of historical process itself. The power of the state to dominate cultural expression results in a tendency to redefine all historical process as derivative from a central core, a historical nucleus, on the model of descent from a single source (or common ancestor). The second reason this process is so obscured from the historical record is that it appears to be associated only with the early stages of state formation; at later stages the state seeks to break down subgroups which provide an alternate identity to that of the state. And third, as a general conceptual category clan structures are tied to ritual structures. As we shall see, the logic of ritual features denies or contradicts historical explanation; ritual action claims legitimacy by placing itself beyond the realm of social process and human constructs.

Nonetheless, where the hegemony of the central court was incomplete, as on Ijwi, there remain clues for understanding the factors involved in the formation of a new set of clan identities. Central to the construction of a new set of social relations—in a changing social context—was the arrival of new groups on Ijwi. The Banyakabwa were one of those immigrant groups, but there were other groups too, and their interaction with each other as well as with earlier inhabitants significantly influenced the evolution of social identities on Ijwi.

Part 2 considers some of these immigrant groups. Chapter 4 examines the conditions which led some groups to settle on Ijwi from the east: the expansionist policies of the Rwandan central court served as an important catalyst to such movement for the peoples living west of the Nile-Zaire Divide, people who shared many of the cultural characteristics of the Kivu Rift Prototype Societies, as described in chapter 2.[35] The early histories of two Ijwi clans, the Banyakabwa and the Beshaza, will be drawn on in chapter 5 as illustrative of these processes. Chapters 6 and 7 consider two other immigrant groups from the east, the Banyambiriri and the Baziralo. As the kingdom on Ijwi developed, members of these clans were incorporated into the structures of the kingdom to provide important ritual roles; the historical antecedents of these groups east of the lake and their settlement on Ijwi were essential components in the later construction of a kingdom on the island.

4
Rwanda and the Rift

During the late eighteenth century, Ijwi society was transformed by the arrival of new groups from the east. These were essentially refugee groups, some fleeing the political pressures of an expanding Rwandan power, some fleeing the increasing population densities and decreasing productivity of the highlands on the Nile-Zaire Divide. Although they often arrived as small groups, their effect on Ijwi social structures in the long run was far greater than their numbers alone might indicate. We have already explored some of the social dynamics which resulted from contact between one of these groups, the Banyakabwa, with early populations on Ijwi. But there were other groups to arrive as well, many with a specific contribution to make to the emerging Ijwi social universe.

The historical antecedents of those who arrived, and the manner by which they settled on the island, were important factors in the construction of a kingdom on Ijwi. Therefore, it is important to consider the political evolution of the Rwandan state during the eighteenth century and to account for the impact of such changes on the area immediately east of Lake Kivu. Rather than present a comprehensive history of the Rwandan state, the objective in this and the next three chapters is to identify those features of Rwandan history which help explain the later social transformations that occurred on Ijwi—transformations which served as a prelude to, but also as an essential complement of, the later process of royal establishment there. Only then will it be possible to discuss the significance of such developments for Ijwi Island.

In the chapters to follow, I will draw on the examples of four immigrant groups, the Banyakabwa, the Beshaza, the Banyambiriri, and the Baziralo. Two of them claimed earlier ritual status east of the lake, and subsequently became important in the royal rituals of the Basibula kingdom on Ijwi. But the various historical antecedents which the immigrants brought with them did not stem from the structure of royal rituals in the Rwandan state, as Rwandan sources aver. Contact with Rwandan state power may have enhanced, redefined, and focussed these ritual configurations, but ultimately they derived from the ritual inventory of the pre-Nyiginya polities near the Zaire-Nile Divide—those discussed in chapter 2. The similarities between the ritual codes in Rwanda and on Ijwi, therefore, were more a result of parallel derivation from a common pool of ritual knowledge than of direct transmission from one state to the other. Ijwi's claims to sovereignty were premised on its role as a functioning member of a community of similarly constructed states, not as a dependent client of one of those states.

Early Rwandan History

In their earliest forms, the state structures of Rwanda began to emerge near Lake Mohasi, on the open grasslands between Lake Victoria and Lake Kivu. This was pastoral country *par excellence,* and the various states which gradually took shape there were originally based on the alliance of pastoralist groups. The Abanyiginya, later to emerge as the dynastic core of the Rwandan state (or, more precisely, as the clan from which the royal lineage was drawn), were only one among several like units in the area, and the traditions relating to this early period of Rwandan history are preoccupied with the intricate pattern of marriage alliances among these units. But relations among such competing factions were also marked by political turbulence; the traditions are replete with references to intrigue, confrontation, and dynastic shifts of fortune.[1] (See Map 6.)

As a result, over time the nucleus of the Rwandan state was gradually displaced to the west, until by the late sixteenth and early seventeenth centuries the history of the Abanyiginya dynasty had come to focus on the eastern slopes of the Nile-Zaire Divide. According to the traditions of the central court, four kings were particularly instrumental in this shift to the west. Kigeri Mukobanya and Mibambwe Mutabazi both acceded to power from the west (though originally they were from Bugesera, in south-central Rwanda). Ndahiro Cyamatare, the second successor to Mutabazi, was killed while waging a campaign in the west, during which the royal drum is said to have been lost to the western armies. After a 12-year interlude, Ruganzu Ndori conquered Rwanda from the east, established a new dynasty, and, like his predecessors, proceeded to undertake many campaigns in the western areas. (See Table 1.)

Such intense relations with the populations of the Nile-Zaire Divide left their mark in many ways. This period saw at least one dynastic shift, possibly two. It appears also to have been a period during which a second genesis myth of the Abanyiginya dynasty was elaborated.[2] The first dealt primarily with pastoralist interests and was explicitly located on the grasslands of eastern Rwanda; the second was quite different, and clearly preoccupied with

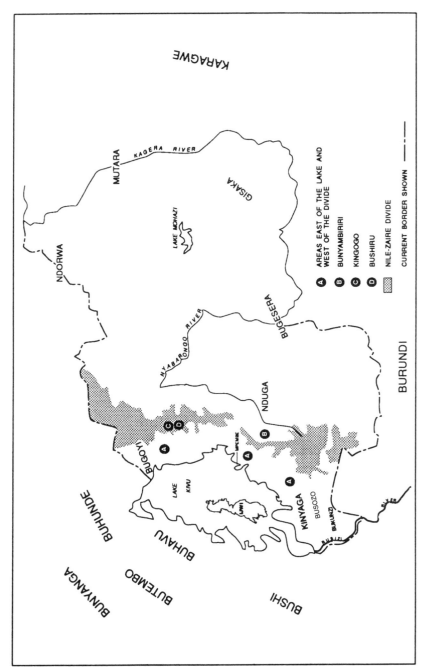

Map 6. Regions of Rwanda

KARAGWE

MUTARA

KAGERA RIVER

GISAKA

LAKE MOHAZI

NDORWA

BUGESERA

NYABARONGO RIVER

NDUGA

AREAS EAST OF THE LAKE AND
WEST OF THE DIVIDE

BUNYAMBIRIRI

KINGOGO

BUSHIRU

NILE-ZAIRE DIVIDE

CURRENT BORDER SHOWN

Ⓐ
Ⓑ
Ⓒ
Ⓓ

BURUNDI

BUGOYI

BUHUNDE

LAKE
KIVU

BUHAVU

BUTEMBO

BUNYANGA

BUSHI

KINYAGA

BUSOZO

BUKUNZI

MPANDE

RUSIZI RIVER

Table 1. The Kings of Rwanda

Mutara Rudahigwa	1931–1959
Yuhi Musinga	1896–1931
Mibambwe Rutarindwa	1895–1896
Kigeri Rwabugiri	1860–1895
Mutara Rwogera	1830–1860
Yuhi Gahindiro	1797–1830
Mibambwe Sentabyo	1792–1797
Kigeri Ndabarasa	1765–1792
Cyilima Rujugira	1756–1765
[Karemera Rwaka	1738–1756]
Yuhi Mazimpaka	1711–1738
Mibambwe Gisanura	1684–1711
Kigeri Nyamuheshera	1657–1684
Mutara Semugeshi	1630–1657
Ruganzu Ndori	1603–1630
Ndahiro Cyamatare	1603–?
Yuhi Gahima	1593–1603
Mibambwe Mutabazi	1588–1593
Kigeri Mukobanya	1586–1588
Cyilima Rugwe	1559–1586
Ruganzu Bwimba	1532–1559

Source: Adapted from J. K. Rennie, "The
Precolonial Kingdom of Rwanda."
Note: The estimated dates are very approximate.

the general cultural features still today associated with the mountainous western regions of the country. It provides a narrative on how Gihanga ("the Founder") brought fire, ironworking, and seeds to Rwanda. He was a great hunter who travelled widely in the area west of the divide, marrying women from local units. (Their sons, in turn, left to establish Rwanda's neighboring kingdoms—hence the ascribed genealogical subordination of such states to Rwanda, and the ideological basis of Rwandan claims to hegemony in the area.) According to this narrative, Gihanga forged especially close ties with families which were to play particularly important roles in the later elaboration of the royal rituals; he introduced the royal drum, the symbol of royalty, to Rwanda, and it was he, according to this myth-charter, who appointed certain families to serve as ritualists for the Rwandan state.

Taken in all its variants, this narrative obviously relates to a form of understanding that goes far beyond its retention of discrete historical "events" alone. Nonetheless it is still instructive to note the remarkable conjunction of the Gihanga narratives with other accounts relating to the period of Rwandan penetration into the forest areas along the divide. Most prominently these deal with the reign of Ruganzu Ndori, portrayed in the Rwandan traditions as the archetype of the warrior-king.[3] In these sources Ruganzu's battles in the west are recounted in epic proportions, and they directly recall the accounts of Gihanga's exploits in the same region, so much so that the Gihanga narrative appears in part to serve as justification for Ruganzu's wars. Furthermore, like Gihanga, Ruganzu too is said to have inaugurated a new royal drum, to replace that lost under Cyamatare (perhaps an allusion to the expropriation of the drum of one of the small polities of the region). The Gihanga tradition clearly relates to a whole epoch; it does not serve simply as an etiological prelude to Ruganzu's reign. It was Mukobanya's reign, for example, which apparently saw the conquest of the areas from which the principal ritualists were to be drawn, areas which later served as central foci for Rwandan royal rituals.[4]

Finally, the shift of interest from the eastern plains to the western mountains appears to have been accompanied by significant religious transformations within Rwanda as well, including the spread of religious forms and cults very different from the veneration of family ancestors or local spirits alone. The worship of the spirit Ryangombe, for example, came to assume an ambiguous relationship to royalty.[5] On the one hand, the central figure is portrayed as having opposed Rwandan kingship, and specifically as having resisted Ruganzu: many vivid traditions portray the epic struggle between Ryangombe and Ruganzu; indeed, in some respects Ryangombe can be seen as a model for resistance to Rwandan royalty. Nonetheless there were also features within Ryangombe religious practices that appear to have reinforced Rwandan royalty. At the most obvious level, Ryangombe is presented as a figure fully in the tradition of the Rwandan epic hero, and thus the corpus reinforces the specifically Rwandan vision of history as applied to their kings—heroic military figures commanding supernaturally endowed powers. In addition, the worship of Ryangombe required initiatory rites—therefore retaining the sense of exclusive membership and hierarchy—and the structures of initiation to Ryangombe directly reflected the structures of the royal enthronement ceremonies. Finally, as an exclusive religion with a body of initiates, it was open to co-optation by the central court; indeed under Rujugira in the mid-eighteenth century, the Ryangombe cult was formally incorporated at the court, with its own resident representative there.[6]

When taken together, these (and other) indications all suggest that during this period the kingdom was substantially reconstituted and Rwandan royalty was virtually reconstructed. Certainly many significant changes in the political culture of the Rwandan state were undertaken at this time. It is perhaps not coincidental that this same period of "reconstruction" also marked a shift in interest from the eastern plains to the western forest and the first intensive contacts with the culturally distinct population on, and west of, the Nile-Zaire Divide. But early conquest and occupation of the areas along the divide remained tentative; effective administration and permanent over-rule did not occur from first contact.[7]

Even though the long-term structural trends of increasing Rwandan involvement in these areas are clear, the consolidation of power over these autonomous populations was not a continuous process. Ritual appropriation and religious hegemony provided one dimension to this process. But military power and administrative penetration were more important to Rwandan control, and these were developed during three particularly important reigns. The most recent was that of Rwabugiri, who ruled during the last third of the nineteenth century; though his policies had a significant impact both on Rwandan political structures and on Ijwi history, his reign falls outside the period of our interest here.[8]

The reign of Yuhi Gahindiro during the early nineteenth century was also important, in two respects. First, he restructured the corporation of royal ritualists. By appointing many of his own favorites to these positions, he both enlarged the corporation and concurrently reduced the political autonomy of this group of ritual functionaries; the formerly exclusive office of hereditary ritualists henceforth shared their positions with delegates of the king. Such a policy may well have been seen as defaming the ritual character of the office; surely it was seen as a threat to the political prerogatives of the hereditary ritualists.

Gahindiro's reign was also a time when the court appears to have ex-erted much greater control over access to land than hitherto.[9] Gahindiro had acceded to power at a very young age; in fact it is likely that he was not the son of his predecessor (who had died after a reign of only five years). These two features made him particularly susceptible to the influence of the queen mother and other councillors. Many of his policies were undoubtedly de-signed to strengthen his personal court ties at the expense of the hereditary positions, especially the ritualists, those who might most strongly harbor reservations regarding his legitimacy as claimant to the kingship. But it is likely that the combination of increased tensions at the court and increased administrative prerogatives over land led to greater mobility of the popula-tion in the area, and that some of those people left the lands east of the lake to settle on Ijwi.[10] Thus the changes under Gahindiro had a direct impact on the areas of the Kivu Rift Valley; later chapters will trace these insofar as the data permit.

But population mobility of this type was not new. In fact administrative consolidation under Gahindiro was likely only an extension of policies initi-ated under Cyilima Rujugira, who ruled in the mid-eighteenth century (ac-cording to Vansina's chronology), three reigns before Gahindiro. One of the innovations of Rujugira's reign, as we have noted, was the attempt to incor-porate Ryangombe at the central court. At a time of increasing state penetra-tion into regions formerly culturally distinct and politically autonomous from the central court, this was clearly part of a larger attempt to reinforce court domination over the ritual and ideological underpinnings of the state, perhaps in an attempt to control popular protest. Although specific data is lacking, it may well be that the independent ritualists were threatened by such policies.[11] Some, indeed, may have sought refuge elsewhere; we will explore that possibility in the chapters to follow.

But military and administrative dimensions to Rujugira's policies were more important to his reign, for Rujugira had likely come to power as a usurper, and it was essential for him to retain the allegiance of the army corporations.[12] It is not surprising then that during this time army corporations assumed increasing importance in the political arena, substantially altering their functions to include administrative duties as well as military operations. Therefore in addition to attempting to increase control over ritual and ideological factors, the Rwandan state under Rujugira embarked on a period of significant external military expansion and internal political-administrative consolidation (including a significant increase in internal social stratification). And the conjunction of ritual and military initiatives under Rujugira was directly related to the new interest in and conquest of the western areas: the ritual features were in part drawn from the western areas; the military dimension was ultimately directed against these areas.

The institutions which most linked military expansion and administrative consolidation were the army corporations, so central in this period both to court power in general and to Rujugira's power base in particular.[13] These changing political influences affected the people of the Nile-Zaire Divide and the Lake Kivu areas in two ways. Directly, the expansionist policies of the Rwandan central court increased population mobility throughout the area during the eighteenth century. This initially intensified the ties within the region, including those between Ijwi and the eastern mainland, because immigrants to Ijwi from the east often maintained close ties with the area of the Nile-Zaire Divide. But over time the introduction of Rwandan cultural norms to new areas (such as the Nile-Zaire Divide) increased the perceived differences between Ijwi and the eastern mainland. Thus indirectly, too, political consolidation within Rwanda was to prove important for Ijwi history, by bringing about changes in social relations and social identities east of the lake. Eventually this was to have important repercussions on Ijwi; as their sense of identity with social groups east of the lake gradually diminished, the island inhabitants came to intensify their interaction with each other.

Mid-Eighteenth-Century Rwandan Expansion

Rwandan traditions provide a relatively detailed record of central court activities from the mid-eighteenth century, roughly from the reign of the king

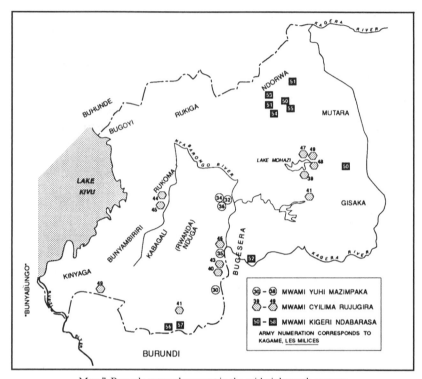

Map 7. Rwanda army placement in the mid-eighteenth century

Cyilima Rujugira.[14] At the time of Rujugira's accession to power, the central
heartland of the Rwandan polity was located in Nduga, on the highland
plateau just east of the Nile-Zaire Divide, with an extension northward and
eastward into the areas of Bumbogo and Rukoma, areas of long-standing
ritual importance to the kingdom.[15] According to central court traditions, the
primary threat to Rujugira was the combined military alliance of Rwanda's
three most powerful antagonists at the time: Ndorwa to the north, Gisaka to
the east, and Burundi to the south (see Map 7).

As in the case of Rwanda, the form of expansionist policies associated
with wide-ranging pastoralist traditions distinguished these kingdoms from
those in the forested areas of the divide, and those farther west. Since the
eastern kingdoms were primarily formed of alliances among pastoralist-
oriented groups, their policies during this period were directed more towards
extending the territory available to these essentially pastoral peoples than
towards incorporating those living within that domain (agricultural and forest cultures as well as pastoralist). Although agriculturalists in Rwanda did
not remain entirely autonomous of effective state control until Rujugira's
reign, the restructuring of Rwandan society that occurred during the eigh-

teenth century still represented a significant departure from earlier periods, altering the nature of both the external expansion and internal consolidation of the polity.

Rujugira had acceded to power with the strong support of the army commanders. Both to reinforce his own political base and to respond to the threat of the military coalition against Rwanda, Rujugira formed an unusually large number of armies during his reign. Others had been formed in the previous reign, that of Yuhi Mazimpaka, but probably these armies were retained in the traditions and within the military establishment because of the demands and honors bestowed on them for their campaigns during Rujugira's reign. This tradition of rapid army formation continued under Kigeri Ndabarasa, Rujugira's successor, but many of these corporations, too, can be attributed essentially to the army formation which occurred under Rujugira, as individual regiments broke away to form their own autonomous armies under Ndabarasa.[16]

In all (though some of the earlier armies may have been lost to the historical record) one-third of all the armies noted for Rwanda are attributed to the reign of Rujugira or his immediate predecessor or successor.[17] Not surprisingly, these were initially stationed in the areas of the greatest external military threat, along the borders between Rwanda and Burundi-Bugesera, Gisaka, and Ndorwa. There is also a clear evolution in the regional distribution of these armies which correlates with the expansionist policies noted in the traditions. Whereas Rujugira's armies were concentrated in the south (Burundi-Bugesera) and east (Gisaka), Ndabarasa's were located in the north (Ndorwa) and extreme south (Burundi), moving beyond those of Rujugira in this area (see Map 7). Even during the reign of Rujugira, army postings show a movement to the north and to the west of the western bend of the Nyabarongo River; significantly, several of the armies located in the west were formed of Hutu, or included a Hutu section—referring to the predominantly agriculturalist peoples generally excluded from the positions of power in the Rwandan state structures.[18]

Expansionist policy strengthened the ties between individual pastoralist groups and the court in several ways. The growth in armies provided new positions of leadership to delegate to the court's supporters. Successful raids and expeditions also provided increased booty to distribute as rewards. Moreover, with the growing role of the military, there developed an increasingly prominent court ideology glorifying such military endeavors, the omnipotence of the Rwandan state, and the importance of the royal court itself as the central institution of the state. Ultimately, new military organization provided the basis for a new and (from the point of view of the court) highly effective administrative framework for the emergent state structures of Rwanda.

The crucial institution in this intensification of administrative control was the army organization itself, for armies were not always maintained exclusively for their role as fighting units. Initially individual armies may have been raised for military purposes, but under Rujugira some of these corporations (or "social armies") began to develop an enduring institutional identity which long outlasted their military effectiveness. For example, of the 29 armies formed before the reign of Mazimpaka, Rujugira's predecessor, only 2 have complete recorded histories. Nineteen have recorded histories only from the reign of Rujugira or one of his successors, and it is only from Rujugira's reign that the concept of perpetual armies becomes generalized.[19] It is also primarily from this period that there appear to have been armies formed predominantly of Hutu.[20] In other words, the changes in army organization show both an enduring institutionalized structure and an increasing intensity, incorporating a wider range of inhabitants of the realm.

This structure was eventually to evolve into the principal administrative framework of nineteenth-century Rwanda, with the army corporations (as *umuheto* groups) eventually serving primarily as prestation-paying units.[21] Many of the armies formed under Rujugira, for example, did not begin paying annual prestations until the reign of Rwogera, in the mid-nineteenth century. Associated with this development of administrative functions was the assignment of permanent cattle herds attached to the armies. As elaborated especially during the reigns of Gahindiro and Rwogera in the first half of the nineteenth century, this institution provided a continuing material base for the perpetuation of the group.[22]

Thus over time the administrative functions of these army corporations gradually became more important than their military functions.[23] Indeed, the two functions were closely related historically. Fighting units were expected to provide their own food and supplies, and often did so by drawing on the resources of the families of the individual members, a tradition easily transformed over time to an annual prestation payment irrespective of the military mobilization; a portion of these prestations was expected to be passed on to the court.[24] As they developed, the armies gradually became less regionally specific in recruitment: members were chosen from widely separated areas throughout the country. Drawing recruits from many regions, these corporations also served to educate and socialize elite youth to common cultural perceptions, inculcating court norms and etiquette as well as providing military training.[25] Such a role undoubtedly helped reinforce and extend the internal class distinctions within Rwanda society—separating those who had served at the court from those who had not.[26]

The reorganization of Rwanda's military structure under Rujugira was accompanied by significant internal transformations in central institutions. Such changes, which included the establishment of a new cycle of royal names and the institutionalization of the Ryangombe cult at the royal court, reflected a greater formalization of many features of Rwandan culture at the level of the court.[27] Increased institutionalization was probably also accompanied by greater standardization, as increasingly the court served as an arbiter of social norms. In general, this process reflects the greater participation of the court, if not also a greater control by the court, in the affairs of the people of the kingdom. On a more general level, this was a time of reassessment, one which would lead during the nineteenth century, especially, to a restatement of the role of kingship in society. Thus in terms of internal politics, the growing military capacity provided a valuable resource for enforcing the expansion of state structures throughout the kingdom.[28] At the same time, the rise of the army as an essential political mechanism of the Rwandan state also established a new type of political faction at the court, one whose interests were furthered by continuing wars.[29]

The Impact on the Western Areas

Most Rwandan historical sources associate Rujugira's military activities with Ndorwa, Gisaka, and Burundi, all large-scale kingdoms organized on a model similar to that of Rwanda in the mid-eighteenth century. But, as noted above, Rujugira's expeditions were also to have an important impact on the highland polities of the western areas; and in some ways, despite their relative neglect in the sources, these western expeditions were to have the greater historical effect on the development of the Rwandan state. Some of the small states to the north and west of the Rwandan core area were attacked directly.[30] But the wars themselves, and the increasing mobilization of men to fight them, appear to have had important secondary repercussions. Across the area as a whole, there is evidence both of markedly increased population mobility in these years and of demographic growth, in part through the incorporation of immigrants from the defeated states east and south of Rwanda.[31]

Population movements, resulting from the military reorganization of Rwanda and the expeditions against the larger states, were particularly important for these western areas. Gisaka and Ndorwa, for example, the two major targets of the wars of Rujugira and Ndabarasa, were the most common points of origin for immigrants to the western regions at this time.[32] In addition two other corporations "created" under Rujugira may have been former Rundi armies incorporated into the Rwandan military organizational structure.[33] Although detailed demographic data is lacking, these traditions indicate the likelihood of substantial immigration to Rwanda (or to areas that had recently been—or were about to be—incorporated into an expansionist Rwandan state) during this period. Such demographic changes may well have affected both agricultural production and security (of land and of persons) within the areas of recent settlement. Indeed in areas of poor soil where agricultural systems depended on long fallow periods, the changes in agricultural practices and declining productivity brought on by such immigration may well have been a cause of further mobility.

Bunyambiriri, one of the highland areas located along the crest of the Nile-Zaire Divide, is one of those areas which has historically experienced food shortages because of its marginal soils and precipitation patterns. But Bunyambiriri also attracted many of these displaced families, because it had remained until that time largely outside the direct political control of the Rwandan court.[34] Bunyambiriri, in turn, became a major secondary dispersal area; traditions from Bugoyi (northeast of Lake Kivu), Ijwi Island, and Kinyaga (along the southeastern shores of the lake) all indicate that significant numbers of people moved out of Bunyambiriri, to the north and west.[35] Often the same groups which immigrated to Bunyambiriri were those which later emigrated, and their departure from Bunyambiriri frequently occurred in the same generation as (or the generation succeeding) their immigration. (The story of the Abagwabiro lineage, to be discussed below, is illustrative: originally from Ndorwa, they first moved to Suti in Bunyambiriri; from there they left for Bugoyi during the reign of Rujugira.[36])

The influx of immigrants from the eastern areas likely contributed to the growing population pressure which appears to have characterized Bunyambiriri's subsequent history. General emigration from Bunyambiriri apparently coincided with a particularly severe famine which occurred under Rujugira,[37] and throughout the region's subsequent history the people of Bunyambiriri suffered periodic famines.[38] Whether in part a product of warfare or a result of increased population pressure with immigration to Bunyambiriri, these famines surely contributed to the eighteenth- and nineteenth-century emigration from this area.[39] Thus secondary emigration out of Bunyambiriri may well have been an indirect result of political and military activities undertaken elsewhere during this period.[40] Immigrant groups arriving in large numbers with the intention of settling permanently in the area, and bringing with them concepts of political organization and patterns of behavior different from those of the highland areas, may well have increased social tensions and contributed to later emigration from Bunyambiriri.

Distinguishing the causes of their arrival from the impact of such refugees on the area helps explain the Rwandan sources on this point. Court sources imply that these mobility patterns are directly related to Rwandan expansion during the time of Rujugira. The first "Rwandan" ties to Bugoyi, for example, are recorded for the reign of Rujugira, who is said to have sent an army there to defeat "invaders" from the west; the members of this army then remained there (so the accounts claim) as central court representatives in Bugoyi.[41]

The most renowned of these new "Rwandan" immigrants was a man named Macumu, the eventual head of the Abagwabiro lineage.[42] Identified as "Hutu" in most sources, he had originally lived in Ndorwa; from there he had moved to Bunyambiriri, then to Bugoyi. This pattern suggests more that he was a refugee from Rujugira's wars against Ndorwa, continually seeking autonomy from Rwandan state control, than that he was acting as its agent, as the court sources claim. Nonetheless in later generations the Abagwabiro were able to parlay their local prestige in Bugoyi into ties with the court; their orientation towards Rwandan cultural values provided a basis for claims by the Rwandan court that they were "official representatives" in the area. In fact, their ties to the court probably resulted from a process of co-opting locally established families to serve central authority, a process similar to that which occurred elsewhere on Rwanda's periphery.[43] The Rwandan court sources on this point are clearly *ex post facto* oversimplifications; viewed as such, the court traditions are easily reconciled with other local traditions.

Nevertheless, in an indirect fashion there is validity to the interpretation that such immigrants were in fact Rwandan "emissaries." Despite being refugees from Rwandan military expeditions, the new immigrants came from areas which shared similarities to Rwandan culture. When juxtaposed against the western Rift Valley cultures, their similarities to Rwandan cultural norms may have been more important than the political differences which opposed such peoples to the Rwandan court. Even as refugees from Rwandan court politics, immigrants from Gisaka and parts of Ndorwa helped introduce Rwandan-like culture norms to the areas of the Nile-Zaire Divide. In a sense, therefore, when judged by later events, they did in effect serve as informal and unintentional emissaries of Rwandan culture to these regions, and their presence west of the divide can be seen (both by the Rwandan court and by inhabitants of the western areas) as a prelude to Rwandan expansion in the area. Nonetheless, emissary status was not the condition of their arrival in the west; the results of their presence were not the same as the intentions which brought them there. Here, as in many oral traditions, cause and effect are conjoined.

Internal Transformations in the Western Areas

Thus from the time of Rujugira, and especially after the reign of his successor Ndabarasa, Rwandan expansionist policies affected the Kivu area in two ways. It intensified population mobility towards the west, and thus increased the heterogeneity of the Ijwi population; Ijwi traditions today associate the arrival of many families on the island with the reigns of the Rwandan kings Sentabyo and Gahindiro, second and third successors to Rujugira. More important, military and cultural expansion westward also led to the increasing incorporation of these western regions into the Rwandan polity. The consolidation of Rwandan political power in these areas became most apparent during the reign of Gahindiro in the early nineteenth century. By the middle of the nineteenth century, the Rwandan court had established its military hegemony as far as Lake Kivu. A few small enclaves remained formally "independent," to be sure, but even these were encapsulated within a larger political and economic framework which was increasingly dominated by the expanding Rwandan state.[44]

Developments in army organization were paralleled by the growth of institutions which placed increasing control over land in the hands of the political elite. The reign of Gahindiro saw the consolidation of political resources in the countryside which accompanied this intensification of political activity at the central court.[45] New forms of clientship emerged and class differentiation intensified, particularly from the reign of Rwogera in the mid-nineteenth century; several "Hutu" armies, for example, were deprived of their associated cattle herds at this time.[46]

These changes in the intensity of Rwandan central court penetration had significant repercussions for the area west of the divide. One result was to tie the people east of the lake increasingly to the socio-political network of the Rwandan state system, while differentiating them from their former kin and colleagues who lived on Ijwi and west of the lake.[47] Thus the differences between these areas, so readily apparent today, resulted more from the rapid evolution of such ties within Rwanda than from the simple "dilution" and "deterioration" of Rwandan forms as they spread to neighboring areas; a diffusionist interpretation is inappropriate.

Close commercial and social interactions (e.g., marriages) had originally characterized relations between early immigrants to Ijwi and their relatives east of the lake. These ties to the east had differentiated groups on Ijwi from one another and thus helped sharpen social distinctions on the island. With the internal changes that occurred in Rwanda, economic ties between Rwanda and the west continued and may even have intensified as the demand for certain types of commodities changed. But the character of these contacts altered; they became increasingly formalized as time went on, and involved fewer individuals on Ijwi. Often they took the form of client ties, illustrating the degree to which norms of interaction between Ijwi and Rwandan communities had changed. But even in these cases, it is clear that the Ijwi interpretation of such clientship differed from the conceptualizations prevalent in Rwanda, in ways which retained some of the flavor of earlier, less formalized relationships.[48] Bloodpacts, for example, also characterized these client ties—something common on Ijwi but less frequent (within clientship) in Rwanda.[49]

The alterations of these translacustrine links, primarily a result of the transformations on the Rwandan side of the lake, had significant repercussions on Ijwi. Identity groups, defined anew, came to correspond more closely to the geographical realities of the island: an emergent sense of community on the island also contributed to the formation of new political perceptions. But the early distinctions among groups on Ijwi, formed and nurtured by linkages to different areas east of the lake, nonetheless remained important in the definition—the creation—of this new island kingdom.

Part 2
The Island Context

5
Immigrants to Ijwi
Ties across the Lake

The Banyakabwa

The Banyakabwa represent a significant refugee group arriving on Ijwi from Rwanda, providing a historical link between the Binyalenge period and the establishment of the Basibula dynasty on the island. As we have seen, their arrival was an important factor in the process of social transformations on the island, especially because they affected the nature of group identity on Ijwi in the late eighteenth and early nineteenth centuries. Subsequently, they were also instrumental in the arrival and establishment of the Basibula royal family, to be discussed below. But the Banyakabwa were important to Ijwi for their own heritage as well as for their relations with other groups, for they were representative of a new type of social entity arriving on Ijwi.

Among all Ijwi clans, the traditions of the Banyakabwa display the greatest internal coherence and time depth. They are consistent over widely separated areas and comprehensive for certain episodes and time periods. As noted above, the time depth retained in family traditions tends to be associated with the group's later contact with royalty. The Banyakabwa fit into this category of clans with royal tie-ins, but their contacts with the Basibula differed from those of other clans in two respects: they were ephemeral rather than enduring, and they were, on the whole, antagonistic rather than incorporative.

In these two respects the Banyakabwa help illustrate certain features common to all clan contacts with royalty: royal contacts changed over time for all clans, and the emergence of institutionalized interaction arose from the recognition of differences. The rituals which bound other clans (but not the Banyakabwa) to royalty were associative, but they associated groups which were otherwise distinct. Such types of formal interaction did not dissolve group autonomy; on the contrary, they reinforced it. The ritual ties associated with royalty, therefore, developed from a sense of increasing differentiation between groups correlated with an increasing awareness of a common overall Ijwi identity distinct from other areas on the mainland.

This chapter examines the arrival and settlement of two groups from the east, the Banyakabwa and the Beshaza. Unlike other groups with strong identities, they were not incorporated directly into the royal ritual on Ijwi—perhaps because of their (implicit or explicit) claims to royal status elsewhere. These newcomers, then, provide an illustration of the strong sense of historical identity and social cohesion resulting from their experiences as outsiders and their continuing ties off Ijwi. In these respects they are representative of the general pattern among immigrants arriving on Ijwi from the east during the late eighteenth and early nineteenth centuries, immigrant groups whose identities have since been redefined by their incorporation into the Ijwi royal rituals.

The Rwandan Heritage of the Banyakabwa

Today on Ijwi the Banyakabwa are universally referred to (by others as well as by themselves) as members of the Bahande clan, taken to be "the same as" the Basibula, the clan of royalty. In an analogous fashion, they also refer to themselves and are known by others as Banyiginya, the clan which includes the royal lineage in Rwanda; they claim structural equivalence to royal families among the Havu and Tembo as well. To be sure, evoking former royal status, whether Banyiginya or Bahande, can be seen simply as a device to reinforce their prestige on Ijwi today; indirect evidence, however, supports their claims, at least in part.[1]

Genealogical indications and other evidence, both from Ijwi and from Rwanda, suggest a tie-in with Rwandan kings of the early nineteenth century. Many Banyakabwa genealogies trace back to Ngulumira, the father of Balimucabo, the earliest and best-known Munyakabwa on Ijwi, four to seven generations from the present elders of the clan. But from these traditions little is known of Ngulumira, aside from his genealogical position. He is said to have lived at Nyirakaronge near Nyanza (the principal site of the Rwandan royal court in the early nineteenth century). Some claim that Ngulumira "begat" Rwogera, the Rwandan king of the mid-nineteenth century (who acceded to power around 1830).[2] But Ngulumira was clearly not in the paternal descent line of the Rwandan kings; it is more likely that this refers to a connection to the maternal line of Rwogera, since Banyakabwa traditions also refer to Nyiramavugo, the queen mother for Rwogera.[3] This was a time of exceptionally intense competition at the Rwandan court, a time in which extraordinarily powerful and ambitious queen mothers figured prominently; Nyiramavugo and her family were therefore deeply implicated in the court struggles.[4] Four kings in a row had to struggle against their matrilateral relatives; at least two had their queen mothers executed. These same traditions retain other references to Gahindiro, Rwogera's predecessor, expelling his "brother" (either Nyamuziga or Ngulumira, in these Ijwi traditions) from Rwanda.[5] Another refers to the early Banyakabwa as "the sons of Rwogera" (meaning the family of the king, junior in status to him).[6] Others too refer to Ngulumira as the contemporary of Gahindiro, the predecessor to Rwogera (ruled, 1797 to c. 1830), whose reign was a time of significant internal restructuring in Rwanda, as we have seen.[7]

Thus the Banyakabwa traditions provide a cluster of references around the Rwandan kings Gahindiro and Rwogera. Imprecise though these may be, because many other royal names from Rwanda (and elsewhere) also appear in these traditions, they nonetheless give credence to the widespread acknowledgement of Kabwa "royal" origins, and are in turn corroborated by genealogies showing a time depth of "Kabwa" identity roughly in line with an early-nineteenth-century succession dispute.[8] Though there are no specific references to "the Banyakabwa" in the Rwandan sources, this period was replete with power stuggles and intrigue over the favor of the king and control of the Rwandan throne, and the queen mothers figured prominently in such intense competition. It is not unlikely that the losing party to these disputes should have withdrawn to an area remote from central Rwanda. An area such as Bugoyi, in the extreme northwest of the country would have been ideal as such a refuge; Bugoyi was, in fact, a Banyakabwa center prior to their arrival on Ijwi.[9]

Although we lack unequivocal direct references in the Rwandan sources to confirm such assertions, indirect testimony abounds. One person on Ijwi, for example, noted that in Rwanda the Banyakabwa are referred to as Banyakaji.[10] Though he was able to add no more on this, it is possible that this refers to the followers of a certain Rugaju, the favorite of Gahindiro and the power behind the throne at Gahindiro's court. His followers were dispersed shortly after Gahindiro's death, early in the reign of Rwogera, after Rugaju had tried to assassinate Nyiramavugo, and was himself executed by a brother-in-law of Nyiramavugo on her orders; her own brother was one of the principal beneficiaries of the fall of Rugaju.[11] Their implication in Rugaju's death might well explain the presence of Nyiramavugo in the Kabwa traditions on Ijwi.

The family history in the Rwandan sources which most closely approaches the early history of the Banyakabwa as pieced together from these fragmentary Ijwi sources, however, is that of Nyarawaye-Urutesi. He was of the family of Nyiramavugo and husband to her daughter, the younger (full) sister of Rwogera. Thus his descendants would have been considered the "sons" of Gahindiro (with one matrilateral link through Gahindiro's daughter). He would also have been of the family which "begat" Rwogera, because Nyarawaye was the brother of Rwogera's mother. Banyakabwa traditions on Ijwi make both these claims. Because of his influence and behavior at the court of Rwogera, Nyarawaye was killed and his brothers then led the family (and their army) in resistance against the court until they too were killed (or dispersed).[12]

Thus there are several possibilities to explain Banyakabwa claims to royal origins in Rwanda. To pursue the matter further would be of only marginal significance in understanding the Banyakabwa historical role on Ijwi. Nonetheless it should be noted that independent of the written sources the Banyakabwa retain a familiarity with Rwandan history which is extraordinary in the Ijwi context, and that these references, fragmentary and imprecise as they are, are not incompatible with Rwandan traditions. Nor are they incompatible with the larger contours of regional history of the day. The convergence of their Ijwi traditions with both Rwandan and regional historical traditions enhances the likelihood that the Banyakabwa do indeed represent the remnants of royal refugees from Rwanda. More than that, the data do not say.

Banyakabwa Patterns of Alliance

Most Banyakabwa on Ijwi trace their immediate antecedents to a place called Cimbiri in Bugoyi (northwestern Rwanda).[13] Others associate Banyakabwa origins with Buhunde, the region just west of Bugoyi, now a part of Zaire, and indeed certain other evidence supports this.[14] In historical perspective, however, the distinction between Bugoyi and Buhunde is largely irrelevant, since Bugoyi shares many cultural and historical ties with Buhunde, and in cultural terms, especially at this historical remove, there is no firm "boundary" between them. Banyakabwa claims to relations with both Bugoyi and Buhunde therefore are not incompatible; what is important is the continued strength of Banyakabwa ties off Ijwi.

Even until well into this century in certain communities, the Banyakabwa maintained strong external ties, testimony to their relative autonomy of the Ijwi political sphere.[15] Today Banyakabwa engage in frequent commerce, visiting, and travel to the mainland: from Kirhanga (in the extreme north of Ijwi) to Bugoyi, Buhunde, and certain islands; from Buzigaziga, Nkuvu, and Boza (on Ijwi's eastern shore) to Mwiiru and Kalengera on the Rwandan shore opposite (see Map 8). Their present external activity may reinforce their lack of integration into the Ijwi royal line, but it is not a creation of their more recent history on Ijwi. Instead, it clearly reflects a continuation of earlier ties and pre-colonial personal mobility in general.[16]

In addition to personal mobility, continuing contacts were assured by marriage alliances and cattle contracts. Within the senior descent line, for example, the Banyakabwa maintained marriage ties with Buhunde in every generation.[17] In later generations these were extended to include other areas west of the lake, especially Buzi (an area formerly populated by Bahunde) and Mpinga (on the western mainland). In all these areas marriages and

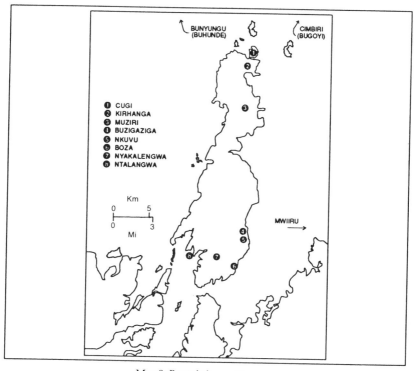

Map 8. Banyakabwa settlements

friendship ties (by bloodpact) were contracted with members of "royal" or high-status families similar to the Banyakabwa on Ijwi.[18]

Banyakabwa marriage ties and other forms of social alliances have also been contracted on Ijwi with members of both branches of the Ijwi royal family (in more recent times, especially with the northern branch) and with other families connected to the royal family such as that of Mushaho, the principal ritualist of the kingdom.[19] Cattle ties, where these can be reconstructed for more recent years, show a similar pattern.[20] (For the distant past cattle contracts are no longer remembered, either because they are a more recent form of social compact or because the social bonds so formed have since lapsed.) In the early part of this century, at least, Banyakabwa cattle contracts were distinguished from those of other Bany'Iju, both by their number and by the fact that Banyakabwa remember having given many cattle but having received few. It is clear that the Banyakabwa, at least the senior line, were relatively rich in cattle; they remain so today despite the difficulties of finding access to pasturage.

One outstanding feature of the Banyakabwa traditions is the focus given

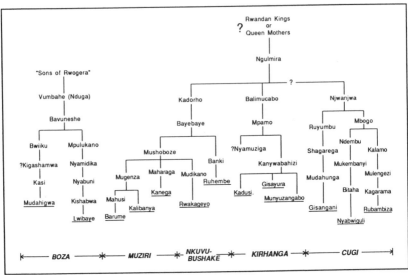

Figure 1. The Banyakabwa (underlined names were people consulted)

to the descent line of the original settlers associated with Balimucabo. This descent line centered in Kirhanga (in the far north of Ijwi), an area still today the "domain" of the Banyakabwa in terms of settlement and administration (see Figure 1).[21] Most Banyakabwa groups identify with this descent line, which serves, in the eyes of others, as representative of all Banyakabwa. Such a clear focus on one descent line has provided the Banyakabwa with a strong sense of cohesion relative to other groups on Ijwi. But it has also lent an intensity to the disputes and secessions among the Banyakabwa, which has produced a tradition of segmentary opposition unusual for Ijwi groups; today there are several secondary centers on Ijwi associated historically with important Banyakabwa personalities.[22] The most important of these was at Buzigaziga, in the highlands overlooking the eastern approaches to Ijwi, with a commanding view of the Rwandan shore opposite. Other communities were located in the south, and from these there broke off still others, some returning to the north (see Map 8). The various Banyakabwa settlements developed a distinct pattern of relations among themselves, a pattern which was to be instrumental to Basibula arrival in the early nineteenth century.

Thus in many respects the Banyakabwa were precursors of later settlers on Ijwi; the most important legacies of the Banyakabwa early residence were also apparent among many of the later immigrants from the east. Just as the Banyakabwa were set apart from other clans as well as from the Binyalenge, the new clans mirrored that social distance in their relations to other clans as well as to royalty. Like the Banyakabwa, the later immigrants too cultivated contacts outside Ijwi, contacts which both preserved their distinctions from other groups on Ijwi and (initially) impeded the development of an Ijwi focus to their social perceptions. These aspects were reflected in their later relations with royalty. But the Banyakabwa failed to reach out to other groups and to transcend their internal orientation; the later arrivals, in smaller but more numerous groups, changed the Ijwi environment by their later interaction with each other—and eventually by their involvement with the growth of royal power.

The Beshaza

As probable fugitives from Rwanda central court politics, the Banyakabwa represent one type of immigrant to Ijwi. A very different (and much more common) form of immigration, caused by Rwandan political penetration of areas west of the Nile-Zaire Divide, is illustrated in the history of the Beshaza clan. This was not a group with close ties to the Rwandan court; to the contrary, Beshaza antecedents are associated with Mpembe, one of the small polities of the type discussed briefly in chapter 2. As such, people of this group appear to have fled not from court intrigue but from invasion, in one form or another. They arrived on Ijwi not as a small group seeking anonymity, but as many autonomous families with continuous ties to the eastern mainland areas, and a common identity derived from shared regional origins rather than membership in a specific lineage. In both these aspects they were more representative of other groups (to be discussed in the next two chapters) than were the Banyakabwa.

The Beshaza constitute the largest and most widely dispersed clan on Ijwi today. In their size and dispersion they show certain similarities to the Balega. But the formation and evolution of Beshaza identity on Ijwi and the relations of this group to the Ijwi royal family were very different from those of the Balega. The latter emerged as a heterogenous group formed of many previously autonomous segments sharing a common relation to newer immigrants on Ijwi. The Beshaza, on the other hand, hold very strong and consistent claims to recent immigration from Mpembe, a prominent peninsula stretching along the eastern shore of the lake, located within the larger region known as Bwishaza (see Map 1). Until conquered by the Rwandan armies, probably in the nineteenth century, Mpembe formed one of the small polities of western Rwanda independent of the Abanyiginya dynasty. Almost all Beshaza on Ijwi today claim descent from—or at least affiliation with—the former kings of Mpembe, and this ideology has served as the foundation for an aura of royal status associated with the Beshaza on Ijwi.

Aside from a few royal names—Nyakabeja, Njeni, Mugombwa, and Rugaba are frequently cited—little is known on Ijwi of the kingdom on

Mpembe;[23] with only a few exceptions, the published Rwandan sources also ignore the former polities of this area.[24] But Ijwi sources do indicate that the kings of Mpembe maintained political contacts, through marriage ties, with some families in Bugoyi in the northwest of Rwanda, bordering on Buhunde (and an area which still today includes many marked cultural traits associated with the Kivu Prototype Society discussed above), and with Bukunzi, another small polity located in the southwest corner of present Rwanda, now a part of Kinyaga.[25] (The kings of Bukunzi, historically associated with the areas west of the Rusizi River, were renowned over a vast area for their control over rain; they were to remain independent of the central Rwandan court until well into the colonial era.[26]) Little more is known of these relationships between Mpembe and Bukunzi, but the very fact that they are cited confirms the sense of shared identity and the pattern of widespread interaction among these polities throughout the region, as postulated in chapter 2.[27]

Such patterns of mobility and interchange also included areas which were not organized into kingdoms before the mid-nineteenth century. Beshaza familiar with the history of the Mpembe kings are found in many areas around the lake today, both on Ijwi and on the mainland peninsulas. Some Beshaza on Ijwi, for example, maintain contacts with other Beshaza communities on Nyamirundi (now part of Rwanda, just south of Ijwi), Ishungu (southwest of Ijwi, today in Zaire), Mabula (on the western shore of the lake), and Buzi (a prominent peninsula in the extreme northwest corner of Lake Kivu).[28] Outside Mpembe itself, however, Ijwi Island is the area of greatest concentration of Beshaza, and the area of their greatest impact.

The Beshaza clan on Ijwi shows many characteristics which would seem to foster an important role in Ijwi royalty. Along with other clans associated with royalty, they share eastern origins, dominance within an important village in the eastern region of Ijwi, and strong royal ties of their own, off the island. Their own descent from royalty, as well as their size and dispersal, would appear to make the Beshaza an important ally for the incoming Basibula on Ijwi. (These factors could also render them a potential threat to the new dynasty, but this would only accentuate the need for co-opting them within the emergent royal structures of the kingdom.) It is surprising, then, that the Beshaza are almost entirely excluded from formal roles within the royal rituals; their only role as ritualists—and a relatively passive role it is—is to provide a wife for the king.[29] (Although she is the only woman with an important public role to play in the royal ritual of Muganuro, preparing the flour from the new sorghum harvest, she does so more as wife of the king than as representative of the Beshaza clan at large, and there is no general identification with this role by other Beshaza.) Yet despite their relatively marginal relations to the royal rituals, the Beshaza are not withdrawn from royalty as are the Banyakabwa; they are well integrated to the social patterns of the island and not localized in a single region.

The explanation for these apparent contradictions in the Beshaza roles on Ijwi is found, in part, in the history of their settlement on the island. Initial contacts between Ijwi and Mpembe clearly occurred before the arrival of the Basibula,[30] but Beshaza immigration continued over a long period and the largest immigration probably occurred in more recent times.[31] Genealogical data, local histories, settlement areas, and clan dispersal data all indicate that the Beshaza probably did not achieve their size on Ijwi or their present status among Ijwi clans until after royal establishment in the southern parts of the island.[32]

The major center of Beshaza immigration on Ijwi is in the village of Bwando, on the eastern shore of the island, just opposite Mpembe on the mainland. From this dispersal area, the Beshaza have diffused widely, but they are particularly numerous in the north of the island.[33] This dispersal and their concentration in the north help confirm the hypothesis of a more recent arrival for large numbers of Beshaza; it appears that royal penetration or the presence of earlier clans in the south made it more attractive to settle in the north. Similarly, the wide dispersal of the Beshaza and the lack of any residential concentration among them (a few centers excepted) also indicate their more recent arrival: the pattern contrasts clearly both with that of other immigrant clans from the east and with their own stated identity with the area of Bwando as their "home community" on Ijwi.[34]

Because of their more recent arrival and perhaps also because of the strength of the ties to the Rwandan shore, the Beshaza illustrate another important aspect of settlement on Ijwi, a characteristic which in all probability can be generalized to other groups immigrant from east of the lake. Although they may well have left Mpembe to escape the turmoil associated with Rwandan military moves in the area, it is clear that, far from being political refugees in any conventional sense, the early Beshaza settlers arrived on Ijwi with the blessing and support of the Mpembe community, and especially of the Mpembe kings. Close contacts were maintained between the new Beshaza settlers on Ijwi and their families in Bwishaza on the mainland; visits between the two areas were frequent. Testimonies such as the following illustrate the point:

> They [the Beshaza ancestors on Ijwi] came to Ijwi to look for land. But not the whole family; they left other brothers there [on Mpembe].[35]

> Nviri [the first remembered ancestor of the respondent's family] used to go from time to time to Mpembe. . . . Nviri carried bananas and beer. He didn't bring

anything back; he was only taking things for his family. There was no "commerce" then.[36]

When one lacks something here, one always goes to Rwanda to look for it; and those in Rwanda when they lack something they always come to Ijwi to look for it. . . . In the old days they sent beer and beans to Rwanda.[37]

The Beshaza often visit Rwanda after coming here. Often they return there to visit. They bring back cows to Ijwi. . . . The settlers came with cows, but also all those who remained on Mpembe sent cows here to be guarded.[38]

There was continuous visiting back and forth; people had cattle both on Ijwi and in Rwanda.[39]

Before the old men died, the Beshaza went to Rwanda-Mpembe for the commemoration of their ancestors [*"kurherakera"*]; but now [the respondent] never does it any more.[40]

In earlier periods it thus appears that these settlements on Ijwi were agricultural colonies, with the new settlers sending back agricultural goods to Mpembe. Indeed, it is possible that a large number of immigrants to Ijwi saw themselves as only temporary settlers, and the turnover in the population may have been quite high.[41] Thus the "visits" between Mpembe and Ijwi sometimes took more enduring forms of population movement. One man who was born on Cugi (in the extreme north of Ijwi) had left Ijwi as a boy to live with some of his family on Mpembe. During Rumanura, the devastating famine of 1916–1918, he had returned to Ijwi. He then left yet again for Rwanda taking sorghum with him. There, his Ijwi relatives sent him goats, which he exchanged for cows in Rwanda, where he stayed for several years before returning again to Ijwi.[42] This sense of mobility in both directions is also illustrated by the man who stated: "The Beshaza on Mpembe are Bahavu because they came from Bwando," the principal Beshaza residential center on the eastern shore of Ijwi.[43] The commercial nature of the earlier ties is in fact explicitly denied by some:

AUTHOR: What did they do when they first came here?
RESPONDENT: They cultivated beans.
AUTHOR: Did they ever engage in trade?
RESPONDENT: No. But if there were many beans, then they would give them for a goat.[44]

Even the kings apparently participated in these movements: "Rugaba [the last king of Mpembe] was also a *mwami;* he came here to visit his family."[45] This was confirmed by another: "The kings were chased [from Mpembe] by the Rwandan kings; then they went back [from Ijwi] to Rwanda."[46]

Thus in the beginning, the social ties and identity orientations of the Beshaza, and probably of other clans as well, were strongly directed off Ijwi, away from other clans on the island. As seed agriculturalists sending harvests off the island, they differed from earlier populations on Ijwi, not just in origins but in material production as well. These differences in material production—and the social relations to follow from this—may have been an important distinction between the Binyalenge and other immigrant groups. Focussing on a particular area and heritage off the island helped distinguish the different groups on Ijwi from one another all the more, at the same time that it strengthened the sense of internal cohesion within these groups.[47]

However, as the Ijwi community became more settled, and increasingly separated from their Rwandan brothers by time and by the diverse forms of political and cultural evolution occurring in Rwanda and on Ijwi, the nature of relations with the mainland altered. Rather than visit their families and provide goods through familial obligations, people on Ijwi increasingly sought "friends" in Rwanda who could provide them with cattle and other material goods. Thus in later years, the exchanges (of agricultural goods for cattle and cattle for marriage) assumed a more formalized, if not entirely commercialized, character.[48] Similarly, differences among groups on Ijwi became expressed increasingly within a common arena, rather than being directed through separate outlets to different mainland communities.

Such ties between Ijwi and the eastern shores of Lake Kivu were not confined to the Beshaza. The nature of these early gifts of agricultural goods from settlers on Ijwi to families on the mainland obviously reflected Ijwi's economic advantage, above all that of a superior climate and good soil. But the form of these ties from Ijwi communities east to the mainland also fell into a more widespread pattern, that of a flourishing export of cattle (and other livestock) from east of the lake in exchange for other products from the west—especially iron, ornamental items, and agricultural products. From the generalized nature of these later transfers across the lake, as well as the generalized character of early mobility patterns in the region as a whole, it is clear that other clans also shared in the type of relations best shown in the traditions of the Beshaza. As noted above, the Banyakabwa retained linkages with Cimbiri in Bugoyi and Mwiiru in Bwishaza, as well as elsewhere north and west of the lake, and these ties helped reinforce their autonomy from the rest of Ijwi society. Other groups living in the same area (such as the Banyambiriri, considered in the next chapter) maintained similar external ties. It is probable, therefore, that many of the earlier distinctions among the small immigrant groups in the eastern highlands of Ijwi, where many of the newcomers from east of the lake had settled, resulted from their continuing ties farther east across the lake.

Since meaningful dynastic integration of the eastern areas on Ijwi did not occur until later in the island's history, it is probable that the primary stimulus for this changing nature of ties across the lake was the changing context within Rwanda, not the process of political centralization on Ijwi. Changes on the Rwandan mainland, especially the apparent in the intensified political climate and the associated cultural integration of Rwandan norms into the area west of the Nile-Zaire Divide, increasingly differentiated mainland culture from Ijwi and other western regions, and tended to diminish the intensity of such interactions across the lake. Reducing the intensity of these external relations altered the focus of the Ijwi groups away from their homelands and contributed, in turn, to more intensive interaction among the different clans on Ijwi.

Ironically, such interaction among the new communities only reinforced the distinctions which had originated in the settlers' ties to different homeland areas east of the lake. The new social context to emerge on Ijwi encouraged the political consolidation of the island at a level above that of clan identity. However, because of the nature of this new political context, such a unification of Ijwi did not break down clan loyalties but tended to consolidate them: in order to be a member of the emergent Ijwi polity it became increasingly important to identify first of all with one of the recognized clan groups, the litmus test of true Ijwi identity.[49]

Changing ties east of the lake therefore provided two of the important factors in the evolution of Ijwi royalty. Enduring ties to the east initially distinguished the clans among themselves. Paradoxically, the changing Rwandan scene brought these emergent clans together—but as autonomous clan units—within a common Ijwi focus. This strongly suggests that the indirect influences of changes on the Rwandan mainland were in some respects more important for the timing and nature of the formation of kingship on Ijwi than were more direct factors of integration which flowed from the new social context emerging on the island. The next two chapters will look at the arrival of two groups from the east, groups which became important to the ritual configurations that came to define royalty on Ijwi.

6
Immigrants to Ijwi
Claiming Ritual Status

During the late eighteenth century Ijwi society was transformed by the arrival of new groups from the east. These were essentially formed of refugees, some fleeing the political pressures of an expanding Rwandan power, some seeking agricultural security away from the increasing population densities and decreasing productivity of the highlands on the Nile-Zaire Divide. Their arrival led to various types of settlement on the eastern shores of the island, and the historical processes thus set in motion were to affect Ijwi's later receptivity to royalty in a profound way. Some groups maintained ties with the Rwandan mainland, sending back agricultural products to homeland areas east of the lake. Others established themselves as permanent settlers from the beginning. And a few apparently brought with them the prestige associated with ritual knowledge from areas of western Rwanda. Whether these ritual ties were directly linked to the Rwandan state rituals is not always clear. But it is clear that the immigrants shared a cultural orientation towards the meaning of royal rituals similar to those later apparent in Rwanda, and that they came to Ijwi with precise knowledge of the forms of such rituals.

Most clans among these immigrants (the Beshaza are in some respects an exception) shared certain social and historical characteristics. They immigrated to Ijwi from the eastern side of the lake, bringing with them similar concepts of social relations which were developing east of the lake. They arrived on Ijwi before the royal family, the Basibula, or at least before the establishment of royal power in their particular area of settlement. They settled in localized (non-dispersed) groups. Their similar cultural background, early arrival, and localized settlement helped generate a strong corporate sentiment as these groups established themselves in this new environment. They were seed agriculturalists with more emphasis on sedentary residential patterns, distinct patterns of labor organization, and a more pronounced seasonal rhythm to their agricultural activities than appears to have been the case for earlier social formations in the area.

Their initial settlement was concentrated in a single area, the moun-

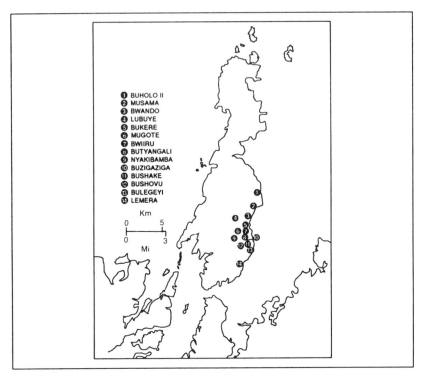

Map 9. Eastern villages on Ijwi

tainous eastern highlands just south of the east-west forest belt traversing the middle of the island (see Map 9). This area was one of the last to be incorporated fully into the administrative structure of the Ijwi kingdom: with one exception, royal residences were not located there; with the exception of one family, royal marriages were not common there; and the general center of gravity of royal presence in the south rather significantly avoided this area. Eventually, however, this eastern region turned out to be important for royalty, particularly in articulating the new agricultural basis of social organization on Ijwi, and several of the clans in this region became significant participants in the development of the royal rituals. Strong ties with the royal family through ritual proved, in turn, to be an important determinant of the future status of these clans on Ijwi.

Such insignificant royal presence in the east contrasted markedly with the ritual strength of the clans who settled there: the same factors which accounted for minimal royal presence also made these groups important for royalty. The early settlement of these communities, their internal coherence, and their external ties to the Rwandan mainland may well have provided a potential threat to the hegemony of the Basibula dynasty on its arrival. Even the ritual relationships forged between these settlers and the royal dynasty were fraught with tension and ambiguity, for while integrating these groups into a wider polity, ritual roles in some respects acknowledged—and intensified—the autonomy of the area from royal control.

The Eastern Highlands

Whereas the Banyakabwa arrived on Ijwi from the northeast (Bugoyi) and originally settled in the north of the island, other immigrants came from the Nile-Zaire Divide southeast of the lake, and settled on the mountainous eastern shore of the island. This highland region is distinct from other areas of Ijwi in several characteristics. Residential patterns in general consist of smaller villages, which maintain a higher degree of clan homogeneity than exists elsewhere on the island. The people here often retain close ties with groups in Rwanda. They live still today in more markedly nucleated clusters. Religious forms, speech patterns, and foods all differ somewhat from those found elsewhere on the island.

The east is also seen as a difficult area for the administration today, and always has maintained a high degree of autonomy both from colonial authorities and from Ijwi central court authorities. The inhabitants here never accepted the colonial headmen imposed on the area from the north, for instance; it was (and is even today) an area viewed as a place of potential confrontation to the central court over such issues as tax collection, pasturage, and land rights. To be sure, certain prominent allies of the court have come from these eastern highlands, especially those of the Baloho clan (as will be discussed below), but they are seen more as representatives of the area to the court—as men with their own power base autonomous of court prestige—than as delegates of the sovereign. As in the case of the Banyakabwa, all these factors are related to the relative age of settlement of these clans on Ijwi and their strong and continuous ties to areas outside the island. But unlike the Banyakabwa, the historical importance of the clans in this area also derives from the ritual roles they have come to assume in the structures of kingship, and from their historical relations with the royal family—very different in some cases from that of the Banyakabwa.

Most villages in the eastern highlands of Ijwi were settled before the Basibula arrival, and were (and are still today) characterized by the predominance of a single clan (sometimes two clans), a pattern rare elsewhere on Ijwi. For recent times, this settlement pattern is illustrated in Table 2, where the number of married males in the predominant clan or clans for each village is expressed as a proportion of the total number of married males for the village as a whole.

Table 2. Clan Localization in Eastern Villages

Village (Clan)	Ratio of Married Males in Predominant Clan to Those in Total Village Population	Percentage of Married Males in the Predominant Clan
Bwiiru (Baziralo)	59/62	95
Butyangali		
(Banyambiriri and Badaha)	57/61	93
(Banyambiriri alone)	44/61	72
Bushovu (Balega)	59/69	86
Bukere (Bahande)	42/53	79
Lubuye (Balega and Bashaho)	69/90	77
Nyakibamba (Beshaza)	21/28	75

Even where two clans predominate (as in Lubuye or Butyangali) each clan tends to settle within its own domain, separate from the other.[1] This pattern of cohesive clan homogeneity is markedly different from the settlement pattern of the earlier period, during the time of the Binyalenge settlement, and also of the later period, after royal establishment, in other parts of the island.

The Banyambiriri and the Basibula

Banyambiriri Arrival and Settlement

The paucity of precise references to people and events of the late eighteenth century on Ijwi serves to underscore the apparent autonomous existence of the early Banyambiriri on the island. Most testimonies note that Mutyangali was the first Munyambiriri on Ijwi and founder of the Banyambiriri center at Butyangali. He arrived alone; there was no one before him. Although this is often claimed only with reference to the hill of Butyangali, the implication is that the Banyambiriri were early arrivals in the area, and that their interaction with others on the island was severely limited and socially unimportant. Typical of the statements to this effect are:

> There was no one here when Mutyangali came; there were no other clans. But Nyamuziga preceded them.[2]

> Mutyangali came alone; there were no others. No one lived here; there was only forest.[3]

> Mutyangali was the first man at Butyangali. No one was here when he arrived; he came up from the lake. There was only forest here. . . . The king here was Nyamuziga.[4]

There was only forest here. Mwendanga followed them; they [the Banyambiriri ancestors] were here before him [the Basibula]. Balimucabo [a collective reference to the Banyakabwa] was here before [the Banyambiriri]; then Mwendanga came to chase Balimucabo to Rwanda.[5]

Most imply or state that Nyamuziga (the Banyakabwa dignitary in the south) was the principal authority in the area at the time of Banyambiriri arrival, and that this was before the arrival of the Basibula royal line; some state that Nyamuhiva was the "*mwami* on Ijwi" then.[6]

Where references to other clans occur, these tend to confirm that the Banyambiriri were among the earliest of the immigrant clans from the east, and that interaction among different localized groups on Ijwi at this time was minimal, as some state directly.[7] The most frequent reference is to the Balega—as we have seen, most likely a composite group formed of very old population segments on Ijwi.[8] Another clan mentioned in early Banyambiriri traditions is the Bahande. But this name is often used to denote the Banyakabwa (as well as the Basibula and other Bahande groups) today, and therefore can be viewed as referring to the Banyakabwa or to the prestige of the "ruling" group.[9]

One of the most interesting references is that which groups the clans encountered by the Banyambiriri on Ijwi into three distinct categories: the Bahande-Basibula; the Balega, Bashaho, and Badaha; and the Bahunde.[10] The first denotes the royal groups (and those which share claims to such prestige); the second includes that group of clans which, each in different areas of the island, share an institutionalized joking relationship with the Banyambiriri (to be discussed below); and the third reflects a perception sometimes associated with the Binyalenge: Hunde culture is seen as (and probably in some respects is, in fact) similar to the Binyalenge culture of Ijwi's past.

Early Banyambiriri Contacts with Royalty

The Banyambiriri of eastern Ijwi are presently divided among three principal residential communities. The senior line is located at Butyangali; a historically related group is settled at Cibishwa, to the south (an autonomous segment of Lemera village); another line is found at Ishungwe, part of the village of Mugote, not far from Butyangali. Although there appears to have been some historical association of these three communities, the nature of these ties is not always clear. Because of its association with Mutyangali, Butyangali is assumed to be the oldest of the three communities; everyone accepts that the Cibishwa community is an offshoot from Butyangali. The genealogies to Mutyangali are variable in the names and number of generations included; some apparently include collateral lines.[11] Although three to five generations are commonly cited, the shorter genealogies appear to have been telescoped, and thus the founding of Butyangali, despite the difficulties in genealogical reckoning, would seem best situated around five generations from today's elder residents.[12] Independent data, primarily tie-ins with other clans, confirm this approximate timing.

But locating Banyambiriri arrival relative to that of the Basibula is more important than determining an absolute date of their arrival. The Banyambiriri unanimously claim to have arrived before royal establishment, and there are many independent data to confirm this. There was no early contact with the Basibula; there was no land payment by any Banyambiriri community; and there was no administrative interaction of any Banyambiriri community with the royal infrastructure. In fact, the Banyambiriri have little record of tie-ins with any other communities, and traditions from other groups as well as the spread of Banyambiriri among the three settlement centers, each one clan homogeneous, all indicate early arrival.

However, neither the Banyambiriri nor the Basibula mention the other in their early traditions. The absence of the Banyambiriri from Basibula traditions pertaining to the east of the island is all the more remarkable because the Banyambiriri are now one of the three most important ritual clans of the kingdom. Despite their proximity to the hill of Buzigaziga, there is no mention of Banyambiriri participation in the Banyakabwa-Basibula struggle over royalty that occurred there (discussed in chapter 9). Furthermore, although the first Basibula residence on Ijwi was at Cimenwe, the summit strategically located directly above Butyangali, the Banyambiriri are not mentioned in the royal traditions nor is any royal presence included in the Banyambiriri traditions.

The Timing of Banyambiriri Settlement

On the other hand, Banyambiriri traditions relating to Nyamuziga, the Banyakabwa leader in this area, assume a prominence which is very different from the scanty general knowledge applying to the time of Banyambiriri arrival on Ijwi. As mentioned, traditions relating to their earliest time on Ijwi refer only to the Banyakabwa; there is a complete absence of references to other clans.[13] This places the argument from silence relative to the royal clan in a new light. It suggests that the Banyambiriri (perhaps in small numbers) were indeed at Butyangali during the time of Nyamuziga, the leader of the Banyakabwa at Buzigaziga, or shortly thereafter. But in his competition with the Basibula, Nyamuziga was forced off the island and his family never subsequently exercised political influence outside Buzigaziga; had the Banyambiriri arrived only later, it is unlikely that they would have retained such clear references to Nyamuziga's presence in this area. The Basibula also withdrew from this area after their conflict with Nyamuziga; the royal family was unwilling or unable to establish effective rule in the east until much later.

It is the absence of effective royal presence in the area, therefore, rather than the absence of the Banyambiriri, that best accounts for the silence of Banyambiriri traditions on the Basibula. In estimating the date of Banyambiriri arrival, we must take greater account of Banyakabwa presence in their traditions than of Basibula absence from those traditions.

A similar conclusion can be drawn from the ritual autonomy of the two Banyambiriri segments, one at Butyangali (including the Cibishwa line) and one at Ishungwe (part of the present village of Mugote). The perceived contemporaneity of these two lines is illustrated by their similar genealogical depth and in the identification of Mutyangali as a "brother" of one of the ancestors claimed by the Ishungwe community.[14] Though roughly contemporaneous, however, the two settlements exhibit important historical differences. The community at Ishungwe seems to have been formed of a line parallel to but independent of the Butyangali descent line. People in Ishungwe, for example, do not recall having attended the annual "lineage" rituals at Butyangali in the past, as do those at Cibishwa, nor do they cite Mutyangali in their genealogies.[15]

The two Banyambiriri communities at Butyangali and Ishungwe have also developed autonomous ritual roles; there is no indication of their having been derived from what was formerly a single common ritual source. Those at Ishungwe preserve the cowrie diadem (called the Ishungwe—hence the name of the community) worn on the *mwami's* forehead during ritual ceremonies; those at Cibishwa, on the other hand, provide the millet essential for the First Fruits ceremony. These two Banyambiriri communities, therefore, deal with different segments of the royal ritual, and each performs its ritual functions exclusively of the other.

In the absence of other commentary, the complete autonomy of ritual functions between these two communities confirms that their separation preceded their acquisition of ritual status in the Ijwi kingdom. It suggests that the different ritual functions were introduced separately, in a pattern which corresponded neither with early royal contacts arising from the court's proximity to Butyangali nor with a sense of a larger Banyambiriri community. Regardless of the timing of their initial settlement on the island, therefore, Banyambiriri interaction with the royal family occurred only well after the arrival of the Basibula. Combined with the indications of Banyambiriri presence on the island from before the time of the Basibula-Banyakabwa conflict, this indicates that the growth of royal institutions and the establishment of a royal infrastructure took place only over a long period of time. The establishment of kingship in its present form, then, was not contemporaneous with the arrival of the royal family.

Thus the early picture of the Banyambiriri on Ijwi is that of several small groups of people arriving roughly contemporaneously, probably driven

out of a common homeland by famine, land pressure, or dwindling productivity. They settled in two communities, quite close to each other, on the
eastern shore of the island. While we lack direct confirmation on this point,
indirect evidence indicates that they maintained some ties with their home
area, although these were not likely to have been very intense. The Banyambiriri do not seem to have had any significant interaction as a group with
other clans on Ijwi at this time (although individual relations undoubtedly
did take place), and there is no indication of any conflict. It would appear,
then, that the arrival of the royalty (and particularly the co-optation of this
group within the royal rituals) consolidated Banyambiriri identity, despite
the fact that the two communities seem never to have maintained any organic
ties beyond sharing the same clan name.

Banyambiriri Ritual Roles on Ijwi

The differences between the Banyambiriri and other clans are particularly
evident with regard to their ritual status in the kingdom. In fact, particular
roles within the shared universe of royal rituals constitute one of the principal
distinguishing characteristics among the clans on Ijwi today. The most important ritual role of the Banyambiriri (performed by those from Cibishwa) is
associated with Muganuro, the annual First Fruits ceremony of the kingdom.
Because the Muganuro ritual will be explored in greater length in chapter 12,
this discussion will focus only on elements which relate to the external relations of the Banyambiriri participants in this ritual.

We have noted that the Banyambiriri were not incorporated within the
rituals of royalty on Ijwi until well after Banyambiriri arrival; the question
remains as to why they should have acceded to such status at all. The eventual association of the Banyambiriri with royal ritual functions and the significance of this association may help explain some aspects of the clan's early
history on Ijwi; thus it is especially important to explore the nature of Banyambiriri relations with groups other than the royal family.

Neither the timing of their arrival nor their present clan size account for
the current ritual importance of the Banyambiriri on Ijwi. It is clear that they
did not arrive on Ijwi with the royal line, and hence their ritual association
does not stem from a commemoration of an early alliance between the two. It
is equally clear, from the data presented in chapter 3 and the localization of
the Banyambiriri even today, that this ritual status does not reflect a historical status as "owners of the soil." Furthermore, the Banyambiriri are not a
particularly large clan and certainly not widespread, nor were they likely to
have been so in the past. Therefore, neither age, nor size, nor dispersal
correlates with ritual status in this case. But the nature of the rituals themselves, and particularly their regional diffusion, may provide some clue to the
Banyambiriri role within them.

The Ijwi Muganuro rituals, for which the Banyambiriri are primarily responsible, are similar to those of Rwanda but clearly distinct from those of other Havu or Shi kingdoms (except for Kaziba, south of Lake Kivu).[16] In Rwanda, the region called Bunyambiriri (to which the Banyambiriri on Ijwi trace their origin) is known as the former home of one of the small pre-Banyiginya polities located on the Nile-Zaire Divide east of the lake.[17] One person specifically noted that the Banyambiriri on Ijwi came from Nyunyi ya Karonge in Rwanda "at the time of the sorghum harvest" (which is precisely the time of the Muganuro festival on Ijwi).[18] Rwandan sources note that among the Basinga clan—which included very early holders of ritual power in the area now included in Rwanda[19]—was a group known as the Bahinza b'I Suti ("Bahinza" is a term that refers to the former royal families of these small polities before Abanyiginya conquest). These were "politico-religious chiefs residing at Suti in Bunyambiriri . . . [who] had all the honors and attributes of kings: drums, tribute, and double names. Those from Suti were called Kings of the Harvest *(Umwami w'Imyaka)."*[20] The title *(umwami w'imyaka)* attributed to the Bahinza b'I Suti in this source was the same title as the one used for the ritualist from Butembo (a region farther to the east in Rwanda) who was responsible for carrying out roles within the Rwandan ritual code which were virtually identical to those the Banyambiriri performed for Ijwi royalty.[21] Thus, although no explicit claim is made by Banyambiriri that they were formerly ritualists east of the lake, considerable indirect evidence suggests that, simply by association with the region of their origin, they arrived on the island with ritual status of some kind.[22]

Therefore, the important ritual role of the Banyambiriri on Ijwi is an indication of the incorporation of rituals primarily derived from outside but only indirectly introduced to Ijwi, by the intermediary of what was essentially a refugee group autonomous of the royal line—in this case by the integration of the Banyambiriri within the larger framework of royalty on Ijwi—rather than by the devolution of ritual power (and ritual knowledge) from the Ijwi royal family itself. Moreover, the ritual incorporation of the Banyambiriri into kingship on Ijwi by way of the Muganuro ceremonies also speaks to the manner of social integration of the Banyambiriri into Ijwi royal structures. It is thus another indication that Ijwi royalty was derived from a much wider ritual and conceptual universe than that which characterized the Basibula royal family alone.

Through the same process by which the rituals of Muganuro were incorporated into the royal structures on Ijwi, the Banyambiriri were integrated with the larger Ijwi society. Therefore, the construction and formation of the ritual character of the Ijwi kingship is at one with the social integration of the kingdom. But the corollary is also true: that because population elements on Ijwi were drawn from such a wide social field, the important ritual role of the

Banyambiriri on Ijwi need be explained by historical factors internal to Ijwi, reflective of the politics at a particular time in Ijwi history, and the changing and inter-related aspects of social realities on the island. In this context, the strong Banyambiriri corporate identity, their localization in an area of prior settlement (and one of importance to the new royal line), and probably also their association with ritual in Rwanda (although perhaps only in the perception of others), all seem to have been significant factors.

Banyambiriri Relations with Other Clans

The place of the Banyambiriri within the larger social and ritual context of Ijwi is also illuminating for the history of the relations among the different clans during the period of the consolidation of Basibula rule. For example, there is some evidence of competition among Ijwi groups vying for ritual supremacy on the island. This competition would have strengthened internal corporate clan identity and divided one clan from another. The institutionalization of ritual ties with royalty would also have diminished overt competition among clan groups, by focussing clan interactions instead on the institutions of royalty. In this way, divisiveness and integration were complementary, with each contributing to the other; by this same process royalty became the principal focus both for clan identity and for "relations" between the clans.

The Banyambiriri today hold one of the three most important ritual positions on Ijwi: they are responsible for producing the millet—a very old seed crop in the area—that is ritually consecrated at the time of the new harvest.[23] In this role they assure the agricultural productivity and hence the economic welfare of this island community as a whole. Consequently, through the symbolic representation of shared production and shared consumption of agricultural produce, Banyambiriri ritual roles are more closely identified with popular participation in the kingdom than are the ritual roles of other clans, which deal principally with either the person of the king or with the entourage or paraphernalia surrounding the king. More directly than those of other clans, therefore, the ritual role of the Banyambiriri establishes a link between the population, on the one hand, and royalty and the king, on the other.[24]

The only other clans to approach the ritual significance of the Banyambiriri as a whole are the Baziralo of Bwiiru, responsible for the royal drums, and the Bashaho, responsible for many aspects of ritual associated with the enthronement and the personal well-being of the king. Of the three most important ritualist clans, the Banyambiriri show the least corporate identity with their ritual roles, and their formal ritual contacts with royalty are limited to once a year (at the Muganuro ceremony), with only occasional other responsibilities (e.g., at the death of Rusanga, the royal bull or the royal ram).

The Baziralo (referred to in their ritual status as Beeru) are the most autonomous of the person of the king; they form almost a ritual counterbalance to royal power, more identified with Ubwiiru, with the legitimacy of royalty, than with the person of the king. In terms of fields of action, the Bashaho ritual role is more closely identified with the royal family than is that of the other two important clans. Mushaho, the principal ritualist among the Bashaho, has daily contact with the king and the royal household, and he derives an exalted status from this fact. In addition, there are many other Bashaho ritualists, more than in any other clan, and the clan has a strong corporate sentiment focussing on these ritual functions; the Bashaho clan as a whole, for example, identifies with the enthronement. Through the role of Mushaho they all enthrone, or "create," the king: "The king cannot reign without us."[25] In no other clan except the Baziralo (a small and highly localized group) does identification with ritual extend to such a broad segment of the clan.

The oppositions among the several Ijwi groups possessing these important ritual powers on Ijwi are particularly strong. The potential conflict over control of ritual in the Ijwi kingdom is exemplified by the testimony of a Mushaho clan member, speaking of *kumbi* clans, those clans carrying a joking relationship with each other. Having first mentioned that the Bahande were the same as the Basibula—the Basibula are a subclan (on Ijwi, a lineage) of the Bahande—he then explained by way of illustration that the Banyambiriri and the Bashaho derived originally from the same father and mother. They became very numerous and quarrelled over who could choose the king; consequently they split into two clans.[26] No other evidence supports this statement. Normally the Bashaho are linked with the Beshaza in this type of vague identity as "sibling" clans; in this case not only were the Bashaho tied explicitly with the Banyambiriri, but this linkage (actually a separation: they were united only in their mutual differentiation) was also associated with ritual competition, the quarrel over who could choose the king. Therefore, at a stroke this testimony serves to explain Bashaho-Banyambiriri connections with regard to their *kumbi* relationship and to the tension which accompanies social proximity stemming from ritual ties to royalty.

The Formation of Banyambiriri Joking Relationships with Other Clans

The proximity which creates tension between the Banyambiriri and the Bashaho conforms to the classic functional analysis of joking relationships as an institutionalization of potential stress brought about by ambiguous social relations.[27] It is significant that between these two clans there are no evident points of compatibility or proximity in residence, origins, or precise occupational/ritual specializations. Instead of representing friendship or shared community, the *kumbi* (joking) relationship between these two clans seems

intended to mitigate the potential tensions which result from their complementary ritual roles, their major point of contact. It is their shared responsibility in ritual roles which brings them together, causing them to act within
the same social network. But it is also ritual distinctions which define their
differences, and which therefore create the distinctions between them. Furthermore, the Bashaho constitute the primary *kumbi* counterpart of the
Banyambiriri. Other clans cited as *kumbi* by the Banyambiriri differ from one
region of the island to another; only the Bashaho appear consistently in all
areas and among all respondents as *kumbi* partners of the Banyambiriri. Yet
their relationship with the Banyambiriri cannot be explained by any other
factors, and this reinforces the strength of ritual competition in the development of this *kumbi* tie.

　　Banyambiriri *kumbi* relations with other clans appear to have developed
from precise historical factors, discrete, identifiable, and different from the
nature of the Banyambiriri-Bashaho *kumbi* tie. But they all share one common function and conceptual purpose: that of uniting two groups in a relationship that both brings them together and, by this very process, recognizes
and promotes the fact that they are different.[28] The *kumbi* relationship of the
Banyambiriri with the Badaha, for example, seems to be particularly important in the area of Butyangali, where these two clans together form an overwhelming proportion of the married male population (93 percent). It is
therefore likely that the very proximity of these two groups has led to a *kumbi*
relation acting to preserve their social and historical distinctions.

　　But the relations between the Badaha and Banyambiriri may well ante-
date the community at Butyangali; their *kumbi* relations prior to arrival may
have determined their common settlement at Butyangali, rather than having
resulted from this settlement. Otherwise it is difficult to explain why they did
not in fact unite to form a single settlement community, as happened in the
case of the Balega clan formation. The Banyambiriri come from an area in
Rwanda of predominantly Abasinga clan settlement; the proportion of
Abasinga in Bunyambiriri is almost twice as high as the Abasinga average for
Rwanda as a whole.[29] The Bahinza b'I Suti, mentioned above, are also considered Abasinga in Rwanda.[30] Most Bany'Iju, in fact, equate Banyambiriri
status on Ijwi with Abasinga status in Rwanda.

　　The Badaha, on the other hand, are universally associated with the
Abagesera in Rwanda. In Rwanda the Abasinga and Abagesera are said to
be two of the oldest clans in the country; they are Abasangwabutaka, "those
who were found on the soil." Along with the Abazigaaba, they perform for all
the other clans in Rwanda the same functions which on Ijwi are performed by
members of two *kumbi* clans for one another. (These responsibilities, known
as *ubuse* in Rwanda, include ritual blessings and attendance at hut-building,
burial, and succession.[31]) But in Rwanda the Abasinga and the Abagesera

perform these functions for each other; along with the Abasinga and Abazi-gaaba, they are the only pairs to act in this capacity.[32] The Banyambiriri and Badaha in Butyangali interact in the same way, by virtue of their *kumbi* status; it is possible that the relationship which characterized the Badaha and Banyambiriri in Butyangali was a continuation of their previous relationship in Rwanda.

The ties of the Bashaho with the Banyambiriri, however, seem to have been of a different nature. Because there is no evidence of intensive ties of the two groups in Rwanda, their *kumbi* relations on Ijwi cannot be ascribed to a retention of pre-Ijwi patterns of interaction, nor is it likely that they result from early Ijwi contact; most early Bashaho groups on the island lived far from the Banyambiriri centers. Historically, in fact, the Bashaho form a rather heterogeneous group, with various segments arriving from different directions at different times. There seems to have been no sustained cultural or geographical association of the two clans on Ijwi, as exists for some *kumbi* clans; the Bashaho are least cited as *kumbi* by Banyambiriri in the very area of closest residential contact. Therefore, Bashaho-Banyambiriri ties are not localized to the area of their geographical contact point; other factors must account for their institutionalized relationship.

Both in its origin and in its reinforcement, therefore, the Bashaho-Banyambiriri *kumbi* relationship can best be explained by the ritual contacts focussing on royalty, complementary and reinforcing on the one hand, but also competitive. Interaction between the two focussed on their central ritual roles within kingship. This process, therefore, seems to be an indication in the ritual sphere of what occurred in some respects also, at a wider level, in the political sphere. A focus on kingship in general brought about new inter-actions among social groups at the same time that it sharpened their dif-ferences. Kingship defined and enhanced these differences while also provid-ing the conceptual arena within which such interaction occurred. The ritual focus on the royal court thus increased perceived clan distinctions at one level while it integrated and unified their interactions at another. It is this "shared competition" which perhaps best accounts for the historical as well as the functional role of the *kumbi* tie between the Banyambiriri and Bashaho.

In certain areas the Banyambiriri claim yet another *kumbi* tie, to the Balega. (No particular Balega group is specified.) This *kumbi* identification, however, is not universally held among the Banyambiriri; instead, it is re-gionalized in the west of the island and in the Havu mainland areas. It is curious that this *kumbi* relationship is not cited also in the east, in Butyangali (home of the Banyambiriri in the east) or Bushovu (the home of a large and important Balega subgroup), because they inhabit opposite slopes of the same massif. So the conditions that apply to other *kumbi* relations (geograph-ical proximity, as in the example of the Badaha) do not apply here. (The

Table 3. Banyambiriri *Kumbi* Ties

Clans	Region of *Kumbi* Association	Hypothesized Origin/Reinforcement
Bashaho	everywhere	shared "ritual competition"
Badaha	Butyangali	pre-immigration interaction in Rwanda (Abasinga-Abagesera)
Balega	western areas	early interaction
Beshaza	northern areas (Malambo)	clan ties of isolated families with dominant clan (also Badaha at Butyangali)

Bashovu do not fulfill significant ritual roles at the court, nor is the timing of Bashovu settlement clear—they may have been later arrivals.) It is therefore most likely that this localized *kumbi* tie emerged from a general identity and inter-relationship with the Balega as settlers on Ijwi with whom the Banyambiriri in the west had early contacts.

Thus three different patterns of interaction seem to account for different pairings of joking relations between the Banyambiriri and other clans on Ijwi: pre-immigration interaction east of the lake, diffused contact among early settlers, and later ritual ties emerging after the dynastic arrival. (These same principles can be extended to *kumbi* ties among other clans as well.) What unites them all is the strength of the differentiation which *kumbi* ties preserve among groups otherwise closely associated. Aside from serving as simply ethnographic curiosities, joking relationships carry with them historical lessons; like other social factors, they are historical products, not just "superstitious customs." *Bukumbi* was therefore one of the mechanisms which impeded the formation of higher-level identities, as occurred in the case of the Balega; the formation of *kumbi* ties contributed to the separation of identity groups.[33]

One exception to the general pattern appears in areas far removed from Banyambiriri localization. In those areas *kumbi* ties seem to have been influenced by geographical proximity among settlements; they fall into the pattern of very small clan representation identifying with a very large group. In the north, where Banyambiriri are nowhere very numerous, and especially in those villages where only one or two families of Banyambiriri are found today, Banyambiriri cite *kumbi* ties with the Beshaza, the most numerous clan in the north in general and dominant in the villages in question. This illustrates the simple alteration of *kumbi* clans to conform to geographical and social differences, but also a basic underlying feeling of compatibility. Members of these two clans share common cultural origins; they share a common interest in and association with royalty; and they share a common area of geographical focus on Ijwi (the east).

Chapters 5 and 6 have considered three of the new clans to arrive on Ijwi from the east; the following chapter will consider another. Regardless of their differences, which were significant, all four of these groups shared similar characteristics on their arrival. They settled in clearly defined geographical units and they appear to have remained relatively independent of each other, thus maintaining separate identities. This provided a new dimension to Ijwi social organization, different from the broad categorizations which previously characterized it (of which the Balega are an example). This pattern was distinct also from the apparent loose criteria of social identity, stemming from easy interaction, which characterized the Binyalenge period yet before that. The emergent society was characterized by more narrowly defined identity patterns of increasing intensity. This was reinforced by historical distinctions deriving from their arrival as separate groups, their settlement in different areas, and perhaps, too, from claims to different statuses associated with these historical differences, statuses which were to take shape as differences between ritualists.

7
Immigrants to Ijwi
Creating Ritual Status

Like the Banyambiriri, the Beeru of the Baziralo clan are a relatively small group, highly localized and with a strong corporate sentiment. They are also tied to royalty as important royal ritualists, responsible for the royal drums. Although ritual functions within the clan are carried out by only two individuals, most Baziralo (even those outside the Baziralo center at Bwiiru) identify strongly with the role of "drum-makers." The tendency towards corporate identity is more pronounced among the Baziralo than among any other clan on Ijwi except the Bashaho, the principal ritualists of the court. This case, therefore, illustrates the importance of ritual in generating corporate sentiment—the more so because the mainland origins of the Baziralo are an insignificant factor in the construction of this corporate sentiment.

I have argued above that a strong corporate sense tends to correlate with ties to royalty and a sense of pre-Basibula clan history. But from internal sources alone, it is difficult to establish the early history of the Baziralo, despite their strong corporate identity—much more difficult than in the case of the Banyambiriri. Baziralo traditions retain even less indication of their place of origin, the nature and timing of their arrival on Ijwi, and their relations with other groups (including the royal family) than do the Banyambiriri traditions; in short, they retain less sense of an early common identity. This implies that their functions as ritualists on Ijwi developed later than did those of the Banyambiriri. Nonetheless references in Baziralo oral testimony to ritual functions in Rwanda similar to those they perform on Ijwi, and indirect tie-ins of the Baziralo on Ijwi with corresponding ritualists in Rwanda, provide more suggestive leads than was true for the Banyambiriri. Therefore, this consideration of the Baziralo on Ijwi will focus more on the spread of ritual functions in the region than on the movement of specific people. The discussion will focus particularly on the timing of the incorporation of Baziralo ritual functions into Ijwi royalty; in so doing it will illustrate the complex nature of the ritual tie-ins within the region.

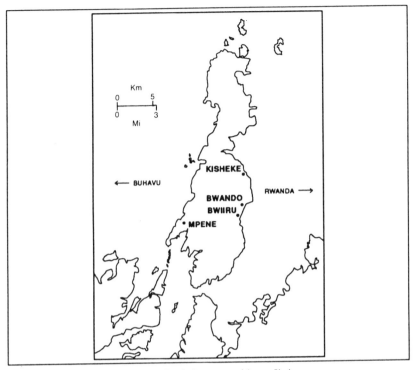

Map 10. Baziralo communities on Ijwi

Baziralo Settlement

Current Baziralo Settlement on Ijwi

The primary residential center of the Baziralo ritualists on Ijwi today is known as Bwiiru, a locative correlated with their appellation as "Beeru" (see Map 10). The term "Beeru" is widely associated with important ritual status in the region of Lake Kivu, although the precise functions associated with this status differ from place to place. In Rwanda, for example, the Abiiru are guardians of the ritual code (the Ubwiiru); in Buhavu and in Butembo, west of Lake Kivu, the Beeru bury the king. Even on Ijwi the term "Beeru" has two different applications. While one group of Beeru serves as guardians of the royal drums, another group has functions similar to those of the Beeru in Buhavu; they are responsible for the preparation of the corpse and the burial of a deceased king. But on Ijwi these Beeru, also known as Banjoga, have a clan identity as Badaha and are completely distinguished from the Beeru of the Baziralo clan, the drum-makers. Ijwi clearly serves as an intermediary between these two traditions, east and west of the lake, combining elements of both. Among the Baziralo on Ijwi, the term "Beeru" in its most restricted sense applies only to those Baziralo who inhabit the hill of Bwiiru; other Baziralo are known only by their clan name, although some recent emigrants from Bwiiru may attempt to retain their status as Beeru.

In terms of clan membership the Baziralo center is one of the most homogeneous on the island. Virtually all the inhabitants of this locale belong to the Baziralo clan.[1] Corporate sentiment within the Beeru community (the people of Bwiiru) is also reflected by the character and content of the traditions, which are consistent, if not entirely standardized.[2] The genealogies often trace back to a single founder, thus emphasizing the "lineage" character of the village. Furthermore, the Baziralo inhabitants of Bwiiru show few signs of widespread contacts outside the village, expressed through blood-pacts, cattle contracts, commerce, or immigration/emigration. Even their joking relations *(bukumbi)* reflect a much narrower focus than those of most other clans.

Village corporate character in Bwiiru is manifested in the person of the "lineage" head (who is also the "village capita"), accepted as such both by members of the hill and by outsiders. Symbolic of his autonomy from the Basibula *mwami* of Ijwi, he is known as a *mwami emwage*—a *mwami* within his own domain (i.e., in Bwiiru). The term of reference for the lineage head as ritualist is "Munyakalinga"—the possessor of the Kalinga (the royal drum). His wife's title is Makamba, the same as that used for the king's wives. Munyakalinga's position and prestige are such that he is even able to express overt opposition to the *mwami* in public. This conforms to the suggestion above, that Munyakalinga's ritual role is that of "possessor of the royalty," a guardian of royalty, even superior to the *mwami* in some respects. There is indeed a certain ambiguous tension between the two dignitaries.

Like the Banyambiriri, their immediate neighbors to the south, the Baziralo are strongly localized in the east. Elsewhere on Ijwi, there are few Baziralo settlements emanating from Bwiiru. The two largest of these secondary settlements are in villages dominated numerically by the Beshaza, the sole *kumbi* clan of the Baziralo. One of these Baziralo communities is located at Bwando, not far from Bwiiru; another is at Kisheke, on the eastern shore just north of the Nyamusize forest area.[3]

Baziralo Arrival from the East

Despite the sense of strong common identities among the Baziralo, the historical traditions of their arrival and establishment on Ijwi are extremely vague. One frequent reference is to Lugyaka, the founder of Bwiiru. But there are difficulties of interpretation or lack of agreement among the various genealogies relating to Lugyaka. For example, two respondents provided the following genealogies (reading back in time from the present):

Baziralo Genealogies as Given by:

Mungazi[a] (6/3/72)	Mugala[a] (6/3/72)
Rutubuka	Mwenyantore[b]
Mutemura	Rutubuka
Murogoyo	Mutemura
Ruhwiza[c]	Murogoyo
Lugyaka	Bagalwa[d]
	Lugyaka

[a]Each respondent also serves as the last generation in his respective genealogy.

[b]Mwenyantore was later cited as a brother of Rutubuka. It is not uncommon that a child lives with his uncle for one reason or another, and that such a relationship is reflected in the genealogy as a relationship of descent. This name is therefore uncertain as a genealogical entry. The agnatic relationship of Rutubuka and Mwenyantore is further brought into question because Mungazi is considerably younger than Mugala. Such an age difference would be acceptable in more than the first ascendant generation, but it is difficult to accept that a second-generation descendant should be much older than a first-generation descendant of the same man, especially when the latter is considered to be "head" of the lineage, in a society where primogeniture is the norm. There is no indication that "Mungazi" refers to the father of the man who presently is known by that name, although such positional succession is occasionally the case on Ijwi.

[c]Ruwiza was the key figure in a separate Baziralo descent line of considerable influence in western Ijwi, at the time of Ndogosa (the early twentieth-century king of Ijwi). Although the traditions nowhere state this unequivocally, this line may result from segmentation related to a power struggle within the family. It is therefore possible that Ruhwiza came to his present residence from Bwiiru, as this single genealogy would suggest. But according to the sons of Ruhwiza on Mpene, Rwamakaza, Ruhwiza's father, arrived from Mpinga during Kabego's reign. It is thus unlikely that Ruhwiza was a "son" (descendant) of Lugyaka; it is clear that "Ruhwiza" (if he were the same man as "Ruhwiza" on Mpene) did not historically occupy this genealogical position. It is curious, nonetheless, that both name lists above include a "generation" between Lugyaka and Murogoyo in lists that are otherwise compatible. The name Ruhwiza was omitted from the genealogy cited by Mungazi 28/6/72. As will be discussed later, there is a possibility that Mutemura was the first ritualist among the ancestors of Mungazi, and that Ruhwiza is viewed as the ritualist, if not also the genealogical, ancestor of the present "Munyakalinga."

[d]It is possible that "Ruhwiza" and "Bagalwa" are two names for the same individual, but given the problems surrounding the name Ruhwiza at this point on the list, it is likely that the two are collateral names. Several other Baziralo genealogies, for example, include Ruhwiza, but never in this genealogical position. His direct offspring are still alive and cite an entirely different genealogy. It should also be pointed out that other genealogies (not presented here) are in general shorter, though this does not in itself invalidate either of those shown above.

Regardless of the exact genealogical ties, it seems evident that the Baziralo arrived at Bwiiru only relatively recently—probably after royal arrival on Ijwi. In Bwiiru, there are no traditions of early interaction with the royal line, nor any recall of the royal conflicts with the Banyakabwa at Buzigaziga, very close to (and within sight of) Bwiiru.[4] There is, however, no indication that the Beeru lived elsewhere on Ijwi prior to their establishment at Bwiiru. The nature of these traditions therefore conforms to Baziralo status as ritual guardians independent of the royal line, almost in ritual opposition to it.

The Baziralo of Bwiiru do, however, maintain one very distinct reference to origins outside Ijwi: they state clearly that they came to Ijwi from Kabagali in Rwanda, where they were also ritual specialists.[5] This is confirmed by all Beeru (and by other non-Baziralo as well[6]), excepting only the descendants of Ruhwiza at Mpene. But despite the unanimity of this common citation, that is all there is. The Baziralo have no other traditions relating to the distant past, and there is no other evidence on Ijwi to confirm or amplify this claim to Kabagali origins. One must turn to the Rwandan sources for help on this account.

Rwandan traditions and ritual give prominence to a group called the Abiiru, the corporation of Rwandan royal ritualists.[7] Within this group, the guardians of the royal drums held an exalted position, in recent times second in status only to the ritualists responsible for the Umuganura ceremony.[8] The head of this subgroup of drum-keepers was referred to in ritual contexts as a *mwami,* and he enjoyed other perquisites of royalty as well, as does Munyakalinga on Ijwi; his principal residence was, indeed, in Kabagali, an area of ritual importance in Rwanda. Such similarities with the Ijwi context could derive either from more recent transpositions or from very ancient common cultural forms widely spread in the region. Taken alone, they are of too general a nature to establish direct historical tie-ins between the two communities. However, the particular aspects of the rituals and associated traditions, and their distinction from general patterns of royal ritual on Ijwi (especially in their timing), suggest that the Ijwi and Rwandan patterns are cut from a tightly interwoven historical fabric. The strands that tie the Beeru on Ijwi to the Rwandan Abiiru may not be very strong, taken individually, but they are multiple, precise, and (in some respects) drawn from independent threads.

Baziralo Ritual Roles

The Ritual Contexts of Rwanda and Ijwi

Social characteristics and geographical settlement patterns on Ijwi associate the Baziralo with the general ritual context in Rwanda. But more precise tie-ins also exist. For example, individual and corporate names related to the drum ritualists in Rwanda consistently appear in traditions relating to the

Baziralo on Ijwi. One non-Muziralo whose parents lived in Bwiiru (or Butyangali) noted that the residents of Bwiiru at the time of Mutemura were known collectively as Bakaraza, and their original home was in Kabagali in Rwanda.[9] In the Rwandan sources, the "Abakaraza" are the social army associated with drum rituals in the earliest periods of Rwandan history.[10] According to these traditions, their authority in the region of present-day western and northwestern Rwanda stems from a period even before the Banyiginya Rwandan dynasties acquired royal drums. The leader of the Abakaraza corporation was a certain Rubunga, ancestor of Nyabutege, who was himself the second ritualist of the Rwandan court in more recent times, and whose official residence was indeed at Kabagali.[11]

This provides yet another indirect tie-in: "Nyabutega" also figures in the Ijwi traditions of the Baziralo, though in a context unrelated to the Bakaraza. The present head of the Beeru on Ijwi, the ritualist Munyakalinga, refers to the Beeru as the Abateege.[12] Another Muziralo cited Nyabutega as the "original" ancestor who begat all the Baziralo, including Mutemura; Nyabutega lived at Kabagali, and was never on Ijwi.[13] The name Nyabutega also appears in the genealogy of the Baziralo family living at Mpene on the western side of Ijwi;[14] as will be discussed later, this descent line is antagonistic to that of Munyakalinga at Bwiiru with an ambiguous relationship to the royal drum ritual (but it is possible they were earlier ritualists, since displaced).

In addition to the simple nominal referents, the references to Nyabutega and the Bakaraza provide other indirect tie-ins to Rwandan identity groups. Gihanga, the mythical first "king" of Rwanda, is said to have learned the secrets of the drum-esoterica from a man named Rubunga, the ancestor of Nyabutega. Rubunga, a member of the Abarenge subclan, is said to have been incorporated into the royal ritual complex as permanent ritualist of the Abanyiginya.[15] Although one part of this ritual was later given to a section of the royal lineage, the family of Rubunga was associated with drum rituals for many reigns.[16] In this way the functions of the drum ritualists in Rwanda were historically related to the Abarenge.

Recent Rwandan traditions represent the Abarenge as an extremely old group in Rwanda; they are referred to in various traditions in much the same manner as are the "Binyalenge" on Ijwi—as former inhabitants who no longer retain their identity, but whose culture was significantly different from present-day culture, at least in material items.[17] Traditions on the history of this group are inconsistent,[18] but in the Rwandan sources the Abarenge are frequently portrayed as an early (pre-Banyiginya) dynasty of Nduga (in what is now central Rwanda). Because of this dynastic tradition the Abarenge are sometimes identified as Tutsi.[19] Although there is no reason to identify the Abarenge in Rwanda directly with the Binyalenge on Ijwi in historical terms, the structural perceptions of each group held by other clans are similar: like the Abarenge in Rwanda, the Binyalenge on Ijwi are differentiated from today's society in material culture, they are thought to represent an early "dynastic" affiliation (e.g., Nyamuhiva, in the case of the Binyalenge), and they are without contemporary social referents.

Another similarity in the two perceptions relates to the drum rituals. In Rwanda there is a direct historical association of the Abarenge with the early drum rituals of the kingdom. On Ijwi, the association of early inhabitants to royalty is much less direct, mediated by incoming clans (such as the Baziralo). In chapter 3, it was shown that the "Binyalenge" of Ijwi's past are frequently identified with the contemporary Balega. Given the association of the Abarenge with early rituals in Rwanda, it is interesting that there is also a faint association of certain Balega groups with drum rituals, either on Ijwi or elsewhere. By extension, the Baziralo, as drum ritualists on Ijwi, share in this vague Balega identity; such structural association of Baziralo with the Balega thus parallels the Rwandan association of drum ritualists with the former Abarenge.

There are other, more specific, examples of this conjunction of Balega and Baziralo. At the time of the research one Muziralo was in the process of changing his clan identity, seeking incorporation among the Booze; he claimed that his Baziralo background related him both to the Balega in general and to the Booze in particular.[20] He justified this move on the premise that the Beeru, the drum ritualists on Ijwi and his former clan, are actually constituent elements of the Balega clan, as are the Booze; therefore, as a Muziralo, he had been a "latent" agnate of the Booze all along. But the Booze, as noted in chapter 3, are frequently linked with the former Binyalenge, as their contemporaries and associates if not as their descendants, and hence the indirect tie of the Baziralo to the Binyalenge/Abarenge. But these ties are traced through the drum rituals, and thus may well be etiological.

In another case, a recent immigrant to Ijwi and a member of the Banyintu, a "clan" from the west not well represented on Ijwi, stated that "the Banyintu are Balega; they are Beeru. They make drums for the king; they live at Bwiiru."[21] Other evidence also indicates that immigrants from the west are absorbed within the Balega without great difficulty. What is significant here is that this person associates his own identity with the Baziralo and does this through a putative "common" Balega identity—that the Balega are associated with drum rituals. Finally, a Munyambiriri made the linkage more explicit still: "The people of Kabagali who made the drums are Balega; [that is,] they are Bakaraza."[22] Thus on Ijwi the drum ritualists are associated with the Binyalenge indirectly, through a more recent clan identity (the Balega), one which incorporates the former Binyalenge. In Rwanda also, the drum ritualists are ultimately associated with a people no longer extant (the

Abarenge), but who share a comparable position in the "historical land-scape" of the society as the Binyalenge on Ijwi.[23]

On Ijwi, however, there is no hint that the drum rituals were expropri-ated directly from these earlier populations, despite the fact that certain tra-ditions ascribe previous "royal" ties to the Binyalenge, through Nyamuhiva, their *"mwami."* Most direct Ijwi testimony on the matter asserts that the rituals came from Kabagali; nonetheless the people who possess them, al-though themselves immigrants from the east, still retain some ascribed socio-logical tie with the Binyalenge, however vague. The confusion arises from failing to distinguish between historical criteria and structural criteria in the portrayal of the Baziralo past.

Rwandan Drum Histories

Rwandan traditions do more than merely confirm a few isolated snatches from Ijwi traditions, however; they attempt to account directly for Ijwi cul-tural similarities with Rwanda in terms of two sets of specific historical events. One of these, relating to the original transfer of drum rituals to the Rwandan Abanyiginya kingship, is only indirectly associated with Ijwi. Ac-cording to these accounts, Gihanga, the first putative Umunyiginya king in the area now composing Rwanda, received the regalia of kingship from the Abarenge, an early ruling dynasty of the Abasinga clan.[24] The king who provided the royal drum was named Jeni, a name which reappears almost invariably among the Ijwi genealogies of the Beshaza clan from Bwishaza, roughly the area where Rwandan traditions locate the drum transfer. The Beshaza also have a *kumbi* tie with the Banyambiriri, but the Banyambiriri on Ijwi claim to be Abasinga in Rwanda, the same clan which the Rwandan traditions claim for Jeni.[25] Thus by a series of transformations in the tradi-tions, there is a conjunction of Rwandan and Ijwi traditions relating similar clans ultimately to a single historical context.[26]

Historical transformations of this type also link the Beshaza and Bazi-ralo on Ijwi, in *kumbi* ties and in settlement patterns. The Rwandan tradi-tions state that the royal ritual of the Abasinga was transferred to Gihanga (an Umunyiginya) by a "servant" of Jeni or a follower of the daughter of Jeni.[27] On Ijwi today, there is a *kumbi* relation between the Baziralo (the clan of the guardians of the drums) and the Beshaza (who claim descent from Jeni—but who do *not* claim to be Abasinga), but this *kumbi* relationship is only one way: the Baziralo claim the Beshaza as their *bakumbi,* but the Beshaza do not reciprocate by referring to the Baziralo as their proper *bakumbi.* Fur-thermore, the Beshaza are the only *bakumbi* of the Baziralo; this is unique among Ijwi clans today, and serves to emphasize and reinforce the autonomy of the Baziralo on Ijwi from other identity groups as well as royalty. The secondary Baziralo settlements are all located in strongly Beshaza-dominant areas, as is Bwiiru itself. The Baziralo are one of the smallest clans on Ijwi, whereas the Beshaza are the largest, and concentrated close to the Baziralo center. This circumstantial evidence from Ijwi reinforces the allusions in the Rwandan historical traditions to some form of common associations of the Beshaza and Baziralo with the drum histories in the area that is presently western Rwanda.

A second set of more explicit Rwandan traditions refers to particular events to explain the similarities in the drum rituals: a direct transfer from Rwanda to Ijwi.[28] These accounts revolve around the story of Sibula, the eponymous ancestor of the Basibula, and the epic king of the Havu: it is a commentary on the Havu (or Rwandan?) traditions that one is forced to rely most heavily on the Rwandan (and Shi) traditions to fill in the story.[29] According to Kagame, the *mwami* Mibambwe Mutabazi of Rwanda, seeking refuge from invading armies, fled to "Bunyabungo" (referring to the general area west of Lake Kivu; the term sometimes includes the entire area west of the Nile-Zaire Divide). There his mother was seized and killed. On his return to Rwanda, Mutabazi enlisted the support of the kings of Burundi and Bugesera, it is said, for a coordinated attack against Bunyabungo to avenge his mother's death. The armies of Bugesera wreaked havoc on their western victims and killed the king there; they then returned to Bugesera, taking with them the pregnant wife of the slain king of Bunyabungo.[30]

In Bugesera, continue the Rwandan traditions, this woman gave birth to a son whom she named Sibula. Many years later, following a succession crisis in Bunyabungo, Sibula, disguised as a trader of *butega* bracelets, returned to Bunyabungo to assume the throne there.[31] On the death of Mutabazi's successor, Rwanda itself was thrown into a period of turmoil, amounting to a civil war which was to last intermittently over several generations.[32] This provided Sibula and his "innumerable warriors"[33] the chance to avenge the death of his father; allied with several of the Rwandan factions, they attacked, ravaging what is today the western part of Rwanda and killing the *mwami* Ndahiro Cyamatare. Rwandan court traditions claim that during his long intervention in Rwanda (11 years, according to Kagame) Sibula seized the royal drum and the ritual specialists associated with it; he is said to have placed both on Ijwi, where the descendant of these ritualists was later "found" by the Rwandan king Rwabugiri at the end of the nineteenth century.[34]

The elaborate detail presented in the Rwandan traditions is not reciprocated in the Havu traditions. Neither on Ijwi nor in Buhavu, for example, is the drum associated directly with Sibula; nor is there any direct testimony to the presence of Sibula himself on Ijwi. Furthermore, there is no reference to royal drums on Ijwi until the arrival of the present dynasty; even clans such as the Banyakabwa, whose interests such a reference would serve, make no claim that there were royal drums on Ijwi prior to the Basibula "arrival." It would thus appear that the details in the Rwandan traditions are *post facto* reconstructions building on the general historical association of Sibula's attacks with a change of dynasty in Rwanda, and hence with a change of drums (which are associated with the concept of "dynasty").[35] The available traditions make it clear that only after the conquest of Ijwi did Rwabugiri become aware of the historical explanations of the similarities between the ritual forms of Ijwi kingship and those of Rwanda.[36] From all indications, therefore, it is only from the time of Rwabugiri's conquest that these episodes entered the Rwandan corpus of historical traditions.

Circumstantial evidence from the Rwandan traditions confirms this conclusion. Rwabugiri had attempted to conquer Ijwi for a decade or more before his armies finally killed the Ijwi king; had the tradition formed a part of Rwandan historical knowledge prior to Rwabugiri's attempts to conquer Ijwi, the recovery of the former royal drums would have seemed an excellent justification for these prolonged attacks.[37] It is surprising therefore that the court—in a kingdom with such an apparent interest in historical events and precedents—did not base its case for attack at least in part on this point, esoteric or not.[38] But during this time the details of Sibula's conquest and the loss of the original royal drums apparently remained obscured even from the reigning monarch. The traditions in question emerged explicitly to account for the "similarities" of Rwandan and Ijwi ritual forms, which Rwabugiri discovered only after his military successes.

Other evidence also suggests that these traditions were unknown before the time of Rwabugiri. Associated with the histories of Cyamatare's death are tales claiming that the Rwandan king Ruganzu had ravaged Ijwi after the death of Sibula. Yet Ruganzu apparently found no drum or ritualists.[39] In fact the Ijwi traditions make no mention of attacks by Ruganzu on the island; only one group (the Booze) makes any consistent reference to Ruganzu, and they do not associate him with Ijwi, or with the drums.[40] Therefore it appears that the loss of the Rwandan royal drums to Sibula was unknown to Ruganzu, successor to Cyamatare, as indeed it was later to Rwabugiri. Both are implausible assertions. Thus the very explicit character and the precision and particularities noted in the Rwandan traditions all seem to date them, in their present recorded form, to the time of Rwabugiri.

Rwandan Interpretations of Havu Ritual History

As we have seen, the Rwandan traditions imply that Ijwi drum rituals derive directly from the implantation of Rwandan ritual forms on Ijwi during the "reign" of Sibula. The common conception of royalty on Ijwi, however, claims that the first Basibula king arrived on Ijwi with all the institutions of royalty (and personnel to make them function), and that therefore all aspects of royalty derived directly from the mainland Havu forms; Havu traditions on the mainland concur. The historical development of these institutions, however, was much more complex than either account would aver. Ijwi data suggest, rather, that local political developments—both on Ijwi and in Rwanda—contributed to the parallel development of similar ritual institutions in those two kingdoms, institutions which ultimately derived from a common general source, and that these internal factors were at least as important in the development of Ijwi ritual institutions as influences from outside. Clearly we need to broaden our perspective and examine the drum histories within a broader regional context. This section considers the historical influences acting on the Ijwi ritual forms from Buhavu as well as Rwanda. Later chapters will analyze the internal evolution of these forms.

As noted above, the names associated with the drum ritualists on Ijwi such as the Abakaraza and the Abateege, as well as the claim of Baziralo historical ties to Kabagali, all lend credence to the Rwandan traditions in their broad outline: there was a tie of Ijwi ritualists to Rwandan ritualist groups. But these were not direct ties: no memory is retained on Ijwi that the Havu king Sibula placed there the drum ritualists captured from Rwanda or that Rwabugiri "re-patriated" them. The very imprecision of the traditions on Ijwi discredits the details of the Rwandan traditions; the Rwandan court traditions are suspect not just because they are said to relate to Ijwi, but also because they are said to have been derived from Ijwi. And even that assertion surfaced only from the time of Rwabugiri in the late nineteenth century. Consequently, although there have indeed been interactions of some sort between Ijwi and Rwanda, the Rwandan traditions considered above do not reliably account for the nature of these interactions.

The traditions of the Baziralo and Banyambiriri also fail to correlate with the Rwandan court traditions concerning the ritual functions of the two groups. The name Myaka is important in Rwandan royal ritual contexts, and this would seem to be reflected in the prominence of Lugyaka, claimed as an important ancestor of the Baziralo on Ijwi. But "Myaka" in Rwanda is distinct from those groups in Rwanda carrying out ritual roles analogous to those of the Baziralo on Ijwi. Myaka, a title associated exclusively with the Umuganura rituals in Rwanda, is a title held by a family associated with, but distinct from, the Abatsoobe ritualist protectors of the drum named Rwamo. Inhabitants of Bumbogo, these titleholders were also distinct from the Abateege, who lived in Kabagali and held other named drums; it was the latter group which commanded the Abakaraza.[41] Thus Ijwi traditions not only combine separate traditions relating to different social groups; they also combine traditions relating to two distinct ritual functions on Ijwi, those relating to the Muganuro ceremony (performed primarily by the Banyambiriri on Ijwi) and those relating to the drums (the Baziralo on Ijwi).

The fluidity of the concepts associated with these traditions is also apparent in the roles of Munyakalinga (the drum ritualist and head of the Baziralo clan) at the Muganuro ceremony on Ijwi. In addition to presenting the drums formally, he is responsible for the ritual cleansing of the kingdom through the use of Ngobosa, a delicate, pronged, wooden instrument. Rwandan traditions, too, refer to a bident as an essential element of the royal regalia in Rwanda. But in Rwanda the Ngobosa rituals are the responsibility of the descendants of Myaka, who are also responsible for the Umuganura celebration and whose duties therefore coincide with those of the Banyambiriri on Ijwi.[42]

Thus the various ritual forms said to derive from Rwanda do not represent discrete, independent lines of interaction with the east. They appear more to derive from a general corpus of ritual concepts and forms than from any exact precursors in Rwanda. Derivation from a common regional pool of ritual conceptualization rather than precise transfer of Rwandan and Ijwi ritual forms is evident in the nature of Ijwi traditions, which do not correlate exactly with Rwandan traditions on this point: there are confusions and crossing of categories. These differences emphasize the flow of ritual functions not only between polities in the area but among different clan groups as well. Part of this can be explained by historical changes in Rwanda as well as on Ijwi since the time of the putative tie-ins; where Ijwi ritual patterns may have cumulated ritual responsibilities, Rwandan patterns may have divided them among more specialized practitioners. But one conclusion is clear: although they may draw on a common source, royal rituals on Ijwi and in Rwanda clearly did not interact in such a direct, precise manner as that portrayed in the Rwandan traditions; there was no direct transfer.

Ritual Ties in a Broader Context: Buhavu, Rwanda, and Ijwi

A comparison of ritual forms indicates that the pre-Ijwi Havu forms shared certain affinities with the early Rwandan forms, but that Havu and Rwandan ritual traditions later grew distinct from one another. This of course is very different from what the Rwandan court traditions claim: that all rituals of kingshp in the west derive from fully developed Rwandan practices. For example, the principal dynastic drum in Buhavu, on the western mainland, is named Rwamo,[43] the same name as the early drum associated with the Abatsoobe ritualists—but not the principal drum of the Abanyiginya dynasty—in Rwanda.[44] But Rwamo is also a secondary name given to the drum on Ijwi, whose principal reference is "Kalinga," the same as the more recent Rwandan drum name. Present Ijwi forms thus appear to derive from both "Havu" and "Rwandan" sources. Most likely they result from the conjunction of two ritual traditions, an earlier (Kivu) form represented in the Havu terminology ("Rwamo"; also the early Abatsoobe drum name in

Rwanda) and a more recent form expressed in the title "Kalinga," as in Rwanda under the Abanyiginya. This cumulated heritage on Ijwi is also evident in the duplication (noted above) of the Beeru concept: the functions of the Beeru in the east (so closely associated with Baziralo identity) correlate with the ritual functions of certain Abiiru in Rwanda who guard the drums; the functions of those in the west (of Badaha clan affiliation) correlate with the functions of the Beeru in Buhavu, who bury the king. Thus present drum rituals on Ijwi apparently were not derived exclusively from Havu forms of kingship, as normative ideology on Ijwi would hold, any more than they were from "Rwandan" forms, as Rwandan traditions assert.

From common influences of royalty east and west of the lake, it could be argued that ritual forms more recently appropriated—and elaborated on— by the Abanyiginya dynasty of Rwanda had formerly been practiced in areas of western Rwanda (or along the Nile-Zaire Divide; see pp. 60–64 above), and that these earlier ritual forms had been characteristic of general royal institutions on the western mainland. In any case, they were not directly implanted to Ijwi from either east or west. Independent traditions from the Baziralo in the west of Ijwi (on Mpene) support such a conclusion. This family claims relatively recent arrival from Irhambi (on the western mainland just south of present Buhavu), where the senior Havu line was located at the time (in the mid-nineteenth century);[45] it was also this family that cited Nyabutega in its genealogy.[46] The two families of Baziralo are further distinguished by their different relationship to the term "Shamvu," the title of one of the Havu drum ritualists in Mpinga, on the western mainland.[47] On Ijwi the term "Shamvu" is found in the genealogies of the western family of Baziralo, those on Mpene; the Beeru (Baziralo) in the east do not include Shamvu among their cited ancestors, but they are nonetheless indirectly linked to the term: "Bushamvu" is the name of the specific area of Bwiiru where the drums are kept, and others on Ijwi occasionally refer to the section of the Baziralo responsible for the drum rituals as Bashamvu.[48]

A similar reference, confined to the western Baziralo, cites Nyagihindula ca Hindamula Omutwingoma as an ancestor and very early drum ritualist. This reference finds no correlate among the eastern Beeru genealogies, but the Rwandan sources, again, do mention a Nyamuhindula in a roughly analogous context, referring to a very early period of Rwandan ritual history.[49] From these indications, the western lineage of Baziralo on Ijwi (on Mpene), although much smaller and lacking any present drum affiliation, appears to have been more closely tied to drum rituals in the past. This lineage may even have served as a historical tie-in between the present-day Beeru-Baziralo in eastern Ijwi and the mainland Havu (Mpinga) ritual forms, on the one hand, and at least some (perhaps very old) Rwandan forms, on the other. Since there has been no direct contact between Rwandan ritual forms and the western Baziralo on Mpene (genealogically independent of the eastern Baziralo), the similar references in these two groups argue for separate derivation from a common source, once again, not specifically Rwandan origins.

Testimony from the Beeru at Bwiiru (in the east) confirm that their function as drum ritualists may be of more recent derivation than their settlement on Ijwi—that is, that they did not arrive on Ijwi as drum ritualists. Ijwi traditions are consistent enough to establish Lugyaka as an early historical personage on Ijwi, but they do not relate Lugyaka or the Baziralo clearly to any particular contemporary Rwandan group, nor do they firmly establish the relationship between the early eastern Baziralo (at Bwiiru) with the Rwandan drum histories. The most frequent references to the earliest Baziralo contacts with Ijwi royalty imply that the Beeru assumed their status as ritualists only during the reign of Kabego (the second Ijwi king, who reigned during the mid-nineteenth century).[50] This correlates with many other indications (to be discussed below) that royal presence was probably not established in the eastern highlands until the reign of Kabego. Although Lugyaka is frequently cited as the first settler in Bwiiru, the drums are almost universally associated with "Mutemura," often cited as the "son" (or "grandson," though both terms are imprecise at this genealogical remove) of Lugyaka, and grandfather of the present Munyakalinga ritualist.[51] Thus apparently independent traditions on the ritual recognition of a royal drum on Ijwi (under Kabego, in the mid-nineteenth century) and genealogical information on the first Munyakalinga (the grandson of Lugyaka) coincide. This evidence suggests that the drum rituals on Ijwi were invested among the Beeru only from the mid-nineteenth century at the earliest—a significant deviation from the "state created whole" ideological statements referring to the introduction of royalty with the arrival of Mwendanga, the first Basibula Ijwi king.

The Ritual Construction of Kingship

Thus the ethnographic tie-ins with drum ritualists in both Buhavu and Rwanda suggest that, before the time of Mutemura (or the latter part of the nineteenth century), the drums were held by the Baziralo lineage now located on Mpene. Indeed some members of this descent line rather obliquely claim that they at one time held the drum; it was only following a power struggle that Mutemura (the acknowledged first Munyakalinga among the present-day Beeru) dispossessed Ruhwiza, a prominent ancestor of the western line, of the drum ritual.[52] Still other testimony, independent of either of the Baziralo lines, asserts that Kalinga had become the royal drum of Ijwi only during the reign of Kabego, and that a different drum existed prior to that time.[53] It is possible therefore that the early Ijwi drum ritualists originally were associated with Mpinga (mainland Buhavu) traditions, but that subsequently these ritual functions were performed by the eastern branch of the Baziralo; the term "Baziralo" finds no reflection in Rwandan sources. It consequently appears likely that the present forms of the drum rituals of the kingdom are very recent, perhaps dating from as late as the middle third of the nineteenth century, and that they were altered during the last third. Therefore the complex set of similarities apparently derives from multiple interactions among Rwandan, Havu, and Ijwi forms, combined with the internal evolution within each ritual form between these interaction periods. The ritual status of the Baziralo emerged from—or was created by—such cultural blending.

More important than precise dating is the timing of these processes of ritual establishment relative to other social changes. Though spotty, the evidence suggests that the Ijwi drum rituals stem from mainland Havu forms (hence the echoes of Mpinga terminology on Ijwi), and that important Rwandan influences are more recent. This would explain the significant differences apparent today between Ijwi and Mpinga in the royal drum rituals and terminology.[54] The similarities of Mpinga Havu rituals with those of Rwanda are suggestive, but the differences are important enough to indicate a very long period of separation or, indeed, divergent variants of a single regional ritual tradition. Thus it is still possible that the Rwandan traditions were essentially correct in asserting that early "Rwandan" (actually, pre-Abanyiginya) ritual traditions were incorporated into Havu ritual; they would have been equally correct to assert that early "Havu" (pre-Basibula) drums had been incorporated into Rwandan rituals.[55] This very early "contact"—actually parallel derivations from a common ritual substratum—is all the more likely because, especially at the royal level, there has been very little recent contact between Rwanda and the mainland Bahavu (west of Ijwi). Furthermore, the Shi drum rituals are markedly different from the Havu rituals, and the differences between the rituals of the Havu and Shi are greater than those between the Havu and Rwanda.[56]

Thus, though perhaps deriving originally from Havu forms, Ijwi cultural traditions were apparently subsequently strongly influenced by more recent ritual forms from east of the lake after the schism of the Ijwi royal family from the mainland Basibula dynasty. But these differences occured at a time when both Havu and Rwandan forms had much evolved from their earlier closer affinities. It would seem then that the early Havu kingship indeed possessed a form of drum ritual with similarities to those also incorporated into Rwandan forms. Ijwi drum rituals appear originally to have been derived from this pattern; later, with the consolidation and reconstruction of the kingdom and especially with the expansion of ritual functions among the various lineages, these drum rituals were invested in the Baziralo lineage of Mutemura living at Bwiiru (Bushamvu).

Thus what was important in this history of ritual forms was the developing social context on Ijwi, which bestowed significance on ritual forms already present, not the simple diffusion of royal forms. It was a process of stimulating a new social awareness and crystallizing new social identities, not one of relying simply on importing and transplanting specific royal institutions and ideas. More recent influences seem to have brought the Ijwi and later Rwandan forms more into line with each other following their earlier divergent development, and the Ijwi drum rituals then appear to have been reconstructed along the model of Rwanda. This can be seen as part of a general process of the separation of Ijwi norms of royalty from its parent line in Mpinga during the nineteenth century.

Conclusion

The last several chapters have considered groups coming to Ijwi just before, or approximately contemporaneously with, the arrival of the royal family. Focussing on the ritually important clans of the Banyambiriri and Bazialo, the analysis provides a basis for evaluating the later claim that the royal family on Ijwi brought with it all the royal rituals and regalia, and that they were accompanied by the ritualists of the kingdom. The ideological predisposition of the immigrant Basibula may have been clear, as shown by the broad similarities of Ijwi norms with those of Mpinga. Contacts with Rwandan state power may have enhanced, redefined, and focussed these ritual configurations, but ultimately they derived from the ritual inventory of the pre-Abanyiginya polities near the Zaire-Nile Divide—those polities briefly discussed in chapter 2. Similarities between the ritual codes in Rwanda and on Ijwi were more a result of parallel derivation from a common pool of ritual knowledge than of direct transmission from one to another. Kingship on Ijwi was constructed in large part from the resources and demands of the people and social environment of the island itself.

The political evolution discussed below illustrates the degree to which royal prestige had to yield to local social and historical realities. Although certain political structures may have been introduced to Ijwi from the outside, they penetrated and adapted to—ultimately they were rooted in and expressed through—the local texture of Ijwi society at the time. Even within royalty, the continuities that existed can best be understood less as elements within some specific Basibula dynastic tradition than as continuities on a broader regional scale. Many groups which achieved status under the new regime could claim to be associated in some way with ritual status elsewhere before their arrival on Ijwi. But that does not mean that dynastic integration was automatic. Ritual concepts and associated concepts of legitimacy were drawn from within the ideological and conceptual pool of resources in the area, just as concepts of ritual efficacy and legitimacy also interacted widely within the region.

At a more local level, too, certain general patterns emerged from the local histories, and these were patterns which did not, in every case, coincide with historical assumptions. The boundaries between clan groups became more clearly defined and took on a new significance only as the several criteria of social definition emerged along roughly similar lines in the pre-Basibula context. Local settlement patterns, ties outside Ijwi, ritual functions on the island, later relations with the royal family and with each other, all combined to reinforce the new lines of social differentiation.

But these were not the only criteria: the new social orientations were consolidated by the later emergence and gradual consolidation of a new political focus on the island. This development will be discussed below. What is important here is that participation in royalty and influence in its forms and evolution were not limited to those who arrived with the king; even those who had settled on the island before the royal arrival were to relate to the changing Ijwi social context in diverse ways. It has been the purpose of these chapters to explore some of the pre-conditions to this diversity and to identify the factors which were significant. The chapters to follow will discuss how these processes became expressed in events associated with the establishment of royalty on Ijwi.

Part 3
The Court Context

8
The Antecedents of Basibula Royalty

The Basibula form the royal family in several kingdoms west of Lake Kivu today, and everywhere they are recent immigrants. They arrived in their present areas of settlement only during the early nineteenth century, and within each of these kingdoms they form only a small group; on Ijwi, at least, they did not gain prominence through weight of numbers or force alone. Furthermore, the vast majority of people within these Havu kingdoms had strong historical roots with a variety of other groups beyond the limits of the new kingdoms, and hence these societies were culturally heterogeneous.

Yet the success of the Basibula went beyond simply legitimizing themselves as the royal dynasty in these areas. Over time they also succeeded in defining these areas as "Havu"; these kingdoms were all considered Havu because their royal dynasties shared common historical roots, not because the populations necessarily shared common cultural antecedents. The process by which Basibula royalty became integrated into these areas therefore constitutes an essential theme of the history of the area.

The next several chapters focus on this process of political restructuring—how it was that the Basibula validated their claims to legitimate authority and became recognized as royalty on Ijwi. This chapter explores the historical contacts of the Kivu Rift societies with the area to the south and sketches out, as far as current knowledge permits, the political profile of the Rusizi Valley in the mid-eighteenth century. The next chapter considers the struggle on the mainland which led to the segmentation of the Basibula royal line, and examines the conflicts among the Banyakabwa on Ijwi at the time of the Basibula arrival. But these conflicts form only a part of the story; while they may have provided the opening for Basibula arrival on Ijwi, the effective establishment of royal power resulted from structural processes occurring over a much longer time. Thus the three chapters to follow will explore in turn the social, economic, and ritual dimensions to these long-term structural transformations which were so essential to the creation of a new kingdom on Ijwi.

The Rusizi Corridor

By the end of the eighteenth century the peoples of the Kivu Rift Valley were able to draw collectively on the cultural traditions of both the forest areas (to the west and northwest) and the Interlacustrine regions (east of the Nile-Zaire Divide). But these were not the only areas with a tradition of historical contacts in the region: influences from the Rusizi River Valley south of the lake also affected the Lake Kivu Rift. As the only outlet from Lake Kivu, the Rusizi River flows south from Lake Kivu to Lake Tanganyika. At its north end, it cuts sharply through mountainous massifs on both its east and west flanks, but at its southern end, where the Rusizi flows into Lake Tanganyika, the river valley broadens into a wide, open plain. As with the cultural corridor directly north of Lake Kivu, discussed in chapter 2, this area served as a corridor of important historical interaction between the forest cultures on the high plateau west of Lake Tanganyika, on the one hand, and the Interlacustrine culture of Burundi, east of the Rusizi, on the other. And as in the area of the Nile-Zaire Divide, so too did the Rusizi Valley include a constellation of many small polities, with highly mobile populations; very likely the political institutions were variable and flexible over time as well.[1]

Traditions from neighboring areas indicate frequent interaction between the areas around Lake Kivu and Lake Tanganyika, both in recent periods and in the more distant past. Although the areas along the current Rwanda-Burundi border, now included in southwestern Rwanda, may have been politically autonomous of the Burundi court, the consolidation of Rundi political structures had their effect, most notably in military terms. Rundi armies penetrated far into the Lake Kivu area; the frequency of these expeditions suggests that this contested area (now included in Rwanda) formed a zone of enduring Rundi influence. However, the cultural similarities of these regions with what are today Rundi populations are greater than could be expected from sporadic military encounters alone; even the Rwandan sources confirm the strength of Rundi influence in the southern Kivu Rift during the late eighteenth century and well into the nineteenth.[2] Tracing Rundi movements north of the present border with Rwanda suggests the intensity of these ties.

Historical Interaction South of Lake Kivu

Most documented traditions refer to Sibula, the eponymous ancestor of the Basibula dynasty, as deriving from the Shi royal family. According to Shi traditions, Sibula's mother, the sister of an unspecified Shi king (and of Nalwanda, the king of Rwanda) became pregnant from an incestuous relationship with her brother; she was expelled (hence the name Sibula Nyebunga—

"Sibula the one who fled," or "the one who emigrated") and gave birth to Sibula, the man who would ultimately become the founder of the Basibula royal line. The metaphorical allusion implies that Basibula royalty derived from a Shi prototype—a "prototype" because Shi institutions have gone through a period of dramatic evolution over the last 200 years, and descent from the present Shi royal family is not established by this story. Though the Shi version is the most detailed, it differs from both the Havu and the Rwandan versions. All variants concur, however, in claiming institutional and conceptual linkages between Havu, Shi, and Rwandan kingship forms at a very general level of abstraction. Consequently, lacking confirmation even among those people they presume to speak for, these Shi traditions appear to be metaphorical statements—more valuable as statements of shared antecedents at the level of institutional concepts and categories, as reaffirmation of the perceived structural equivalence of the three dynastic lines, than as literal accounts of precise historical ties, still less as accounts of specific historic personages and events.[3]

Except those living in areas of heavy Shi influence, the Basibula do not themselves share this tradition; on Ijwi there is no mention of direct ties to the Shi dynasty. But Ijwi traditions do refer to shared common origins with the Shi kings in Lwindi, the land of "Munganga."[4] Located on the southwestern periphery of the present Shi states, Lwindi is clearly of central importance in the development of kingship in the area. Because Ijwi traditions omit important elements of the Shi traditions, it is unlikely that these Shi traditions, claiming Havu biological descent from Shi ancestors, encapsulate authentic historical presence. The configuration of these data suggests instead that the dynastic status of the Basibula descent line shares traditions of royalty deriving from the same core concepts as the present central Shi dynastic line (the Banyamwocha), but developed independently of the Shi forms.

In some respects Ijwi royalty shares stronger similarities with other kingdoms in the Rusizi Valley than with the central Shi kingdoms. Indeed, despite central Shi claims to anteriority, these smaller peripheral kingdoms may well represent the older forms; ethnographic distribution patterns suggest that central Shi forms are intrusive within the wider cultural context, more recent in their current structure, and thus less representative of core political concepts for the area than the peripheral polities. Bufuliiro, for example, located just northwest of Lake Tanganyika, though not itself Shi, is one of those kingdoms whose royal family claims to have come from Bunyindu ("Lwindi")—but its royal family does not claim descent from Banyamwocha.[5] The Fuliiro term for "ritualist," as on Ijwi, is *"mugingi"* (not *"mujinji,"* as in Bushi), and this is a consistent sound shift, distinguishing Ijwi from Shi pronunciation. Although formal linguistic studies are lacking, to the untrained ear the language spoken in Kaziba, a peripheral Shi state very

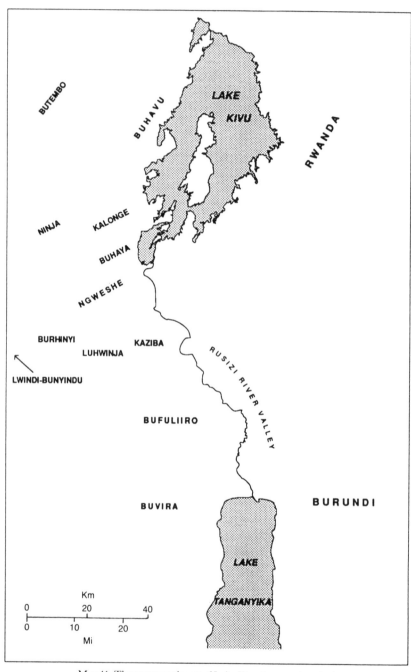

Map 11. The states southwest of Lake Kivu (present location)

148

near Bufuliiro, appears closer to Kiny'Iju, the language spoken on Ijwi, than does Mashi-Mahaya, the language spoken in the central Shi states (which are geographically closer to Ijwi).[6] Kaziba is said to share closer royal traditions with Bufuliiro than with other Shi states, and Kaziba and Ijwi share similarities in royal ritual which distinguish them from the central Shi state of Buhaya.[7]

The Basibula dynasty also exhibits general cultural features similar to those of Rundi royalty. The dynastic name Ntare is a generic name for Havu kings of the senior royal line on the mainland (but not on Ijwi); Ntare is also a royal name for individual Havu kings. This name is shared with the Rundi and Ha dynasties (and areas east and northeast of Rwanda as well), but not with Bushi and Rwanda, the more immediate neighbors of the Basibula. The annual First Fruits ceremony (Muganuro) on Ijwi also bears more similarities to the ceremony of the distribution of the seeds (also called Muganuro) in Burundi than with recent forms of the analogous ceremony in the central Shi states.[8] In general social relations, an institution such as cattle clientship (known on Ijwi and in Burundi as *bugabire,* from the verb *kugabe*) is much more similar to Rundi forms of cattle clientship than to the more hierarchical forms found in Rwanda, where the more recent Ijwi ties have been concentrated.[9] Thus in many ways the Havu areas share in the general culture traits that are associated with Burundi, as well as with the Rusizi Valley—but are different from Bushi and Rwandan norms.

In oral literature, too, there is a pattern of Rundi and Basibula traditions sharing certain forms and specific names. For example, Ijwi traditions concerning the royal arrival to the island provide a prominent role to a diviner named Lubambo, who lived just east of the lake (in what is now Kinyaga), and who was to become the maternal grandfather of Mwendanga, the first king on Ijwi. Lubambo sheltered Mwendanga's father as he fled a succession dispute; eventually Lubambo's daughter, named Nkobwa in the traditions, gave birth to Mwendanga. The conjunction of the roles of Lubambo as diviner and Nkobwa as his daughter is significant. In Burundi, the name Rubambo (Lubambo) is associated with diviners; he is said to be their representative to the spirit world. Furthermore, Rundi diviners often use a calabash doll named Nyabukobwa, sometimes explicitly referred to as Rubambo's cohort.[10] Clearly, the traditions on Lubambo in Burundi and Kinyaga draw on a common cultural substratum in associating the names with the roles portrayed.[11] And clearly, too, there is in these references much evidence to refute the assertions that Basibula antecedents stem directly from the central Shi states.

Rundi Influence in the Rusizi Valley

The political dynamics of this area were not confined to shared internal characteristics. Direct evidence of important interchange and contact east and west across the Rusizi Valley exists from a considerable time depth. For example, Luhwinja, one of the small kingdoms on the "southern tier" of Bushi, is said to have derived from Bukunzi, a small polity (independent of the central Rwandan court until 1925) located east of the Rusizi. But Bukunzi itself was apparently established by members of the Shi royal family, fleeing into political exile (to escape Rundi incursions), following a family dispute.[12] Similarly there are traditions of Rwandan influence moving west of the Rusizi from the eighteenth century, and perhaps from long before, affecting political activity in what is now Bushi.[13] If these traditions are taken as even roughly indicative of personal mobility and institutional interchange within the region, they testify to rather intensive contacts in the very area which saw such an important proliferation of traditions of royalty.

Such politically significant activity was not limited to east-west contacts across the Rusizi River. North-south movements in the area have been important too, and as a result the political frontier between Rwanda and Burundi has been historically unstable. Both Rundi and Rwandan traditions refer to numerous occasions when Rundi forces penetrated north of the present Rwandan border, particularly into the western portions of Rwanda and the Rusizi River Valley—and often with considerable success. Paradoxically the Rwandan data are much more complete than are the Rundi sources on these wars; consequently in areas of weak Rwandan presence (such as the Rusizi Valley) it is possible that much of the record has been lost.

But even from the Rwandan sources there is a clear pattern of Rundi influence north. The Rundi king Ntare I (c. 1700–1725) is said to have attacked both Rwanda (in the present Prefecture of Butare) and Kinyaga (which was not at that time a part of Rwanda).[14] Near the end of the eighteenth century, the two powers joined forces to overthrow the dynastic line of Bugesera, a kingdom located in the border area between Rwanda and Burundi well to the east of Kinyaga. Rundi military activity north of the present border is also noted in the Rwandan sources for the reign of the Rundi king Mutaga I, during the mid-eighteenth century. Another Rwandan source notes the attack of a large Rundi force north through the Rusizi River Valley and from there along the eastern shores of Lake Kivu as far north as Mpembe (a peninsula just south of present-day Kibuye), also in the eighteenth century.[15] The derivation of Basibula royal forms from the area of the Rusizi Corridor appears to have followed a similar historical pattern—displacement of royal forms and politically significant social groups north, from the Rusizi Valley to the southern reaches of Lake Kivu.

The clearest sources on this intense activity in the Rundi traditions are those that relate to Ntare II, who reigned from the late eighteenth to the mid-nineteenth centuries. These sources specifically note the importance of Rundi contacts with the Rusizi Valley area—and with Kinyaga and Bushi.[16] Ntare II is said to have fought all along his northern border, from Bugesera to Kinyaga. But he also had direct contact with Bushi, where he was so successful, according to these traditions, that he had to build a road through the forest to bring back all the cattle captured.[17]

It seems clear that Rundi incursions into the Rusizi Corridor—and perhaps informal Rundi control over the area as well—date from the time of Ntare II, and hence the early part of his reign may have been particularly turbulent for the regions southwest of the lake. Ntare's expeditions may indeed have been one factor inhibiting the growth of large political units in the Rusizi Valley, and even at the end of the nineteenth century this area was divided into small quasi-independent units.[18] Regardless of any direct links with the Burundi state, the evidence suggests that the Basibula dynastic line represents one (or an off-shoot from one) of the small semi-autonomous royal families in the area, moving north perhaps in response to increasing Rundi pressure. The exact mechanics of the process are less important than the clear evidence of regional influence being exerted over these small polities sharing a common cultural heritage. If the Basibula derived from such a historical context, certain elements of this heritage would likely be retained in Ijwi kingship; and this in fact appears to be the case.

But turbulence in the Rusizi Corridor also affected Burundi. During the late nineteenth century two major threats to the Rundi throne issued from just these areas northwest of Burundi. One was a challenge to Mwezi Gisabo's succession to Ntare II in the mid-nineteenth century, mounted by Twarereye, another of Ntare's sons. Rundi traditions claim that during his military campaigns Ntare had established royal enclosures in Bushi and on Ijwi, and that Twarereye had been born on Ijwi. Ijwi traditions, however, retain no references to the wife of Ntare, to Twarereye, or, indeed, to Rundi presence of any kind, despite the fact that all the events claimed in Rundi accounts fall within the chronological range of other Ijwi traditions. It is likely, therefore, that "Ijwi" is used in these Rundi traditions (as elsewhere, in the Rwandan traditions), simply as an expedient locale to identify an external origin of threats to the local (i.e., Rundi) political order.[19]

Later in Mwezi Gisabo's long reign (c. 1850–1908) another such challenge was mounted by a man named Kilima. He too is said to have been the son of Ntare II by a Shi wife whom Ntare married at the time of one of his military campaigns to the northwest; such an account claims Kilima as a potential legitimate successor to Ntare. Others say he was Ntare's grandson—and that Mwezi had killed Kilima's father (thus providing a motive for

Kilima's opposition). Rundi court traditions, on the other hand, claim Kilima was a simple Mushi renegade; Shi sources make no reference to him at all. We may never know his true genealogical antecedents for sure. Nor do we need to: here, as elsewhere, genealogical arguments are used only to legitimize political claims. Whatever his origins, Kilima was clearly an effective leader with strong local support, and he successfully opposed Rundi court penetration into the area; whether for political or genealogical reasons, many people believed in the legitimacy of his struggle.[20]

But in the late nineteenth century, there was an important new element in the political balance in the area: from 1896, German forces fought Kilima as a powerful local leader; after 1899 they sought his support in their joint struggle against Mwezi, and subsequently (on Mwezi's capitulation in 1903) once more turned against him in their attempts to shore up Mwezi as a unifying focus for German power. Three years later (1906) Kilima was captured and exiled to a German post on Lake Nyasa.

Though Kilima did not succeed in overthrowing Mwezi, he did successfully defend the autonomy of the Rusizi Valley from Rundi court control before the imposition of German rule. For although this area appears to have been partially incorporated into the Rundi state under Ntare II, it again reverted to a system of small autonomous polities as soon as Kilima's wars made this possible. Kilima's struggle with the Rundi court occurred only in the late nineteenth and early twentieth centuries, but in fact the presence of opponents such as Kilima was probably not unique: it is likely that his struggle was representative of a type of recurring resistance in the area. Even the Germans recognized that the chiefs of the Rusizi Valley had always been "more or less independent" of the Rundi monarch,[21] and they could not have succeeded without strong support from the local population. Thus Rundi incorporation of the Imbo—the Rusizi Valley plain—was clearly a long, uneven process. The implication is that this area was formed of independent royal families which had maintained their claims to royal status even under Rundi rule; it was finally incorporated into the Rundi political order only by German force of arms. These earlier conditions of autonomy and confrontation may well have contributed to the movement of some groups north of the Rusizi Corridor into the Lake Kivu Rift.

One can therefore safely discount the claims of the direct presence of Rundi individuals on Ijwi. But the claim to Rundi political or cultural influence may carry some weight, if the Basibula royal presence in this area is seen as at least an indirect result of Rundi royal activities. Although the data do not allow for precision in citing direct Rundi ties, it is entirely plausible that influences from the south were present in the Lake Kivu region at about the time that the Basibula royal dynasty became established at the south end of the lake, just prior to their arrival on Ijwi. How it was that the members of one small descent line of the region moved off the mainland to settle on Ijwi will be discussed below.

The Southwest Shores of the Lake: The Havu and the Shi

Over the course of the eighteenth century, the Shi states had emerged as important political poles on the high plateau southwest of the lake, and their presence there was to alter the political geography of the region in many ways.[22] But their growth did not create the kingdom on Ijwi in any direct fashion. Instead, the Shi expanded into the region between the two Havu royal segments, forcing one branch north along the lakeshore and permitting the other to hive off to Ijwi. By reinforcing their separation, Shi expansion contributed to the growing autonomy—and eventual sovereignty—of the Ijwi royal family.

The early centralization of Shi political structures was associated with a long-standing dynastic rift between two branches of the Banyamwocha, the Shi ruling family. This struggle lasted most of the eighteenth century, but the expansion of Shi influence towards the lake occurred only later, in part as a response to this internal confrontation, as each faction sought outside resources (through alliance or conquest). Until the end of the eighteenth century, therefore, Shi influence directly along the lakeshore appears to have been relatively unimportant. Since this area was home to the Basibula dynasty, direct contacts between the Basibula and Banyamwocha (the Havu and central Shi ruling lines) occurred only from early in the nineteenth century.

At its southern end, Lake Kivu constricts into a narrow funnel before opening out into a broad bay just north of the outlet to the Rusizi River. The narrow throat of the lake (the "funnel") was clearly Havu territory, with family members forming a single community on both sides of the lake. The areas of Luhihi, Cishoke, and Lugendo west of the lake were conquered by the Shi only a short time before the arrival of colonial troops in the area, and are now administratively part of Bushi. But they include a population which still today claims strong Havu affinities: linguistic patterns, cultural features, and social networks link these people more closely to Havu than to Shi communities; the island of Ibinja is still administratively a part of Buhavu— a reflection of earlier Havu historical claims to the area.

East of the lake the island of Nkombo (now part of Rwanda) and the lakeshore populations are seen, both by the people inland from the lake and by the lakeshore peoples themselves, as being Havu. In other words, even more than normally was the case, this mosaic of small islands and irregular peninsulas provided the home for a single community tied by culture, trade, and intense social interaction—marriage ties, bloodpacts, economic bonds, and formal friendship exchanges. Thus the close ties among members of the

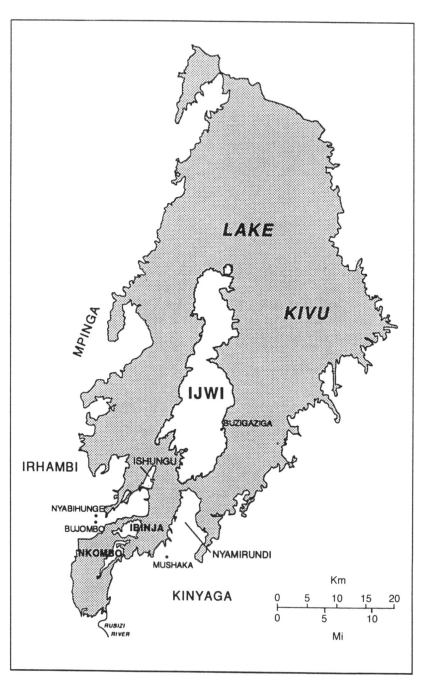

LAKE

MPINGA

KIVU

IJWI

BUZIGAZIGA

IRHAMBI

ISHUNGU

NYABIHUNGE

BUJOMBO

IBINJA

NKOMBO

MUSHAKA

NYAMIRUNDI

KINYAGA

RUSIZI
RIVER

Km

| 0 | 5 | 10 | 15 | 20 |

| 0 | 5 | 10 |

Mi

Map 12. The Basibula domain

Basibula family across the narrow channels of the lake, discussed in the next chapter, were magnified many times over for the local population in general. And despite current administrative divisions and international boundaries, such relations continue with great intensity still today: in cultural terms, these people clearly see themselves as different from the Bashi. Historically, in turn, Shi political actors appear to have viewed the area east of the lake as one of political refuge, as a separate area, autonomous of Shi authority, in a pattern remarkably different from Havu relations and transactions across the lake.[23]

So all the evidence—and even if circumstantial, it is consistent and broadly based—indicates that early Shi political energies were concentrated on the plateau, west and south of the lake.[24] Shi incursions into these lacustrine communities of Lugendo, Cishoke, and Luhihi appear to have been sustained only from the mid-nineteenth century, when the central Shi state entered into a period of expansion under Makombe and his son Bigomokero. Even then, direct Shi lakeshore influence was stronger farther north (in Luhihi, Katana, and Irhambi) than at these southern reaches of the lake.[25] Consequently, although the pressure of growing Shi power at the end of the eighteenth century may have indirectly affected the schism in the Havu royal line at the south end of Lake Kivu, neither mainland Havu nor Ijwi traditions refer to direct contact with Shi political personnel at that time. But certain Havu traditions do recount, in colorful detail, the increasingly strained relations among the Basibula themselves.[26] Eventually these tensions led to a classic tale of ignominious flight, pitiable orphanage, and triumphant return—of the exile, rebirth, and restoration of one segment of the Basibula family. It is a story of pedestrian deeds told in mythic terms. It is the story of the establishment of a new royal line, eventually to come to power on Ijwi Island.

9
The Arrival of the Basibula Dynasty on Ijwi

As we have seen, Basibula antecedents link the history of the Kivu Rift with the region of the Rusizi Valley to the south of Lake Kivu. But neither the references in the oral record nor indications from the ethnographic record include detailed substance. The earliest traditions to address the issue of Basibula royalty directly date only from the late eighteenth century, and locate the Basibula on the southwest shores of Lake Kivu. Their primary residence was at Nyabihunge, a hill whose prominent summit commands an expansive view of Ijwi, the entire southern shores of the lake, and the plateau to the southwest. Here a succession dispute among the sons of the Basibula king Bamenyirwe led eventually to the breakup and dispersal of the Havu ruling family.[1] The two primary contenders at Nyabihunge were sons of different mothers: one contender, named Kabwiika, was the eldest son of Bamenyirwe; the other, named Kamerogosa (Bamenyirwe's eventual successor), was the son of the most prominent wife.[2] Kabwiika, the unsuccessful contender, left the royal center at Nyabihunge and moved east across the lake, to Kinyaga; there he took up residence with some of his supporters, the family of a man named Lubambo.[3]

On the Mainland: The Basibula and the Babambo

The Babambo, the family with whom Kabwiika sought refuge as he fled Nyabihunge, had also apparently come from the south; by the late eighteenth and early nineteenth centuries this group was established along the southernmost shores of Lake Kivu.[4] Lubambo himself had managed to translate his skills and reputation as a healer into strong social and political ties with the Rwandan court.[5] His numerous sons were strategically placed on both sides of the lake, and they had achieved considerable importance in the area as well. Kabwiika was well received by this powerful family in Kinyaga, and eventually he fathered a child by Nkobwa, one of Lubambo's daughters. As the name implies, Kabwiika and Nkobwa were not married. (The name

156

Nkobwa derives from the Rwandan term *"umukobwa,"* meaning "unmarried woman" or "girl.") The child, therefore, a boy named Mwendanga, had an inauspicious introduction to the world: he was an illegitimate son born to a political refugee in exile.

To provide for the visitors who would assemble to celebrate the birth of his child, Kabwiika sought fish from some fishermen at the lakeshore. But a dispute arose, and in the confusion that followed, Kabwiika was accidentally speared by one of his own men. His death meant that Mwendanga, henceforth paternal orphan as well as illegitimate child, became heavily dependent on his matrilateral relatives who raised him. Thereafter the sons of Lubambo served as Mwendanga's political benefactors as well as his maternal uncles, a most influential role within the kinship context of the area.

These sons of Lubambo were unable to sustain their father's favored position at the Rwandan court, however. Instead, focussing on the areas of their strength, they turned their ambitions westward, across the narrow straits of the southern pedicule of the lake. With their encouragement and essentially with their support, Mwendanga made an attempt to reclaim the Basibula throne, then occupied by his paternal uncle, Kamerogosa. Although Mwendanga was unsuccessful in this attempt, the Babambo, in their zeal, managed to kill Kamerogosa.

The sources unanimously portray Mwendanga as seized with remorse on hearing of Kamerogosa's death, and they imply that this was the reason he refused to claim the throne for himself.[6] To the Babambo, however, Mwendanga's action was seen as a failure of will, a betrayal of the cause. They saw Kamerogosa's death as an element of outright conquest and the establishment of a new "order," under Babambo protection. But Mwendanga apparently saw it in narrower terms as simply part of a family dispute within the bonds of the established order, as the continuation of a power struggle within the family intended to drive off Kamerogosa and assert Mwendanga's "rightful" claims denied Kabwiika; he had not intended to kill Kamerogosa. The tension between the protégé and the benefactors, a stress resulting from their different structural positions, is evident in the traditions.

In contrast with accounts of other episodes, the Ijwi traditions tell of Mwendanga's relations with the family of Lubambo in detail and in eloquent terms.[7] Although narrated almost exclusively by the Babambo (on both the mainland and especially on Ijwi), these traditions underscore the depth of Mwendanga's continuing association with the Basibula and imply that these ties were directly opposed to the interests of the Babambo. For example, the different positions taken by Mwendanga and the Babambo on the question of Kamerogosa's succession reflect divergent perceptions of Mwendanga's social status (and responsibilities). The differences revolved primarily around the conflict between Mwendanga's paternity (as Musibula) and his proper

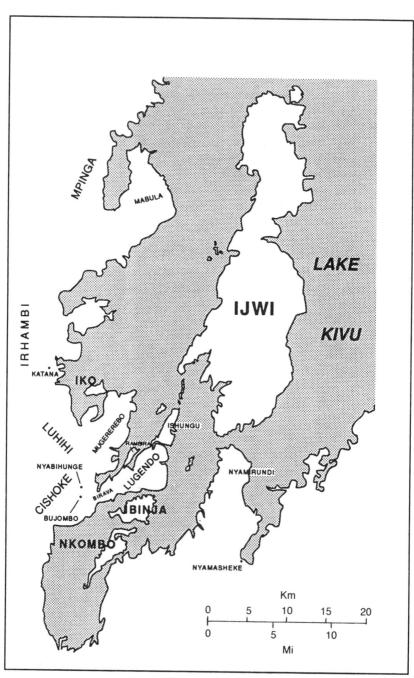

Map 13. The south end of Lake Kivu

lineage membership (as Mubambo), and soon they led to the partial estrangement of Mwendanga from his ambitious Babambo supporters.[8]

Mwendanga moved to the western side of the lake—the Basibula royal
family at Nyabihunge having since departed north along the lakeshore—
where he established a residence at Bujombo, a hill neighboring Nyabihunge
to the southeast. The position of Bujombo represents Mwendanga's paradox.
The hill is a twin to Nyabihunge, very close and of roughly the same height
(though slightly lower). It thus implies an identity with the Sibula (as opposed
to the Babambo); but it is separate from, and almost a challenge to, the
traditional seat of the Basibula royalty in the area. At the same time, by
setting up his own residence at Bujombo (and also by refusing to seize kingship by force) Mwendanga retained his identity with the Basibula, and hence
with the fiction of "royal heritage."[9]

In a most skillful manner, therefore, the sources simultaneously accept
the "facts" of Mwendanga's illegitimate paternity and yet assert his "royal"
identity. He has an ambiguous status, as befits the first king of a new dynasty.
By emphasizing the strength of Mwendanga's ties to the Babambo, these
traditions also foreshadow (and hence intensify the impact of) the subsequent
Basibula-Babambo struggles which were to occur at the time of Mwendanga's
death. In both the traditions on Mwendanga's youth and those on the succession dispute which was to dominate Basibula royal history on Ijwi in the early
nineteenth century, the Babambo are shown to be ruthlessly ambitious in
support of their sororal nephew. Their precipitate action leading to regicide
in both cases reinforced this interpretation of Babambo political character.[10]

The traditions on Mwendanga's early (pre-Ijwi) career can thus be seen
as part of a larger corpus of traditions which emphasize the features common
to such struggles. The traditions also portray other members of the Ijwi royal
family as struggling to free themselves of their maternal uncles, the Babambo.
Their emphasis on the common elements of similar episodes reflects the
cyclic character of royal traditions throughout the area.[11] The sense of struggle is intensified by Mwendanga's inauspicious childhood and the detail with
which the traditions stress the dependent position of his youth. The ultimate
outcome, known by all Bany'Iju today, and the present position of the
Babambo, collectively, as "maternal uncles" of the kings, also heighten the
sense of competition between the Babambo and Basibula conveyed in the
traditions.[12]

The Babambo, however, were not Mwendanga's only source of political
support and alliance in the mainland areas. Mwendanga also had ties with
Kamo, a man who had originally lived farther west, in Butembo, and whose
descendants, today known as the Baloho, were to play a leading role in the
establishment of the dynasty on Ijwi.[13] The traditions dealing with Kamo are
of a character entirely different from those treating the Babambo. They are

brief, fragmentary, and evocative (rather than narrative). In short, they relate how Kamo, a diviner, met Kabwiika. On Kabwiika's death Kamo raised his son Mwendanga and travelled with him, protecting him from his enemies by carrying him in a sack.[14] Kamo later shared his knowledge on divination with Mwendanga, and accompanied him to Ijwi as his court diviner. Although there are no confirmed details on the nature of Mwendanga's (or Kabwiika's) mainland ties with Kamo, it is highly probable that their later alliance on Ijwi derived from earlier links on the mainland. It is thus clear that Mwendanga was able to draw on the political support of several alliance networks formed prior to his arrival on Ijwi.[15]

There is no direct testimony that people or groups arriving on Ijwi with Mwendanga were important in his initial establishment as king. But indications in non-royal traditions suggest that other groups arrived on Ijwi at roughly the same time as Mwendanga, perhaps as a reaction to the unsettled political climate on the mainland (illustrated by the events associated with Nyabihunge and Bujombo). Consequently the Baloho probably formed only one of the groups accompanying Mwendanga to the island. In addition to direct alliances, therefore, it is possible that Mwendanga succeeded in establishing his influence as "royalty" on Ijwi by a deft strategy drawing on the general support of immigrant families familiar with the Basibula traditions of royalty on the mainland, in addition to combining the use of force (vs. the Banyakabwa) with policies of both distancing and incorporation of earlier immigrants into Ijwi.

On Ijwi: The Basibula and the Banyakabwa

Mwendanga's successful arrival and establishment on Ijwi are most directly related by groups already there. Babambo traditions on the mainland state that it was they who encouraged Mwendanga and in essence "sent" him to rule on Ijwi, but most probably this assertion is simply an ideological extension of their more general role as political mentors.[16] Traditions from the island associate Mwendanga's arrival more precisely with cleavages within the Banyakabwa community. According to these traditions, Mwendanga was "requested" to provide aid to one of the parties in these disputes.[17] Mwendanga's arrival on Ijwi can therefore be related to the spread of the Banyakabwa from their settlement center in the extreme north of Ijwi to other areas of the island, mostly in the south.

It is difficult to be precise about the causes of conflict among the Banyakabwa. It is clear, however, from both Banyakabwa settlement patterns and the frequency of internal disputes that the pattern of segmentation and dispersal among the Banyakabwa differed from former patterns of mobility associated with the Binyalenge. It may well be that segmentation was a structural feature of Banyakabwa descent groups, and that therefore it is less important to identify the immediate precipitating incidents than to recognize the structural features of the particular social environment within which these events occurred. At any rate, the "conflict" which accompanied segmentation among the Banyakabwa testifies to a pre-existing sense of solidarity, since in these circumstances the fact of separation conflicts with the ideal of solidarity. This sense of solidarity among the Banyakabwa is essentially what distinguished them from the Binyalenge.

The traditions themselves reflect this sense of solidarity by focussing on the fact of segmentation rather than on specific causes. The cause of conflict among Banyakabwa groups is expressed in terms of a common cliché, that of the refusal to share food. Consequently, it is impossible to ascertain the precise objectives and goals of the parties to the conflict; but neither is it necessary. The specific object of contention is viewed as merely secondary, as post facto justification for the situation of separation. What was significant, the traditions indicate, was the fact of segmentation; the immediate catalysts are less important than the structural aspects which make it necessary to create (or invent) such a catalyst in the first place.

This diffusion of Banyakabwa settlement took place shortly after (one or two generations after) Banyakabwa arrival, and (significantly) was directed to areas quite distant from Kirhanga, the Banyakabwa center in the extreme north of Ijwi. At the time of Basibula arrival, the Banyakabwa in the south were concentrated at four principal centers: at Buzigaziga, the home of Nyamuziga; at Boza, the home of Kazi and Bavuneshe; at Nkuvu, the home of Bayebaye; and at Ntalangwa, the home of Kambi (see Map 8). No reasons are given (except a conflict over "succession" and prestige), but the move is essentially portrayed as a conflict between Nyamuziga (in the south) and Balimucabo in the north. In more general terms it becomes a conflict between Kirhanga in the extreme north and all the other Banyakabwa settlements. In some respects all four southern groups were in opposition to the northern Banyakabwa branch at Kirhanga, the home of Balimucabo and Kanywabahizi.[18]

But conflicts also apparently existed among these families in the south, specifically between Nyamuziga, the senior member of the southern Banyakabwa contingent, and Kambi, the most junior member. Kambi had left Buzigaziga in the eastern highlands (the home of Nyamuziga) to establish himself on the southwestern peninsulas of the island. He was therefore within easy contact of Bujombo, the new home of Mwendanga, and he was undoubtedly well aware of the events associated with the Babambo and Basibula on the nearby mainland. From there, Kambi is said to have sought Mwendanga's assistance in his conflict with Nyamuziga.[19]

The two versions of Mwendanga's early relations with the Banyakabwa are both partly conflicting and mutually reinforcing. One portrays Kambi as an ally of Mwendanga, and hence as historical intermediary between Mwendanga at Bujombo and Nyamuziga at Buzigaziga. According to this version, Kambi asked for Mwendanga's support in his conflict with Nyamuziga. Mwendanga agreed, and with Kambi's assistance he drove Nyamuziga from his eastern residence to Mwiiru, on the eastern lakeshore.[20] (Part of Rwanda today, Mwiiru is still the center of a significant Banyakabwa community, with continuing ties to Ijwi.)

The other version, focussing on Nyamuziga, relates that Nyamuziga sought Mwendanga's assistance against the Banyakabwa of the north; Kambi is not mentioned.[21] In this account, Mwendanga arrived on Ijwi ostensibly to make a bloodpact with Nyamuziga. In fact, this turned out to be a ruse; having discovered Nyamuziga's poor state of military preparedness, Mwendanga later returned and forced him to flee. Mwendanga then set up his own residence on the island, again at a hill neighboring (but this time dominating) the former residence of his adversary. From there he established his reign.[22]

The precise historical events in this takeover are neither clearly established nor important. What is important is that Mwendanga eventually drove out Nyamuziga and subsequently set up an enclosure at Cimenwe, adjacent to Buzigaziga and overlooking the eastern lacustrine approaches to Ijwi. This was a most strategic location; not only was it near—and above—the former home of his immediate adversary but also it was in the immediate settlement area of other early clans, including the Banyambiriri and the Baziralo (see Map 9). During the establishment of the Basibula kingship on Ijwi this was the only example of expelling a rival from another clan; the Banyakabwa were the only group with the potential of providing coherent opposition to the Basibula immigrants and the subsequent establishment of their dynasty. The use of deceit (by contracting a bloodpact before driving out Nyamuziga[23]) and the use of force also belie the ideological tone of more generalized traditions on the royal family's arrival and establishment, which assert that Mwendanga was asked to come to Ijwi and was so well received because he was generous and well loved (and of "royal" blood).

Although this story is told in terms of only two dramatis personae, Mwendanga and Nyamuziga, various other immigrant groups were also present in the eastern region of Ijwi at this time (as discussed in chapters 6 and 7 above). Their presence (and potential opposition) may have been one reason why Mwendanga did not stay long in this particular area. He soon left the eastern highlands to establish residences elsewhere on the island without, apparently, having made any significant contacts with the other communities in the east—certainly without having institutionalized any administrative presence there.

The Meaning of the Basibula Arrival on Ijwi

In assessing the validity and significance of these traditions, the essential problem is their imprecision. They are seldom comprehensive or complete, and are usually limited to a single clan or area. Thus there is little independent confirmation, and few other sources (aside from clan population figures, which confirm the traditions, in this case) against which to compare or assess the traditions. The analogy to be made here is with a jigsaw puzzle where the colors of the different pieces have faded, where edges have been rounded and broken off so that the pieces no longer fit, where many of these overlap or duplicate each other, and where most of the pieces, indeed, have been lost.

Viewing traditions as part of a historical "puzzle" in this sense, however, touches on a more fundamental problem still. Essentially such a view presupposes that the constituent pieces form part of a single larger image, and that the total picture can be reconstructed by the careful assemblage of the various fragments. But it is an optimistic assumption that there previously existed a single perception of the past from which all the fragments derive; even where there presently exists a unified perception of the past, that condition cannot always be guaranteed to have held true in the past. Therefore it is dangerous to view the essential task of the historian as that of "reassembling" traditions to form a single coherent picture of the past. The character of historical traditions as perceptions rather than as accounts is especially clear in those discussed here. They need to be treated as clues to motive and significance, as interpretations themselves, rather than as statements of immediate causes.[24]

There are, however, some inferences to be drawn beyond the facts stated directly in Ijwi traditions. First, the external ties of the Banyakabwa were of great importance. Nyamuziga, for example, sought both assistance (from Mwendanga) and refuge (at Mwiiru) off the island. This was a common pattern: as we have seen, numerous external alliances characterized early Ijwi history, and this pattern was to recur frequently in political competition on Ijwi. In each succession struggle political contenders appealed to political and military resources outside Ijwi. Such external ties resulted both from precise historical links (on the part of the individual contenders) outside Ijwi, and from Ijwi's general political history as part of a wider field of historical interaction. In political terms, as with social interaction and alliance during the earlier periods, then, Ijwi was not an exclusive domain: the boundaries of political activity and political alliances during this period did not coincide with the obvious geographical boundaries of the island.

Significantly, those who sought assistance outside Ijwi to fight their political battles within were eventually overtaken by the very changes which their initiatives introduced into the political environment. As in the case of Nyamuziga, those basing their support on outside alliances were ultimately overcome by their inability to control the forces that they themselves had called upon. Their reliance on (or preoccupation with) outside sources of support led to a disregard for the internal network of power, and this ultimately doomed the claimant.[25]

A second significant aspect of these traditions is the opposition which appears so prominently in them between practical politics and normative statements. This is particularly apparent in Mwendanga's "expulsion" of his blood-brother, Nyamuziga, the man who is said to have appealed to Mwendanga to come to Ijwi.[26] Such a clear contradiction suggests an important transformation of the political context on Ijwi; in the "new" context one political actor simply overcame the other by sheer force, acting outside the conventional norms of social behavior. (One account explained that this deceit—the betrayal of the bloodpact—eventually caused the deaths of Mwendanga's sons, the implication being that Mwendanga was not entirely above the social proscriptions of the bloodpact.[27]) Still, the conflict of principles and eventual dominance of one (force and practical politics) over the other (social convention and norms of friendship) are boldly apparent in the traditions accounting for the introduction of a new political epoch on Ijwi.

Finally, this episode is also portrayed as a battle over "royalty": Mwendanga's drums, the symbols of royal legitimacy, were stronger than was Nyamuziga's claim to royalty.[28] What distinguished Mwendanga from Nyamuziga in this context was his success in breaking away from reliance on a single narrow kin group for political support. Whereas Nyamuziga relied exclusively on his own kin group,[29] Mwendanga was more successful, over time, in incorporating himself within a widening alliance pattern, and thus in widening the perceptions of political action. His status was essentially the product of his ties to—and ability to mobilize—people outside his own kin group. Although Mwendanga drew much of his initial mainland support from the Babambo, there were clearly other groups associated with his early years on Ijwi. Mwendanga may well have already worked within this wider political framework on the mainland before his arrival on Ijwi; indeed, his political position there virtually compelled him to do so.

But Mwendanga's initial arrival did not create instant integration. In his battle with Nyamuziga, for example, there is no evidence that others participated on either side; in fact the indications are that the eastern inhabitants remained outside that struggle. The process of incorporating new peoples into a new social framework continued long after his arrival on Ijwi. Indeed, it was only over time, and especially under Mwendanga's successor Kabego, that the Basibula kingship gained legitimacy and established itself politically by doing what the Banyakabwa, or at least what Nyamuziga, had failed to do. Thus although Mwendanga's success resulted in part from his ability to integrate many groups within his growing alliance network, his personal capacities do not provide the whole explanation. More important were the long-term processes integrating kingship as a norm and as an institution within the growing social identification of individuals, both as Bany'Iju and as members of particular clans.

Royalty was not, therefore, imported to Ijwi, still less imposed by single individuals. Ijwi royalty was created on Ijwi itself by the interaction of many peoples and individuals. The integration of kingship into Ijwi—which proceeded apace with the increasing differentiation of its constituent social groups—was therefore not the achievement of the royal family exclusively. The next three chapters will explore the various ways in which others participated in the process of integrating Ijwi kingship within Ijwi social structure; they will discuss the social, economic, and ritual dimensions of creating a kingship on Ijwi.

10

The Social Alliances of the Basibula on Ijwi

Mwendanga does not seem to have been directly accompanied to Ijwi by large numbers of followers. Nevertheless, the schism and segmentation within the royal family at Nyabihunge had apparently contributed to (and perhaps also been a symptom of) a climate of insecurity on the southern mainland, and many families from these areas sought refuge on Ijwi. Therefore new people arrived on Ijwi roughly simultaneously with the royal family, although they were not always directly associated with the Basibula. These immigrants from the south again altered the social situation and may well have contributed to a political climate within which the Basibula came to be accepted as royalty on Ijwi.

The arrival of new population elements from the southwest, however, provided only one factor in the establishment of Basibula royalty on Ijwi. Another consisted of alliance patterns which created common affinities of people on Ijwi with the Basibula line. Marriage alliances were especially important in this regard. These were essentially of three types: marriages with the earlier populations, marriages contracted with the new arrivals, and marriages with important families outside Ijwi. Different dimensions to these alliances are illustrated by two clans, each of which formed early ties to royalty. The Bashaho case illustrates how the larger clan identities, formed of the fusion of new arrivals with earlier settlers, both resulted from and strengthened ties to royalty. The Baloho illustrate another type of alliance with the Basibula: several generations of intensive marriage ties between these two families provided royal linkages to an area of weak Basibula presence.

Thus widespread marriage alliances helped provide immediate political support in the establishment of the royal line on Ijwi. But over time they also produced potentially disruptive succession struggles within the Ijwi dynasty, as each contender drew on separate alliance networks. External marriage ties were important in two respects. In the earlier years of Mwendanga's reign, they served as alliance mechanisms between the royal family on Ijwi and the mainland areas claimed by Ijwi kings. However, during the reign of Mwendanga's successor, Kabego, external alliances became increasingly important for their effect on internal Ijwi politics—not just as mechanisms of adhesion between two different areas of Basibula influence. These external alliances were to become especially significant as sources of support for the various protagonists in Ijwi's succession disputes.

Conflict over succession usually opposed the sons of different wives of the king (as noted in chapter 2). Where the important wives were drawn from within Ijwi society, this posed a threat to the political integration of the kingdom. But the earliest succession struggles invariably opposed an "Ijwi" candidate (one born on Ijwi to an Ijwi woman) to another whose essential power base lay off the island. In this situation the low level of royal integration—the inability of different factions within the royal family to generate popular support on Ijwi for their internal political struggles—may itself, paradoxically, have contributed to the longer-term political unity of the island. During the early years of Ijwi's kingship the external focus of these royal marriage alliances cushioned Ijwi society from the most divisive aspects of succession struggles, largely containing them within the royal family (and its outside allies). But in return, such external alliances (which were later based on other alliance mechanisms as well as marriage) widened the sphere of competition for the Ijwi throne, and over time they threatened the autonomy of Ijwi kingship itself, by including Ijwi within the political space of other more powerful kingdoms. Both because of their importance to Ijwi event-history and because they tell us much about the deeper nature of historical process on Ijwi, the following chapter will examine these external alliances and their changes over time. This chapter will focus on internal alliance patterns of the Basibula royal line.

The Bashaho Allies of Mwendanga

At the time of his arrival on the island, Mwendanga's allies included those who came with him and those who had been on Ijwi earlier but had nonetheless retained strong ties with the western mainland areas. It is possible that some families moved to and from Ijwi several times during the period of Mwendanga's establishment, for there always has been much interchange in this region. Even today, the people of the lakeshore areas on the southern mainland, a region long since annexed by Shi authorities, are accepted as "Havu" by themselves and by others, and they share strong linguistic and cultural similarities with Ijwi.[1] Therefore, though statements which associate the arrival of a given family with the arrival of Mwendanga need be handled with caution, as stereotypical, their general portrayal of the situation seems justified: that there was a general intensification in the exchange of people between Ijwi and the mainland at the time of the Basibula schism. The

Basibula move to Ijwi appears related to a much wider flow of population in the area.

Even for those who claim to have arrived earlier or later than Mwendanga, their very mobility indicates potential support for the new arrival, and it is likely that they proved to be an important political resource for the immigrant pretendants to royalty. The groups on Ijwi most likely to have lent such support were those who previously held ties west of the lake as well as on Ijwi, for Mwendanga's influence was never exclusively (or even primarily) associated with Ijwi. The principal areas of the Basibula domain at this time were at the southern end of the lake, and especially on the mainland peninsulas and islands nearby, rather than on Ijwi itself.[2] Therefore, regardless of its exact relation to Basibula politics, movement of this sort may have helped build up common loyalties and a common identity with Basibula kingship traditions, instead of threatening them.

The Bashaho provide an example of this historical pattern, one which may have been repeated within other family groups on the island. There was clearly a substantial Bashaho population established on Ijwi well before the arrival of the royal line. The oldest Bashaho genealogies and traditions point to early residence (long preceding the Basibula arrival) in the central portion of southern Ijwi, in the locales of Lubuye, Mushovu, Bugarula, and Kihumba, with a secondary settlement at Bushake. This early population seems to have been widely dispersed, however, for although there were several settlement centers for the Bashaho, not all early Bashaho identify with these centers.[3]

Other Bashaho, or people who came to identify themselves as Bashaho, also arrived from Bushi at about the same time as the royal family.[4]

> AUTHOR: Why are the Bashaho the most important clan [among the ritualists]?
> RESPONDENTS: Because they arrived together [with the Basibula]; one cannot forget those who arrived [settled] with you.[5]

> Gahindo came with his brother Muguma to enthrone the king here.[6]

> The Bashaho were at Mulyamo [a hill in south-central Ijwi], then later came Gahindo [ancestor of Mushaho, one of the principal ritualists on the island]. He came with Camarage, the son of Mwendanga. Mushaho is the ritualist of the *mwami;* that is why he came later.[7]

But not all the Bashaho arrived as a single immigrant group; they speak of different entries to Ijwi from different origins. In historical terms, therefore, the Bashaho form a heterogeneous group. They also form a large group—larger by far than most groups of Rwandan origin in the east, for example. Thus in their size and historical heterogeneity the Bashaho show similar characteristics to the Balega (also from the west). Nonetheless, despite general agreement on common origins to the west, there is another form of historical heterogeneity which speaks to the wide variety of contacts within which Bashaho identity operates. The Bashaho identify themselves with a multitude of other clans outside Ijwi: the Abashambo, Abega, Abashingo (Ababingo), and even the Abanyiginya in Rwanda; the Bashinjahavu and Bashoho in Bushi; and even the Beshaza and the Basibula on Ijwi. Yet paradoxically they have a strong corporate sense on Ijwi, one explicitly tied to their ritual role: "I am a Mushaho, and the king cannot rule without me."[8] In their corporate identity and their ties to kingship they share characteristics with the eastern groups (from Rwanda); indeed it may well have been the identity with kingship that reinforced their corporate identity.

One significant feature of the Bashaho settlement pattern is the proximity of the early royal residences to the old Bashaho communities.[9] The pattern also holds for more recent Bashaho arrivals, and even today there are several Basibula descendants of the first king in the area of the Bashaho primary ritualist.[10] Their strong ritual ties to kingship, their locations on the island, and their claims to have had earlier ties with the west—with the Zaire mainland, rather than with Rwanda—all indicate that the more recent Bashaho immigrants were likely to have been strong supporters of the king, as indeed they claim to have been.[11]

The outstanding link of the Bashaho with the Basibula today is in their ritual positions. Of the five principal ritualist roles involved with the Muganuro ceremony (discussed in chapter 12), three are those of Bashaho ritualists. In addition, the ritualist most closely identified with the king is a Mushaho. He is constantly in attendance at the court. He shares in the king's taboos. He has the specific duty of preparing the king's bed. And, he, like certain other ritualists, is a *"mwami emwage,"* a *mwami* in his own right and in his own restricted domain. His title (and term of address as well as a term of reference) is Mushaho; he is the only ritualist on the island to take the corporate clan name as his ritual title. Many of these features are widely associated with Bashaho roles elsewhere in the region,[12] but the discrepancies between the rituals on Ijwi and their mainland counterparts indicate that those on Ijwi resulted from historical interaction on Ijwi at least as much as from direct importation.[13]

The strong corporate sentiment of Bashaho on Ijwi today is at variance with the heterogeneity of the group's origins; the diversity of their pre-Ijwi locations and their separate arrivals suggest that their current identity is only a recent development. Because their identity is most strongly asserted in the context of royal rituals, it is likely that their participation in royalty served as a focus for the emergence of a wider Bashaho identity. The combination of these two aspects—the corporate identity among all Bashaho groups, regardless of their origin or time of arrival on Ijwi, and their ties to kingship—

indicates that those Bashaho who arrived with the king served as important intermediaries with the earlier Bashaho settlers on the island. The close alliance of some Bashaho families with royalty apparently served as a nucleus for the wider coalescence of various Bashaho segments into a corporate group, at least relative to royalty. This, then, is clearly one indication of how contact with royalty has contributed to the sense of common identity and to the cohesion of clan groups as they are presently defined.

Joking relations also indicate early Bashaho support for the king. The Bashaho most consistently claim *kumbi* ties with the Basibula and the Banyambiriri. There is no direct evidence on the historical evolution of such ties. Nonetheless, looked at within the context of other historical data, Bashaho *kumbi* ties with the Basibula appear to retain an early alliance tie between the two. This is also true of Bashaho joking relationships with the Banyambiriri, which reflect the proximity of the early settlements at Bushake-Butyangali, and perhaps also the common ritual significance associated with the two clans. Thus in a general way *kumbi* ties confirm the general hypothesis proposed here: that the Basibula and the Bashaho had close contact from near the time of Basibula arrival, and that this is indicative of a strong politically significant alliance, as most traditions state.

The Basibula and the Baloho

Another clan, the Baloho, has traditions which relate them in very explicit terms to Mwendanga, both on the mainland and later during the establishment of his kingship on the island. Baloho traditions include no reference to the actual causes of Mwendanga's arrival on the island, but the subsequent history of this clan makes it clear that they were important allies and collaborators of Mwendanga and that they had come from the west, where they claim to have been associated with Mwendanga before his arrival on Ijwi.[14] On Ijwi, the Baloho also served as important administrative intermediaries to the royal family in the east of the island. Because of their important role in integrating kingship to an area of the island where social distinctions were so sharp, the Baloho were one of the most important allies directly accompanying the Basibula to Ijwi.

Marriage alliances were particularly significant in the Baloho role as royal intermediaries. The specific marriage ties formed between the Basibula and Baloho were associated with their common arrival as two small immigrant families on Ijwi. In addition, the alliance network based on these marriage ties illustrates the strong corporate identity which accompanied dense interaction of this sort. Indeed, marriage ties can be viewed as alliances only when the two groups have a clear sense of corporate identity, distinct from one another; in turn, their use as political alliance mechanisms, especially when repeated over several generations, probably reinforced a sense of internal cohesion and identity within the group. Certainly in this case the depth and coherence of remembered genealogies among the Baloho stem at least in part from this phenomenon.

Some Baloho claim "originally" to have come from Gisaka (in eastern Rwanda), and to have derived from the Abagesera, the ruling clan there.[15] From Gisaka, these accounts continue, they moved to Kinyaga,[16] and after stopping briefly there they continued west of the Mitumba Mountains, into the area now included in the kingdom of Buloho (a Tembo kingdom today). Their current clan name on Ijwi derives from this association; in fact, those genealogies that reach back prior to their arrival on Ijwi include the name Mwandulo, the present common dynastic name of Buloho.[17] A migration of this sort is rarely found in Ijwi traditions, and these accounts are at odds with the general character of Baloho traditions; the historical veracity of the details of such traditions is very much in doubt. At a general level, however, postulating such a move reaffirms the strength of the concept of mobility among peoples in the area; by reflecting such ease of movement, it also evokes the common cultural characteristics of the region at that time (the mid- or late eighteenth century or before), as discussed in chapter 2.

The first direct tie-ins of the Baloho with Ijwi history center on the person of Kamo. According to Baloho traditions, it was he who befriended Kabwiika (Mwendanga's father); it was he who is said to have carried Mwendanga in a sack to protect him from enemies and eventually directed him to Ijwi; and it was he from whom virtually all Baloho on Ijwi claim descent.[18] Some traditions, the most elaborate (and possibly elaborated), portray Mwendanga's appreciation for Baloho assistance and counsel in the form of a division of the island between the two groups; some Baloho traditions even imply that the Baloho once held the insignia of royalty.[19] One Muloho expressed this relationship in the following manner:

> Kabwiika, the father of Mwendanga, died there [on the mainland]. My grandfather [actually fifth ascendant generation] was named Kamo. . . . Before Kabwiika died, he said to Camukenge, or rather to the father [actually grandfather] of Camukenge: "You, the father of Camukenge, I am dying, but you have always been my friend. Stay close to him [Mwendanga]. And if he ever obtains a country for himself, you must share it between you two. Then when we had made it possible for Mwendanga to arrive here, Mwendanga was not selfish; he divided the country into two parts. Two parts. He divided the part near the forest, or rather bordering on the lakeshore and the islands [here he named several peninsulas]. . . . [He took those areas.] That part located above [near the mountainous forest] was for us. . . . "You will be like my child," [said Mwendanga]. . . . And he said to Camukenge: "You Camukenge, you are my child. I will give you authority over all the people and all the cows that you raise there. Only pay court to me here, as it should be done. . . ."[20]

The tie between the early Baloho and Basibula is strengthened by the fact that Kabwiika's mother, the paternal grandmother of Mwendanga,[21] named Mwakabugubugu, was herself from Mubugu, another Tembo kingdom west of the Mitumba Mountains. In more recent times, with the northward displacement of the Basibula dynasty, Mubugu has had very close contacts with the "Havu" peoples from Mpinga and Bubale along the western lakeshore; it is possible therefore that this reference—or the assumption drawn from it—is an etiological anachronism. Nonetheless, from the assertion that the mothers of Kamo and Kabwiika shared a common "ethnic" identity derives the assumption that Kamo shared an affective relationship with Kabwiika, which presaged that which he was later to show towards Mwendanga.

Though a small lineage themselves, the Baloho came to hold positions of authority over a vast area in the east of the island. In later years, members of this family served as delegated authorities, virtually as *in loco regis* in status, although their effective power (like that of royalty itself) was never very great. In the years following Mwendanga's arrival and during his reign, however, this status was reflected more in their role as allies of the king, as his personal advisors and friends, than in the administrative powers they held. The evolution of these ties between the Baloho and Basibula illustrates the range of alliance forms and their possible expression. In the early years, Baloho proximity to the king was based on personal affinity, on friendship, and on service: Kamo is said to have been the king's diviner (*mulaguzi* or *murhonga*).[22] Later on, the alliance was reflected in the pattern of recurring marriage ties between one descent line of the Baloho and the royal family. Only in more recent times do cattle contracts appear important in the expression of this alliance tie, and these only reinforce the marriage alliances. More recently, these ties have been expressed in terms of delegated authority to the Baloho and in their ritual roles performed for the kingship.

Marriage ties between the Baloho and the Basibula formed a particularly dense alliance network and consequently are relatively well remembered. They occurred in every generation from Kamo's son, Nculo, to very recent times, a total of five Baloho generations. In addition, they are often reciprocal, with a woman from among the Baloho marrying into the royal family and a daughter of the royal family marrying a Muloho. (See Figure 2.)

In the first generation, the alliance was not direct: Mwendanga was an only child and when he arrived on Ijwi his children were very young, but his daughters married into the next two generations of Baloho. Nonetheless, even in Mwendanga's generation there was an indirect marriage tie between Mwendanga and Kamo's son, Nculo: Nculo's wife was the full sister of Mwendanga's wife Mongera.[23] (Among all the early royal wives, Mongera was to have the greatest impact on Ijwi; her residences are still remembered.) Both Nculo's son Camukenge and Camukenge's son Nyacinywa married

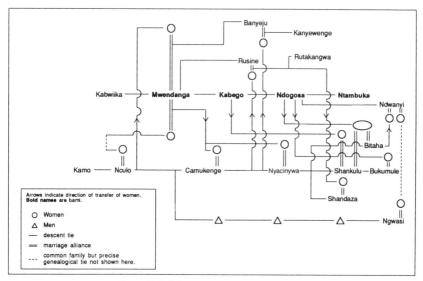

Figure 2. Baloho marriage ties with Basibula

daughters of Mwendanga.[24] Nyacinywa's son Shankulu, a renowned warrior
of the mid-nineteenth century, married the daughter of Mwendanga's son
Kabego; she was the uterine sister of Ndogosa, Kabego's son and successor.
When she died, Ndogosa offered his own daughter to Shankulu—both
women (Kabego's daughter and Ndogosa's daughter) having the same personal name, Bizininka.[25] Shankulu's son, Bakumule, married another of
Ndogosa's daughters, the full sister of Ntambuka, Ndogosa's successor as
mwami.[26]

In formal political terms marrying out the king's daughters is more
important than marrying women into the royal family, for the distribution of
women by the king represents the *mwami*'s assurance of fertility and perpetuation for non-royal lineages. In a sense, it is more prestigious for a lineage to have one of their members marry the king's daughters than to give a
daughter to the king. The king's daughters often maintained their royal status and partly reflected this status on their affines (and especially their own
children). But other forms of marriage alliances were significant as well:
exchange marriages between the Baloho and the Basibula and the marriage
of Baloho women with sons of the kings helped strengthen these direct alliance ties to the court. One such marriage was that of Nculo's daughter to
Mwendanga; she was to become the mother of Banyeju and the grandmother
of Kanywenge, both important Ijwi representatives on Ishungu, the mainland peninsula just southwest of Ijwi.[27]

Still other Baloho women married sons (or grandsons) of the *bami*. In terms of political alliance these may not have provided as strong a tie as marriage directly to the *mwami* himself, but they greatly reinforced other ties to the court. In ideological terms also, they increased the strength of the concept of affinity between the two families.[28] Although Kabego did not take a wife from among the Baloho, at least two other sons of Mwendanga (Rusine and Banyeju) married daughters of Camukenge. These women gave birth to Rutakangwa and Kanywenge, both important royal figures in their own right.[29] Each of these marriages was embedded in the alliance network more deeply than might be at first apparent, however. Banyeju was himself the son of Camukenge's sister, and thus this was a matrilateral cross-cousin marriage (a favored marriage relation on Ijwi) as well as a strategic political alliance.[30] On the other hand, the marriage of Camukenge's daughter with Rusine was part of an exchange, because Camukenge himself had married Rusine's full sister.[31] The exchange was to continue in the next generation, when one of Nyacinywa's sons (a grandson of Camukenge), named Shandaza, married a daughter of Rusine (and Camukenge's daughter, the full sister of Nyacinwa), and Shandaza's brother Shankulu married daughters of both Kabego and Ndogosa.

   In political terms the most important of these "secondary" marriages (to sons of the king) occurred in more recent times, when Ndwanyi, a son of Ndogosa (he himself the second successor, after Kabego, to Mwendanga) moved into the eastern area. There he married into the Baloho family, cementing, in this particular locale, the earlier more general alliance of the two families. This was especially significant because Ndwanyi was (with one exception) the first Musibula to live in this eastern area.[32] His wife was the daughter of Camukenge Bitaha, the Muloho who lived closest to Ndwanyi's new homestead, and also the Muloho closest to the court in personal terms. Yet Bitaha (the grandson of Camukenge, Nculo's son) himself had married a daughter of the *mwami* only when his older brother, Shankulu, had provided him with the daughter of Ndogosa, formerly Shankulu's own wife. This process illustrates the corporate perspective involved in these exchanges of women. It is otherwise surprising that Bitaha did not himself receive a woman from the *mwami*'s household, because he appears to have been personally closer to the court than was Shankulu.[33] Another, though more distant, tie between these two families in this area is shown in their marriages into a common third family. The second wife of Ndwanyi was the granddaughter (through the paternal line) of the paternal great-grandfather of the wife of Ngwasi, the great-grandson of Nculo.[34]

   In later years the Baloho alliances forged and maintained with the Basibula were expressed in more direct political terms. From their initial status as *barhunyi*, or court intimates (reinforced by their affinal ties), the Baloho were to serve under Mwami Ndogosa (the grandson of Mwendanga), and later under colonial rule, as *barhambo,* administrative representatives. At the regional level, a Muloho served as a "notable," responsible for 13 villages in the eastern portion of southern Ijwi. At the level of the local village community, Baloho were to serve as capita in several villages.[35]

The number of such villages has varied over time as the designation of village boundaries altered (for administrative purposes). Also the family and immediate locale of an important personage with direct ties to the court were autonomous of normal village administration. For a man of Shankulu's status, this autonomy applied to the whole area of his principal residence at Kisheke. By his direct ties to the court, Shankulu even tended to overshadow the delegated capita of the larger village (Bulegeyi), a man who was in any case the subordinate of Shankulu's brother Camukenge, the *murhambo* of the wider region which included Bulegeyi.

In addition to their posts in Kisheke and the central village of Mugote (the homes of Shankulu and Camukenge, respectively), Baloho have in recent times been appointed as authorities in two other villages, Lubuye and Musama. Each of these villages was relatively recently designated an autonomous administrative unit, and this provided the opportunity to appoint new *barhambo* from outside. Both appointees were Baloho. Lubuye is composed of two major clans, one accounting for 40 percent, the other for 37 percent of the total village population; Musama, though boasting only one strong clan (63 percent), actually consists of several sharply differentiated locales. In neither village were the Baloho originally resident there, and thus in both villages the *murhambo*'s clan forms only a small proportion of the total population—in essence only the immediate relatives of the *murhambo* himself. (In Lubuye only 4 families out of 90 are Baloho today; in Musama, the figures are 5 out of 35.) These men were sent out one generation ago as administrative delegates and thus represent a recent extension of Baloho administrative authority in the area.

Within the eastern region the Baloho held a sort of quasi-royal status stemming from their political pre-eminence. They express this in their own traditions by referring to their former possession of royal regalia—though they are careful to note that these regalia held different ritual names from those of the Basibula kingship.[36] Associated with these claims, there is a strong sentiment that when Mwendanga arrived on Ijwi he divided the island between Kamo (or Kamo's sons) and himself, and that he then withdrew to the extreme southwestern peninsulas, leaving the central and eastern areas of southern Ijwi to the Baloho.[37] (The Baloho make no claims to areas in the north.)

But the Baloho were not the only ones reputed to have held the ritual items of kingship in this area of the eastern highlands. They themselves refer to the former royal status of the Banyambiriri (something to which the Banyambiriri make no reference in their own traditions) and note their defeat of the Banyambiriri as support for their own claims to such high status: they had to instruct Mwendanga in the status and etiquette of royalty.[38] One lasting testimony of their claims to former royal status today is seen in the Ijwi enthronement rituals, where a Muloho bestows the dynastic name on the new king. (For the Baloho this is a reflection of their former historical role, where they bestowed kingship itself on the Basibula family.) Yet Baloho status as former retainers of royal regalia themselves and as participants in the ritual of enthronement is subordinate to their roles as political-administrative authorities—and as political allies to the king by their repeated marriage ties. It is in these contexts that the Baloho most closely identify with kingship on Ijwi.

This chapter has considered two factors which facilitated the integration of Basibula royalty within the Ijwi social network during the early nineteenth century: still new immigrants to Ijwi, represented by the Bashaho experience; and marriage alliances, represented by the Baloho. The arrival of significant numbers of family groups from the southwest provided the original impetus for the establishment of royal status. Arriving as part of a general pattern of two-way mobility—a demographic interplay between the islands and the southern mainland—these small familial groups did not polarize the social context on Ijwi, but their combined presence served to balance the eastern orientation of earlier Ijwi immigrants. Basibula settlement in the southwest of the island capitalized on this general immigration pattern, building on a momentum which was to transform the Basibula line from political exiles on the mainland to royalty on Ijwi. Marriage ties provided a second aspect to this transformation, by perpetuating earlier alliances and extending the alliance system to new families on Ijwi.

Despite their intensity, however, marriage relations with the Baloho were insufficient in themselves to subordinate the eastern areas to Ijwi royalty. Integrating this area within the royal structures would depend on other mechanisms, primarily the ritual incorporation to be discussed in chapter 12. But ritual incorporation was also undertaken in the context of power relations—and power implied superior access to material resources. For such a small and poorly endowed group, the Basibula were extraordinarily successful in mobilizing such resources. Unfortunately, the available data do not permit us to trace how this was accomplished in any precise fashion. Nonetheless, there are broader indications suggestive of this process.

The historical development of royalty on Ijwi was shaped by the changing pattern of relations to the mainland. As we have seen, other groups had ties to mainland areas also, but where these existed, changing conditions on the mainland eroded the sense of common identity between mainland and island factions of groups which formerly considered themselves as integral units. The Basibula on Ijwi did not retain close ties to the mainland Basibula descent line. But they did retain, develop, and expand their alliances with other wealthy and powerful groups on the mainland, groups like the Babambo, discussed in the preceding chapter. The next chapter will look at these external relations of the Basibula, first exploring the material resources available to them and the manner in which they were utilized (within the limits of the data), then examining the political alliances of members of the royal family with mainland groups.

11
External Alliances and the Establishment of Royalty on Ijwi

Over the course of the early nineteenth century, a new kingdom took shape on Ijwi Island, one in which the concept of kingship focussed on the island itself. It did not happen this way by pre-ordained writ. In fact, many of the most powerful groups on Ijwi tried to maintain politically salient ties with mainland areas, both east and south of the island. In most cases they failed, not because of events on Ijwi but because events on the mainland reduced the political significance of such social ties. It was outside the design of the most prominent actors—but very much following the interests of the "less visible" elements of emergent Ijwi society—that Ijwi political evolution occurred in the way it did. Looked at in terms of historical process, Ijwi political change took the form of a narrowing, rather than an expansion, of the political arena. Clan organization was not a synecdoche of later dynastic political order, not a scaled-down version of a later full-blown political form. Clans grew and took new forms as part of that very context within which kingship itself was conceived, nurtured, and shaped; and within this context kingship eventually assumed a character of its own even while sharing the wider regional cultural and historical characteristics which formed its origins.

The political salience of these earlier ties to the mainland declined not for want of a base there; such ties continued throughout Ijwi history—at all levels of Ijwi society—through the colonial period and right down to the present. Nor was it for want of trying; in each reign the most powerful contender to royal succession attempted to draw on outside resources—and failed. It was because Ijwi concepts of royalty made sense only on Ijwi, and members of the royal family did not have the power to impose other forms, or provide a different logic from that which evolved from interactions among the people who lived on the island. (The Basibula benefitted from royal hegemony, to be sure, but the conceptual logic by which new relations were defined was derived from local concepts.) Nor, indeed, did other outside actors have the power fully to control the people of Ijwi. Even colonial power was ineffective in the early years; only after several decades of struggle, stretching into the

1930s, did colonial power successfully impose its own set of social relations and economic obligations on the people of Ijwi.

Nonetheless, the legacy of ties off Ijwi was a powerful one. Strong contacts had existed, and formed an integral part of the history of many groups on Ijwi. And strong individuals had worked to maintain such external ties. Indeed, such ties had served individuals well in the past, and were instrumental in the early period of Basibula arrival on Ijwi. They provided the key elements for the consolidation of political resources in the hands of the Basibula. If outside influences did not prevail in every case, they clearly affected the nature of historical process on Ijwi during this period (and subsequently). The history of Ijwi cannot be understood without accounting for the sense of community reaching across, rather than being limited by, the bays and channels of the lake. This chapter will discuss these early networks and their limited utility for consolidating later Basibula power. The increasing importance of internal factors in the consolidation of royalty on Ijwi—the formation of a ritual field proper to Ijwi royalty—will be the focus of the next chapter.

The Material Basis of Royal Arrival

The period dealt with here, 150–200 years ago, is too remote to be covered by comprehensive narrative traditions. The most serious gap in the traditions relating to this period, however, is the lack of references to economic data. This problem is encountered elsewhere in the region as well—in Bushi and Rwanda, for example, where the oral record is in general much more complete and appears to provide a much greater time depth than do the Ijwi data. Yet even there the record is still very selective; even in such areas few economic data are forthcoming. For the region as a whole, data relating to economic relations within a given society do not reach back much before the beginning of this century, essentially covering the period of colonial rule. [1]

Thus the material basis of kingship on Ijwi in the early nineteenth century is problematic; the data simply do not account for institutionalized forms of material flows. There was, first, no payment for land occupation until much later periods on Ijwi; virtually all descendants of early settlers deny that their ancestors ever paid *Kalinzi,* tribute in return for royal recognition for land claims. The availability of land, the historical mobility of the family unit, and the lack of power of the royal family to enforce such payments all militated against the imposition of centralized control over land rights. Although from the early years of Basibula arrival there was a certain prestige derived from the delegation of "land grants" *(akabindi),* these could not be enforced as territorial domains within the kingdom until much later.

Similarly, cattle transfers are almost entirely absent from the traditions pertaining to the nineteenth-century politics of royalty. There are two exceptions to this which help confirm the general point. First, cattle distribution appeared important during the late nineteenth century, when Nkundiye, a son of the Ijwi king (Kabego), attempted to mobilize the support of the Ijwi population in his struggle to combat the military occupation of the Rwandan king Rwabugiri.[2] This episode will be discussed in greater detail below; in the present context it is noteworthy both because it is such an outstanding exception to the general pattern of cattle distribution for political purposes during this period and because it was such a spectacular failure: although they doggedly resisted Rwabugiri's attacks, the Bany'Iju did not support Nkundiye in his struggle. In addition, Nkundiye is invariably portrayed as the most "Rwandan" candidate in the succession struggles. As an ally of Rwabugiri, he fought in many of Rwabugiri's wars to the west, and (according to these Ijwi traditions) became a prominent figure at Rwabugiri's court. It is therefore not surprising that the traditions portray him drawing on a "Rwandan" alliance mechanism such as cattle clientship to try to fortify his claims as Kabego's successor; such behavior was well within his character— and fits well with the Ijwi perception of Nkundiye.

There is a second exception to the general absence of cattle distribution used for political purposes. Many Ijwi individuals obtained cattle by their own personal endeavor in Rwanda, rather than from the Ijwi royal court. The fact that Bany'Iju turned so readily to Rwanda as a source of cattle is significant beyond its implications for continuing historical patterns of inter-action between certain Ijwi families and the areas east of the lake; it also speaks to what was not occurring within Ijwi royalty. Since for the early years there is no reference to cattle distribution by royalty on Ijwi, it seems clear that the court did not control cattle as a major pillar of its political power. (When this occurred in later years it concerned only the political elite, and the form it took followed more or less a pattern of alliance among equals rather than hierarchical integration.)

Although there are no references to the use of cattle for political alliances on Ijwi, however, there are references to such use on the mainland. Therefore despite the fact that cattle played such a small role on Ijwi, it is entirely possible, indeed likely, that they were used by the Basibula in external alli-ances. The most intriguing sources on such mainland cattle ties refer to a relationship between Mwendanga and Gahindiro, the king of Rwanda. And indeed, Rwandan sources (and some Ijwi accounts) imply that Mwendanga was sent to Ijwi as the representative of Rwandan royalty. Most Ijwi sources, however, give no support to such an assertion; in Ijwi interpretations, the transfer of cattle in this fashion simply demonstrated Mwendanga's claims to royal status equivalent to that of other kings in the region. If indeed such an alliance existed, it is likely to have referred to one of a series of external alliances of the Basibula (that with Rwanda being the most prestigious, at least in more recent terms). Cattle received from Rwanda, therefore, were more likely to have been important for mainland alliance formation; if cattle distribution was a political resource in the hands of the Basibula, the returns from this were probably applied to the Ijwi context in a different form.

There is also no indication that the Basibula derived material support directly from taxing or participating in external commercial networks, such as the trade in *butega* bracelets around the lake.[3] They may have benefitted from this trade in a general way, but they did not control or affect either the production or the trade in such items. Indeed for the most part this trade took place without formalized markets; even where early markets did form, they did so in those regions most removed from the direct control of centralized political authorities. In addition the Basibula controlled no other form of commodity production—in iron, canoes, or salt, for example. Thus the fundamental categories of land, cattle, canoe transport, material production, and trade were outside the control of the Basibula, and did not serve as the material basis of their emergent rule on Ijwi.

There were, nevertheless, considerable material resources available to the incoming royal family: Mwendanga's immediate successor, Kabego, is said to have married over 30 wives (although only 16 are remembered on Ijwi today—those who had sons who lived on the island). Many of these women, including the mothers of all the later contenders for the throne (and therefore the most powerful wives) were drawn from mainland areas. Kabego's accumulation of wives on such an extraordinary scale attests to considerable accumulation of resources and indicates that the Basibula probably drew much of their political and material support from the mainland areas rather than from the island population, even after their arrival on Ijwi. But since he did indeed marry other wives from Ijwi as well—other than the (mainland) mothers of powerful political contenders—it appears that Kabego was drawing on material resources from the mainland and successfully applying them to the Ijwi domain. This implies that the material basis of Ijwi royalty derived primarily from earlier Basibula royal status on the mainland. The fact that they had such resources to draw on gave them the political advantage on Ijwi, over rivals (such as the Banyakabwa) or others.

Kingship on Ijwi also drew on the mainland resources in another sense: in the prestige of Basibula royal status accumulated there and carried over from outside regions. For the Basibula heirs to royal status, prestige therefore became the capital good of royalty, and control over the allocation of this scarce resource was a principal component of Basibula status on Ijwi. Prestige served the Basibula as a capital good both as a means of defining relationships within the context of royalty and as a tool for acquiring certain productive ends (such as accumulating wives). In addition to serving as a capital good, therefore, prestige was also currency, and one that could be produced in as great a quantity as the central court found expedient, simply by increasing the titles and functions tied to the central court. It could be attached to any of various statuses, each qualitatively different from the next. As long as the court controlled access to this prestige they retained the focus for developing royalty.

Thus part of the power of royalty on Ijwi was not the control over material items alone so much as the power of prestige and the accompanying influence over people's minds—the belief in kingship, and the belief that the Basibula held the legitimate rights to kingship. It was through the prestige of royal status that external sources of material wealth could be converted into a powerful political resource within Ijwi. The material flows that did gravitate to the court probably consisted of goods immediately consumed (beer, pre-eminently, and goats or food) rather than control over land or economic processes such as production or trade. Such gifts to the court are items which are not retained in the Ijwi traditions, nor would they necessarily be thought of as "tribute"; Bany'Iju also sent them to families in Rwanda without thinking of them as political tribute.

The prestige of royal status did not exist in isolation, however. It was both a product of and a legitimizing factor for the use of force. The position of the Basibula depended on monopolizing access to royal prestige, and therefore on removing or co-opting any alternate sources of that prestige. The mobilization of army organizations under Mwendanga provides an illustration of the way in which external resources could be effectively applied within the Ijwi context. The Ijwi sources do not refer to the supporters of Mwendanga used against Nyamuziga. This struggle is portrayed as a struggle of individuals, duelling with mystical powers: Mwendanga sent a basket of flour with arrowheads in it; ultimately he was victorious because his "drums"—his claims to kingship—were the stronger. But in other contexts, traditions both on Ijwi and on the mainland refer collectively to the Bahimuzi as the army of Mwendanga. Today this name is associated with the members of the regional organization from Ishungu, the mainland peninsula extending north and east from Bujombo, towards Ijwi. The association of the Bahimuzi with Mwendanga—even in Ijwi traditions—underscores the mainland focus of Mwendanga's domains; but it also illustrates one of the primary means by which mainland resources were translated into the social context of an island kingdom, once the changing social context had made that feasible.

The use of force in establishing Basibula royalty on Ijwi was nonetheless very selective. The conflict with Nyamuziga is the only recorded case where this occurred on Ijwi until the time of the succession disputes following Mwendanga's and Kabego's reigns. Force was used only against direct threats to Basibula royal prestige. One dramatic example of the use of force outside this framework helps illustrate the point. At the arrival of Mwendanga on Ijwi, the Babambo (Mwendanga's allies and protectors) are said to have taken food by force and to have seized the daughters of the island inhabitants without returning bridewealth.[4] Such arrogant behavior is said to have alienated the population and led to the eventual expulsion of the Babambo under Kabego.

These traditions are interesting on two counts. First, they illustrate both the reaction of the Ijwi people to behavior of this type and Kabego's ability to use such widespread antagonism against the Babambo for the purposes of consolidating Basibula rule on Ijwi, as distinct from and opposed to Basibula rule of Ijwi from the mainland. There were, then, limits on the extent to which force could be used within the kingdom against its own people, without jeopardizing—even threatening—the prestige of royal status, at least at this stage in its history.[5] Equally important, however, these traditions also imply that such behavior—material demands based on perceived differences in prestige—may have characterized mainland political behavior at this time. If so, this confirms the pattern noted above, that political resources (defined both in terms of prestige and material resources) accumulated on the mainland areas could be applied to the Ijwi domain. The Babambo were apparently trying to use similar processes in the opposite way: to expropriate resources from Ijwi to consolidate their position on the mainland.

The material bases of kingship therefore followed the lines of prestige. Indeed in the initial stages, where one of the essential components of power was illustrated in the alliance ties formed by the circulation of women, and where prestige was a major factor in accumulating women, the two were close complements in the process of the establishment of royalty.

The material basis of kingship also followed the patterns of prestige in another sense. The Basibula kingdom was first established on the mainland, and although the sons of Kabwiika (or Nkobwa) were no longer kings on the mainland, they still were able to draw on the prestige of royal status and apply those resources in new areas. Thus the process of schism within these kingdoms was more than one of division into two autonomous units, for both drew on the same resources even in the new area. Though Kabwiika was vanquished within the Nyabihunge context, his descendants retained the status of royalty in new contexts and were able to mobilize the resources needed to make good on that claim.

What follows will trace the efforts of other contenders for Basibula power to continue that policy. In every case they failed. In every case, by controlling the rituals that legitimated kingship, those who laid claim to local power resources prevailed against contenders who, over time, called upon increasingly powerful outside alliances. The next section will consider these alliances; in doing so we will transgress the strict chronological limits of this study by a considerable margin, tracing succession disputes into the 1920s.

Nonetheless, the principles involved in later succession disputes illustrate some basic principles of earlier political power.

Succession Disputes and Royal Integration on Ijwi

The integration of the Basibula within Ijwi society was more than a series of distinct events; it was also a long-term continuing process, whose evolution can be traced through the succession disputes which marked each reign. These conflicts demonstrate the dialectical opposition of two themes present throughout Ijwi history. Powerful external alliances forged by ambitious individuals were ultimately opposed to the internal integration of Ijwi society and its increasing collective identification with royalty. In the succession episodes—always the critical juncture for the reproduction of royal power— the most ambitious contender invariably sought assistance from outside Ijwi, and each succeeding dispute brought alliances with increasingly powerful and increasingly distant allies. But invariably also, the eventual victor relied on support from within Ijwi rather than on powerful external allies: those who sought such allies were, in every case, eventually rejected. Over time, this consistent pattern served to reaffirm the integration of kingship on Ijwi specifically with Ijwi society.

Marriage ties were initially important in the formation of external alliances based on support from a contender's maternal uncles. But paradoxically, external alliances deriving from marriage ties off Ijwi came to serve as a divisive threat to the integrity of the Ijwi kingship; they came to be seen as a means by which external influences sought to dominate the Ijwi throne. Ultimately the marriage bond proved too narrow to serve as an incorporative mechanism, an effective integrative device for the kingdom as a whole. As a form of alliance whose boundaries were clearly defined, the marriage bond related two distinct families; its integrative efficacy varied directly with the extent of corporate sentiment which tied those families to wider group identities. But by singling out a specific family as an ally, a royal marriage also distinguished that group, separating it in conceptual terms from the rest of society. Thus although marriages helped tie the royal family to certain other families, the exclusive nature of these ties impeded the larger integration of society as a whole, the more so because it tended to intensify the feelings focussing on that one family and differentiate them from others around them. Over time, therefore, marriage bonds were superseded by other forms of alliance ties.

The internal Banyakabwa dispute discussed earlier set the pattern for the type of alliance formation which was to recur in the later succession disputes. One Banyakabwa faction sought external support, and it was within the framework of this alliance that Mwendanga arrived on the island. Those who sought Mwendanga's aid, however, were unsuccessful in maintaining their position on the island, being overcome by the very "ally" they sought to use for their own ends. This was the constant tension apparent in such alliances with a powerful outsider: how to achieve one's own internal goals without in the end becoming merely a tool of the external allies, and therefore jeopardizing the integrity of the entire structure one sought to control. This pattern became especially apparent in the succession conflicts following the reigns of Kabego and Ndogosa, when the external allies were indeed sufficiently powerful to use the alliance as a lever for establishing their own presence on the island, as Mwendanga himself had done with Nyamuziga.[6]

Succession to Mwendanga

The first succession dispute within the Basibula dynasty on Ijwi occurred at the time of Mwendanga's death. The two primary contenders were Vuningoma, the son of a Mubambo woman, and Kabego, whose mother was of the Badesi clan. Although all four of Mwendanga's principal wives were originally from the mainland, only Vuningoma from among their sons had lived on the mainland, with his maternal uncles. Kabego lived on Ijwi, as did many of his brothers, and apparently had little contact with his own matrilateral kin on the mainland.

The conflict between Kabego and Vuningoma can be looked on primarily as a territorial struggle, almost as a struggle of secession (with Kabego seceding from the Basibula territorial base on the mainland), rather than as one of succession.[7] The integrity of the domain as a whole was at stake, and the lines of dissension were essentially drawn between Ijwi and the mainland areas, represented by the Babambo. Originally, the Babambo, who claim to have "sent" Mwendanga to Ijwi in the first place and some of whom had settled on the island, had so antagonized the Ijwi population by their arrogant behavior as to alienate themselves from any support on Ijwi. The climax of the struggle is portrayed in terms of Kabego's defeat of the Babambo on Ijwi: he rounded up all the Babambo on the island and had them placed on a small island between Ijwi and the mainland. Some escaped by swimming to the mainland, but those who could not were slaughtered to a man. The only exception to this pogrom was a single Babambo family retained on Ijwi as the ritual maternal uncles of Mwendanga's descendants (in the context of "perpetual kinship"), a recognition of the Babambo role in Mwendanga's youth. Even in pursuing his political ends, Kabego was therefore careful to preserve—or to re-create—the ritual depositories of kingship.

This episode illustrates the principal way in which Kabego was able to succeed Mwendanga as the focal point of Ijwi kingship. Rather than fighting to possess Mwendanga's royal regalia, Kabego apparently moved to establish his own ritualists, regalia, and indeed his own kingdom based on Ijwi rather than on the mainland.[8] For although Vuningoma held the king (Mwendanga lived out his old age on the mainland, not far from Vuningoma's principal homestead), and probably also some of the regalia, Kabego held the allegiance of the *bagingi* (the royal ritualists) responsible for enthroning the king and legitimizing his reign. It was thereafter the legitimacy of enthronement, or public participation through the *bagingi* as king-makers, that was paramount in the succession process; control of these factors was crucial to the Ijwi political process. The contenders who fought for control of kingship on the basis of strong external ties alone tended to alienate the Ijwi population. In each case, the successful contender held fewer external ties than his opponents but maintained closer ties on the island, thus implicitly recognizing that the ultimate power of kingship was extrinsic to the political position itself and "belonged" to the social context. From this perspective, it is not surprising that Ijwi traditions give much more prominence to the struggle between Vuningoma and Kabego than to the arrival of Mwendanga on the island. For it was with the defeat of the Babambo that the Basibula redefined their own royalty and that Ijwi Island became its own kingdom, at least as defined in terms of external autonomy.

The sequel to this struggle on the mainland indicates that there had been but little ritual component to Mwendanga's kingship. The fact that Mwendanga did not possess the full ritual components of kingship may explain why—given that the succession dispute was essentially a regional struggle between Ijwi and the mainland—there did not develop two independent royal lines following Mwendanga's death, one line on Ijwi and one on the mainland peninsulas. Although Mwendanga's principal political bases were located on the western mainland, many of the most important ritualist families on Ijwi today originated from the east. This reinforces the view that in these stages the ritual component of kingship was more important than outright political power. The centralization of the ritual aspects of kingship developed most strongly in areas where segmentary tendencies were strongest, areas removed from centralized political strength. Had there been a ritual component to Mwendanga's rule on the mainland, there would have been little to prevent Vuningoma from establishing a separate kingdom on that basis. It is possible that Vuningoma's allies and mentors, the Babambo, alienated the population on the mainland as much as they did on Ijwi, and that this inhibited the growth of a mainland kingdom there. But this would also indicate that Vuningoma had only shallow support in the area and hence lacked any general acceptance on the part of the population—and the effective ritual power to create it.

Competing political pressures in the region during the mid-nineteenth century also help explain why Ijwi was more suitable than the mainland as a locus for royalty. To the east, the Rwandan state was beginning to exert considerable political influence in Kinyaga (south and east of the lake). The Shi states, whose power was expanding in the plateau areas to the southwest during this time, probably also had growing influence in this lakeshore region; indeed Shi expansion may have been related to the extension of Rwandan power into Kinyaga. It is even possible that the senior Havu line then settled in Irhambi, west of the lake, still had some influence in the area. By transforming the mainland area of Mwendanga's domain of influence from a political nexus to a political buffer area, a "no man's land," the combination of these growing regional forces may well have inhibited the emergence of a new kingdom on the mainland under Vuningoma (or even under Mwendanga). But the lack of any such claims to royalty indicates also that Mwendanga and Vuningoma had succeeded only in creating a political alliance with the Babambo, but had moved no further in creating a social context amenable to the growth of patterns of kingship.

This implies that Mwendanga was originally less a king than a regent for a latent or potential kingship, one which only later came to full flower on Ijwi, one nurtured by the Ijwi social context. Ijwi was close enough to the mainland to draw on the general traditions of royalty in the area, but at the same time it was distant enough from these pressures to develop its own royal tradition independent of these competing contexts. Later, with the growth of Ijwi royal traditions, the island kingdom came to dominate the shoreline areas of the mainland and the peninsulas and islands of the lake, including in its domain much of Mwendanga's former territory. But in the new context these areas were only extensions of the Ijwi domain.[9]

The Succession to Kabego

The second succession dispute was much more complex, linked as it was to several competing parties, with varying alliances between them.[10] It was also tied to the larger context of internal politics on the island, in particular the growing distance between the northern and southern sectors of the kingdom. Finally, this succession dispute was inextricably linked to Kabego's wider regional ties, to the ambitions of the Rwandan king Rwabugiri, and to the eventual conquest of Ijwi by Rwabugiri's forces. However, though situated within a larger political context and thus including many individuals and a wider framework of events, this succession struggle can still be viewed as part of the pattern outlined above, and it reinforces the argument that external power was less significant than ritual identity in gaining the allegiance of the population.

Three contending parties (each a son of Kabego) played key roles in the disputes to determine Kabego's successor. One of these, a man named Lwahamire, was the son of a Mudesi woman, of the same clan as Kabego's maternal line. Significantly, however, the Badesi had not been a factor in the dispute between Kabego and Vuningoma, nor had they moved to Ijwi in any numbers after that time.

Lwahamire made the first overt move in this struggle, by requesting Kabego to name him as successor. But this had occurred during the absence of another prime contender, Ndogosa. He had been sent to the mainland to provide military support to the Havu king at Mpinga, at the time fighting against the attempts of the Shi royal family to move into the area of Irhambi on the western mainland, till then claimed by the Havu. Ndogosa's absence, it is implied, seems to have been devised to clear the Ijwi "political land-scape" to lay the groundwork for Lwahamire's eventual succession. If so, the similarity with the previous succession dispute is evident: Mwendanga had apparently favored the son of a wife from his own maternal line; Kabego, it is implied, was following in a similar pattern.

But Ndogosa heard of the plot and returned home to accost Lwahamire on this point. The confrontation led to a dramatic showdown, one widely recounted in Ijwi traditions. Ndogosa and his men seized Lwahamire and took him to the blacksmith's forge. There, continue these accounts, he had the smith heat the coals to red hot. They then placed a spearpoint in the coals and heated it to glowing white. Ndogosa seized Lwahamire, struggling, and threw him to the ground, where he gouged out his eyes with the heated spear. Blinded, Lwahamire henceforth was unfit for kingship, and no threat for the throne.[11]

They took Lwahamire to recover on Nyamisi, an island off the south-west coast of Ijwi, near the mainland peninsula of Ishungu. Ishungu at the time was the site of one of the enclosures of another son of Kabego, the third principal antagonist in this dispute. His name was Nkundiye, and he was to prove the most ambitious of all in his quest for power. For while Ndogosa was willing to remove his adversaries from contention in a brutal fashion, Nkundiye was willing to go further and betray the king himself.

On the mainland, not far from the island where Lwahamire recovered from his frightful wounds, lived the Badesi, Lwahamire's matrilateral relatives (and hence, collectively, his maternal uncles). Nkundiye's first move in this political game was to encourage Lwahamire's maternal uncles to seek vengeance against the uterine family of Ndogosa, as indeed they were entitled to do. Rugina, the elder brother of Ndogosa and eldest son of Kabego, lived on an island neighboring that of Lwahamire's convalescence. It was here that the Badesi directed their blow.

One dark night, while Rugina, having drunk with his night watchmen, was deep asleep, Lwahamire's maternal uncle, Gatumwa, arrived silently, stealthily, and entered the compound through the hole in the reed enclosure intended for cattle. The night watchmen slept, and from outside the hut where Rugina slept, Gatumwa reached through the thatch to cut through

Rugina's intestines, even while he slept with his wife beside him. Instantly she awoke to find them both covered with gore and Rugina dead. In the furor that followed, Gatumwa was able to return to his canoe, and on Ishungu he reported to Nkundiye, who rewarded him with several cows for his work.[12]

This episode, widely known on southern Ijwi and told frequently and with great drama, serves to draw together two important themes. On the one hand, Gatumwa's role recalls the importance of the matrilateral line in alliances of this nature. At the same time it illustrates Nkundiye's first external alliance—and one not with his own kin—in forwarding his claim. The episode as a whole, then, marks a transition from the earlier pattern of matrilateral ties to one of forging external alliances beyond kin ties.

Subsequent to these internally motivated conflicts, the Rwandan king Rwabugiri, whose domestic policies were closely tied to an expansionist military policy, turned his attention to the Kivu area. Ultimately all the regions bordering on Lake Kivu, both east and west of the lake, were to feel the impact of his regiments. But the area which served as a focal point in this western policy was Ijwi Island, the object of his earliest attacks and of his most prolonged interest (spanning his reign).[13]

His earliest attacks were unsuccessful, however, because of the mastery of the lake maintained by the Bany'Iju rowers. Thwarted in his initial attempts, Rwabugiri was to try for a decade and more to overcome the Havu control of the lake. And these attempts played perfectly into the stratagems of Nkundiye (and others) on Ijwi. It was Nkundiye, so the Ijwi traditions recount, who eventually led Rwabugiri successfully to Ijwi, permitting him to assassinate Kabego, and thus accomplish the conquest of the island.

In return for this assistance Rwabugiri established Nkundiye as the *de facto* chief on the southern part of Ijwi. Nkundiye continued to fight for Rwabugiri in the wars to the west, where he achieved such distinction as to overshadow even Rwabugiri's own warrior-favorites, and thus earn their profound envy. During one famous expedition, Nkundiye is said to have personally saved Rwabugiri's life and one of his regiments. During the same campaign one of the Rwandan elite armies was annihilated and one of the great heroes of the Rwandan court was killed. Suspicion fell on Nkundiye's troops for not having fully protected this army, and so in the process eliminating a rival for status and influence at the court.

It was not long before Rwandan court intrigues against this "barbaric" hero from "the land beyond the mists," combined with Nkundiye's own ambitions, were to lead to his disfavor at the court. For Nkundiye not only surpassed the military efforts of Rwanda's most celebrated warriors, he flaunted the fact. In addition, Nkundiye sought to control the entire island, as his father before him had done, not just to serve as the delegated authority to half the island. But Rwabugiri had delegated authority in the north to another representative who was, like Nkundiye himself, a grandson of Mwendanga. In a dispute over terrain, Nkundiye captured this man and had him killed in yet another "heroic" episode in Ijwi's drama.[14] To do so of course was to challenge Rwabugiri's ultimate authority—and his power to enforce it.

Meanwhile, on the death of his father, Ndogosa had fled far to the southwest of the lake, to Ngweshe, or (according to some reports) to Bunyintu, in the forest region southwest of Bushi's current boundaries.[15] Having thus eliminated most of his rivals, Nkundiye proceeded to declare himself independent of Rwabugiri. On the imposing headland of Bushake (ironically sharing the same summit with Buzigaziga where Mwendanga had routed Nyamuziga), high above the eastern shoreline of Ijwi and facing Rwanda across five miles of water, Nkundiye had his own drums sounded until the echo resonated off the Rwandan shore in a gesture of symbolic defiance to the Rwandan king, his nominal overlord and former benefactor.

Nkundiye's audacity was nothing less than treason in the eyes of Rwabugiri. And so for the third time the Rwandan king organized a campaign against Ijwi.[16] Nkundiye fled to an island off the mainland (near Kalehe); Rwabugiri's troops pursued him there. True to his heroic character, Nkundiye vowed not to be taken alive, broke his own spear across his knee, and hurled himself into the lake, drowning within sight of the Rwandan boats. Finally overtaken by his own "ally" and his own ambitions (which collided with Rwabugiri's larger plan), Nkundiye thus lost his own bid for succession. In the process, his external alliances had directly threatened the autonomy of Ijwi kingship itself by ushering in a decade of Rwandan rule on Ijwi. On Rwabugiri's death a decade later, Ndogosa returned from exile in Bunyintu to accede to the vacant throne.

The important element in this episode was Nkundiye's reliance on powerful external allies to achieve his aims. In his alliance with the Badesi, the parallel of Nkundiye's strategy with that of Vuningoma is very close; the regional identification of the Badesi and the role of maternal uncles supporting their sororal nephew both recall the Babambo support of Vuningoma a generation earlier. But the Badesi alliance was not the focus of the succession struggle to succeed Kabego. It was a transition from one form of alliance to another, much more dramatic, form, one with potentially much more significant repercussions for Ijwi and the whole region.

The most important difference between Nkundiye's alliance patterns and those of Vuningoma was that Nkundiye did not rely for support on his maternal uncles. Instead, he made an external tactical alliance to achieve a specific political goal—that of succeeding Kabego. But this form of alliance lacked the stability inherent in ascribed alliances with matrilateral kin, who themselves might have an interest in preserving the internal structures. In situations where these matrilateral kin lay outside the system—and from there, Nkundiye's alliance pattern was but a small step away—the security provided by their common interests is endangered. And in this case, the narrowing focus of Ijwi royalty to the island alone had left matrilateral kin off the island increasingly alienated from the kingship.

Nkundiye's tactical alliance also did not account for the nature of Rwabugiri's ambitions and strategies in the area. It was clear that aside from their common goal of removing Kabego, the ultimate aims (and hence strategies) of these two leaders were incompatible. Rwabugiri's goal was expansionist. Both the tactics used on Ijwi and the Rwandan traditions claiming earlier Rwandan antecedents on Ijwi suggest that his long-term aims were to incorporate Ijwi within the Rwandan political framework, as he had attempted to do with other regions (such as Gisaka and Kinyaga). But this was incompatible with Nkundiye's goals of an independent sovereign state (as under Kabego) under his own control.

At one level, therefore, Nkundiye was thwarted by Rwabugiri. But it could also be argued that in fact he failed in his objectives of attaining kingship by his inability to attract local Ijwi support. His incapacity in dealing with Ijwi society, his failure to become responsive to it, is the outstanding if unspoken characteristic of Nkundiye as portrayed in the Ijwi traditions. He was "heroic," perhaps even admirable, to some; but he was also unapproachable. By his very achievements (as well as by his inordinate ambitions) he was set apart from society, separate, alone. Even his attempts at forming alliance patterns on Ijwi, conscious political alliances again, are striking in their contrast to more common Ijwi alliance patterns. The traditions speak of him as distributing large numbers of cattle—"whole hills of cattle" at a time. Behind the hyperbole is the unspoken difference from Ijwi norms, in which (except in marriage ties) cattle are simply not prominent in the Ijwi past as alliance mechanisms. Although friendship cattle were sometimes exchanged, this was not, it appears, done on any great scale until recent times; cattle were more often exchanged as part of commercial ties.

Thus paradoxically, even Nkundiye's attempts at forming alliances are noteworthy by the manner in which they articulate differences between the contracting parties. In the traditions of today these alliance forms only highlight the essential distance of Nkundiye from Ijwi society. It was this distance, more than anything else, which doomed his attempts to succeed Kabego. For without the support of the ritualists, and beyond them Ijwi society as a whole, he could neither be accepted as king nor mobilize Ijwi support for his cause against Rwabugiri.

The Succession to Ndogosa

Although the political context of the 1920s was far different from that which had prevailed 50 years earlier, the struggle to succeed Ndogosa followed some of the same patterns. The principal protagonist in this drama was

Mugenzi, the eldest son of Ndogosa. Like Nkundiye, he was a man of heroic proportions, physically as well as in his character. A man of great ambition, boldness, and sense of the dramatic, Mugenzi was to attract his own personal following and to force the succession issue to a crisis long before his father's death. Like Nkundiye, too, he was to alienate himself from the rest of his brothers, and to turn to powerful outside assistance—in this case, to the Europeans now entering the area. But his chosen allies were more powerful than he at first realized; they had their own aims independent of those of Mugenzi himself, and independent sources of power which were in no way affected by their alliance with him. Beyond tactical concerns, they had no stake in Mugenzi's ultimate success, and therefore no commitment to the alliance with him. As in the case of Nkundiye, the rebel on Ijwi had no influence over the policies, resources, or goals of his political associates, and no share in defining the limits to those goals. In reality, then, this was not a relationship of alliance; it was clientship.

In the end Mugenzi was to fail in his objectives because he did not successfully integrate his cause with that of the Bany'Iju as a whole, and tie his fate to theirs. Like Nkundiye, Mugenzi perceived effective kingship essentially as the ability to exert power, even power externally derived. Therefore kingship was to be obtained essentially through the exercise and mobilization of power, from whatever source. This concept represented a fundamental alteration in the concept of kingship on Ijwi. It was a fatal miscalculation on his part, for Mugenzi failed entirely to understand the essential integration of power within Ijwi society. In focussing only on the exercise of power, he failed to see that the power of kingship on Ijwi ultimately derived from authority provided by the *bagingi,* the group of ritual specialists. Even in their humble roles, they were, collectively, the ultimate king-makers on Ijwi.

Ndogosa's first-born son, Mugenzi, was born sometime before 1890, during Ndogosa's exile in Ngweshe. On his father's return to Ijwi, Mugenzi quickly entered the political context of early European arrival in the area. He attended the (German) Protestant mission school on Ijwi and became an early political adept of the Germans prior to World War I. During the war he was a partisan of the Germans, fighting the Belgians with guns captured from Belgian soldiers sent to Ijwi. After the war he was deported from Ijwi, but he nevertheless impressed the Belgians with his character, pride, and organizational abilities.

The Belgians were to spend a decade and more trying vainly to administer Ijwi Island—to force the population to work, cutting timber, providing sand, and constructing buildings on Ijwi and in Bukavu, the new administrative center at the southern end of the lake. In addition the colonial authorities expected the population to provide food of many sorts—cattle, chickens, goats, sheep, and fish, as well as grains and bananas. And their instrument for achieving all this was to be the *mwami* Ndogosa.

But Ndogosa would not—and indeed he could not—acquiesce in this intrusion on the lives of the Bany'Iju. Although royal status brought with it power, such demands were simply beyond the capacity of royal power on Ijwi to assure. After delaying as long as possible he fled to the high mountainous forest called Nyamusize, where he lived in self-exile for several years. To the Belgians, of course, this was only proof of his complicity in the truculence of the Bany'Iju, in their refusal to become simply servants of the colonial regime. For many years the colonial regime sought him with every means at their disposal. As their frustration grew, they deported Ndogosa's sons one after the other until virtually none of his family remained on Ijwi. The Belgians even killed Ndogosa's delegated ambassador to them, Camukenge, in the most gruesome fashion, an event which has come to symbolize the brutality of colonial rule in the traditions on Ijwi. And still Ndogosa was not forthcoming.

But Mugenzi saw collaboration with Europeans in a different light. From his exile, having seen European power and judging that the Belgians were there to stay, Mugenzi negotiated for his own release. He promised to locate Ndogosa and turn him over to the Belgians within six months of his return to Ijwi, if they would let him serve as their administrative authority. They agreed, and Mugenzi returned to Ijwi. Once again, as with Kabego and Nkundiye, the Ijwi king was betrayed by his own son, who was attempting to harness external power to his own ends.

Mugenzi was no more successful than his predecessors had been before him. Though he deported several of his brothers who had also returned, refused to permit others to return, and hunted vigorously for Ndogosa, the king remained secluded. Thus even having cleared the field of other contenders and backed by European power, Mugenzi was unable to win over the population. In the end he failed to produce Ndogosa to the European authorities, and was exiled once again. But it was not the Belgians who ultimately thwarted his ambitions; it was the people on Ijwi who did so, or rather it was his own failure as an aspirant *mwami* to see the importance of their support.[17]

The sequel to this illustrates again the importance of the ritualists in defining—creating—the king. Having seen the enormous suffering inflicted on his people and the futility of remaining a fugitive, Ndogosa presented himself to the Belgian authorities. He was deported, and died in exile in 1928.[18] Following Ndogosa's death the ritualists had refused to enthrone Mugenzi as his successor; instead they bestowed the kingship on Ntambuka, Mugenzi's younger brother. But Ntambuka himself was exiled in 1943, and his half-brother Muhamiriza was placed as colonial "chief" of the southern half of Ijwi. At independence 17 years later, it was Ntambuka who was returned as *mwami* to Ijwi after an overwhelming vote of confidence by the population, thus removing from power Muhamiriza, who for so long, and with such diligence to colonial policy, had administered southern Ijwi for the

Belgians. The choice of the *bagingi,* determined some 17 years previously, had prevailed. One of Ntambuka's first concerns was to reassemble the *bagingi* on the island, summoning to Ijwi those who had left to seek work off the island. In so doing he reconstituted the essential basis of royalty—and of his own kingship—on Ijwi.

The Politics of Kingship

In the oral accounts available today, the struggle over kingship was most evident as a struggle within the royal family to accede to clearly defined positions. Over time, however, these positions were more fluid, not defined in absolute, unchanging terms but molded by the interaction of the interests of many individuals. The end result was less a maximization of social well-being than a continuously fluid statement among competing parties; even the rights and powers of the king could vary over time with changes in the political constraints acting on the king at any given time. The participants involved in this process included many more people than the members of the royal family or their immediate associates alone. Furthermore, defining the shifting contours of royal power was not always a positive, "progressive" process. Although overt opposition was not always prominent in this process, underlying currents of thought and alternate channels of activity did much to redirect action and reorient thinking on political relations.

The politics of kingship therefore went far beyond alliance mechanisms and integration. Royalty on Ijwi emerged from a process of juggling opposition, confrontation, and competition among factions. The various actors drew on diverse material, demographic and ideological resources. Increasingly pervasive factionalism—such as that involved in the intensification of clan identity—was one obvious result of this. Another was the growing significance which emerged between court and countrymen; as the stakes became higher, with greater differentiation in political power among factions, so the political salience of status distinctions increased, too. But this was not a unidirectional process, nor a clear-cut cause-effect relationship. Political centralization transpired within a context of social fragmentation just as social segmentation occurred within the process of political centralization.

Similarly the opposition between the court and the *bagunda,* the commoners, was an opposition shot through with ambiguity and paradox. For example, the struggle between court and commoners on Ijwi was often overlayed by the struggle of Bany'Iju against outside powers—against the Rwandan king Rwabugiri in the 1870s, against Belgian colonial authorities in the 1920s, against the post-colonial administrative policies in the 1980s. In each case, some individuals and classes on Ijwi benefitted at the expense of the vast majority, who suffered through occupation, taxation, and expropriation.

But king and commoners were most often united against the external foe and their internal allies.

Court and commoner, therefore, were not always the most salient categories of political activity, and the political fault lines among factions on Ijwi became blurred. In fact there were many political fault lines involved. In different contexts, different criteria were operative; in any given instance, multiple definitions might be at work simultaneously: region, status, ritual prominence, alliance ties, and a variety of short-term political considerations all molded the shape of confrontation over and beyond the simple categories of court and commoner. Access to outside power and the availability of external resources were just additional factors to be seized on by one or another of the internal competing factions. But in most cases they were utilized by court actors. Even while some commoners have benefitted from outside occupation (by Rwandan, Belgian, or Zairean officials), and even while the secular trend has been to strengthen the presence of outside power, many more Bany'Iju have struggled—and still do—against the intrusion of such outside power; many have had no choice. Kings and commoners were often united in these struggles, and the struggle against court exactions was often phrased in terms of the struggle against outside power—often fought in the name of preserving "traditional" (i.e., reciprocal more than exploitative) court relations to the population. In recent times this form of struggle has become less prominent, as court members (and others) have tightened their ties with the outside administrative powers (and as such influences have become increasingly dominant). But historically, political relations on the island have been expressed more eloquently through the ambiguities of the struggle between "kings and clans" than through the struggle between "court and commoners," appealing as that imagery may be.

But to note that kings and clans were the major categories of social identity on Ijwi in the early nineteenth century is not to diminish the political dimension of social change on the island. Viewed as a historical phenomenon, the concept of clan is pre-eminently a political concept. It includes ethnicity, class, and faction, but goes beyond each. When the empirical record is examined carefully, clans can be seen as both political constructs and important factors of political dynamics. To phrase the essential character of political dynamics on Ijwi as a simple opposition of court and commoners is to misconstrue the complexity of the record and misportray the subtlety of historical process on Ijwi. Acting through their clan identities, individuals came to see themselves as members of groups which simultaneously opposed and extended court power. Clans set clear limits on court power even while they served as channels of diffusion and indeed as the generators of dynastic hegemony, validating royalty as a political order; this represented a fundamental change from the earlier periods of Ijwi history.

Clan membership provided validation for certain leaders who enhanced their personal status by being simultaneously tied to royalty (through ritual) and by opposing royalty—by being in some contexts "above" the king, by representing a "correct" social order beyond the immediate power of the king, by naming the king, by providing the elements essential to proper kinghood, by guaranteeing the fertility of the island through Muganuro, and by serving as validation of the ties of the *bagunda* (the commoners) to kingship. Looked at in full historical perspective, therefore, the situation was not so bipolar as the phrase "court and commoner" might suggest. Despite the difficulties of defining "court" and "commoner" as opposed concepts, kings and clans still served as the operative concepts in understanding this fluid process of social change; the relations of these two groupings better capture the opposition-cum-encapsulation of the two categories (court and clans) which so typified the processes at work.

Conclusion

As the last three chapters have shown, the establishment of Ijwi kingship was a complex process extending over a long period. It was affected by the evolving conditions in Rwanda east of the lake and the mainland south of the lake, as well as by the particular events that occurred on Ijwi itself. But the establishment of kingship was a process which was more than the sum of these discrete events; it was also a product (as well as a cause) of changing conceptions on the island itself. Taken alone, the events which tell us how this happened are not sufficient in themselves to explain why it happened.

Kingship was more than simply the presence of a king, and ultimately the establishment of royalty could not be achieved (and certainly could not be accounted for) by marriage patterns, choice of residence, and alliance ties alone. These were necessary, but not sufficient, conditions for royalty. Just as marriage ties which first seemed to provide alliance later appeared as a limitation to the integration of kingship, other factors soon became more important than the mere presence of a royal family. Political integration of this type takes place on a much wider scale than can be accounted for in terms of marriage alliances and personal interactions alone.

Earlier chapters have attempted to bring out some of the initial processes which contributed to the establishment of royalty. This and the preceding chapters have discussed the condition of Basibula arrival, the types of alliance patterns they entered into, and the widening identities they may have encouraged. But a major concern has also been to supplement the previous chapters by indicating how the earlier deepening distinctions within Ijwi society reinforced the growing Ijwi focus, by making it possible for separate groups to relate independently to the new power. From this a new type of interaction emerged based on prestige, and thereby encouraged still further the growing clan awareness by encouraging a common Ijwi-wide focus.

Thus by the end of the eighteenth century the Basibula had been established as a royal lineage at the south end of the lake. But a succession struggle led to the expulsion of Kabwiika, one of the contenders to the "drums" (the royal succession). Later, Kabwiika's son Mwendanga, allied with the powerful Babambo family, returned to contest the drums yet again. Although Mwendanga did not succeed in claiming the drums, his Babambo allies killed the *mwami* (Kabwiika's former rival). As a result, the Basibula royal family withdrew from the area and established their rule farther north along the lakeshore, at a place called Irhambi (in the area of present-day Katana). Mwendanga stayed in the area of the earlier Basibula kingdom, but he also extended his influence to Ijwi Island. Here he was close enough to the mainland to maintain his earlier influence, but enough removed to escape the competing influences which began to be felt in the area from the east (Rwanda), south (Bushi), and west (Buhavu, the kingdom of the mainland Basibula). From genealogical data, tie-ins with the Rwandan traditions, and supporting data from several different clan groups, Mwendanga's arrival on the island can be placed towards the end of the first quarter of the nineteenth century, perhaps during the decade 1815–1825; it is likely that he was already a mature adult, probably in his late thirties or forties at the time.[19]

Mwendanga's ties on Ijwi were never very strong; his influence there was exerted primarily through other clans serving as intermediaries. He maintained his ties with the western mainland, and his principal residences remained there. It was not until the time of his successor that kingship on Ijwi became a significant influence on the island and recognized as distinct from other areas. The political separation of Ijwi from the mainland areas—from the east, as discussed in the chapters of part 2, and from the west, as discussed here in terms of the succession disputes—was crucial to the centralizing process on Ijwi. Rather than being related to a process of political expansion, centralization on Ijwi was related to an intensification of social relations on the island, to a narrowing of the political arena, both geographically and socially (as political activity became increasingly confined to the court and excluded many others outside this prestigious elite).

The declining political significance of external ties altered the nature of social interaction on Ijwi, and thus forced the question of the nature of power on the island. No clan was so predominant as to control power, as the succession disputes clearly indicate, with contenders in each dispute reaching outside the island. Instead of one clan predominating, power developed from the social interactions of the several clearly differentiated groups on Ijwi. These were reflected in the rituals of kingship, which tended to differentiate the groups still more, for they articulated their differences as corporate groups in the context of interaction within royalty. But royal rituals also brought groups together by their common focus on the kingship—formed of a small weak lineage whose major resource was the influence it derived from its claim to royal status.

Thus royalty was both a product of social interaction of a particular sort and an important element in the definition of this interaction. But most important, while it drew on traditions of royalty throughout the region, Ijwi royalty flourished because it was cut off from direct involvement within those emerging political spheres. Both interaction and autonomy were important. But interaction occurred in a much less direct fashion than the simple "diffusion of institutions" as portrayed in many sources on African history. Autonomy, on the other hand, was itself a product of events elsewhere in the region. Its role can be fully appreciated only by considering regional historical processes; it was less a product of independent evolution than the term may imply. What was unique to Ijwi Island was the way in which these derived concepts interacted with and accommodated to the perceptions and demands of the evolving social context.

The last two chapters have considered two factors which facilitated the integration of Basibula royalty into the Ijwi social network during the nineteenth century: still new immigrants to Ijwi, this time from the southwest; and marriage alliances. The arrival of significant numbers of family groups from the southwest provided the original impetus for the establishment of royal status. Arriving as part of a general pattern of two-way mobility—a demographic interplay between the islands and the southern mainland— these small familial groups did not polarize the social context on Ijwi, but their combined presence served to balance the eastern orientation of earlier Ijwi immigrants. Basibula settlement in the southwest of the island capitalized on this general immigration pattern, building on a momentum which was to transform the Basibula line from political exiles on the mainland to royalty on Ijwi. Marriage ties provided a second aspect of this transformation, by perpetuating earlier alliances and extending the alliance system to new families on Ijwi. And both immigration patterns and marriage alliances were significant for the material basis of kingship and the struggles over control of external resources.

The fourth and most important aspect of the formation of kingship on Ijwi was the creation or legitimation of ritual alliances and of royal ritual itself. Certain features of this process have been discussed in chapters 6 and 7 above. The next chapter will explore this aspect of the integration of kingship on Ijwi by describing the most important ritual of royalty and analyzing the roles of the various clans within it. For the rituals had meaning only within a given social context; the clan identities of the actors provided the social context within which that ritual meaning became manifest. But the collective rituals of royalty provided the arena for another dimension of the dialogue. Clan identities—defined in relation to other clans not by internal criteria— were articulated, reinforced, and given meaning by the roles which clans performed, through the ritualists, in the ritual performance of the kingship.

12
Kings and Clans on Ijwi
The Muganuro Ceremony

At the time of my research, Ijwi Island had witnessed only three enthronement ceremonies over the last 150 years, and no king had yet been buried on
Ijwi with the full royal ceremonies. Therefore the annual First Fruits ceremony, called Muganuro, was incontestably the most important single royal
rite on Ijwi. In many respects it still is. It is the only ritual which regularly
brings together all the ritualists *(bagingi)* and, beyond that, much of the population on Ijwi.

Although celebrated at the time of the sorghum harvest, the importance
of Muganuro on Ijwi does not revolve around its efficacy in assuring the
fertility of the crops, for the agricultural fertility of the island was not affected
when Muganuro was suspended on Ijwi, during Rwabugiri's occupation and
during most of colonial rule. On the contrary, fertility and well-being are the
justification for, not the consequence of, Muganuro.[1] Muganuro is important
because it reaffirms or re-creates the spirit of well-being through common
participation in royalty. It is pre-eminently a ritual celebrating royalty.

More than any other single factor, it is the participation of Ijwi ritualists
within the Muganuro ceremony which relates kingship to Ijwi society. But
Muganuro clearly draws on a set of ritual forms and symbols and concepts
common throughout the area. Therefore, while the participants in Muganuro
relate royalty to the specific Ijwi context, the structure of the rituals relates
kingship historically to the wider regional context. These two dimensions—
Ijwi historical specificity and regional cultural legitimacy—most clearly intersect in Muganuro.

An explanation of the nature of kingship on Ijwi therefore has to account
for both the structural continuities of the ritual throughout the region and its
local evolution on Ijwi. This chapter will try to account for this dialogue of
regional and local factors within the ceremony of kingship. It will first provide a brief description of the ceremony. It will then consider the groups
participating (or not participating), and discuss the historical evolution of the

ritual. Finally, it will examine the Ijwi Muganuro ceremony within the wider historical perspective of similar rituals held throughout the region.

Behind the ideology of participation lies the potential of royal power on Ijwi, to be sure. But that power is today limited—not only by state power from outside but also by the hegemony of popular participation, manifested in the rites of kingship from within. And this seems always to have been the case. The historical data strongly suggest that this ritual of royalty derives not from the royal family (as royal ideology would hold), but from ritual concepts common to the region at the level of the family, as well as at the level of royalty. An interpretation based on the historical record therefore is at odds with the ideological hegemony of the royal court. In what follows, the data presented in previous chapters will be drawn on to explore the forms and limits to the prevailing hegemony of popular participation.

The Muganuro Ceremony[2]

Muganuro is an important ritual occasion, but it is also a social occasion—*the* social occasion of the island. To most Bany'Iju this is its primary characteristic. Time and again, Muganuro was described to me as the occasion when people come together, dance, drink beer, and greet each other and the *mwami*. Almost no one described the ceremony in terms of the prescribed ritual forms, and this seems not to have derived from any esoteric character of the ritual but from the fundamental way in which the ceremony—and the ritual itself—was thought of.

As a public ceremony, then, Muganuro is both social and ritual. But in Muganuro the social and the ritual spheres are not separate categories; they are united, for Muganuro is the ritual expression of the social unity of Ijwi. As ritual, Muganuro is simultaneously an expression of social organization and the source of social organization, because social structure is perceived in the same categories as those articulated in the course of the ritual. In this sense the ritual, the expression of kingship, "creates" the very classifications by which society is ordered. Muganuro, "a ritual of royalty," plays the central role in the reproduction of social categories.

During the week before the ceremonies the *mwami* visited the former residence of his father at Cisiiza, near Buholo, the site of the Muganuro celebration. (Buholo and Cisiiza are near the center of the southern portion of Ijwi.) From that time normal activities of the court were suspended; throughout Muganuro the *bagingi* paid court in a continuous séance. This is the one time (aside from enthronement) when all three major *bagingi*, in fact all *bagingi*, come together in their ritual roles. Muganuro represents in a literal way, therefore, the integration of Ijwi society and the integration of kingship within that society.

The formal ceremonies began with the arrival of the royal drum, Kalinga, at dusk on the evening before the public ceremony. The elaborate cortege accompanying Kalinga was headed by Munyakalinga, the drum ritualist; it included three drums, all wrapped in fine woven mats. Munyakalinga, each of the drums, and many of the crowd of accompanying people wore the red flowers of the *omugowha* tree *(Erythrina)*, a plant prominent in many of the public rituals on Ijwi, both royal and non-royal. The arrival of the drums set off a flurry of excitement in the failing light of dusk; many drums beat out their welcome, and throngs of people sang, danced, and clapped their greeting to the drums. The *mwami* himself came out of the enclosure and enthusiastically clapped his greeting to the drums. It was a moment of gaiety and rejoicing, and the general festivities and drumming continued well into the evening.

The drumming began again well before sunrise the next morning, and would continue throughout most of the day. But the major focus of this prelude to the events of the day was the slaughter of a bull, a process carried out in an elaborately formal manner. This took place in a courtyard directly behind the principal hut, Kagondo, where the ritual drum Kalinga was kept throughout the ceremony. The bull was killed with a long knife *(ngorho)*, and placed on its back with the horns impaled in the ground. Through the upper lip was placed an *olusiro*, a bouquet formed of the branches of *eralire, omugohwa, olushasha,* and *umuhunjuhunju* leaves (to be discussed below), and Nyarushara, the principal iron ritual element. Against Nyarushara were placed two other iron implements, Walengere and Olugusho.[3]

The blood from the slaughtered bull was carefully collected in wooden bowls, and the hide was removed with great care, because it would later be used in making one of the royal drums. Portions of the carcass were carefully excised and placed on two stakes, one on each side of the bull. Mushaho (one of the three principal ritualists) sat at the head of the bull, separated from it by the bouquet and the iron regalia, and seated between the two stakes holding the portions of meat. The meat was then taken to Kagondo, the hut where it was later to be prepared and communally eaten by the *bagingi*.

The central Muganuro rituals took place later in the day. The king, dressed in a long robe draped over his right shoulder, wore a leopard skin over that, and the prescribed regalia. The single most important ritual item was the *ishungwe*, the royal diadem formed of three cowries, worn on the king's forehead and fastened with a leather thong. Small pieces of ivory strung together (with red beads separating them) formed the *icirezi*, another headband worn below the *ishungwe*. Aside from the headbands, the *mwami* wore an *enyonga*, a long leather necklace that hung almost to his waist; the pendant hanging from this is said to contain certain remains of his predecessors. On his right arm, the *mwami* wore the *gahengeri,* a bell amulet attached to his biceps, and the *olulinga,* a massive copper bracelet. The *bashibahali,* an amulet in woven fiber worn on his left biceps, and the *olugolo,* an ivory bracelet worn on his left wrist, completed the *mwami*'s regalia. In addition, two *bagingi* wore regalia: Mushaho wore an *ishungwe* with two cowries, an ivory bracelet, and a copper bracelet, and Cirunga (also of the Bashaho clan) wore an *ishungwe* with two cowries. Both *bagingi* were dressed in white cloth and wore pure white cattle egret feathers on their heads.

The actual ceremonies began very simply. Holding the ritual bouquet, the *mwami* left Kagondo, the hut where he had donned his regalia and where the principal drum, Kalinga, was kept throughout the ceremony. Two Bashaho *bagingi* accompanied him: Mushaho carried the iron regalia and Cirunga held a wooden bowl of water. The *mwami* strode onto the portico in front of Kambere, the hut facing the entrance to the enclosure; hundreds of people had jammed into the area directly in front of Kambere.[4] Dipping the leaves into the water carried by Cirunga, the *mwami* asperged the population.

Then began the public ceremonies. The *mwami* entered the hut directly and was seated on the *ntebe* (the wooden seat) just inside the entrance, flanked by Mushaho to his right and Cirunga to his left. During most of the events to follow, the *mwami* was almost completely hidden from the outside; he assumed the role of quasi spectator. The important actors in the rituals were the *bagingi* and regalia. Prominently displayed at the center of the raised portico to Kambere were the iron regalia; they were placed in the same formation as at the head of the bull earlier in the day: Nyarushara in the center, with Walengere leaning against the right arm and Olugushu against the left. In front of these regalia were four spears standing upright. Slightly to the right was Ngobosa, a delicate, forked, wooden instrument about six feet in height. Fifty feet or so in front of the hut were the two smaller ritual drums of the kingdom, Ndamutsa (also named Murhatwa) and Cihumuliza. The *mwami* sat directly behind the regalia, aligned with Kalinga (the principal royal drum, located within Kagondo, the hut directly behind Kambere), the iron regalia (Nyarushara, Walengere, and Olugushu), and the smaller drums (Ndamutsa and Cihumuliza). This pattern was maintained throughout the ceremony. In many respects, as this pattern illustrates, the *mwami* served as a surrogate Kalinga; rather than glorifying the *mwami* personally, the ceremony was built around the concepts of testing and strengthening him—and "placing him," that is, assigning him a place—within the context of kingship.

The first portion of the ceremony was initiated when Munyakalinga took up Ngobosa, on the portico of Kambere. Among the leather thongs hanging from Ngobosa was an *ngisha,* a ritual whistle made from an antelope horn. This type of whistle is often associated with occult power capable of being directed with devastating effect. Munyakalinga first took the Ngobosa and made a speech glorifying the strength and power of the kingdom and its king, Ntambuka; no enemy of the kingdom, it was said, could escape the power of this curse, and all those who held ill feelings against the kingship (ubwami) would be destroyed. During this speech, Munyakalinga turned Ngobosa first towards the mwami and then towards all the neighboring countries, directing Ngobosa to the three directions outside the hut: along the axis of the hut first, then right, then left. He blew into the ngisha, producing a long piercing whistle.

Munyakalinga then left the portico and went to the drums Ndamutsa and Cihumuliza. There, he repeated the words, extolling the kingdom and cursing its enemies. Again he whistled into an ngisha, this one attached to Ndamutsa. He took up Ndamutsa, greeting the kingdom in a loud voice (in common speech, "ndamutsa" means "I greet you"). In a very dramatic pose held in silence for some time, he placed the drum on his left thigh, the drumstick in his right hand poised above the drumhead. Suddenly and very deliberately, he beat a single beat on the drum. The population, including the mwami himself, broke into applause. Munyakalinga then proceeded with three equally deliberate beats on Ndamutsa, with long pauses and a dramatic stance between each one. This time there was no applause, but following the fourth stroke a single tone, drawn out for several seconds, was sounded on Mpembe, the ritual ivory trumpet.

Carrying Ndamutsa, Munyakalinga then advanced about 10 feet towards the hut, quickly assumed his earlier dramatic pose, poised over the drum and paused thus for several seconds in the absolute silence, before again striking Ndamutsa a single stroke. Immediately Mpembe was sounded, this time with several short blasts preceding another long drawn-out tone, and the process was thus repeated. Several times Munyakalinga advanced, paused, and struck. And each time, to a total of four, Ndamutsa was answered with one tone (or sometimes several short tones and one long) on Mpembe, until Munyakalinga stood with Ndamutsa on the very edge of the portico. Here the sequence was repeated once again, but with still longer and more deliberate pauses. The tension by then had mounted until it was almost perceptible—in the people's faces, in their poses, in the silence around, and in the repeated drama of the pose and response.

After striking Ndamutsa on the very edge of the portico and after the long extended response of Mpembe, Munyakalinga stepped onto the portico himself and struck four moderately spaced beats on Ndamutsa. Another Mwiiru then took up Cihumuliza, the smaller of the two smallest ritual drums, and with very little ceremony beat a steady one-beat rhythm directly up to the portico.

As Cihumuliza joined Ndamutsa on the portico with the iron regalia, the tension was released. A long ululation by the women was immediately joined by the rhythms of nine non-ritual drums. Inside Kambere, Mukwiza-nyundo, one of the Bashaho *bagingi,* took up the iron regalia. He moved Nyarushara in a circular motion over the head of the *mwami,* then placed the tip of Walengere at the chest of the *mwami,* moving it up over his face and forehead, and also passed it once around the head of the *mwami.* Immediately the applause, cheering, dancing, and movement shattered the earlier crystal-line silence. The sounds of Mpembe, the drums, the dancing were to con-tinue for 45 minutes and more. The royal bull (Rusanga) and ram (also Rusanga), each accompanied by other cattle and sheep, were brought into the enclosure (to be led out after a short time), and the *bagingi* left Kambere to dance in a large circle before the royal hut. From time to time others dashed out from the crowd in front of Kambere and recited their praise poetry to the drums, to the regalia, and to the king.

The next episode occurred about an hour later. Six of the non-ritual drums were taken out of the enclosure to meet the procession accompanying the new harvest of sorghum and millet. By the time this procession reached the gates of the enclosure, it had attracted a large and excited crowd. It was led by six of the large royal drums and a troop of special dancers. These were followed by Kakomere, the Munyambiriri ritualist, carrying an *omugohwa* flower in his hair (as indeed did many others in the entourage) and with a garland of leaves of various types (including *eralire*) around his neck. Behind him came two men, each carrying on his head a container of grain; one brought *bulo* (millet), the other *mahemba* (sorghum). As they entered the en-closure, the excitement again reached a high pitch, with drumming, ulula-tions, and trumpet blasts joining in the deafening welcome.

Amid the noise and general pandemonium, Kakomere, the *mugingi* responsible for the cultivation of the *bulo,* walked slowly and deliberately to the portico of Kambere. He took some of both the millet and sorghum and sprinkled them over the king, over himself, and over the people just outside Kambere. The *mwami* took the grain and immediately passed it back to others, who took it to the kitchen area behind Kambere. There the grain was ground into flour by the ritually prescribed wife of the king, of the Beshaza clan; later she was joined in this work by other wives of the king and the *bagingi* as well. The sorghum and millet flour were mixed with water, and short bamboo sticks were dipped into this mixture. Kakomere took up each stick separately and sucked the mixture off it. The ground millet and sor-ghum flour was mixed with a variety of leaves and other substances, includ-ing some of the *mubande,* the substance made of ritual prescribed earth and dried herbs. Later still, this mixture was taken out in front of Kambere where it was fed to the two *nsanga* (Rusanga-bull and Rusanga-ram).

Shortly after, four drums left yet again, this time to return accompanying the procession of the fish, the third element of the ceremony. Once again a crowd accompanied the arrival of the fish, and once again the *mugingi* (this time, Nzuki, a Mulega) wore an *omugowha* flower and a garland—and he carried an *omugera*, a thin iron spear about four feet long. The live fish was carried in a pot of water. In front of Kambere, it was impaled on the *omugera* and presented to the *mwami* and the *bagingi*. Once again the *mwami* took the *omugera* and returned it so the fish could be prepared with the other food.

This ended the public rituals, and for most people, the rest of the evening was left to dancing, drumming, and meeting: "All the people come together and dance and share beer." Finally, the *mwami* and *bagingi* alone ate the fish, the *mubande* (mixed with flour prepared from the sorghum-millet grain), and the selected portions of meat taken from the bull slaughtered that morning.

The following day, parts of the ceremony—the ritual attire, the asperging of the population by the *mwami,* and the drama of the drums (with the Ngobosa and the drums Ndamutsa and Cihumuliza)—were exactly repeated. But this time the enclosure was virtually empty; only those directly involved with the ceremony or with the king's entourage were present. And the public ceremony included only the presentation of the drums. The repetition of the drum ceremony alone therefore tended to bracket the presentation and consumption of the grain and the fish; by their very omission, these two elements of the preceding day's ceremony found renewed emphasis. The ceremony of the second day also emphasized the significance of the popular participation in the previous day's festivities, again by its very absence on the second day.

The Bagingi and the Muganuro Ceremony

Each of the three principal clans involved in Muganuro, the Bashaho, the Baziralo (Beeru), and the Banyambiriri, plays a different role with regard to kingship on Ijwi, and these different roles are best reflected in the rituals. The personnel of Muganuro therefore illustrate the specific relations of social groups to kingship on Ijwi. But the meaning of the social relations expressed through ritual is best elucidated by the nature of the rituals themselves: in the recurrent themes apparent in them, and in the relationships among the different segments of the ritual. This and the next section will consider these two aspects of the ritual as it was performed in the early 1970s, whereas the two sections to follow will look at the Muganuro in historical perspective, on Ijwi and in the wider region.

The Bashaho are the most numerous actors within the ceremony. Their role is enhanced because in the Muganuro context they always appear with the king, dress similarly to him, and handle the same (or similar) regalia.

The three most important Bashaho *bagingi* are Mushaho, Cirunga, and Mukwizanyundo. In addition to serving the *mwami*, Mushaho presides over the slaughter of the bull and the division of the meat, sitting in a position exactly analogous to that of the *mwami* during later ceremonies: facing the regalia and aligned with the regalia and the bull.[5]

The two other prominent Bashaho in the ceremony, Cirunga and Mukwizanyundo, are ritual blacksmiths, responsible for the iron regalia.[6] But the Bashaho do not have a reputation as smiths on Ijwi outside this ritual context; no one I spoke with could recall other Bashaho smiths of the past. The most renowned blacksmiths on Ijwi are the Balega of Bushovu; during the forging of the iron instruments, Mirimba, a Mushovu,[7] must be present to strike the first blow with the *nyundo* (the forging hammer) on Nyarushara. But no Mushovu takes part directly in the public ritual ceremonies of Muganuro.[8] The Bashaho role as ritual smiths in Muganuro therefore seems to result more from the conjunction of Bashaho domination of the royal rituals with the prominent symbolic role of the iron regalia than as a reflection of earlier Bashaho economic activities (as smiths) on the island.[9]

The relationship of the Baziralo (and especially that of Munyakalinga) to the king has been discussed in chapter 7 above. Of all the *bagingi*, the keeper of the drums is the most independent of the king and court; he maintains the greatest sense of being a *mwami emwage* (i.e., a *mwami* in his own domain), and he is the most likely to speak out against the *mwami* in meetings of the *bagingi*. Throughout Muganuro, Munyakalinga received great deference; especially at the arrival of the drums, the *mwami* greeted him effusively. A representative of the western line of Bashamvu (the Baziralo on Mpene) was also present and took an active part in Muganuro. His role, however, was markedly different from that of Munyakalinga: rather than being in ritual opposition to the king, he appeared only with the *mwami*.

The Banyambiriri are another important clan in this ceremony. Most important among them is Kakomere Bilali, from Cibishwa (Lemera village); he is responsible for planting, cultivating, and presenting the *bulo* (millet) and the *mahemba* (sorghum) used at the Muganuro ceremony. On a command from the king, the *bulo* is planted at night, on a tiny plot. Transporting the *bulo* to Muganuro is a ritual in itself: Kakomere and members of his immediate household must wear the red flowers of *omugohwa* and a garland of leaves around their necks, and Kakomere himself is dressed in a white robe. There is a degree of license involved, because Kakomere can demand gifts from those he meets on the way, and others line the way to greet him as he passes with the *bulo*.[10]

Birahinda, another Munyambiriri *mugingi*, is also referred to as Kakomere ("Kakomere k'Ishungwe"). Although he himself does not take part directly in the Muganuro ceremony, he is responsible for the preparation of the *mubande* which is mixed with the *bulo*. This food is then fed to the two *nsanga* and eaten by the *mwami* with the *bagingi* in the central rite of Muganuro.[11] As with the Bashaho smithing ritualists, Birahinda's association with the *mubande* is largely ritual; generally, the man most closely associated with the *mubande* is Gahamire Mondo, a specialist in herbal medicines and an expert in the preparation of *mubande* in other contexts (outside Muganuro). Although not directly involved in Muganuro, Gahamire is included in some of the other royal rituals (such as those at the death of Rusanga). The indications are that he has been only recently included in these rituals, through his personal ties at the court and his status as elder *mushake* (herbalist).[12] He is the only member of the Bakanga clan incorporated into the rituals.

The third episode of Muganuro is the presentation of the fish. This function is undertaken by Nzuki, a Mulega (of the Babambo subclan), who lives at the extreme southern tip of Ijwi, very close to the mainland. As noted, the fish is brought live to Muganuro and is presented to the *mwami,* impaled on an *omugera,* a long, thin, iron rod formerly used for fishing.[13] This is one of three roles performed by the Balega as *bagingi*. Aside from Nzuki, however, the other two Balega ritualists are not prominent in Muganuro. The role of Mirimba has been discussed above, with that of the Bashaho blacksmiths; the other Mulega ritualist is Njogero, a Mubambo, the ritual maternal uncle of the kings, who plays no part in the Muganuro ceremony.

In addition to the principal *bagingi* mentioned, many others are involved, directly or indirectly. Some of those are in charge of Rusanga, the royal bull, or the royal herd associated with Rusanga (either as herdsman or as milker for this herd). Others are in charge of various forging tasks, such as Mirindi, or Kasindi (another Mushaho ritual smith, responsible for forging Olugushu), or Ntandira (who brings water from a designated spring to cool Nyarushara as it is forged, and to contain its vital force during its transition from iron bar to potent ritual instrument). Ruzuba, the Muloho who publicly pronounces the name of the new king at the time of accession, is present but plays no direct role. And there are many others with individualized functions.

Each *mugingi* looks to Muganuro as his celebration, whether or not he has a formal task in the ceremony. Muganuro is important to *bagingi,* for even while they act as intermediaries, Muganuro separates them from the commoners. But perhaps even more important is the way in which Muganuro separates the various *bagingi* from one another. The nature of the tasks and the clearly defined division of ritual tend to distinguish each *mugingi,* clarifying his own unique identity against the others. At the broadest level, however, the ceremony as a whole brings the *bagingi* together, as illustrated in the core of the ritual, the presentation and consumption of food. These agricultural products are not presented to the king alone; they are presented, through the king, to the entire kingdom and consumed by all the *bagingi* (and entirely consumed at Muganuro). Muganuro is therefore a social ritual *par excellence:* both symbolically and literally it brings people together.

The Social Meaning of Muganuro

Muganuro does much more than bring people together in kingship; it also unites them as social groups—and divides them into social units. The ritual of Muganuro is the most dramatic expression of the fact that the unity of kingship is forged of many different elements. These diverse social elements, whose independent evolution has been described in the preceding chapters, are both distinguished from each other by kingship and collectively embedded in the concept of kingship. The lines of demarcation between clans are more clearly articulated in this ritual than in any other social context on Ijwi. This section will illustrate how this underlying conception is expressed in different aspects of the Muganuro ceremony.

The heart of the Muganuro ritual is the opposition portrayed between centralization and differentiation. In the royal rituals each clan performs its ritual functions autonomously of the others, and the ritual roles therefore stress the exclusive nature of clan identities. Indeed participation in the rituals may well be an important factor in creating, or perpetuating, these social identities, even where they may have derived originally from other historical circumstances (such as independent arrival). But in addition to the focus on clan participation in Muganuro, the focus on kingship itself is also important to the royal rituals. While rituals such as Muganuro and enthronement help define clan classifications, they also define the king and thus re-create kingship. They are the purest expression of *ubwami* on Ijwi and the ultimate legitimizing factor of kingship; it is only in these ritual contexts that the *mwami* is said to "reign" *(ayimiika).*

Because clan differentiation is central to the expression of the integration of the kingdom, the royal rituals are strongly preoccupied with the separation of the various elements of kingship.[14] Many aspects of the ritual illustrate the process of defining, legitimizing, and separating the elements formerly (or subsequently to be) combined in kingship: the different cuts of meat from the bull, the different clans among the *bagingi,* and the different foods presented. Once separated, these elements are then recombined in a new context: the meat, grain, and fish are consumed by all the *bagingi* together as well as by the *mwami* (and the two *nsanga,* bull and ram). The importance given to *mubande* in the ceremony reflects the same theme: *mubande* is both earth and plant, soil and food, productive quality and produced element. It is a powerful protective medicine as well as a potent healing element; it is used in sorcery cases as well as to heal physical illness. Part of its potency and danger stems from the very fact of the conjunction of categories represented in the physical elements of which it is composed.

The slaughter of the bull and the division of the meat reflect these processes of separation and recombination. A segment of each portion of meat—heart, lung, liver, intestines, as well as many other cuts—is placed on two stakes near the head of the bull; these portions are later prepared and eaten by the assembled *bagingi*. Thus the various constituent parts are separated—and in the process identified. They are then reintegrated in the communal feast, which brings together all the *bagingi*. By consuming the sacrificial victim in common, the participants share in the sacral nature of the sacrifice at two levels: they share of the victim, and they share with each other. As sacrificial victim, the bull thus mediates on two axes. The first is the opposition of one constituent element to another within the same analytical plane. This applies both to the segments of meat taken from the bull and to the separation of the clans within the kingdom. The second level of meaning is represented in the opposition of the whole to the parts, since the bull is first divided into its "constituent parts" and then "reassembled" and eaten communally. In an analogous process Muganuro separates the clans (by identifying each with a separate function) and reunites them in kingship.[15]

As with the meat, the plants used in asperging the population also represent the concept of separation, but this is expressed through the symbolism of the plants themselves rather than by their relation to each other. One plant within the *olusiro* (the bouquet carried by the *mwami*), named *eralire*, is a potent symbol of power, purity, and separation; it is often planted near a house to ward off harm and protect the inhabitants from sorcery. Another (*umuhunjuhunju* or *umutudu*) is planted at the homestead enclosure; it thus separates the domestic realm from the outside world. A third plant *(olushasha)* is used in the burials of the king and the two *nsanga;* it thus helps mediate between (but also symbolically establishes the boundaries between) the worlds of the living and the deceased. *Olushasha* is also spread on the portico of Kambere before the ceremony of Muganuro begins (and was used in the past at the doors of commoner homes). The fourth plant of the *olusiro, omugohwa,* is used frequently to define ritual occasions; it is present at weddings, births, the accession of a new homestead head, during the first presentation of a newborn child to his or her grandparents, at Ryangombe rites and blood-brotherhood ceremonies, and at royal rituals. Thus it, too, has a connotation of separation, that of defining the ritual and sacral realm apart from the profane, and is associated with defining the boundaries between different statuses.

Similarly the various clans involved in the principal episodes of Muganuro arrive at the ceremony separately. The distinct functions which make up Muganuro are each performed by one clan alone (though the ritual roles may be duplicated within that clan[16]). A given ritual function therefore provides an exclusive identity to a particular clan. But if this is the only time when the individual clans act in such exclusive roles and identify in a quasi-corporate way, it is also the most prominent occasion when the clans (or certain clan members) come together with each other in prescribed clan roles.[17] While the drums, the regalia, the grain, and the fish are each the responsibility of one clan individually, each element—and each *mugingi*—becomes ritually powerful only when combined with the others. Therefore despite the exclusive nature of clan identity expressed in Muganuro roles, these identities do not emerge simply by direct interaction with other clans, but rather through their common participation in kingship. In this way Muganuro reaffirms the role of kingship as providing the essential structure for social identification.

Throughout the ceremony then there is a constant juxtaposition of the two concepts of separation and unity. The division of the bull into its constituent elements and their recombination in the ritual meal is analogous to the separation of the clans by their different functions and their recombination when the *bagingi* consume the meal together. The analogy can be carried further, since the bull (formed of the different portions of meat) and the kingdom (formed of different clans) also appear in analogous situations in the ceremony. While the bull is slaughtered the iron regalia are placed at his head in a formation that is exactly replicated during the public Muganuro ceremonies, when the regalia are placed at the entrance to Kambere. During the slaughter of the bull Mushaho sits at the bull's head in a position analogous to that of the *mwami* during the public ceremony; the iron regalia thus mediate between the king and clans (the kingdom), just as they do between Mushaho (a surrogate in some respect for the *mwami*) and the bull.[18]

The significance of kingship as a context for interaction among the clans is expressed in the markedly restrained role of the king during Muganuro.[19] (This posture was duplicated during the enthronement ceremonies I witnessed several years later, when a younger and more vigorous king acceded to power—and during a ritual that one might expect would celebrate the king.) In fact the rituals underscored the king's subordination to the larger ritually defined kingdom. Thus the role of the *mwami* in this instance was a ritually prescribed stance, not a personal characteristic. During Muganuro (as during the enthronement ceremonies), the king for the most part remains within Kambere, and the action focusses on the non-royal participants and regalia. He formally receives the items brought by other *bagingi;* these items must pass through his hands before being prepared for communal consumption, but the king remains a passive recipient, not an active initiator. The participants clearly do not derive their power from him, but from their communion with one another. The king represents their union, and his ritual power derives from that fact.

Therefore the king is not thought of as "divine" in the sense of being the unique depository of sacred forces of productivity and power. Instead he serves as mediator among the various conceptual categories which compose kingship; his mediation defines these categories by separating the constituent elements of the ceremonies even as he unites them in kingship. The ritual intensity of the position removes kingship from any clearcut space within the classificatory schema. But this ambivalence is a product of combining several categories simultaneously in kingship; kingship is not independent of or "above" the constituent elements of the kingdom. It is in its role as mediating between conceptual categories that kingship is thought of as sacral; the sacral aspect of kingship does not derive from the "divinity" of the king.[20]

The centralizing aspects of the ritual conceptions of kingship contrast with the centrifugal aspects of the political dimensions of kingship. At least during the initial stages of Basibula rule on Ijwi (up to c. 1870), political competition focussed on controlling the source of ritual power, and the ideological factors of kingship which reinforced the integrity of the whole (as expressed in the Muganuro rituals) were greater than the political forces acting towards segmentation.[21] But ritual centralization, although essential to the formation of kingship, did not guarantee political centralization. The two concepts were not identical, and the discrepancy between them marked the political evolution of the island. In fact the centralized ritual focus intensified the political struggles; it was in defining the arena of the struggle, not in the effectiveness of the political institutions, that the island was politically centralized in this early stage of kingship on Ijwi.[22]

Thus within the Muganuro ceremony on Ijwi, social differentiation reached its clearest articulation through the common participation in kingship by the different units of which it was composed. The clan structure of the island as it exists today is in large degree the product of the centralizing process that occurred on Ijwi and the emergence of the rituals now associated with kingship, even though those centralized structures were products of broader transformations within Ijwi society that occurred independently of kingship. Royal rituals in a sense created, validated, and reproduced the structure of clan identities on the island.

The meaning of the royal rituals goes beyond the ceremonies themselves, of course. They validated clan identities in a society which held no other corporate expression of clan membership (except, to some degree, in *bukumbi* relations). The ceremonies belonged to the *bagingi,* and the ritualists set limits on the power of any given individual to rule, at least in the long run; collectively, the ritualists served as an autonomous depository of political proprieties and a political sense of proportion. And on Ijwi they were both jealous guardians of their own (and others') autonomy and full participants in the royal rituals at the court. In fact, effective autonomy and active participation were mutually reinforcing characteristics of *bugingi* ritual status; the full practice of one assured the continued viability of the other.

But if they strengthened social categories within kingship, royal rituals also created a hegemony of social domination, by establishing and validating the hierarchical relations of kingship and the central role of the Basibula clan and court. We do not know with any certainty the emergent relations of production which accompanied this form of political power and social hierarchy (although chapter 10 has sketched out some broad possibilities). To confront the hegemony of the ritualists, those in power needed to accumulate resources. But after the accession of Kabego, the power base of the kings was essentially limited to Ijwi Island. Until the attacks of Rwabugiri, king of Rwanda in the late nineteenth century, the population (and the ritualists) on Ijwi were able to threaten withholding support for actions not within the range of royal behavior legitimated by the rituals and social consensus (as defined by the ritualists); ritual hegemony legitimized such forms of opposition—for example, in the refusal to recognize Nkundiye as sovereign or the refusal to accede to Mugenzi's demands on the population to provide tribute to the Belgian authorities.

To break through this barrier of local hegemony, various claimants to power on Ijwi had sought to turn elsewhere—off Ijwi—to accumulate resources for the purposes of political consolidation; in each case they failed, as we have seen. Outside power could be exerted in the short run: Mwendanga had driven off Nyamuziga; Rwabugiri had established some administrative presence on the island over a generation; colonial power had kept various pretenders in place for a time. But the hegemony of local ritualists was such that these outsiders were never able to acquire local power bases on the island. In each case, when the external context changed (e.g., with Rwabugiri's death or with decolonization) those who had based their power on access to outside resources lost their positions; they were never able to establish their own authority or their own local bases of support. (The situation today is of course very different, since it is not only royalty but commoners who seek outside resources; their solidarity as Bany'Iju is eroding.) Thus in the early years of emergent kingship the social hegemony was a hegemony of ritualists; their effectiveness in retaining this hegemony—defining right ways of thinking about social relations—was in combining strong political autonomy from the court with full ritual involvement with the kingship.

Parallel developments in Rwanda and Bushi appear to confirm this general conclusion. In Rwanda the balance seems to have been broken essentially because external warfare provided the court with access to outside resources. These were not material resources alone, but offices, status, and prestige to distribute, and the development of a new court ideology stressing hierarchical relations, social stratification, and court power. During the nineteenth century, the Rwandan court was able to use these externally derived resources against the internal population, and to enlarge the ritualist corporation to allow the king to name his own representatives among the ritualists. More important, these resources provided an alternative to the ritual hegemony which had previously confined court actions. Once the earlier cultural consensus had dissolved, power concentrated in the hands of the court could be used in new ways—for land control, taxation, or new forms of corvée. From the time of Cyilima Rujugira (in the mid-eighteenth century) through the reigns of Gahindiro (early nineteenth century) and Rwabugiri (in the late nineteenth century), there were signs of increasingly intense confrontations between court and ritualists, with the court seeking to portray the ritualists as anachronistic and their norms as atavistic: Cyilima introduced new religious authorities at the court, Gahindiro enlarged the corporation of ritual authorities (appointing his own men to their ranks), and Rwabugiri was constantly in conflict with the ritual authorities.

If in Rwanda the decline of ritualist hegemony was characterized by diminished ritualist participation at the court, in Bushi the political culture was marked by a strong sense of autonomy on the part of ritualists: the *bajinji* there appear always to have been more autonomous, and intent on preserving their autonomy at the cost of participation. Hence the ritualist corporation in Bushi was more an association of "former authorities" (increasingly becoming "dignitaries"), sometimes retaining considerable authority at the local level, but gradually losing influence at the central court. Without the full participation of the *bajinji* in the rituals of the central court, the political leaders appear to have become more removed from the population—at least that is the impression received from the sources currently available. "Drinking *mubande*" implies distributing seeds and meal from the central court to the local and domestic power-holders, thus symbolically reinforcing both their authority over others and the hierarchy of the political chain of command. Thus in Bushi the zealous autonomy of the *bajinji* appears to have led to a slow dissolution of ritualist hegemony and increasing independence of the central court; it also led to less administrative centralization than in Rwanda.[23]

The central court on Ijwi, by contrast, seems to have had neither the capacity for external conquest (to provide resources independent of local support) as in Rwanda, nor the political latitude to develop a court ideology autonomous of the ritualists seeking to withdraw from the central court arena (as in Bushi). On Ijwi the ritualists were validated by their role in kingship, but still saw themselves as opposed to the hierarchical powers of a given king. It was only with the changing external contexts in the later nineteenth and early twentieth centuries that this ritualist hegemony began to dissolve. In every case, kings on Ijwi came to power with the support of the ritualists, and found it useful to accept the hegemony of ritually defined institutions—both those of kingship and those of clanship. It was only later that clans on Ijwi—and the ritualists who represented them—would be seen either as points of confrontation and competition for kingship (as occurred in Rwanda) or as irrelevant (as in Bushi).

Changes in Muganuro on Ijwi

The prevailing climate of opinion on Ijwi states that Muganuro rituals came with Mwendanga and have been unchanged since that day, that Mwendanga arrived with all the *bagingi,* that the kingdom was created whole. When focussing on the rituals alone, most *bagingi* (and others) on Ijwi assume that ritualist families "always" filled their current roles; the present is extrapolated back into the indefinite past.

But, as we have seen, other data bring this assertion into question. They challenge both the manner of arrival of these rituals and their continuity. Differences in the meaning of *bugingi* status found on Ijwi today may represent an evolution of this concept. In the north, a *mugingi* is "someone who has his own domain; and no one can remove him from the place acknowledged as his own domain. He stays there in his own domain, like a *mwami* in his domain. That, that is true *bugingi.*"[24] *Bugingi* status in the north, therefore, is associated essentially with autonomy from royalty. In the south, on the other hand, *bugingi* status is more likely to be directly tied to kingship through a ritual role.[25]

The individual family histories of most *bagingi* provide another, and more direct, challenge to the ideology of *bugingi* status, because these histories diverge so clearly from the ideal noted above. In fact, they conform to a regular pattern which suggests that the present ritual forms were structured only during (or after) the reign of Kabego, the second king on Ijwi. Although Kabego's reign has not been our focus in the present study, this was clearly an important period for the institutional consolidation of kingship; both royal institutions and clan identities seem to emerge most strongly in the mid-nineteenth century under Kabego.

Of all the *bagingi,* the Bashaho are the most closely and directly identified with the person of the king. Their own social identity is very closely tied with their central role in ritual kingship, and consequently their conception of royal rituals is the least flexible of all the clans: they came with the king and they "always" enthroned the king, on Ijwi and even before their arrival on the island. Even those groups of Bashaho which retain traditions of an early (pre-Basibula) presence on Ijwi identify with the principal ritual role of the Bashaho at large.[26] Their ritual association with the iron regalia is also accounted for in these terms. Some Bashaho associate their ritual role with Nyiganda, the head of a prominent family in Bushi, of the Bashinjahavu clan; this family also holds the iron ritual instrument called Walengera, similar in shape to Walengere used on Ijwi, and preserved by the Bashaho blacksmith (Mukwizanyundo).[27] By claiming direct descent from a clan with similar ritual traditions in Bushi (and thus, by extension, claiming affiliation with other prestigious clans in the area—the Abega and Abashambo in Rwanda) the history of the Bashaho on Ijwi appears to substantiate the "state created whole" hypothesis: that ritual kingship on the island was imported in its entirety—and fully mature—from elsewhere.

It is possible that there exists some historical tie between the Bashaho rituals on Ijwi and the Bashinjahavu rituals in Bushi. But most evidence suggests that Ijwi kingship resulted from a long slow process of alliance formation on Ijwi, not from direct importation. One reference on Ijwi notes that the Bashaho arrived in a special relationship with Mwendanga, an alliance confirmed by independent data discussed in chapter 10. But it also clearly asserts that it was only under Kabego that the ritual of kingship began to take a recognizable form, with the incorporation of other clans:

> RESPONDENT: Mwendanga came to Ijwi with only two *bagingi*, Muguma and Gahindo [the ancestors of the respondent and of Mushaho, respectively]. Then the children of Muguma and Gahindo enthroned each *mwami*. . . . When Kabego was enthroned[28] he was enthroned by many clans. . . . But when Mwendanga arrived he came with the Bashaho, with Gahindo and Muguma [alone].
> AUTHOR: Since there are many *bagingi* here [now], did Mwendanga change the number of *bagingi?*
> RESPONDENT: No; he added no one. . . . Then they [Kabego, Ndogosa, and Ntambuka] saw the regalia were numerous, so they later distributed the regalia among other clans. But first, with Mwendanga, were the Bashaho.[29]

It is significant, too, that Gahindo is only the grandfather of the present Mushaho, himself a younger man today. In other words, it seems clear that even the *bugingi* status of the Bashaho (or this principal branch in terms of ritual status) stems from Kabego's time at the earliest.

Other *bagingi* also associate the formation of kingship in its present form with the reign of Kabego. In an interview at the Muganuro festivities themselves and in the presence of Mushaho, Cirunga (another important Mushaho ritualist) stated that the first ancestor of his family to serve as ritualist did so at the time of Kabego (not Mwendanga).[30] He added that Mpembe (the ivory trumpet) was also obtained by the ritualists from the kings in Irhambi during the reign of Kabego. This may reflect the ideology that kingship on Ijwi derived from Havu kingship (because Mwendanga descended from the Havu royal line); more likely it reflects the fact that Mpembe is seen as an instrument representative of the forest kingdoms (Butembo, Buhunde; the locative "Irhambi" can be applied either to the mainland Havu kingdom or to the forest kingdoms west of the mountains). But the important point is that—in contrast with the general ideology—it indicates the importance of Kabego's (not Mwendanga's) reign in the process of ritual elaboration.

Although the Bashaho ritual role may derive from a longstanding alliance with the Basibula, the roles of other *bagingi* seem to represent the influences of more local factors; many of them came to be included in the royal rituals through a process of ritual expansion (or devolution). The role of Bashaho as ritual smiths does not reflect any occupational associations of the Bashaho on Ijwi with smithing; on Ijwi it is the Balega who are the renowned smiths in the prosaic context. Mirimba is one of the few Balega with a ritual role, but his role is almost embarrassingly attenuated. It is his job to "reforge" Nyarushara at the beginning of each new reign: he brings banana beer of one-day fermentation *(kibabi)* and pours it on the iron implement. With Nyundo (the smith's hammer), he beats on Nyarushara (once only) and then gives it to Mukwizanyundo (the Mushaho smith) to "forge."[31] In the ritual itself, Mirimba consecrates the forging process; the beer is said to "cool" Nyarushara, or to control its ritual power. Mirimba also provides the symbolic initial blow. This ritual form serves to legitimize the further smithing roles of the Bashaho. Cirunga's statement that his family became ritualists under Kabego means that either the Balega were associated with ritualist status at that time (or after) in order to legitimate Cirunga's function (recalling claims to status as "owners of the soil" in agriculturalist rituals elsewhere) or that Cirunga's family replaced the former ritualist functions of the Balega. Either interpretation represents a significant alteration in ritual functions and casts doubt on the Bashaho arrival as ritualist smiths.

The traditions of the Baziralo also indicate that incorporation of *bugingi* status to kingship did not occur as a result of direct importation to Ijwi with the royal family. Chapter 7 discussed the evidence that the Baziralo line divided, and that the present line of Beeru, the sons of Mutemura, attained ritualist status only after the time of Rwabugiri (i.e., after 1895).[32] Traditions of the western Baziralo family on Mpene, on the other hand, claim that they in fact did hold *bugingi* status prior to Mutemura, and that they had come from Irhambi, bringing with them these ritualist traditions, only during the reign of Kabego.[33] Marriage ties confirm this claim: the first Muziralo *mugingi* under Kabego, a man named Rwamakaza, married a daughter of Kabego. Rwamakaza died shortly after Rwabugiri's first attack (c. 1870), and his son Ruhwiza was brought up at the home of his mother's sister's husband, a man named Mahugo. Mahugo had twice married into the royal family. One of his wives was a daughter of Balikage, Mwendanga's eldest son (who had lived in the north of Ijwi); after Balikage's death, this woman was closely associated with Kabego's household. Mahugo had also married a daughter of Kabego himself. Ruhwiza had therefore been brought up with close ties to the Ijwi royal family and was apparently a favorite at the court. The western Baziralo here still maintain a privileged status as quasi *bagingi* at Muganuro, but it is an unusual situation: they have status but no clearly defined role.

Alterations in the composition of the *bagingi* participating in royal rituals were not simply a matter of the gradual establishment of kingship, which, once implanted, continued unchanged. Changes among the *bagingi* with ritual status continued, extending even into more recent times. In one case, a family was deprived of *bugingi* status when the death of the ram Rusanga was attributed partially to their negligence. As Mbarata, a *mugingi* from the small island of Irhe, escorted the ram to Muganuro, he lodged for the night at Nyakalengwa. There Rusanga was attacked and killed by a leopard. The ram was given a royal burial, but the ritualist family was not reinstated as *bagingi*.[34]

In another case, Rulinda, the present herdsman responsible for the bull Rusanga, notes that his family did not serve as *bagingi* until the time of Ndogosa's return from exile (after the end of Rwabugiri's occupation, i.e., after 1895). Rulinda's father had been a *murhunyi*, a court favorite, of Kabego. As in other cases, marriage ties help record and confirm this alliance: Rulinda (the father of the present *mugingi*) had married the daughter of Kabego's eldest son, Rugina. On Rugina's death (see chapter 11) his children had been cared for directly by the royal court, and this close relationship of Rugina's daughter with the court continued even after her marriage to Rulinda. Thus Rulinda's family, especially the children of Mwarugina (the daughter of Rugina), had been brought up as part of the larger family of the court; Rulinda's later appointment as *mugingi* only confirmed this status.[35] Still another *mugingi*, this time an important participant in Muganuro, also claims recent *bugingi* status for his family. Mushengezi Munyama, the ritualist in charge of presenting the fish, noted that his family had participated in Muganuro only since the time of Ndogosa.[36]

Thus ritualist status is not an unchanging category, nor does Muganuro serve as a charter to Ijwi society as it was constituted on the arrival of Mwendanga. It includes groups which arrived independently of the royal family as well as early allies of the Basibula. But although Muganuro is an evolving institution, it is not necessarily subject to short-term fluctuations. While it is open to change it also tends to retard changes and to channel change. Thus on Ijwi, Muganuro has helped to reinforce and preserve social differentiation within kingship. By focussing clan identities on royalty it has helped maintain identity differences, and simultaneously prevented differentiation from becoming so factionalized as to pose a threat to kingship itself. To the degree that royal rituals remained the principal source of social prestige, and as long as no alternative sources of wealth, prestige, and power provided any serious challenge to kingship in this regard, the rituals of royalty remained the essential "capital good" of kingship—that is, they served as mechanisms that most defined the character of social relations.

Ijwi Muganuro in the Regional Context

In addition to integrating kingship into Ijwi society, the royal rituals also tied Ijwi kingship to the larger region. For while there were alterations in Muganuro resulting from the specific Ijwi context, there were broad regional continuities at work as well. Comparison of the Ijwi Muganuro with similar royal rituals among neighboring kingdoms illustrates the degree to which Ijwi kingship was a product of a set of concepts shared throughout the region, as well as a result of local historical development.

The Umuganura Ceremony in Rwanda

The royal rituals most similar to the Ijwi Muganuro rituals are found in Rwanda.[37] As was the case for Muganuro on Ijwi, the Umuganura ceremony in Rwanda was a First Fruits ceremony. It culminated in public ceremonies after the first harvest of sorghum, during the months of April and May, but as part of the same ritual, shorter ceremonies took place at intervals throughout the year, in August-September, September-October, and February-March. In Rwanda as on Ijwi, the consumption of specially prepared foods, including millet and sorghum, was a central part of the Umuganura ritual. But in Rwanda the ritual focus was on sorghum, whereas on Ijwi the specially harvested ritual grain was *bulo,* millet.

The relations of the Ijwi rituals of Muganuro to their counterparts in Rwanda were complex, and need be addressed at three levels: the oral traditions which link Ijwi and Rwandan ritualist families by direct descent from a common ancestor, the structural similarities apparent in the performance of this ritual in the two countries, and the shared conceptual universe which gives meaning to the ritual in the two kingdoms. Some Ijwi ritualists, as we have seen, claim direct historical ties to Rwandan ritual families. But the form and meaning of the two sets of rituals, and the analysis of the traditions related to these specific families, suggest that there was no direct transfer, no simple derivation of one set of rituals from another; as we have seen in chapters 6 and 7, the links are indirect and pass through various historical transformations. Still, certain Ijwi ritualists retain a strong and enduring sense of identity to their Rwandan ritualist counterparts through their perceived common responsibilities. In their oral testimony the precision of the references to corporate groups and individuals associated with ritual duties in Rwanda is remarkable, and these references are reciprocated, to some degree, in the Rwandan traditions. And some Ijwi ritualists claim geographical origins in precisely these regions associated with high ritual prestige in Rwanda. All these factors provide a strong basis for claiming social identity, if not direct descent, among the ritualist groups in the two kingdoms. Clearly, there has been historical interaction of some type.

Evidence for the historical connections between the two ritual contexts can also be found at the level of ethnographic comparisons—comparing the procedures of ritual performance themselves (including terminology as well as ritual practice). The sacrifice of the bull, the ritual objects used, the presence of the drum, and the presentation and preparation of the grain: as these ritual acts are performed on Ijwi they are very similar to the First Fruits ceremonies described for Rwanda. The forms of the rituals are remarkably close, regardless of the precise historical origins of the specific ritualists involved. And Ijwi rituals are close not only to the Rwandan rituals. In some respects they are even more reflective of the elements in the Rundi Umuganuro ritual than of the Rwandan ritual—a curious fact given the Ijwi ritualists' claims to historical descent from Rwandan ritual groups. But such a pattern is one more indication that in fact the Rwandan ritual derives from a regional prototype pattern, rather than that Ijwi patterns represent a degenerated form of some "pure" unchanging Rwandan ritual practice. (Were that the case, it would be difficult to explain how Ijwi forms evolved along a course exactly parallel to other traditions [Burundi or Kaziba] though independent of them.) By the similarity of functions and titles over such a broad area, the cumulative evidence suggests that, despite the claims of some ritualists to have arrived on Ijwi from east of Lake Kivu, Ijwi rituals are in fact derived from a widely shared cultural form rather than a specific Rwandan ritual.

Beyond the specific claims of oral traditions and the general indications of compared ritual performance, a third level of historical linkage relates to that of conceptual similarities, as shown by a comparison of the structural meaning of the ritual. This too reinforces the importance of understanding each of these ritual fields as variants of a common set of cultural patterns widely spread in the region. For example, as I argue elsewhere, the Rwandan Umuganura ritual did not focus on kingship itself. Instead it explored the wider cultural and conceptual context within which kingship was situated. In fact, the ritual dramatized and articulated the elements of that wider context;[38] the king, though important, was only one among many participants, and was not the central focus of the rite. Instead this Rwandan ritual sought to clarify the relationship of kingship to other aspects of ultimate concern: nature (or ecology), culture (or technology), and society (or the relationships among social groups). Within the structure of the ritual, kingship mediated between these three categories—even in Rwanda, the most centralized kingdom of the area and the kingdom with the greatest degree of political power concentrated at the royal court. And so it does on Ijwi, in very much the same way. The king is mediator; he validates and is validated by the relationship between food (the products of the natural world) and society, between drums (representative of the kingdom itself, the paradigmatic cultural construction) and society, and between the social groups themselves.

The Umuganuro Ceremony in Burundi

Rwanda is not the only cultural context which provides fruitful comparisons with Ijwi ritual; these practices were part of wider regional patterns. But despite general similarities, there were important differences between the Ijwi forms and ritual performance elsewhere. Umuganuro in Burundi differed from ceremonies of the same name in other states.[39] In Burundi, Umuganuro was held at the time of the distribution of the sorghum seeds for planting, not at the time of harvest. It was a ritual of agricultural fertility and, in addition to sorghum, included other major foods (bananas, beans, squashes, and honey), and a ritual hunt.[40] The roles of specific ritualist categories in Burundi also differed from those in Rwanda and on Ijwi. In Burundi the Biru (part of the larger category of Bajiji) were important in the burial of the *bami*.[41] These were roles that were also associated with the concept of "Beeru" in the Havu kingdom in Mpinga (Kalehe), among the Tembo polities west of the Mitumba Mountains, and on Ijwi.

Beyond these superficial differences, however, there were many more fundamental similarities between the Muganuro forms in their Rwanda, Ijwi, and Burundi contexts. They shared the same basic conceptualization of (and some variation of the term) "Muganuro"; they included the common role of the king, and the common ritual importance of the consumption of food, especially sorghum and millet;[42] the ceremonies in all cases unfolded in the hands of commoners (in Rwanda and Burundi, "Hutu" commoners); and both on Ijwi and in Burundi the critical public act was that of sounding the drum. Despite the differences in the sources, it is clear that these three kingdoms shared in a common ritual universe.

Not all important national rituals in Burundi were monopolized by the kingship, however. Another important ceremony occurred at the time of the millet harvest in April; this ceremony, named simply *okury'omwaka* ("to eat the harvest"), was carried out individually by each household head (as in Bushi). Despite the consumption of food at the royal Umuganuro ceremony, *okury'omwaka* was the true "Prémices" (First Fruits ceremony). Thus in Burundi the First Fruits ceremony, properly speaking, was not incorporated within the royal rituals, as in the case of the Rwandan Umuganura rituals (which included both sowing and harvesting at different times within the ritual as a whole). Umuganuro in Burundi was the feast of the king, whereas *okury'omwaka* was the feast of the common people, "the feast of the Hutu and the Tutsi."[43]

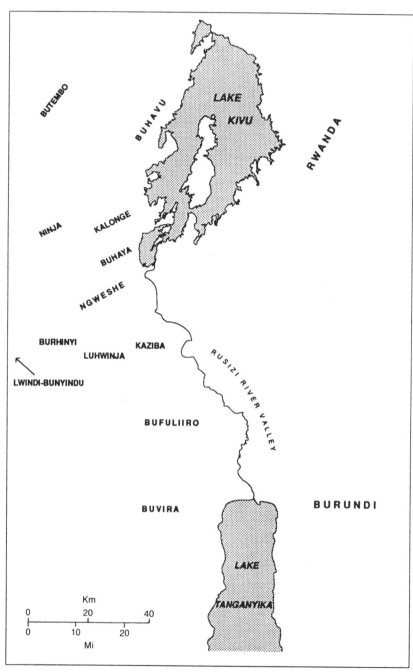

Map 14. The states southwest of Lake Kivu (present location)

The difference in the ritual connotations of kingship between Rwanda and Burundi in this regard may be less important in historical terms than is at first apparent. Their geographical distribution and their association with millet (a very old crop in this region)[44] indicate that these agriculturalist rituals are very old; a consideration of the rituals themselves indicates that the recent Rwandan and Rundi forms derive from a common model, despite the fact that one was part of a royal ritual and one a local celebration. They give every indication of having been everywhere performed at the level of the individual household in the past, and having been incorporated into the rituals of kingship (where this occurs) only relatively recently.

The differences between Burundi and Rwanda are instructive in this regard. In the former, the rituals of the First Fruits were held at the household level, despite the myth—virtually identical to that in Rwanda—that sorghum was introduced by royalty.[45] In Rwanda on the other hand, the Umuganura ritual as a whole consisted of four distinct temporal segments and two functional roles—the distribution and planting of the seeds, and the celebration of the harvest.

Ijwi data provide a historical link between these two models. One man (a "Munyalenge," or a Mulega living in a village identified with the Binyalenge, living in an area of only marginal royal influence) noted that his family had performed ritual celebrations of their own at the time of the First Fruits until the royal family arrived. "That is why," he added, "the royal family celebrates Muganuro at that time."[46] Even today on Ijwi young men are not supposed to plant sorghum before their fathers have begun to plant, lest they expose their fathers to the possibility of contracting leprosy—that is, to do so is taboo. The royal Muganuro provides a clear parallel: it is believed that the *mwami*'s health is endangered by any early consumption of sorghum of the new harvest (e.g., through fermenting beer); one does not endanger oneself, one endangers the kingdom by breaking this taboo. Clearly both these examples from Ijwi evoke the Rundi experience. They emphasize the local familial significance of these ceremonies, not the exclusive royal focus of First Fruits, despite the fact that the present Ijwi forms are very similar to the recent Rwandan forms.

The Rwandan Umuganura ritual as a whole was formed of various temporal (and functional) segments: these were performed intermittently throughout the year, but they were all seen as constituent elements of a single ritual complex, which therefore included both planting and harvest rites. Consequently the recent form of the ritual appears to have resulted from the cumulation of rites which were related but formerly distinct. It is therefore entirely plausible that the First Fruits ceremony in Rwanda was incorporated within the royal Umuganura independently of the rites associated with the distribution of the seeds. On the other hand, it is unlikely that these ceremonies devolved from centralized kingship to the level of the individual homestead in Burundi, where the hegemonic power of kingship and the political powers of the king's court remained relatively weak. Thus comparative structures suggest that these ceremonies, so widespread and focussed on very old agricultural products, were co-opted into royal rituals from more local sources, even while kingship helped reinforce these ritual patterns.

The Mubande Ceremony in Bushi

To the west, in Bushi, a celebration analogous to Muganuro focusses on the concept of "Mubande." As noted in chapter 2, *mubande* is a sacral concept linked to the land, but with very different symbolic expressions in different areas. The term *"mubande,"* referring variously to crystalline rock or a mixture of earth and herbs, is used widely throughout the area, but is especially important west of Lake Kivu. One of the states in which *mubande* plays a prominent role in the annual agriculturalist rituals is Kaziba, on the southern edge of the plateau, intermediary between the high plateau west of Lake Kivu and the low plains around the northern end of Lake Tanganyika. Located between these two different cultural spheres, Kaziba is also one of a series of small states associated with the ancient development of kingship forms in this area of the western Rift lacustrine region.[47] In Kaziba *"mubande"* refers to a material composed of the mixture of earth and herbs, as on Ijwi; it is used in the annual royal rituals (called *okunyw'omubande,* "to drink the *mubande"*) in a manner very similar to that described above for Ijwi.[48]

   In the Shi states to the north of Kaziba, however, the situation is different. There the ceremony is named Mubande-mpundu ("the Mubande celebration"—*mpundu* being the cries of ululation emitted during such public festivities), and people refer to the feast as that of "drinking *mubande."* Yet there is no *mubande* substance included in the ceremony.[49] It would appear therefore that the Shi variant has lost its use of the *mubande* substance but kept the term, and that the Kaziba-Ijwi ceremony represents an earlier form.[50] This conclusion seems confirmed by the central importance of drinking *mubande* in Kaziba and on Ijwi, around the periphery of Bushi proper.

   In the central Shi kingdoms, as on Ijwi, the celebration itself includes a communal meal of sorghum, millet, and meat (in this case reported as that of a ram, offspring of the "ritual sheep" named Nyabulambwi). The millet, we are told, is "bought" in the great forest whence the first Kabare, the first of the dynasty, is said to have come[51]—the only crop with a specified provenience for the ceremony. Mubande in Bushi is said to be a ceremony of the distribution of the seeds (for planting), but it is held in March or April, a time which also includes the harvest of the first sorghum crop; some of the harvest is set aside for "tribute." The timing of the ceremony and the central importance of the communal meal indicate that the ceremony also includes aspects

Table 4. Comparative Elements of Royal Rituals

	Mubande	Sorghum	Muganuro (or variant)	Eleusine	Harvest
Bushi-Buhaya	(x)	x		x	
Kaziba	x				
Ijwi	x	x	x	x	x
Rwanda		x	x	x	x
Burundi		x	x	(x)	(x)
Buha				x	x

Note: Parentheses indicate presence in a partial form or separate ritual from the central First Fruits ceremony.

of the First Fruits. After the *bajinji* share their meal, portions of the meat, millet, and sorghum are sent to each "subchief." Thus, as in Burundi, the official ceremony in Bushi is normatively focussed on distributing the seeds, but in fact is also associated with other ceremonies at the local level; taken together the rituals (at their various levels) span the entire sequence, as most elaborately expressed in the Rwandan ritual.

The evolution of the Shi form of the Mubande ceremony away from a Kaziba-Ijwi type of ritual appears to be linked with the more recent Shi political centralization, by which certain features have been retained at the local level without being co-opted into the higher political levels. In Bushi, for example, a Barhwa ("pygmy") ritualist is married to his half-sister (or at least is portrayed as doing so in the rituals), but this form of *mumbo* (cf. chapter 2) is not reflected within the Banyamwocha ruling family.[52] Also at the sorghum harvest, each family must present part of the harvest to the *chef de village,* and this is termed *okurhul'omwaka,* "the harvest tribute" (or "the annual tribute").[53] In addition, the lower-level authorities go through a ceremony of legitimation each year called *okunyw'omubande,* the same term as that used in Kaziba. The Shi ritual sphere thus appears to be very similar to that of the other Rift Valley areas, but the formal elements of the ritual are markedly different. These differences suggest that the evolution of the Shi political hierarchical structures took place very rapidly, and relatively recently; they apparently did not evolve primarily out of the local-level celebrations, or succeed in co-opting them to the same degree as elsewhere.

Conclusion: Muganuro and Kingship on Ijwi

This discussion suggests that a common conceptualization of ritual and power is widely spread in the region. Though shared by kingship, this conceptualization is not applicable to kingship alone; it exists independently at the level of the individual homestead. Within this conceptual framework, kingship has inserted itself in different forms in different places; thus the historical process described for Ijwi is indicative of broader processes which were present throughout the region.

The specific form of kingship on Ijwi bore the imprint of a particular social context at a particular time. But it grew out of changing forms of social definition and social identity which occurred on Ijwi (partly as a result of events on the mainland, both east and west), and which were perpetuated by the nature of settlement on Ijwi. The significant events in the formation of kingship on the island were those which, although fully situated within the evolving political context of nineteenth-century Ijwi, nonetheless also gave meaning to the basic conceptual patterns found elsewhere in the region. Local events were important but the underlying structural conceptions, common throughout the region and through time, were essential to provide meaning to those events; they helped translate events—discrete, ephemeral, and empirical—into institutions.

Thus Ijwi kingship was no historical accident, no chance occurrence of individuals and events. Kingship did not develop solely from its own internal resources, nor was it imported from a unique source (or from several discrete contributory sources). Instead, the ultimate form of kingship was structured by the conceptualization of society: by the relations of groups to one another, of individuals to larger groups, of the flow of power and force in society. The very concepts of "autonomy" and "sovereignty" were deeply enmeshed in regional mutual influences and interdependence. Just as discrete clan identities both contributed to and grew from increasing political interaction and consolidation, so too the patterns of historical autonomy and the "unique" patterns of change on Ijwi were in constant dialogue with the regional patterns which gave the local patterns meaning and direction.

Conclusion

By the mid-nineteenth century the people of Ijwi had developed political structures very different from those on the island 60 years before. But they had not done so alone; they had drawn on resources, ideas, and new immigrants from off the island. Nor had they acted as a single unit in this evolution; in some ways there were greater differences on the island under the kingdom than there appear to have been before the Basibula arrival. Nor had they simply responded to initiatives of a single small group; the process of political centralization which led to kingship on Ijwi built on transformations which had long preceded the arrival of the Basibula. The actions of the Basibula assume significance only by accounting for these expanded contexts of space, time, resources, and social identity.

Yet each of the themes finds its antithesis in Ijwi's history as well. People and groups on Ijwi often drew their political resources from off the island, but these resources were increasingly applied within the Ijwi domain; in a sense the emergence of royalty resulted in a narrowing of the field of action rather than in an expansion of the kingdom. Second, although the social distinctions on the island intensified, this resulted more from increasing interaction than from a process of separation or a "growing apart." Finally, the initial use of force provided a monopoly over the ritual power of royalty in the hands of the Basibula, but over time force gave way to concepts of ritual integration. These rituals themselves became one of the principal foundations of the political order, because they legitimized the Basibula political position and hence also legitimized their use of force. They also empowered certain important non-royal actors, but this power was power over the court (at certain times), not power over the population; it is striking how ordinary, even poor, the ritualists appear in a material context, despite their prestige at the court.

There are, then, three sets of dialogues discussed here: those between local and regional factors, those between court and clan, and those between physical force and ritual prerogatives. Without neglecting the interaction between them I have concentrated on one element within each pair, not as necessarily more important, but as generally more neglected in the works of historians. For the geographical element this is obvious; although there had been no published work on Ijwi Island or on the Havu, and although other local studies had been produced, no attempt had been made in this area to assess the importance of regional features of historical change—to examine the interacting factors which stimulated and catalyzed change at the local

227

level. This study is intended as a move in this direction. Similarly, among the dyads noted above the concepts of "clan" and "ritual power" have generally been neglected themes in historical studies of this area, and so I have tried to address these aspects of Kivu history as well. What follows is an attempt to sketch out, very briefly, the conceptual framework I have drawn on to do this.

Alterations in clan identities are usually seen as occurring so slowly as to be of little interest to historians. Consequently historians have generally treated clan formation as part of a given social background, something outside their field of inquiry, outside the realm of change in African societies. When considered at all, changes in clan identities have been perceived either in terms of changes in personnel (by the incorporation of individuals within pre-existing clan compartments) or as movement (by the diffusion of a clan group). Less frequently have historians investigated more fundamental changes in the structure of these clan categories themselves.

But while historians have largely neglected the question of changes within clan identities, social scientists have produced relevant work in this field. One of the most influential of these has been J. C. Mitchell, whose study of dance troupes on the Copper Belt of Zambia focussed on the emergence of new identities within the colonial context.[1] He concluded that for Africans on the Copper Belt "the ethnic distinctiveness which they took for granted in the rural areas is immediately thrown into relief by the multiplicity of tribes with whom they are cast into association. Its importance to them is thus exaggerated and it [this "ethnic identity"] becomes the basis on which they interact with all strangers."[2]

Mitchell emphasized the important relationship between changes in these identity patterns and changes in the wider political context. By treating the changing wider context as a catalyst to identity change, he brought into question earlier explanations of ethnic cohesion based on internal institutional characteristics alone. In Mitchell's analysis, the emergence of new patterns of social identity was specifically associated with new perceptions of the boundaries between groups: what was important in this context was the strength of the differences between various groups rather than the shared similarities among individuals within a given group.

> When we talk about tribalism in urban areas we refer not to the linking of people in a patterned structure . . . but rather to a subdivision of people in terms of their sense of belonging to certain categories, these categories being determined by [relative] ethnic criteria. . . . It is thus clear that there is no necessary correlation between a tribal structure on the one hand and tribalism, as I use the word, on the other. The one is a system of social relationships; the other is a category of interaction [among different groups] within a wider sphere.[3]

This concern with categories of interaction as more significant than rigidly determined static qualities (or internally defined "patterned structures" in Mitchell's phrase) foreshadowed more recent work on the analysis of social perceptions and identities, the most influential being that of Fredrik Barth.[4] In Barth's work particular patterns of interaction were viewed as the defining characteristics (rather than as derivative characteristics) of ethnic identity: "The critical focus of investigation becomes the ethnic boundary that defines the group, not the cultural stuff that it includes. The boundaries to which we must give our attention are of course social boundaries, though they may have territorial counterparts."[5]

Although stressing the analytic importance of examining process rather than structure, Barth was still concerned with the maintenance of these "ethnic boundaries" more than with long-term structural transformations in ethnic identities. Changes in these identities were therefore seen at the level of individual changes. For Barth, the principal problem in changing ethnic identity was that of accounting for the magnitude of personal flow, the processes of "social osmosis" through relatively persisting cultural boundaries. He was interested in how this could occur without at the same time grossly upsetting the relative demographic balance of the two (or more) groups involved, for it was precisely their interdependence that assured their individual identities and their boundary maintenance. Beyond this, Barth did not investigate the question of the creation of new ethnic boundaries or the formation of new identities.

Other works, however, have carried the argument further than Barth in this regard, and refer back to Mitchell's work on the emergence—or creation—of new sets of ethnic boundaries. Like Mitchell and Barth, Aidan Southall rejects the significance of rigid "patterned structures" (or internal cultural criteria) as a suitable conceptual framework for understanding identity and ethnicity. Instead, he provides many examples to illustrate both the emergence of new "tribal" identities to confront the demands of the colonial context, and the creation of such identities by colonial participants—anthropologists as well as administrators.[6] (And because of the strictures of the colonial context, these "created" identities often came to be accepted by the colonized people themselves as valid categories of activity and identity within the new arena of social and political interaction.)

Similarly, Crawford Young's earlier work documented the formation of new ethnic identity patterns in the Congo under colonial rule, by processes very similar to those noted by Southall.[7] These encompassed two aspects of social change. One consisted of the direct initiatives of the colonial power, molding the conditions of labor recruitment, local administration, and the distribution of power to local-level authorities to accommodate the colonial perceptions of discrete, mutually exclusive, and clearly defined ethnic units.

From another perspective these transformations also derived from African initiatives to maximize their influence within this emergent colonial context. Often this resulted from attempts to mobilize support of a permanent and exclusive nature along lines that came to be portrayed as "traditional ethnic solidarity." Such attempts solidified the more pragmatic fluidity which characterized the broader and more multifaceted situational identity structures of a previous era. Clearly these processes recurred many times in the Congolese colonial experience, and, as does Southall for East Africa, Young provides examples from several different areas of the Belgian Congo to support his case.[8]

Both Southall and Young focus on the factors of ethnic change rather than boundary maintenance. In this sense they reach beyond Barth. But they also concentrate on the colonial period and stress the importance of the colonial context for the formation of new identity patterns. By implication, these processes seem exclusively associated with colonial contexts. Yet the processes they describe here are equally applicable to other periods as well— and to different levels of identity. All the works noted above indicate that the perception of even marginal benefits can act powerfully on the process of identity formation; there is nothing to indicate that the processes of political change at the local level during the pre-colonial period differed in this respect. Even in the pre-colonial period, the local response to new situations of political centralization and the emergence of changing social identities—the shifting of ethnic boundaries—can be seen as a process similar to those that occurred within the colonial context.

This study argues that similar processes were important at the level of clan formation. What the Ijwi data suggest is not just that such "ethnic" groups existed before colonial rule, but that the general social processes which made salient such identities—and the essential fluidity of ethnic categorization—long pre-dated the modern context. Fluidity was not introduced by European rule; if anything, at the structural level such fluidity was constricted and constrained by the new context of power. But the potential for fluidity was always there—and therefore also the potential for change in social categories—in all periods, as in all cultures.[9]

Thomas Bender's reconsideration of the essential categories which have guided the thinking on United States urban history provides an example of the broad applicability of these broader analytic characteristics of social change. He argues that the growth of cities in many cases enhanced the sense of locally defined communities—both within the cities themselves and outside them. And this process of reinforcing local identities carries over onto the larger social canvas as well: "However paradoxical it may appear, nationalism and localism as basic orientations to life were simultaneously enhanced, and in some respects they even reinforced each other during the first half of the nineteenth century."[10]

Bender brings into question the "bipolar" conceptual framework, by which two elements of a single social formation (communal identity and administrative definition) are isolated from their larger social context and counter-posed to each other. He thus challenges the common assumption that two such perceived elements are opposed to each other, and that one varies in inverse relation to the other—in the case of Ijwi, the assumption that as the strength of court power increased, the strength of clan identities necessarily had to decline. When this conceptual idiom is integrated with a unilinear view of historical development, it is assumed that one of these elements (e.g., kingship) is continuously strengthened while the other (clanship) is continuously weakened and eventually dissolved. But such an argument is premised on the artificial separation of the two elements from the larger social context within which the people themselves acted. As Bender notes:

> Thinking of gemeinschaft and geselleschaft in terms of sequence [with one element simply replacing the other] is thus erroneous. They represent "two kinds of human collective living" in which all individuals are involved. The focus of analytic interest becomes therefore the interaction and interplay [between these two forms of identity]. . . . The task of the cultural historian . . . is not to date the moment when one of the worlds of social relations is replaced by the other; it is to probe their interaction and to assess their relative salience to people's lives in specific situations. . . . What we need is a perspective that will enable us to take an overview of the simultaneous polarity and reciprocity of these two patterns of human interaction. . . .[11]

This study, though drawn from a context far removed from Bender's interests, has attempted precisely that: to explore the development of two kinds of "human collective living" on Ijwi, to probe these "two worlds" of human involvement, and to provide an overview of the "simultaneous polarity and reciprocity of these two patterns of human interaction."

In this work increasingly sharply defined clan identities have been associated with the growth of rituals of kingship. But ritual expressions were more important in reinforcing clan distinctions than in creating them in the first place. They may have sharpened the definition of these identity boundaries, but the processes which led to their emergence were already long at work. The effect of ritual structure was to make social distinctions meaningful, to channel the processes of changing identities, perhaps to redirect them. Therefore royal rituals were an important aspect of social reproduction; through time they reinforced and thus "re-created" clan differentiation.

Other ritualized situations, such as those involving joking relationships or (in certain cases) ancestor propitiation, serve the same role as Muganuro in this respect, but in each case clan identity is nonetheless defined primarily in terms of its ritual forms. Clans were not formed in order to serve ritual purposes, but ritual defined the orientation and validated the process by which clan identities took the shape they did. It is in this perspective that clan differentiation and royal rituals have been considered together in this study.

The work of Maurice Bloch is particularly helpful in illuminating the central role of ritual in defining clan conceptualizations.[12] Bloch argues that a similar set of conceptualizations associated with ritual perceptions also applies to perceptions of "social structure."[13] But he also notes that the formalized idiom of ritualist expression precludes any explanatory role for such ritual contexts.[14] Because of the repetitive nature and narrowed range of communication possible with such a fixed form of expression, ritualist situations can serve only as a surrogate to explanation. In Bloch's assessment ritual is not a form of communication, but a type of "anti-communication": it defines the realm of those concepts that cannot be explained historically.

When applied to clan categorization this analysis explains why "clans" have served as such an unsuccessful focus of historical inquiry in the past, because clan conceptualization belongs also to the realm of "anti-communication," employing a "type of communication which both excludes explanation and hides this exclusion."[15] The issue of clan "origins" (or, on a wider plane, that of social differentiation) thus lies outside the realm of logical (or, in Bloch's terms, "propositional") explanation. This is why the history of clan conceptualization can be traced only by considering the changes in the wider political context, and why it is misleading to view clans as corporate historical groups with their own definable history independent of the wider social context.

Because both central court political institutions and clan organization are thought of in terms of a common set of ritual concepts, the origins of a clan category and the origins of a dynastic structure are conceptually intertwined; they share certain parallels and present similar problems to historians. Historians have worked on the problems of penetrating beyond dynastic ideology much more than they have explored the ideologies of clan origins. By linking dynastic ideology and clan ideology in this way, so that through understanding ritual they are seen as sharing the same intellectual paradigms, Bloch's analysis implies that a major shift in one field will be associated with a shift in the other. This explains why transformations to new forms of identity groups on Ijwi can be seen as closely associated with transformations in the political structures of the island, especially those fostering increased centralization. And it explains why, rather than being seen as opposed categories, clan and royalty can be seen as associated concepts—at least in one particular form of social transformation.

The relationship of ritual to the social order also provides the central focus of A. M. Hocart's suggestive study, a work which yields many insights for the analysis of the Ijwi data.[16] Hocart notes, for example, that ritual establishes an equivalence (a relational identity) between two different elements operating in the same ritual universe. As we have seen, royal rituals on Ijwi do form an equivalence between elements within the ritual (the sacrificial bull and the kingdom, for example). But they are not limited to that role; the equivalence established among the ritual participants (the *bagingi*) during these rites also establishes clan categories as equivalent identity groups, regardless of other differences that may hold between them. The very fact of ritual equivalence suggests that these are not "identical" groups: "The ritual establishes an equivalence that was not there. If it were there already there would be no point in having a ritual."[17] Therefore ritual implicitly but unavoidably establishes the distinctions between groups as well as their equivalence.

As in the present study, Hocart's approach privileges the precursors to institutional change; he focusses on the pre-existing ritual apparatus associated with a given social order, and the ways this ritual apparatus is used in creating social institutions. For the Ijwi case, I have made a slightly different argument—that although the court rituals do indeed draw on a pre-existing ritual code, they were not practiced at the level of a common Ijwi society before the establishment of a "royal" court as a political focus on the island. Societal rituals were brought about by the same changing structural conditions that also facilitated the establishment of new forms of political authority on the island.

Whereas Hocart traces the evolution of society from ritual organization to "government," the approach adopted here avoids such a unilineal argument. The relationship between ritual and politics was critically important in defining the patterns of social change on Ijwi, but this relationship was expressed in more indirect form than that postulated by Hocart. Ritual praxis underlay political perceptions, to be sure, and ritual authority certainly underlay effective political action on Ijwi. But the presence of society-wide ritual structures was not a pre-condition to the development of administrative institutions. The process was—like so much else in human history—one of *bricolage*, with the Bany'Iju drawing on pre-existing ritual elements and restructuring them in new ways to arrive at a new formal structure. Ritual concepts provided the lexicon, the units of expression, but the exact form of expression was a product of the particular actions of particular people, not pre-determined by existing ritual structures. On Ijwi the changing ritual field gave life (and meaning) to a new type of social order, but it did not dictate any particular form to those emergent political institutions. The larger structures of this new social order conformed to the general patterns found throughout the region. But the particularities of these institutions were molded by the people and circumstances of the day. Fully understanding one element to this dyad—societal structures or institutional particularities—requires understanding both.

In the same manner, it is not the internal characteristics of a given clan group which make them a recognizable social unit, but the relational aspect defined by their ongoing ritual functions within the larger social arena. In Barth's terms, again, what is critical is the maintenance (or transformation) of group boundaries. The particular structures of clan identity result from concepts generated by interactions both with other units of a similar analytic type (other clans) and with different types of social unit (with kingship, for example). Consequently, neither clan formation nor clan maintenance can be understood apart from the larger processes by which its members interact with other aspects of society. In this respect (although there are also important differences) the concept of "clan" can be understood only within a conceptual framework similar to that proposed by E. P. Thompson for understanding social classes:

> The notion of class entails the notion of a historical relationship. Like any other relationship it is a fluency which evades analysis if one attempts to stop it dead at any given moment and analyse its structure. . . . we cannot understand class unless we see it as a social and cultural formation, arising from processes which can only be studied as they work themselves out over a considerable historical period.[18]

And again, though Thompson draws on a metaphor of industrialization, a similar analysis could be applied to clans on Ijwi:

> Class is not this or that part of the machine, but *the way the machine works* once it is set in motion—not this or that interest but the *friction* of interests, the movement itself, the heat, the thundering noise. Class is a social and cultural formation (often finding institutional expression) which cannot be defined abstractly or in isolation but only in terms of relationship with other classes; and ultimately the definition can only be made in the medium of *time,* that is action and reaction. . . .[19]

Thus this analysis of state formation has differed from most other such studies in several ways. It has ended with the arrival of the royal family rather than starting from that point. It has focussed on the process of clan emergence rather than that of central court expansion. It has looked at regional historical factors in addition to local factors; therefore it has not focussed on a single domain as defined by present political or cultural boundaries, but has tried to consider historically significant units. And instead of focusing on specific royal institutions as either independent variables unchanging over time, or as dependent variables, adjusting to a pre-existing and enduring social milieu, this study has tried to look at the continuity of the ideas of kingship (over time and area) and to inquire into the transformations in non-royal levels of society to understand how they contributed to, as well as responded to, the emergence of kingship on Ijwi. Such analytic approaches may be different from other studies of this kind, but they reflect aspects which the Bany'Iju shared with other peoples; the people of Ijwi were unique in their history, but in these general processes they were not alone.

What, then, accounted for royalty on Ijwi? Certainly it was not simply the personal qualities of a single man alone. Nor was it the political support he was able to generate. It was, most of all, a receptivity to royalty on the part of the people of Ijwi, generated by new patterns of interaction among groups on the island and new concepts of group belonging which lent significance to the rituals that came to surround the king. The concentration of these rituals at the royal court provided royalty with a major political resource, that of ritual status, legitimized and distributed by the court itself. In a sense then, as noted above, ritual served as a "capital good" of kingship, for ritual contexts determined the relationships among different groups.

The rituals were drawn both from outside Ijwi and from the population on the island. Consequently the combined royal rituals provided a means by which the people on Ijwi simultaneously created their own identity and related to the peoples around them. For at different levels of perception the members of any given clan both shared in the experience of kingship with others and were differentiated from them, just as clans, as social categories, shared in kingship but were differentiated from each other within the context of kingship. This multifaceted aspect of kingship meant that kingship always contained within it the possibility of its own transformation from within. It was, in turn, by their changing inter-relationships that the people of Ijwi of the early nineteenth century generated a royal tradition of their own, one that would serve as a distinctive focus for this island people through the colonial period and beyond.

Appendices
Notes
Glossaries
Oral Sources
Bibliography
Index

Appendix 1
Research Methods

This project was conceived in 1970, while I was teaching in Bukavu, Zaire. I had acquired a certain familiarity with the region and had met several Bany'Iju, including Ntambuka Sibula, the son of the *mwami* of Ijwi, who was supportive of the project. But more important, a historical study of Ijwi Island seemed interesting on grounds other than personal ties alone. Although the Interlacustrine area of Africa had been intensively studied over a relatively long period, historians of the region had concentrated on a few highly centralized kingdoms. More recent work, however, has emphasized regional concepts and themes, and the focus has shifted away from the central courts to include more "peripheral" areas and smaller political centers. The Havu kingdoms presented an excellent opportunity to work within this new framework; they were peripheral to the Interlacustrine area (in particular to one of the major historiographical poles of the region, that of Rwanda), and I hoped they could provide some understanding of cultural interchange in a wider regional context.

My initial interests were in precolonial history. Among the unexplored subjects for this region at that time were the history and social characteristics of the numerous smaller polities which had been incorporated into the Rwandan state. In western Rwanda the last of these (Kingogo, Bushiru, Busozo, and Bukunzi) succumbed to the Rwandan central court only by the direct application of colonial military force. (There were many other cases where colonial power was instrumental in expanding the area under Rwandan central court administration.) But the Ijwi kingdom also had obvious historical ties with the Zairean mainland. Therefore Ijwi Island provided a particularly interesting field of research, as at least indicative, if not representative, of a type of small-scale political organization formerly common in the area. There were other advantages as well. The Ijwi kingdom had relatively clearly defined precolonial origins and, unlike other kingdoms of this region, Ijwi's royal traditions showed a strong continuity through the colonial period (though their political powers had been altered by the colonial context). Ijwi also was unique in the region in providing a functioning kingdom with a king who maintained close political ties to the local community independent of the national or regional administration. The *mwami* was old enough to preserve a real interest in the history of his domain and young enough to be actively involved in the affairs of his kingdom. Having been exiled for a total of 27 years (on two occasions) during the colonial period, the Ijwi *mwami* had himself been bypassed by regional politics. His absence from Ijwi had denied him access to the details of the Ijwi past, but this had only intensified his interest in Ijwi's history. None of the other kingdoms of the region combined these features; elsewhere the *bami* (former sovereigns) were either too old to be active in local affairs, or so young as to be absorbed in national politics; for this latter group, local status was seen as a stepping stone to other interests, rather than accepted as a responsibility in itself.

Other research was underway elsewhere in the area at the time; this enhanced the interest of the Ijwi research and contributed significantly to its ultimate value. Historical projects had recently been initiated by others in the Rusizi Valley (to the south), in Kinyaga (southwest of Lake Kivu), among the Shi states (to the southwest), and among the Nande kingdoms (to the north). In addition, comprehensive studies in social anthropology, in religion, and in cultural anthropology had recently been completed in Bushi. These studies had included Buhavu only marginally; the relative lack of attention given the Havu states in the available literature enhanced the interest of the project, though the near absence of previous work of any kind among the Bahavu presented several problems for both research and writing.

The research for this project was conducted between 1971 and 1975, but was not continuous during that time. The last three months of 1971 were spent in preparation for the project; rudimentary language studies, basic reading on the wider area, and myriad formalities involved with research authorization amply filled my time. There-after during 1972 and early 1973 I worked on Ijwi, on the islands of the lake, in the Havu and Tembo kingdoms on the mainland (Kalonge, Mpinga Sud, Mpinga Nord, Buzi, Ziralo, and Bufumando), in Rwanda, and in archives in Uvira, Bukavu, and several local depositories. From February 1973 to April 1974, illness and teaching responsibilities interrupted the work, but throughout that time I kept close contact with events on Ijwi through continual visits by friends and occasional short visits to the island. I resumed formal research in May of 1974, both on Ijwi and again in several Tembo kingdoms west of the Mitumba Mountains (Mubugu, Buloho, and Kalima); late in the year I worked in the mainland areas both in Zaire and Rwanda. Thus over several years about 18 months were spent on research, of which 10–11 months (discontinuously) were spent on Ijwi.

My research on Ijwi initially received a cool reception. Although medical re-search had been carried out by a team of Belgian doctors, no intensive social studies had been conducted on the island. As I was neither priest, doctor, plantation man-ager, nor government official, and since I lacked the wealth and trappings of other Europeans, I fit into no clearly defined identity mold for the people of Ijwi. It took several months before I felt I was accepted, or at least tolerated, on the island; when it came, the shift in attitude was rapid and noticeable, with a marked change in receptivity both among the population and at the court. From that time, I felt very much a part of Ijwi—and believe that many people on Ijwi accepted me as such. Nonetheless, while I was accepted socially (and even made some good friends), there were still certain topics which eluded me: the recent history of Ijwi's relations with outsiders has seen too much disappointment, deception, and outright brutality to be overcome in a short time.

The political climate at the time of the research was highly volatile, and some important changes took place while I was there. I arrived on Ijwi about one month after President Mobutu had announced the abolition of the *bami* as administrative officials (except those formally co-opted into the position within the state administrative grid). The announcement created uncertainty among both the "elite" and the general population on Ijwi; the latter had suffered on many occasions before, during elite struggles for control of the island. Feelings ran high: the chief of the northern part of Ijwi (from a junior line of the royal lineage; his father had been placed in power by the Belgians) resigned following Mobutu's speech. (A month later he quietly withdrew his resignation.) The king, the court, and others in the south were also perturbed. Mobutu had established his own brand of "authenticity" as the foundation for a new political culture. Since the maternal line of the Ijwi kingdom had come from an area that is today part of Rwanda, it was feared that Mobutu would use this argument as a pretext to abolish kingship on Ijwi, claiming that the present Ijwi dynasty was not "authentically Zairean."

It was an inauspicious time to initiate historical research on the island. External powers had often waged war against the kingdom: at the time of the Belgians, this had been done in the name of "civilization" (and took the form of forced labor, physical brutality, and material expropriation); now it was carried out in the name of "authenticity" (and took the form of forced labor, physical brutality, and material expropriation). Since my presence was otherwise inexplicable (teachers don't walk the hills talking with old men), it was originally assumed that I was involved in this new political policy. In these circumstances, it took a little time to gain the confidence of the people on Ijwi.

In addition to the local manifestations of the new power game in Kinshasa, there was a general intensification of the political climate for the country as a whole during the early 1970s: the name of the country was changed, Christian names were abolished, corvée labor was reintroduced, dress codes were redefined, the state struggled with churches over the control of schools (among other issues), foreign-owned businesses were expropriated (and first distributed to well-placed Zaireans, later re-expropriated and retained by the state), party officials confronted state administrators, the youth league assumed a new prominence in political issues.

By 1974 these changes directly affected Ijwi economic and political life. As part of the policy of expropriating foreign enterprises, the plantation on Ijwi was acquired by the director of the Presidential Office; Zaireans were appointed to plantation management positions. Ambitious plans were drawn up for paving roads, introducing electricity, providing an airport, building a 400-room luxury hotel, and inaugurating other impressive schemes on Ijwi. Simultaneously the administrative structures were reorganized. Ijwi became recognized as its own administrative "zone" directly tied to the regional and national administrative grids; formerly Ijwi had been administratively dependent on Kalehe, on the mainland. A few Bany'Iju found positions as part of the local-level administration, but the principal positions were occupied by outsiders. In addition, some 50 soldiers arrived on Ijwi, local labor was conscripted to widen and improve the roads—actually rutted tracks—for the cars of the new administrators, and the boats of the Bany'Iju were impounded to discourage "smuggling" (of coffee) to Rwanda; in fact the threat of appropriation of canoes simply offered a new source of income for officials. At this time, too, coffee prices paid to producers dwindled, until finally the growers received no payment at all for their coffee; coincidentally, perhaps, this corresponded with a financial scandal in which the president is said to have done quite well on personal profits from coffee exports.

Thus Ijwi was much more closely integrated to the Zairean administrative grid, but the people of Ijwi saw precious few benefits from these new expressions of state power. In fact the firmer the state embrace became, the greater the antagonisms emerged between state authorities and the people of Ijwi. For example, someone had to provide for the new administrative and military personnel—people who did not want to be there to begin with, and who often came with high expectations of the material gains to be realized from their stay on the island. Since the state wasn't going to do it, the task fell, involuntarily, to the least powerful groups on the island. State administrators imposed market prices for Ijwi agricultural goods; in the face of rapidly rising prices for mainland goods and static or falling earnings on their own produce, many people simply refused to take their goods to markets, especially to those markets near administrative centers. By then I was effectively disassociated from any government identification; nevertheless a climate of such intensity and uncertainty clearly affected interview situations on some subjects.

External factors were not the only influences on the research climate I faced; I brought my own conceptual obstacles along with me. Earlier experience in northern Uganda and in Rwanda had only reinforced my image of certain basic institutions which I associated with African societies in general. Society was, of course, divided up into discrete units of "clans" and "lineages," defined by fixed genealogical data. Knowledge was transmitted in oral traditions—of which there were many forms, to be sure, but these were nonetheless seen as formal genres which (to varying degrees) assured the faithful transmission of historical facts from one generation to another, from original observation to the recitation. As I saw it then, my job was simply to record these recitations—part of the mechanical process of "collecting data."

I couldn't have been more mistaken. All these assumptions were misguided; over the years, I had to discard them one by one and embark on a personal odyssey of reconstructing a new understanding of (at least this) African society. Not only did I have to reconceptualize the human patterns of behavior and thought that constituted social structures, but I also had to account for changes over time in these social processes and set them within wider social figurations. In addition, I had to locate myself consciously in the social universe of the Bany'Iju. In short, I needed to contextualize (in time, place, and social referent) both the actions and narrations I witnessed and my own understanding of those data.

I had to face the reality that none of my expected building blocks of society— clans, lineages, genealogies, oral traditions—existed as I had expected, and that even my own observations were products of a particular (and changing) historical context. Instead of genealogies, there were name lists (which included brothers, uncles, in-laws, and sometimes women, often in random order). There were no "traditions" in the classic sense of the term, but multiple (and often conflicting) oral accounts—or perceptions, transmitted in fluid forms; though these were not random utterings, there were no clearly defined and universally accepted norms of social control over content. Historical knowledge seemed to be transmitted in a variety of ways, through time, laterally, and back through time ("feedback"—a process whereby more-recent data are incorporated into historical accounts). In short, there was no single coherent history of Ijwi, there were many of them. But none of this meant that history did not exist, that it was unknowable, or that it was of no significance—as the colonial stereotypes averred. The job became more complicated, to be sure, but no less interesting.

The problems did not end there. It was not simply that Ijwi forms did not correspond with Western orthodox assumptions of the day. It was also a time of profound intellectual change within the field of African history. Penetrating questions were being asked on the generation and reproduction of historical understanding, and especially on the forms and meaning of oral sources. These debates did not take the form of denying all validity of oral sources; they were phrased more in an anthropological tone, more as a part of methodological inquiry—that of defining levels of understanding in sources on the past. The essential argument to emerge in the 1960s—that oral data need be treated as any other historical source, with the same methods of critique applied to them—came to be questioned in the 1970s by two competing schools of thought. "Fundamentalists" felt that the application of critical apparatus led to an excessively subjective and distorted understanding of African history; they argued that one simply had to accept oral data at their word, that oral data were literally true. Structuralists argued that oral accounts represented the expression of deep conceptual values, that the events and persons mentioned in such accounts were less important than the structural coherence on which such accounts rested—in fact that such events and personages were only metaphorical represen-tations of deeper structural values. The field had splintered; understanding his-tory—whose history, and at what level of understanding?—had become a whole new enterprise.

Initially it was a little discouraging for a young researcher; the processes of the social construction of knowledge, its production, structuring, reproduction, and reception, were all elements that concerned me, and answers to such concerns were not immediately evident on Ijwi. And this at a time when I was only learning the language and geography, acquainting myself with the daily work routine on Ijwi, familiarizing myself with the names and faces and the common institutions that formed my new world. Only over time did it become clear that on Ijwi there was no firm cultural hegemony that defined "truth," or that lent itself to a common inter-pretation of experiential awareness. In this book I have tried to convey some of the flavor of the intellectual diversity, discourse, and confrontation which characterizes historical discussion on Ijwi.

I employed a variety of approaches for the research. Oral testimony in various forms was my principal source. This was not only because of the lack of written documents and archeological sites, but also because of the intrinsic value of such an approach in obtaining data on local-level social integration and regional interaction, from people from a wide variety of social backgrounds. But the people of Ijwi do not in general recite texts or narratives in any formal way. There were few singers on the island and their songs were predominantly learned from, and described events in, neighboring areas. There were few historical subjects common to all the island, not even stories of the origin of kingship; in each region of the island my questions concerned historical events or personages specific to that area. Consequently my early contacts were generally conducted as unstructured interviews, in a question-and-answer format, with subsequent elaboration. Such a format obviously has drawbacks, since the information obtained is in large part a reflection of the researcher's particular interests and questions at the time, and thus is directed. I tried to avoid this problem by posing highly generalized topics for conversation, but this technique either elicited responses at a similar level of generality or was simply discarded outright: often I was specifically requested to ask questions to be answered. I was constantly aware of being captive to the expectations of the interviewees. But over time, as they came to know me, my interests, and my interview techniques, and as I came to know them, their interests, and modes of discourse, our encounters became more informal, more like conversations than interviews. Eventually these totalled over 600 on Ijwi alone, providing roughly a 20 percent sample of men over 55. On Ijwi I interviewed in each of the 75 "villages," and sought out at least one interviewee from each clan represented in these administrative units.

Such an extensive technique also helped identify those with the greatest interest in history, those whose thinking covered a wide domain of Ijwi history and culture, and those whose information was confirmed by independent sources. These were the men whom I consider the most reliable witnesses. But reliability is necessarily a subjective concept: accuracy has no necessary tie to breadth of knowledge, nor is it always validated and confirmed by its relation to widely held conceptions and clichés; furthermore, an interest in history does not reduce the bias inherent in a testimony. "Reliability" in this context has little to do with any preconceived notions of factual accuracy. It is more concerned with thoughtful reflection on the issues of Ijwi history. Thus these traditions, or conversations, are more indicative of concepts of history, of explanatory patterns, than "collections of facts" and information. These people were historians in their own right, not simply messengers, transmitting a factual past to the present. They were interpreters, mediating between a complex set of processes which defined past Ijwi experience, on the one hand, with today's diverse range of perceptions of those processes, on the other. There were things they didn't know and they mused about them. There were ambiguities in their understanding and they addressed them. And there was much they felt strongly about and could explain why. They were critical, inquisitive, and self-aware. And so I treated them as historians and their testimony as historical analysis, not as a simple statement of "hard fact." Thereafter I returned to these "reliable" thinkers, sometimes many times, over the course of my research. In this manner I tried to combine an extensive survey approach with a more intimate relationship to a few of the more reflective historians on Ijwi.

Return interviews were less dependent on a question-and-answer format than the initial contacts. They took more the form of open-ended discussions, as researcher and narrator became increasingly acquainted and eventually became two historians sharing common interests (but not always arriving at similar conclusions). Some of these men invited me to visit them when there was some aspect they wanted to discuss (as well as simply for cordiality); in time, informal and unannounced visits were completely accepted. By the end of the research I felt I had exceptional access to many households.

I quickly found that group interviews were difficult to use for these purposes; wherever possible, interviews were conducted on an individual basis, at the home of each person involved. On several occasions early in the research I hosted "soirées" with abundant beer and food, and invited the "best" interviewees, hoping to iron out contradictory information which had emerged in earlier interviews. These were enjoyable occasions and helped immensely in meeting older men in an informal atmosphere. But I quickly gave up all hope of using these occasions for directly historical purposes. Traditions on Ijwi are not held corporately. Discussion among those with contrasting narratives, with a view towards determining a single "acceptable" testimony, were counterproductive, to say the least. Nor did such discussions serve to refresh the memories of the participants; often such mutual "prompting" simply intensified the argument and ended in utter bedlam. Where there were contrasting points of view to be discussed I preferred to bring them up with individuals in a more personal environment.

Individual interviews, then, were preferable in every way. Some were attended by others, but many were conducted with an individual and his family (or close friends) alone; this pattern was especially true of return interviews. Sometimes an earlier interviewee would accompany me to the next interviewee's home, and was often a help in the initial stages of a new interview context. But frequently such a man would leave before the completion of the interview. Similarly, an initial corps of onlookers would quickly thin out or move on entirely, well before the completion of the interview; during the rainy season Bany'Iju have plenty to do.

In some cases capitas attended the initial interviews in the village; where interviewees were reluctant at the start, they often helped improve the research atmosphere. This was especially true because many of the capitas appointed from above were not particularly knowledgeable about the history of a village; often the interviewees eventually felt compelled to correct, dismiss, or confront some of the evident gibberish of the capitas. Since most people interviewed were elder men on their own "turf"—sometimes with little love for the capitas—there was little deference evinced in discussing matters of this type. Only rarely did a capita accompany me except during the first interviews of the first day in a village. Nor did I feel it necessary to consult the capita beyond the initial introduction (though sometimes I would stop by for a courtesy visit); I came and went as my own schedule dictated. As my work became more widely known and my questions became more refined and I came to know personally many interviewees and their families, consultation with capitas was dropped entirely; "interviews" finally became simply visits of friendship, part of the daily round that occurs continuously on Ijwi.

Very few women were interviewed formally, though frequently men would seek the advice of women for genealogical ties and sometimes for historical questions pertaining to family history—even the history of the husband's family. In addition to their detailed knowledge of local family history and genealogies (including marriage ties) women were invariably superior on linguistic matters. For questionnaires dealing with the Swadesh word list, they understood the exercise immediately and had a much surer grasp of the lexical aspects of the language than did the men. Women were also interviewed when specifically indicated by others as knowledgeable either for general historical matters or for certain specializations (such as healing). The absence of women interviewees generally, however, is a lacuna in the data, and an important one, one that I wish I had been more sensitive to at the time.

I learned Kihavu sufficiently well to be comfortable in casual conversation and in the interviews, often preferring to conduct them myself. But most interviews were conducted with an interpreter present, if not directly participating all the time. Over the course of the research I employed three interpreters, but only one worked directly with me at any one time. These men did much more than simply accompany me on interviews; they assisted in a variety of ways to introduce Ijwi society to me (and me to it), to discuss and refine questions and concepts, to teach me the language, and to polish some of my more barbaric renderings of a beautiful language. We lodged, ate, and lived together (except when working near their homes). They were much more than interpreters; they were colleagues.

Most initial interviews were recorded as handwritten notes; later interviews, long recitations, narratives, songs, or subjects of special interest (e.g., clientship) were recorded on tape. It would perhaps have been preferable to have recorded all interviews verbatim, but tapes were difficult to obtain and beyond my budget, and I was consequently neither able to record as much as I would have preferred nor even to retain taped copies of all that I did record.

Other types of oral data were also collected, though not in any systematic fashion. These included songs, praise poetry, and occupational verse (as for rowers or cattle-herders). But songs and praise poetry were often introduced to Ijwi from outside; they were often concerned with events not directly connected with Buhavu and tended to be very fragmentary in form and of marginal historical value for this project. There is a further type of oral data, however, which this study would have benefitted from had I paid more attention to it. At the time of the research, the lines between "myth" and "history" were still rather clearly articulated in the minds of most students of oral history in Africa; while there was an accepted "gray" area, these two categories were still seen largely in terms of ideal ("pure") types. Today it is clear to me that there is much more to the understanding of history and of historical sources. With more time and greater sensitivity to this issue I could have done more to collect a wider variety of Ijwi narrative.

Other data were recorded in more standardized questionnaires. After the initial research, three villages were selected for their contrasts in location, size, age, clan homogeneity, and social context. Surveys were carried out in these units with a 100 percent sample of resident married males on such questions as cattle, land, religion, commercial matters, forms of social contracts, marriages, children (education, residence, marriage). A questionnaire for capitas was also administered to a random sample of 40 percent of the capitas and all the "notables." Lexico-statistical data (adapted from the Swadesh 100-word list) were also completed for various areas in Buhavu and Butembo. (Questionnaires were also drawn up for the contemporary Ijwi educated elite and for Bany'Iju living in Buhavu, but I was unable to administer these.)

Finally, prolonged periods of residence on Ijwi contributed to my own appreciation, and (I hope) understanding, of Ijwi society. I lived in the compounds in the hills, as close as possible to the area which I was researching at any given time, and I travelled only on foot or by boat. I preferred to stay with friends, but in some areas I stayed with the capita or at the king's enclosures when they were convenient and when it would have been awkward not to have done so. Occasionally I lodged at a school or a dispensary. This approach obviously kept me close to the community, and allowed me to continue visits until late at night, or to start as early as necessary. I usually ate with those who worked with me and any visitors who dropped in; sometimes I ate with neighbors or friends.

One important aspect of such participant observation was regular visits to the *bwami*. In the initial stages of the research I visited the court only infrequently, in part to establish my own identity distinct from the court. Later in the work, especially when in the southern part of the island and with increasing frequency towards the end of the fieldwork period, I stopped in once or twice a week and sometimes much more frequently, usually in the late afternoon or evening. I was invariably well received and believe that towards the end of my research, my presence provided no inhibitions on the actions or words of the *mwami*. Nonetheless, the language used at the court is an elaborate (and rather elliptical) dialect of Kiny'Iju. (Sometimes the *mwami* would lean over and explain things in my "commoner" Kihavu for me, or explain issues over dinner, when we usually ate alone.) In other words, there would have been little difficulty in keeping from me what the court did not want me to hear, but I believe that there was no conscious deception, that I observed affairs in their normal course.

A final form of research was access to documentary sources, both government archives and the valuable collection of writings, notes, diaries, and dictionaries of the Missionaries d'Afrique (the "White Fathers") in Bukavu and at the various missions. Missionary documents were consulted at the archives of the Archevêché de Bukavu through the kindness of S. E. Monseigneur Mulindwa Mutabesha, and at the Centre d'Etudes des Langues Africaines (CELA), thanks to R. P. Vermeiren. Other documents were consulted at the missions of Bobandana, Kashovu, Matanda, and Mwanda. Governmental archives were consulted at Rambo (Ijwi Sud), Kalehe, Minova, and Uvira.

Appendix 2
Clan Statistics on Ijwi

Village names are italicized. Population statistics are from the 1969 census. They are to be read as: (total population; adult males) [total of married males, shown broken down by clan statistics for each village]. Statistics on adult males were not available in the 1969 census figures from South Ijwi.

North Ijwi

Notable: Munyuzangabo Bazungu

Kihumba (484; 88) [60]
Capita: Kabona (or Byamera)

Bahande	33
Bashaho	19
Balega	6
Bakanga	2

Kishenyi (918;140) [126]
Capita: Birongo Ngwarha

Bahande	34
Bashaho	41
Beshaza	24
Balega	10
Baziralo	4
Bozi	3
Bakanga	9
Badaha	1

Kimalamungu (409; 80)
Capita: Kanyabeshi

Beshaza	49
Bahande	49
Balega	27
Bashaho	8
Banyambiriri	4

Cugi (391; 82) [77]
Capita: Kakuru

Balega	9
Bahande	52
Bashaho	8
Beshaza	8

Bushusha (383; 84) [97]
Capita: Kashombo

Balega	33
Beshaza	25
Bahande	20
Banyambiriri	14
Bakanga	5

Muganzo (549; 96) [77]
Capita: Mpinja

Beshaza	23
Bahande	20
Balega	8
Bozi	8
Banyambiriri	15
Bashaho	3

249

Villages for which clan statistics are
not available:

Buyumbu (883; 162)
Capita: Kanyange Hurumba

Bulehe (334;65) [137]

Bukole (766; 134)
Capita: Mwandulo

Mulungu (77; 14)
Capita: Rubenga

Katonda (54; 8)
Capita: Mbinja

Notable: Magendo Karhongo

Mulamba (542; 105) [96]
Capita: Nyamurembya Mahuka

Beshaza	59
Bahande	37

Kamole (565; 112) [142]
Capita: Rutega Cuma

Beshaza	118
Bahande	6
Bashaho	7
Balega	4
Baziralo	3
Bozi	1
Badaha	1
Bakanga	1
Banyambiriri	1

Busobe (248; 44) [34]
Capita: Bengehya

Bozi	27
Bahande	4
Beshaza	2
Balija	1

Buruhuka (1,391; 262) [174]
Capita: Kaligisi

Bahande	80
Beshaza	26
Bashaho	30
Balega	25
Bakanga	4
Badaha	6
Bozi	3

Bushonga (469; 96) [100]
Capita: Balike Nyabalinda

Balega	40
Bahande	31
Beshaza	11
Bashaho	9
Basibula	7
Basarazi	2

Bunyakiri (775; 137) [123]
Capita: Mutazamba

Balega	65
Bashaho	37
Beshaza	10
Baziralo	5
Bahande	5
Badaha	1

Villages for which clan statistics are
not available:

Tshirongwe (402; 77)
Capita: Rutega

Kishumbu (678; 125)
Capita: Kaboyi Mugoneza

Bweshu (721; 138)
Capita: Kiyorha Munyampara

Notable: Kampayane Busomoke

Kisheke (615; 126) [110]
Capita: Kalegamire Badafabasheka

Beshaza	56
Baziralo	20
Balega	18
Bashaho	16

Kinji (312; 66) [49]
Capita: Kaboye Mulengezi

Balega	23
Beshaza	20
Bashaho	6

Kibanda (429; 93) [95]
Capita: Yafali

Bakanga	34
Beshaza	33
Bashaho	12
Balega	11
Badaha	3
Banyambiriri	2

Kashiraboba (927; 188) [156]
Capita: Kabanda Camuraye

Beshaza	46
Bahande	42
Balega	44
Bozi	10
Bakanga	7
Bashaho	7

Bugarura (1,043; 217) [181]
Capita: Mbogobogo

Beshaza	79
Balega	59
Bashaho	24
Bakanga	6
Bahande	3
Banyambiriri	3
Badaha	2
Baziralo	2
Balija	2
Banyintu	1

Lweza (346; 71) [63]
Capita: Rukanika

Beshaza	25
Bashaho	14
Bakanga	14
Bahande	4
Balega	3
Banyambiriri	2
Badaha	1

Mafula (237; 50) [35]
Capita: Musheke

Beshaza	19
Bahande	9
Balega	4
Bakanga	2
Bashaho	1

Muziri (581; 127) [127]
Capita: Barume

Bahande	53
Beshaza	21
Balega	19
Bakanga	18
Bashaho	11
Babambo	2
Baziralo	1
Banyambiriri	1
Balija	1

Bukinanyana (808; 190) [131]
Capita: Muhanuka

Beshaza	30
Bashaho	24
Banyambiriri	21
Balega	21
Bozi	13
Bahande	10
Badaha	7
Baziralo	5

Bukenge (561; 118) [72]
Capita: Rusaku

Bahande	26
Bashaho	17
Beshaza	12
Balega	10
Banyintu	4
Bakanga	2
Badaha	1

Ngula (482; 84) [74]
Capita: Mavuta

Beshaza	23
Bahande	27
Balega	6
Bakanga	6
Bashaho	4
Booze	4
Banyintu	4

Kagushu (519; 119) [84]
Capita: Madali Singeni

Beshaza	49
Bashaho	19
Balega	8
Bahande	5
Banyambiriri	1
Baloho	1
Badaha	1

Village for which clan statistics are not available:
Nkola (471; 94)
Capita: Kubehya

South Ijwi

Notable: Kasigwa Zacharie

Mpene (1,245) [198]
Capita: Sangara Constantin

Balega	46
Bashaho	43
Bahande	37
Beshaza	18
Banyambiriri	17
Badaha	15
Bakanga	12
Baziralo	5
Banyintu (Bayange)	3
Baloho	2

Muhyahya (192) [113]
Capita: Nyamwirha

Bashaho	42
Balega	24
Beshaza	24
Bahande	14
Badaha	4
Bozi	3
Baloho	1
Banyambiriri	1

Buhoro I (274) [51]
Capita: Mudasumbwa Thomas

Bahande	22
Balega	18
Badaha	4
Beshaza	4
Bashaho	3

Buzibu (713) [148]
Capita: Njamweru Pierre

Balega	36
Bahande (Basibula)	32
Banyambiriri	26
Bashaho	20
Beshaza	18
Badaha	10
Bakanga	6

Nkonde (534) [76]
Capita: Mahugo

Balega	24
Bahande	19
Bashaho	12
Beshaza	6
Banyambiriri	9
Badaha	4
Bakanga	2

Bugarula (421) [66]
Capita: Kadjibwami Bigeba

Badaha	23
Bashaho	14
Banyambiriri	12
Beshaza	10
Bakanga	5
Balega	2

Kimomo (982) [131]
Capita: Baderha Ildephonse

Balega	45
Basibula	20
Bakanga	19
Bashaho	15
Banyambiriri	11
Beshaza	8
Badaha	5
Bahande	5
Baziralo	3

Buhumba (937) [151]
Capita: Mushagasha Ruhembe

Badaha	43
Balega	31
Beshaza	26
Bashaho	13
Banyambiriri	12
Bahande	11
Bakanga	7
Baziralo	5
Baloho	2
Barhungu	1

Gashara (573) [90]
Capita: Nyasi Elias

Bahande	14
Balega	20
Banyambiriri	15
Beshaza	18
Bakanga	11
Bashaho	8
Badaha	3
Baziralo	1

Ntalangwa (949) [166]
Capita: Bagalwa Benoit

Basibula and	
Bahande	40
Bashaho	33
Beshaza	28
Banyambiriri	22
Balega	16
Baziralo	9
Bakanga	8
Baloho	8
Badaha	2

Kasihe (540) [78]
Capita: Bakengamwami
Ntalwingwika

Balega	23
Banyambiriri	14
Bashaho	19
Bakange	6
Bahande	5
Beshaza	5
Baloho	3
Banyamocha	3

Karhayo (623) [134]
Capita: Saburume Kambarhi

Badaha	35
Banyambiriri	25
Bashaho	30
Beshaza	20
Bahande	10
Bashamvu (Beeru)	6
Baloho	2
Bakiko (Bushi)	6

Villages for which clan statistics
are not available:

Chassi (237)
Capita: Warubwene Mutarushwa

Notable: Zihindula Michel

Mugote (1,209) [218]
Capita: Bizaza Innocent

Banyambiriri	76
Beshaza	42
Baloho	34
Bashaho	31
Balega	20
Bahande	12
Badaha	2
Bakanga	1

Bwando (1,285) [234]
Capita: Ruvugwo Paul

Beshaza	118
Banyambiriri	46
Bashaho	32
Baziralo	32
Badaha	3
Basibula	3

Nyakibamba (137) [28]
Capita: Nyandekwa Mbavu

Beshaza	21
Bashaho	6
Balega	1

Bushake (678) [101]
Capita: Kasisi Chirimwami

Bashaho	60
Basibula	18
Banyambiriri	13
Bakanga	3
Baziralo	2
Balega	2
Beshaza	3

Bukere (350) [53]
Capita: Zahiga Paul

Basibula	42
Balega	7
Badaha	2
Banyambiriri	2

Kihumba (292) [57]
Capita: Nyakosi Zacharie

Bashaho	44
Basibula	6
Beshaza	3
Balega	3
Badaha	1

Lubuye (508) [90]
Capita: Ruzuba Rugadju

Balega	36
Bashaho	33
Beshaza	11
Banyambiriri	5
Baloho	4
Basibula	1

Bushovu (500) [69]
Capita: Byuma

Balega	59
Beshaza	8
Banyambiriri	1
Bakanga	1

Butyangali (329) [61]
Capita: Musoro Venant

Banyambiriri	44
Badaha	13
Balega	2
Basibula	2

Nkuvu (576) [81]
Capita: Machumu Changachanga

Balega	50
Beshaza	11
Basibula	11
Bakanga	3
Baziralo	2
Bashaho	2
Banyambiriri	2

Buhoro II (71) [49]
Capita: Lwahimbwa

Bakanga	23
Beshaza	15
Balega	11

Bwiiru (399) [62[
Capita: Mutemura Mungazi

Baziralo	59
Beshaza	2
Banyambiriri	1

Musama (168) [35]
Capita: Ngwasi Munihuzi

Beshaza	22
Banyambiriri	7
Baloho	3
Bashaho	2
Balega	1

Bulegeyi (1,077) [167]
Capita: Mucura Pascal

Beshaza	108
Balega	49
Balaho	6
Banyambiriri	3
Bakanga	1

Village for which clan statistics are not available:

Kigera (334)
Capita: Mvano Joseph
Notable: Ntawiniga Hyacinthe

Rambo (1,104) [146]
Capita: Bitoga Musaka

Balega	66
Beshaza	26
Banyambiriri	22
Basibula	21
Bashaho	9
Badaha	2

Boza (535) [62]
Capita: Mutanyerera Muhamiriza

Banyambiriri	24
Balega	14
Bashaho	10
Bahande	6
Badaha	4
Bakanga	3
Beshaza	1

Bunyama (642) [105]
Capita: Rubibi Mungereza

Balega	69
Beshaza	19
Bashaho	5
Badaha	5
Bakanga	2
Bahande	1
Bashamvo (Bajinji)	2
Banyambiriri	2

Karama (477) [50]
Capita: Ntibanjura Joseph

Bashaho	17
Balega	14
Banyambiriri	8
Basibula	6
Badaha	2
Bakanga	2
Beshaza	1

Muhungwe (1,007) [225]
Capita: Kushiga Balike

Balega	67
Bahande	30
Banyambiriri	15
Badaha	99
Beshaza	5
Bakanga	4
Bashaho	4
Baloho	1

Lemera (1,099) [180]
Capita: Musafiri Yalumire

Balega	59
Banyambiriri	52
Beshaza	19
Bashaho	19
Bahande	17
Bakanga	12
Baziralo	2

Buhagwa (399) [59]
Capita: Rutega Francois

Balega	22
Banyambiriri	13
Beshaza	7
Bashaho	6
Badaha	5
Bakanga	3
Bahande	3

Mubale (1,164) [216]
Capita: Timbiri Tarcice

Balega	64
Bashaho	33
Banyambiriri	28
Badaha	28
Bahande	25
Beshaza	20
Bakanga	14
Baloho	4

Lushindi (579) [100]
Capita: Bahale Edouard

Bashaho	45
Beshaza	15
Balega	13
Banyambiriri	11
Bahande	9
Bachiiko	3
Badaha	2
Bakanga	2

Kilala (422) [101]
Capita: Batumika Munziginya

Balega	43
Beshaza	19
Banyambiriri	13
Bashaho	12
Basibula	9
Badaha	4
Bakanga	1

Mazina (714) [115]
Capita: Kashweka Déogratias

Balega	42
Basibula	24
Bashaho	22
Beshaza	12
Badaha	3
Baloho	3
Banyambiriri	7
Bakanga	1
Balidja	1

Mulamba (377) [56]
Capita: Mwa Chambu

Banyambiriri	16
Balega	17
Bashaho	10
Bakanga	4
Badaha	4
Bahande	3
Baziralo	2

Kinyabalanga (176) [32]
Capita: Rukeba Nyalumya

Balega	15
Bahande	7
Baloho	4
Beshaza	1
Badaha	1
Banyambiriri	4

Notes

Introduction

    1.   Vansina notes that any cursory perusal of the successive editions of *Notes and Queries in Anthropology* makes this clear ("Deep-Down Time: Political Tradition in Central Africa," *History in Africa* 16 [1989], 345). He has noted the vagaries of clan and lineage concepts on many occasions, and has traced the evolution of ethnographic perspectives in the Belgian Congo (among other references see his "The Peoples of the Forest," in *History of Central Africa*, Vol. 1, ed. D. Birmingham and P. Martin, 75–118 [London, 1983]; and "Lignage, idéologie et histoire en Afrique équatoriale," *Enquêtes et documents de l'histoire africaine* 4 [1980], 133–56). My own argument goes beyond the definitional problem; I try to show how understanding the social dynamics associated with "clan" identities is essential to understanding and explaining the emergence of central political power, and vice versa. On this point see D. W. Cohen, "Precolonial History as the History of 'Society'" (*African Studies Review* 17, 2 [1974], 467–72), a review of M. d'Hertefelt's *Les clans du Rwanda ancien* (Tervuren, 1971).

    2.   One example of observers struggling with multiple concepts of clan identities is that of Nkore (J. Roscoe, *The Banyankore* [Cambridge, 1923]; K. Oberg, "Kinship Organisation of the Banyankore," *Africa* 11 [1938], 129–38; M. T. Mushanga, "The Clan System among the Banyankore," *Uganda Journal* 34, 1 [1970], 29–33; S. M. Karugire, *A History of the Kingdom of Nkore in Western Uganda to 1896* [Oxford, 1971]).

    3.   Some exceptions to this are: L. de Heusch, *Le Rwanda et la civilisation interlacustre* (Bruxelles, 1966); J. Jensen, "Die Erweiterung des Lungerfisch-clans in Buganda (Uganda) durch den Anschlush von Bayuma-Gruppen" (*Sociologus* 19, 2 [1962], 153–66); d'Hertefelt, *Les Clans;* Vansina, "Lignage, idéologie, et histoire"; J. Vansina, "Knowledge and Perceptions of the African Past" (in *African Historiographies,* ed. B. Jewsiewicki and D. Newbury, 28–42 [Beverly Hills, 1986]).

    4.   M. Sahlins, *Islands of History* (Chicago, 1985), vii. I am not in total agreement with all aspects of this work and subsequent sources referred to in this section. Nonetheless I find salutary these authors' approaches to historical understanding, especially their views on the relation of historical and cultural understanding, as discussed below.

    5.   E. Wolf, *Europe and the People Without History* (Berkeley, 1982).

    6.   This approach concurs with that of J. L. Comaroff ("Of Totemism and Ethnicity," *Ethnos* 52, 3–4 [1987], 301–22):

The forces which produce consciousness—totemic, ethnic, or other—lie in the construction and transformation of economy and society. But the terms in which they are understood by social actors have to do with the way in which the world is signified: human beings perceive and act upon their contexts not as they are formally constituted but as they are construed in shared signs and symbols. (p. 311)

7. For French history: E. Le Roy Ladurie, *Montaillou* (New York, 1979); E. Le Roy Ladurie, *Carnival in Romans* (New York, 1981); and Natalie Zemon Davis, *Society and Culture in Early Modern France* (Palo Alto, 1975). For United States history, among many other examples: R. Birdsall, *Berkshire County: A Cultural History* (New Haven, 1959); P. Boyer and S. Nissenbaum, *Salem Possessed: The Social Origins of Witchcraft* (Cambridge, Mass., 1974); R. A. Gross, *The Minutemen and Their World* (New York, 1976); and K. Lockridge, *A New England Town: The First Hundred Years* (New York, 1970).

8. M. Taussig, *The Devil and Commodity Fetishism in South America* (Chapel Hill, 1980), 229.

9. Jean Comaroff, *Body of Power, Spirit of Resistance: The Culture and History of a South African People* (Chicago, 1985), 155.

10. Comaroff, *Body of Power,* 156.

11. Comaroff, *Body of Power,* 6.

12. Comaroff, *Body of Power,* 194.

13. Elizabeth Traube, *Cosmology and Social Life: Ritual Exchange among the Mambai of East Timor* (Chicago, 1986), 133.

14. Sahlins, *Islands of History,* 108; emphasis in original.

15. Maurice Bloch, *From Blessing to Violence: History and Ideology in the Circumcision Ritual of the Merina of Madagascar* (Cambridge, 1986).

16. Bloch, *From Blessing to Violence,* 183.

17. Bloch, *From Blessing to Violence,* 194. On the general points being made here, I have found two works particularly useful: Claude Lévi-Strauss, *Totemism* (Boston, 1963); and de Heusch, *Le Rwanda et la civilisation Interlacustre.* Despite the recent criticism of structuralist approaches, these two works raise important questions about the positivist assumptions that characterize the field; they provide a suggestive framework for understanding the transformation of social identities—and they have done so, not at an abstract level, but by close analysis of the historical and ethnographic record. Although I do not accept every detail of their argument, I find their general approach illuminating; they effectively focus our attention on wider regional patterns, on broader questions of social process, and on the need constantly to reexamine our own conceptual assumptions.

18. Sahlins, *Islands of History,* vii.

19. See, for example, "History and Theory: An Editorial" (*History Workshop Journal* 6 [1978], 1–6); Tony Judt, "A Clown in Regal Purple: Social History and the Historians" (*History Workshop Journal* 7 [1979], 66–94); and E. Fox-Genovese and E. Genovese, "The Political Crisis of Social History: Class Struggle as Subject and Object" (chap. 7 in their *Fruits of Merchant Capital* [Oxford, 1983]).

20. This is discussed further in D. Newbury, "Bushi and the Historians: Historiographical Themes in Eastern Kivu" (*History in Africa* 5 [1978], 131–51). In other

articles I have tried to show how a view from the periphery contributes to a reassessment of Rwandan history: "The Clans of Rwanda: An Historical Hypothesis" (*Africa* 50, 4 [1980], 389-403); "Lake Kivu Regional Trade in the Nineteenth Century" (*Journal des africanistes* 50, 2 [1980], 6-30); and " 'Bunyabungo': The Western Frontier in Rwanda" (in *The African Frontier: The Reproduction of Traditional African Societies*, ed. I. Kopytoff, 162-92. [Bloomington, 1986]).

21. H. Codere ("Power in Ruanda," *Anthropologica* [Canada], n.s. 4, 1 [1962], 45-85) discusses such a set of assumptions of the elite monopoly of history as they apply to this area.

22. I discuss this further, drawing on current theories of ethnic identity, in the Conclusion. But the fact that clan categories *can* change does not mean that they necessarily *did* change (still less, that they changed continuously and at a constant rate). For a different view, emphasizing not changes in clan identities but the reproduction of clan structures over long periods, see, *inter alia*, G. Schlee, "Interethnic Clan Identities among Cushitic-speaking Pastoralists" (*Africa* 55, 1 [1985], 17-38); and G. Schlee, *Identities on the Move: Clanship and Pastoralism in Northern Kenya* (Manchester, 1989).

23. It is a lacuna of this work that I carried out so few interviews with women. I began my research in 1970, before I fully understood the significance of the fact that men and women have very different relations to the hegemonic structures of society. I did consult women, but not on a systematic basis, and mostly on specialized topics and skills (language, farming, healing, etc). In other aspects, too, women's perspectives could have significantly textured the history presented here—perhaps in some respects altering it.

24. For a summary of these approaches, see M. C. Young, *The Politics of Cultural Pluralism* (Madison, 1976); M. C. Young, "Nationalism, Ethnicity, and Class in Africa: A Retrospective" (*Cahiers d'études africaines* 26, 4 [1986], 421-95); and L. Vail, "Introduction: Ethnicity in Southern African History" (in *The Creation of Tribalism in Southern Africa*, ed. L. Vail, 1-19 [London, 1989]). Vail proposes a generalized model rather than a precise theoretical formulation; it is a distinction well taken.

Chapter 1. Ijwi Island Today

1. For the Interlacustrine kingdoms, see *inter alia* M. C. Fallers, *The Eastern Lacustrine Bantu* (London, 1960); B. K. Taylor, *The Western Lacustrine Bantu* (London, 1962); M. d'Hertefelt, A. A. Trouwborst, and J. H. Scherer, eds., *Les anciens royaumes de la zone Interlacustre méridionale* (Tervuren, 1962); E. Mworoha, *Peuples et rois de l'Afrique des lacs* (Dakar, 1977); Karugire, *A History of the Kingdom of Nkore;* M. S. M. Kiwanuka, *A History of Buganda. From the Foundation to 1900* (London, 1971); and G. Hartwig, *The Art of Survival in East Africa: The Kerebe and Long Distance Trade* (New York, 1976). For an introduction to the forest cultures, see J. Vansina, *Paths in the Rainforests: Toward a History of Political Tradition in Equatorial Africa* (Madison, 1990); J. Vansina, *Introduction à l'ethnographie du Congo* (Kinshasa, 1966), 53-115; Vansina, "The Peoples of the Forest"; J. Vansina, "Towards a History of Lost Corners in the World" (*Economic History Review* 35, 2 [1982], 165-78); J. Vansina, "L'homme, les forêts, et le passé en Afrique" (*Annales economies, sociétés, civilisations* 6 [1985], 1307–

34); Vansina, "Deep-Down Time"; D. Biebuyck, *Lega Culture: Art, Initiation and Moral Philosophy among a Central African People* (Berkeley, 1973); W. de Mahieu, *Structures et symboles* (Londres, 1980); C. Turnbull, *Wayward Servants: The Two Worlds of the African Pygmies* (Garden City, N.Y., 1965); and C. Turnbull, *The Forest People* (Garden City, N.Y., 1962).

2. The consumption of fish on Ijwi contrasts markedly with customs in Rwanda, where there is, among the Tutsi, a proscription on fish (J. J. Maquet, *Le système des relations sociales dans le Ruanda ancien* [Tervuren, 1954], 271; F. Simoons, *Eat Not This Flesh* [Madison, 1963], 113).

3. Two celebrated examples of these boats are that described by E. Johanssen (*Ruanda: Kleine Anfange-grosse Aufgaben der evangelischen Mission im Zwischenseengebiet Deutsch-Ostafrikas* [Bethel bei Bielefeld, 1912], 200) and the personal boat of Rwabugiri, the late-nineteenth-century warrior-king of Rwanda. For the Abeeja on Ijwi, see Muhinyuzi M., "Le rôle de la pirogue à Idjwi" (Mémoire de Licence, ISP–Bukavu, 1982).

4. These exchanges occurred long before the imposition of colonial boundaries; these were drawn in such a way that Ijwi was included in the Belgian Congo, whereas areas east of the lake (and all islands east of Ijwi) were considered part of Rwanda. (For a discussion of the border negotiations, see W. R. Louis, *Ruanda-Urundi, 1884–1919* [Oxford, 1963].) So what was formerly a commercial pattern essential to the Bany'Iju, often linking families and friends, at a stroke became "illegal smuggling" within the colonial and post-colonial context; for further consideration, see my "From Frontier to Boundary: Some Historical Roots of Peasant Strategies of Survival in Zaire" (in *The Crisis in Zaire: Myths and Realities*, ed. Nzongola Ntalaja, 87–99 [Trenton, N.J., 1986]). Under the present regime, controlling travel across the lake has become especially brutal in the months of May through July, with the coffee harvest; each year people are shot and many boats and goods expropriated by avaricious Zairean military or administrative personnel; in most cases they proceed to sell such expropriated goods in Rwanda on their own account. In these conditions the colonially defined boundary has simply become the pretext for legalized theft and murder by government personnel.

5. I use the term "banana" throughout to refer to types of plantains as well as various types of bananas. Technically, the fermented banana beverage is prepared as a kind of cider, but I follow the convention of referring to it as beer; socially, bottled beer and banana beer are used interchangeably. On the role of bananas in Ijwi society, see Mastaki L., "Bananier et société à Idjwi" (Travail de Fin d'Etudes, ISP–Bukavu, 1982).

6. This is illustrated in the testimony of one man who explained why his family had originally come to Ijwi: "Warhimba [the first ancestor of his family to arrive] came here so he could have his banana grove and make good beer. The Bahavu *like* their beer!" (Mushayuma Semutwa, 3/5/74). Similar comments were not uncommon.

7. One of the most important members of Ijwi's contemporary elite provides an outstanding example. At the time of my research he was principal of the most prestigious primary school on the island, a scion of the Catholic church community, a valued advisor both at the court and for individual members of the Ijwi community. His home was—and continues to be—a favorite gathering spot, where beer from his natal area (in a remote mountainous region of the island) is continuously on hand for

the reception of visitors, even in his absence. Even at the royal court, this beer is recognized as being the "true" beer of Ijwi, "better than whiskey." Its provenance was easily recognizable by members of the court.

8. It was a sad occasion for many homesteads on Ijwi and on the Zaire mainland when, attempting to enforce a policy of *regroupement de villages* in 1972, the administration sent gangs of youths to cut down the banana groves of people who lived near the main roads—supposedly to make room for all the people who would soon be building within the prescribed distance from the road. The cool, moist shade and fragrance of the banana grove, the homestead "retreat," gave way to the harsh sunlight and dust of the dry season, and the homestead retained no protection against the rains and winds of the rainy season. One of the aspects most missed was the rustle of the wind and the sound of the rain among the banana leaves, and in general the loss of a sense of being "enclosed" in the home. This was one more example of the war of harassment waged by the government against the people.

9. In Rwanda, large clay pots *(ibibindi)* are still the containers used for carrying and storing beer, although beer is consumed from gourds. Although the root *"-bindi"* translates as "pot/gourd" over a large part of the Bantu area, on Ijwi it refers to gourds only in the context of carrying beer—otherwise it refers only to a type of large clay pot. The implications are that beer was formerly associated only with clay pots; sorghum beer (as opposed to banana beer) still is.

10. For example, one man who needed beer for a ritual purpose took a small pig onto a well-travelled path, where he slaughtered it and sold the meat, but only in exchange for bananas, not for money. With the bananas he made beer, used what he needed and sold the rest, making a profit far in excess, he told me, of what he could have expected from simply selling the pig, or the meat, directly for money. Frequently, barter and negotiation over land, animals, canoes, and certain "imported" goods occur in private compounds. Markets are only for selling; they lack the sense of social interchange that accompanies distribution through barter and negotiation.

11. Biraro W. "Evolution des formations médicales à Idjwi, 1928–81," Travail de Fin d'Etudes, ISP–Bukavu, 1982.

12. For an account of its founding, see A. de Ligne, *Africa: L'évolution d'un continent vue des volcans du Kivu* (Bruxelles, 1961); see also Muhinyuzi M., "L'impact socio-économique de la Société LINEA–Idjwi sur la population d'Idjwi (1927–1973)" (Travail de Fin d'Etudes, ISP–Bukavu, 1980). Constituting about a sixth of the cultivatable land area of the island, the plantation is in part responsible for land pressure on Ijwi; the wages it paid during the 1970s and 1980s were abysmal and served as the source of frequent social protest. (This illustrates the contemporary form of confrontation between Bany'Iju and outsiders who attempt to control them and the resources of the island: the plantation is owned by an important member of the "Kinshasa clique," but one who claimed ties with Ijwi.) For a consideration of "customary" land tenure forms on Ijwi, see Bayange M., "L'évolution du régime foncier coutumier et le problème des terres dans la Zone d'Idjwi sous les Basibula" (Mémoire de Licence, ISP–Bukavu, 1984).

13. The "zone" (formerly "territoire") is the lowest administrative level tied directly to the Zairean national administrative grid. While different zones vary in size, a zone usually includes 200,000–300,000 people.

14. Although there are many varieties of this game over a vast area of Africa, as

it is played on Ijwi, *mucuba* is very similar to that described in R. S. Shackell, "Mweso— The Board Game" (*Uganda Journal* 2, 1 [1934], 14–26). See also P. Townshend, "Les Jeux de Mankala au Zaïre, au Rwanda et au Burundi" (*Les Cahiers du CEDAF* [1977, no. 3]).

15. For a consideration of this, see D. Newbury and C. Newbury, "King and Chief on Ijwi Island, Zaire" (*International Journal of African Historical Studies* 15, 2 [1982], 221–46); and for the earlier split in the royal family, see D. Newbury, "Rwabugiri and Ijwi" (*Etudes d'histoire africaine* 7 [1975], 155–75). The local *chef de collectivité* in the north, lacking the ritual authority of the *mwami* (his analog in the south), was officially referred to as the *sultani* in the colonial period. The phrasing was awkward but the rationale was significant.

16. I use the term "village" here, and throughout the work, to refer to an administrative unit with a single administrative representative recognized by the court (and local administration), rather than in the sense of a coherent residential cluster of homesteads. Villages on Ijwi vary greatly in size, clan composition, and age; administrative boundaries were also frequently changed during the colonial period.

17. Material on this point, based on my own village surveys and specific interviews, is confirmed by A. Kashamura (*Famille, sexualité, et culture* [Paris, 1973], 122–28 and passim). These characteristics are still present today.

Chapter 2. An Overview of Kivu Culture, c. 1750

1. General overviews of these cultures are found in many works by Vansina: *Introduction à l'ethnographie du Congo*, 53–115; "The Peoples of the Forest"; *Paths in the Rainforests;* "Towards a History of Lost Corners of the World"; and "L'homme, les forêts et le passé en Afrique." Specifically on this region, see Biebuyck, *Lega Culture.* On the Kumu, a people neighboring the Nyanga to the west: de Mahieu, *Structures et symboles;* W. de Mahieu, "Le temps dans la culture Komo" (*Africa* 43, 1 [1973], 2–17); W. de Mahieu, "Cosmologie et structuration de l'espace chez les Komo" (*Africa* 45 [1975], 123–38, 236–57); and W. de Mahieu, "A l'intersection du temps et de l'espace dans l'histoire des idéologies: L'exemple Kumu" (*Cultures et développement* 40 [1979], 415–37). Many of the characteristics of this culture zone are found east of the Nyanga as far as the Ruwenzori Mountain chain in western Uganda (H. Van Geluwe, *Les Bira et les peuplades limitrophes* [Tervuren, 1957]; R. Packard, *Chiefship and Cosmology: An Historical Study of Political Competition* [Bloomington, Ind., 1981], chap. 1; E. Winter, *Bwamba Economy* [Kampala, 1955]; E. Winter, *Beyond the Mountains of the Moon: The Lives of Four Africans* [Urbana, 1959]; E. Winter, "The Aboriginal Political Structure of Bwamba" in *Tribes Without Rulers,* ed. J. Middleton and D. Tait, 136–66 [London 1958]; K. Alnaes, "Nyamayongi's Song: An Analysis of a Konzo Circumcision Song" (*Africa* 37, 4 [1967], 453–65); and R. Oliver, "The Bakonjo and the Baganda" *Uganda Journal* 18, 1 [1954], 31–33).

2. I use the term "prototype society" in a fashion analogous to the way linguists refer to "proto-languages." Lacking data drawn from direct observations for this period, I seek to reconstruct the basic features of a generalized culture model, from current data extrapolated back through time and from the comparison of diffused elements, just as linguists compare variants of contemporary lexical items to arrive at

a root term. I recognize the limits to this technique, and use it only to identify certain cultural features, not to understand the specific relations among cultural elements— the morphology of culture, how society operated, or how it evolved. This technique provides strong indications of certain important elements which composed the culture of the past, no more. But even that can be useful for understanding subsequent change from this reconstructed model. It may not yield as precise a historical reconstruction as some would like, but it is an approach which is at once honest to the fragmentary nature of the data and serviceable for historical reconstruction.

3. Many of these aspects are portrayed in D. Biebuyck, *Rights in Land and Its Resources among the Nyanga* (Brussels, 1966); D. Biebuyck and Mateene K., *Une anthologie de la littérature orale des Nyanga* (Bruxelles, 1970); D. Biebuyck with Mateene K., *The Mwindo Epic from the Banyanga* (recited by Candi Rureke) (Berkeley, 1969); and D. Biebuyck, *Hero and Chief: Epic Literature from the Banyanga (Zaire Republic)* (Berkeley, 1978). In wider cultural classifications, the Nyanga occupy an ambivalent position; culturally they are part of the forest zone, linguistically part of the Interlacustrine zone (S. J. Van Bulck, *Les recherches linguistiques au Congo Belge* [Bruxelles 1948]); Meeussen notes that some features of Kinyanga can be explained only as representing characteristics of an earlier language associated with the Bambuti (pygmies) (A. E. Meeussen, "De Talen van Maniema," *Kongo-Overzee* 19, 6 [1953], 385–91).

4. Biebuyck reports that in 1956 the population density in Bunyanga was fewer than 5 people per square mile (Biebuyck, *Rights in Land,* p. 7; see also Biebuyck, "L'organisation politique des Banyanga: La chefferie Ihana," Part 2, *Kongo-Overzee* 23, 1–2 [1957], 60–61). The sources on which this and the following sections are based relate primarily to the early 1950s. Therefore, I have used the past tense here, though many of these features continue to be effective today. I am aware of the risks of generalization over space and time; by using the past tense I do not intend to imply that these features were unchanging. Nonetheless, the results of my own fieldwork in these areas indicate that the general principles of social organization discussed here can be fairly applied to the past over a broad area.

5. D. Biebuyck, "L'organisation politique des Banyanga: La chefferie Ihana," Part 1, *Kongo-Overzee* 22, 4–5 (1956), 304–5; Biebuyck, *Rights in Land,* passim. There is a review of social organization in *Rights in Land,* 26ff.; in Biebuyck and Mateene, *Mwindo Epic,* 1–5; in Biebuyck and Mateene, *Une anthologie,* 11–12; and in Biebuyck, *Hero and Chief,* 34–75.

6. Biebuyck, "L'organisation politique," 2:59–83, provides a full discussion of the territorial organization of these polities; see also Biebuyck, *Rights in Land,* passim, esp. 33–43.

7. Biebuyck, "L'organisation politique," 1:307; "fictive unit" is Biebuyck's term.

8. Biebuyck, "L'organisation politique," 1:308.

9. The Tembo, for example, identify with the territorially defined political unit—and this identity can change with time or with a shift in residence. Only very rarely will a Tembo cite another identity independent of family or territory. This indicates that names associated with "clans" elsewhere were formerly associated with political units. But the Tembo situation shows that in such territorial units recruitment is not based on putative descent, as is usually assumed to be the case for clan

structures. Such territorial identity also included a much greater potential for change than usually assumed for clan membership.

10.   For a consideration of how changing state power affected clan identities in Rwanda: D. Newbury, "The Clans of Rwanda." At later stages, however, the consolidation of state power seems to have eroded local-level corporate identities (C. Newbury, "Deux lignages au Kinyaga"; and L. Meschi, "Evolution des structures foncières au Rwanda: Le cas d'un lignage Hutu" [both in *Cahiers d'études africaines* 14, 1 (1974)]).

11.   Biebuyck, "L'organisation politique," 1:305–9.

12.   D. Biebuyck, "De Mumbo-instelling bij de Banyanga (Kivu)," *Kongo-Overzee* 21, 5 (1955), 441–48.

13.   Biebuyck, "L'organisation politique," 1:330, 337; 2:63, 88.

14.   Biebuyck, *Lega Culture*, 38, 40, 115.

15.   Biebuyck notes, for example, that in certain respects blood brotherhood provides a stronger and more stable linkage than other socio-political relations in Nyanga society (Biebuyck, "L'organisation politique," 2:92). Today on Ijwi (whether it was so in the past is not clearly established) blood brotherhood is taken to be more important than kinship in certain respects, because it is voluntary, a wilful commitment. The curse attendant on breaking the bloodpact therefore is seen by some as more forboding than the curse associated with the transgression of a kinship taboo. But in the past Bany'Iju appear to have made bloodpacts freely to obtain cattle in Rwanda, and subsequently blithely to have ignored them without consequence when it came time for return payments. In Rwanda, by contrast, bloodpacts were more discrete, more solemn, and undertaken with fewer people (M. Pauwels, "Le pacte du sang au Rwanda," *Annali Lateranensi* 22 [1958], 9–40; R. Bourgeois, "Le pacte du sang au Rwanda," *Bulletin des juridictions indigènes et du droit coutumier congolais* 25, 2 [1957], 39–42). Bushi is more like Ijwi in this regard (R. Bourgeois, "Le pacte du sang au Bushi (cihango ou kunywana)," *Bulletin des juridictions indigènes et du droit coutumier congolais* 27, 2 [1959], 33–36).

16.   Biebuyck, "L'organisation politique," 1:310; D. Biebuyck, "La société Kumu face au Kitawala," *Zaïre* 11, 1 (1957), 32; this second essay is entirely concerned with the interaction of externally derived institutions within an existing social framework. Also A. Moeller de Laddersous, *Les grandes lignes des migrations des Bantous de la Province Orientale au Congo Belge* (Bruxelles, 1936), 312–16; J. Gérard, "La grande initiation chez les Bakumu du nord-est et les populations avoisinantes," *Zaïre* 10, 1 (1956), 87–94. Biebuyck (*Rights in Land*, 7) notes that roughly 20–25 percent of the population of the administrative Territoire de Walikale was non-Nyanga. In "La société Kumu," Biebuyck stresses the "ethnic" heterogeneity of the territorial groups, including, in some cases, the interspersal of Kumu and Nyanga; on pages 13 and 32, he mentions specifically the interchange of Nyanga institutions with their neighbors (cf. also Biebuyck, "L'organisation politique," 1:309–10). Thus the very fluidity and flexibility of the system provide enormous potential for the rapid adaptation to a new external context, such as occurred on Ijwi in the late eighteenth century.

17.   Biebuyck notes that many individuals trace their ties to an "agnatic" group through one or more women ("L'organisation politique," 1:305–9; *Rights in Land*, 26–27).

18. This is detailed in Biebuyck, *Rights in Land,* 17, 20–23.

19. Biebuyck, *Rights in Land,* 25–27, 32.

20. On the basis of figures from Biebuyck ("L'organisation politique," 2:60; and *Rights in Land,* 7 and 32), the largest Nyanga polity included a population on the order of 3,000 people in the 1950s; most polities were much smaller.

21. Biebuyck, "Mumbo," 441–42; Biebuyck, "L'organisation politique," Parts 1 and 2. Colonial alterations, and thus the potential for systemic flexibility and change in the Nyanga political system, are particularly well illustrated in "L'organisation politique," Part 2.

22. Biebuyck, "Mumbo," passim; Biebuyck, "L'organisation politique," Parts 1 and 2, passim, esp. 1:311–32. Except for *bandirabitambo,* cognates for each of these terms are found elsewhere in the Interlacustrine zone.

23. Biebuyck, "L'organisation politique," 1:308, 319.

24. This is implicitly recognized in Biebuyck, "L'organization politique," Part 2, passim, and in Biebuyck, "Mumbo," passim; it also was apparent from my own fieldwork throughout the Tembo kingdoms and in Kalonge.

25. Biebuyck, "Mumbo," 447.

26. Biebuyck, "L'organisation politique," 1:317: "A state can exist for many years without a reigning *mubake;* it is close to decay and disintegration if there is no *mumbo.* Thus in the present state of disintegration of the Nyanga political organisation [under colonial rule], most local groups though they have lost their political stature [*"la personalité politique"*] have, however, maintained a *mumbo,* and in this manner maintain the possibility of reconstructing their former state."

27. This is a parallel institution, although more prominent because associated with the continuity of the polity, to that mentioned above for the commoner level (see p. 50 and note 17 above). A variation of this institution occurs among the Lega, as noted in Biebuyck, *Lega Culture,* 43: "The Lega like to marry within their clans and are proud when they can boast of being *bitutuma* or *mubake,* that is, when they have several categories of male mothers [maternal uncles] in their own clan."

28. Biebuyck, "Mumbo," 444, gives many examples of *bombo* (plural of *"mumbo"*) who were not biologically related to the *mubake,* but were classificatory sisters. These include the daughter of a chief's wife and a man other than the chief, or, likewise, a daughter born long after the death of the former chief, the daughter of a member of the family of the chief, a daughter of a wife of a client of the former king.

29. Biebuyck, "Mumbo," 445.

30. These mechanisms are specified in Biebuyck, "Mumbo," 443–47: esp. 446–47; also in Biebuyck, "L'organisation politique," 1:314–19.

31. Biebuyck, "Mumbo," 445–46; for specific cases: Biebuyck, "L'organisation politique," 2:77, 79. All these principles are evident in the histories of the Tembo states as well.

32. Biebuyck, "L'organisation politique," 2:81.

33. For the remarkable convergence of the role of "sister marriage" among reigning monarchs elsewhere, see L. de Heusch, *Essais sur le symbolisme de l'inceste royale en Afrique* (Bruxelles, 1958), esp. chap. 3.

34. In addition to the Ijwi cases cited below in chapter 11, two cases of succession conflicts in Kalehe, including the long period of undetermined succession after

the death of Kamerogosa in 1961, illustrate this struggle. Perhaps the clearest example of this in the sources now available is the case of Rwanda, where Rwabugiri appointed his favorite wife to serve as ritual queen mother to the designated successor (who was not her own son). Within two years of Rwabugiri's death in 1895, she had succeeded in removing the designated heir and replacing him with her own infant son, in the famous Coup of Rucunshu. (There are many sources on this, among them: A. Kagame, *Les milices du Rwanda précolonial* [Bruxelles, 1963], 101, 113, 135–36, 162, 167; A. Kagame, *La poésie dynastique au Rwanda* [Bruxelles, 1951], 47; A. Kagame, *Un abrégé de l'histoire du Rwanda de 1853 à 1972*, Vol. 2 [Butare, 1975], 105–28, esp. 122–26; L. de Lacger, *Ruanda* [Kabgayi, 1961], 358–59, 361–69; M. d'Hertefelt and A. Coupez, *La royauté sacrée de l'ancien Rwanda* [Tervuren, 1964], 333–34; and A. Des Forges, "Defeat Is the Only Bad News: Rwanda under Musinga, 1896–1931" [Ph.D. diss., Yale University, 1972], 21–22, 26–32). Political maneuvering of this sort was common in Rwandan succession struggles—and the queen mothers were prominent actors in these struggles. In fact the struggle over "kingship" was often subordinate to the struggle over succession to the female role of queen mother in Rwanda and in many other states. At a more general level (though with some reservations), see R. Cohen, "Oedipus Rex and Regina" (*Africa* 47, 1 [1977], 11–31).

35.   Biebuyck, "L'organisation politique," 1:314–21; 2:81, 86–92; Biebuyck, *Une anthologie*, 12–13.

36.   L. Viaene, "L'organisation politique des Bahunde," *Kongo-Overzee* 18 (1952), Part 1 in no. 1, 8–34, Part 2 in no. 2–3, 111–21. This pattern also seems to have been frequent in Butembo and Buhunde, though it is possible that the present intensity of this practice is a more recent development.

37.   Biebuyck, "L'organisation politique," 1:306–7, 309–10, 316, 321–22.

38.   Biebuyck, "L'organisation politique," 1:326. This role bears obvious similarities to that of *murhwali* on Ijwi; in fact in Kiny'Iju (the language of Ijwi) the term *"muluzi"* refers to a member of the royal family (though many say it is a Mashi term), whereas *"murhwali"* refers to a member of the royal family invested with political power. On the term *"muluzi,"* see R. Sigwalt and E. Sosne, "A Note on the Luzi of Bushi" (*Etudes d'histoire africaine* 7 [1975], 137–41).

39.   Biebuyck, "L'organisation politique," 1:324–26; Biebuyck, "Mumbo," passim. In fact, many of the terms and titles noted above are found throughout the wider Interlacustrine region with remarkably similar semantic fields. *"Baluzi"* (*barusi*), for example, is the term for direct descendants of kings in Buhavu and Bushi; *"bakungu"* is the term used for wealthy persons (or those of high political positions) as far east as Lake Victoria. Among the vast ethnographic literature for these areas are: Fallers, *The Eastern Lacustrine Bantu;* Taylor, *The Western Lacustrine Bantu;* Mworoha, *Peuples et rois de l'Afrique des lacs;* and Hartwig, *The Art of Survival.*

40.   Biebuyck, "L'organisation politique," 1:327–30; Biebuyck, "Mumbo," passim. For the role of Musao in Buhunde, see Viaene, "L'organisation politique des Bahunde," 1:21; 2:114. Musao is the title inherited with the role, but it also becomes the titleholder's personal name as well as the name of his clan.

41.   The material on Nyanga and Hunde *mubande* rituals is drawn from "Le Mpandi ou le Mubandi chez les Banyanga et les Bahunde" (unpublished document, Bobandana Mission, n.d., based on materials collected by L. Viaene from several

sources, including missionaries and Zairean priests). *Mubande* is also mentioned in Viaene, "L'organisation politique des Bahunde," 1:13. Quartz crystals are also used in slightly different contexts in some Nande states (R. M. Packard, "The Politics of Ritual Control among the Bashu of Eastern Zaïre during the Nineteenth Century" [Ph.D. diss., University of Wisconsin–Madison, 1976], 58). In Rwanda, too, 24 quartz crystals were found in the grave of Mwami Cyirima Rujugira. Some of these were polished, perforated, or otherwise worked by hand. Two transluscent crystals were unusually long (F. L. Van Noten, *Les tombes du roi Cyirima Rujugira et de la reine-mère Nyirayuhi Kanjogera: Description archéologique* [Tervuren, 1972], 35; plate 12, items 19, 32, 70).

42.   It is significant that Kalinda was the first *chef de tout le Buhunde* (he was appointed in 1923), and prior to this *mubande* document, he had actively collaborated with the same priest in preparing a document entitled "Histoire des Bahunde," which portrays Buhunde as having "always" formed a single centralized kingdom, a perspective very different from numerous other data. The implication is that the political context within which the sources were collected significantly affected the presentation of Hunde history. The same bias is apparent in the *"mubande"* document. The *mubande* data were obtained, we are told, only after repeated requests to the *mwami* on the part of Pére Viaene. On Kalinda, see Kalinda K., "Essai de biographie du Mwami Kalinda Muteso (André) de la chefferie Buhunde, 1904–1976" (Travail de Fin d'Etudes, ISP–Bukavu, 1982).

43.   I am not arguing here that the Hunde form was identical to the Nyanga form, but that the Hunde data on *mubande* are too unreliable to be used as an indication of an earlier form at all, and that therefore (given their similarities in general culture) we must seek to understand earlier forms of *mubande* among both Nyanga and Hunde through the Nyanga forms alone, until other data are available. Of course in practice, there were certain variations also among Nyanga forms, as among Hunde forms.

44.   B. Corti, *Les mois du sorgho* (Bruxelles, 1955); R. D. Sigwalt, "The Early History of Bushi: An Essay in the Historical Use of Genesis Traditions" (Ph.D. diss., University of Wisconsin–Madison, 1975), 132.

45.   P. Colle, *Monographie des Bashi* (Bukavu, 1971), 260, 264–66; E. Sosne, "Kinship and Contract in Bushi: A Study in Village-Level Politics" (Ph.D. diss., University of Wisconsin–Madison, 1974), Appendix 1; Sigwalt ("The Early History of Bushi," 135) notes the differences in the Kaziba and Haya forms in Bushi.

46.   Moeller de Laddersous, *Les grandes lignes;* J. B. Cuypers, "Les Bantous Interlacustres du Kivu," in *Introduction à l'ethnographie du Congo,* by J. Vansina, 201–11 (Kinshasa, 1965); J. Vansina, "Introduction," in *Les anciens royaumes,* ed. d'Hertefelt, Trouwborst, Scherer.

47.   Bucyalimwe M., "Une rationalisation? Les migrations rwandaises au Kivu, Zaïre," in *Ambiquité de l'innovation: Sociétés rurales et technologies en Afrique centrale et occidentale au XXe siècle,* ed. B. Jewsiewicki and J.-P. Chrétien, 39–54, (Québec, 1984). Bucyalimwe M., "Land Conflict in Masisi, Eastern Zaïre: The Impact and Aftermath of Belgian Colonial Policy, 1920–1989" (Ph.D. diss., Indiana University, 1990), adds greatly to our understanding of the complex layers of interaction during the colonial and post-colonial periods.

48.   On Hunde political organization: Biebuyck, "L'organisation politique," 1:304, 307, 309, 310, 311, 326, 337; 2:62, 66; Biebuyck, *Rights in Land,* 8; Biebuyck, "La société Kumu," 38, note 13; Viaene, "L'organisation politique des Bahunde," 1:111–21. Marriage ties are catalogued in Biebuyck, "L'organisation politique," 1:319; 2:86. On commerce, the Nyanga received goats, sheep, dogs, oil, and iron tools for *butega,* anklet-bracelets of woven raphia fibers (T. Barns, *Across the Great Craterland to the Congo,* [London, 1923], 114–16; D. Newbury, "Lake Kivu Regional Trade").

49.   For example, both A. Pagès (*Au Ruanda. Sur les bords du Lac Kivu, Congo belge. Un royaume Hamite au coeur de l'Afrique* [Bruxelles, 1933], section 5) and I. Reisdorff ("Enquêtes foncières au Rwanda," [unpublished manuscript, Butare, n. d. (1952?)], enquête no. 33) note the intensive population movements in this area: "Les Bagoyi [of northwestern Rwanda] . . . sont presque tous originaires du nord-ouest du Lac Kivu" (Pagès, *Un royaume Hamite,* 638). Further references to the cultural ties between Bugoyi and Buhunde are found in Pagès, *Un royaume Hamite,* 661–62, 667, 676, 682. Pagès (pp. 644–45) also gives a list of *"clans et sous-clans"* of Bugoyi, in which he attributes "western origins" to almost half the groups cited (27 of 57). For commercial interaction, see D. Newbury, "Lake Kivu Regional Trade."

50.   Personal communication from Prof. A. Coupez of the Musée Royal de l'Afrique Centrale (Tervuren, Belgium). Although Kinyarwanda has penetrated the entire area today, there are indications that the tonality of the Bugoyi dialect of Kinyarwanda is similar to that of Kihunde and different from Kinyarwanda elsewhere; verbal conjugations of the language formerly spoken in Bugoyi (before Kinyarwanda became so widespread) were also markedly different from those of Kinyarwanda. A few pockets of this former language remain in the mountains of eastern Bugoyi (on the Nile-Zaire Divide), and the people who speak this language claim distant historical ties to the Nande to their northwest. I am grateful to Prof. A. Coupez for his valuable assistance on these matters.

51.   R. D. Sigwalt, "Early Rwanda History: The Contribution of Comparative Ethnography," *History in Africa* 2 (1975), 137–46.

52.   By "eastern highland," I refer particularly to the villages of Kisheke, Musama, Buholo II, and parts of Bwando, on the flanks of the forested mountain area along Ijwi's eastern shore.

53.   Gahire 27/1/73.

54.   Examples of these are: *"mukungu,"* a respected elder (a term found in many other lacustrine languages as well, but not commonly used on Ijwi); *"cicugwa,"* "goat"; *"bwacere,"* a morning greeting.

55.   Kishake 30/5/74.

56.   Among foods the consumption of *bifunu,* a root crop grown in the forest areas, serves as one example. For material culture, the preference for round clay huts rather than hemispherical thatch huts, and the use of several types of shoulder bags distinguish this locale from other areas on Ijwi.

57.   F. L. Van Noten, "The Early Iron Age in the Interlacustrine Region: The Diffusion of Iron Technology," *Azania* 14 (1979), 61–80. P. R. Schmidt ("A New Look at the Interpretations of the Early Iron Age of East Africa," *History in Africa* 2 [1975], 127–37) also shares this general line of argument. For earlier archeological discussions of this area: J. Nenquin, *Contribution to the Study of the Prehistoric Cultures of Rwanda*

and Burundi (Tervuren, 1967); J. Hiernaux and E. Maquet, "Cultures préhistoriques de l'âge des métaux au Rwanda-Urundi et au Kivu (Congo belge). Première partie," ARSC, *Bulletin des Séances* 2, 6 (1957): 1126–49; and J. Hiernaux and E. Maquet, *Cultures préhistoriques de l'âge des métaux au Rwanda-Urundi et au Kivu (Congo belge), IIe partie; suivi de: Deux sites archéologiques à briques en territoire Walikale (Kivu)* (Bruxelles, 1960).

58.   In a more recent work, Van Noten gives cautious confirmation to this observation, concluding: "There is a clear distinction between the sites along the Lake Kivu axis and those situated to the east" (although he does not directly consider the Zairean sites in this particular work) (F. L. Van Noten, *Histoire archéologique du Rwanda* [Tervuren, 1983], 27–28). See also F. L. Van Noten, ed., *The Archeology of Central Africa* (Graz, Austria, 1982), 72: "[Kawezi ware] is typologically closer to Kalambo ware than [to] any other Interlacustrine wares." Others, however, disagree (M. C. Van Grunderbeek and E.R.H. Doutrelepont, "L'âge du fer ancien au Rwanda et au Burundi: Archéologie et environnement," *Journal des africanistes* 52, 1–2 [1982], 25).

59.   For a discussion of these attitudes, see my " 'Bunyabungo' "; also C. Newbury, *The Cohesion of Oppression: Clientship and Ethnicity in Rwanda, 1860–1960* (New York, 1988), 36, 51. Disdain towards people in the west is a prominent feature of Rwandan cultural stereotypes still today.

60.   J. Vansina, *Oral Tradition* (Chicago, 1965), classifies these sources. Among the older works, Pagès, *Un royaume Hamite,* and de Lacger, *Ruanda,* are outstanding. More recent historical work on Rwandan history based on oral traditions includes: A. Kagame, *Inganji Karinga,* 2 vols. (Kabgayi, Rwanda, 1950); A. Kagame, *L'histoire des armées bovines dans l'ancien Rwanda* (Bruxelles, 1961): Kagame, *La poésie dynastique;* Kagame, *Les milices;* A. Kagame, *Un abrégé de l'ethno-histoire du Rwanda,* Vol. 1 (Butare, 1972); Kagame, *Un abrégé;* C. Gakaniisha, *Récits historiques Rwanda* (Tervuren, 1962); J. K. Rennie, "The Precolonial Kingdom of Rwanda: A Reinterpretation" (*Trans-african Journal of History* 2, 2 [1972], 11–53); J. Vansina, *L'évolution du royaume Rwanda dès origines à 1900* (Bruxelles, 1962). Valuable overviews of recent Rwanda social organization, which also account for historical and regional differences, are M. d'Hertefelt "Le Rwanda" (in *Les anciens royaumes,* ed. d'Hertefelt, Trouwborst, and Scherer, 9–112; and M. d'Hertefeldt, "The Rwanda of Rwanda" (in *The Peoples of Africa* ed. J. Gibbs, 403–40 [New York, 1965]); also see d'Hertefelt and Coupez, *La royauté sacrée,* for a consideration of the ritual culture of Rwandan royalty.

61.   The principal exceptions to this are discussed in M. Pauwels, "Le Bushiru et son *muhinza* ou roitelet Hutu" (*Annali Lateranensi* 31 [1967], 205–322), a valuable case study of one of these polities; F. Nahimana, "Les bami ou roitelets Hutu du corridor Nyabarongo-Mukungwa avec ses régions limitrophes" (*Etudes rwandaises* 12, numéro spécial [1979], 1–25), provides an overview; de Lacger, *Ruanda,* and J. K. Rennie, "The Precolonial Kingdom of Rwanda," both provide overviews of Rwandan history which give due recognition to the historical significance of these pre-Nyiginya polities. Larger states to the east and north have been the study of A. d'Arianoff (*Histoire des Bagesera, souverains du Gisaka* [Bruxelles, 1952]) and, for Ndorwa, J. M. Freedman ("Principles of Relationship in Rwandan Kiga Society" [Ph.D. diss., Princeton University, 1974]; "Joking, Affinity, and the Exchange of Ritual Services among the Kiga of Northern Rwanda: An Essay in Joking Rela-

tionship Theory," *Man*, n.s. 12, 1 [1977], 154–65; "Three Muraris, Three Gahayas, and the Four Phases of Nyabingi," in *Chronology, Migration and Drought in Interlacustrine Africa*, ed. J. B. Webster, 175–87 [New York, 1979]; and *Nyabingi: The Social History of an African Diety* [Tervuren, 1984]). The kingdoms of Busozo and Bukunzi in the southwestern part of Rwanda were conquered with Belgian assistance during 1923–1925 (de Lacger, *Ruanda*, 82–89; E. Ntezimana, "Coutumes et traditions des royaumes Hutu du Bukunzi et du Busozo," *Etudes rwandaises* 13, 2 [1980], 15–39; E. Ntezimana, "L'arrivée des Européens au Kinyaga et la fin des royaumes Hutu du Bukunzi et du Busozo," *Etudes rwandaises* 13, 3 [1980], 1–29; P. Smith, *Le récit populaire au Rwanda* [Paris, 1975], 320–25: "Fin d'un roitelet," narrated by A. Bapfakulera; C. Newbury, *The Cohesion of Oppression*, chap. 4). Bushiru and Kingogo in the north-western part of the country were conquered in the same period (Des Forges, "Defeat Is the Only Bad News"; F. Nahimana, "Les principautés Hutu du Rwanda sep-tentrional," in *La civilisation ancienne des peuples des Grands Lacs*, ed. L. Ndoricimpa, 115–37 [Paris, 1984]).

62.   Pauwels, "Le Bushiru," 244, note 61.

63.   Pauwels, "Le Bushiru," 210–20. *"Muhinza"* is the term usually used in sources influenced by Rwandan central court paradigms. For a discussion of this term, see Nahimana, "Les bami ou roitelets Hutu."

64.   Pauwels, "Le Bushiru," 212. A similar ceremony is also apparent for Buhunde (L. Viaene, "La religion des Buhunde (Kivu)," *Kongo-Overzee* 18, 5 [1952], 394–95) and for certain pre-dynastic groups on Ijwi Island as well.

65.   Pauwels, "Le Bushiru," 211. This observation carries greater significance than simply as a statement that the *muhinza* sought the advice of others. In general, colonial authors equated the ritual pre-eminence of rulers with political "abso-lutism." Because their model of African kingship was based on their understanding of the colonial Banyiginya state, they tended to undervalue the collegial aspect of power within these small polities along the Nile-Zaire Divide. This lends even greater significance to the remark that the *mwami* "took no important decision without first having consulted his council," a remark which also reflects the conclusion of de Lacqer (*Le Ruanda*, 83).

66.   Pauwels, "Le Bushiru," 211. It should be reiterated that the sources here have a very strong bias towards father-to-son succession, the normative rule in the Rwandan (Abanyiginya) state. This lends added weight to the precision of this statement; but it also explains the implication that sometimes a son was chosen. Of course, ideally, the son of the *mumbo* was also the son of the *mubake* (or *muhinza*); although in this case there is no necessary correlation with the institution of *mumbo*, it is highly probable that this fact would not have been disclosed to the European investigators, especially when they were priests (and rather zealous priests at that, as was Pauwels).

67.   Pauwels, "Le Bushiru," 216.

68.   Biebuyck, "Mumbo," 443–47; Biebuyck, "L'organisation politique," 1:314–19.

69.   The sources on Bunyanga and these early Rwandan polities are clearly independent of each other. Although Rwandan sources pre-date Biebuyck's publica-tions, they are scattered within the Rwandan writings and very much concerned with

the Rwandan historical context. It is highly unlikely that they influenced Biebuyck's analysis in any way, which in any case was based on his own fieldwork.

70. However, the political assumptions and structures are not as common as Ntezimana assumes for Busoozo and Bukunzi in "Coutumes et traditions," where he treats these two polities as virtually interchangeable structures. For influential early diffusionist studies of this area: R. Bourgeois, *Banyarwanda et Barundi*, Vol. 1, *Ethnographie* (Bruxelles, 1957); J. Gorju, *Entre le Victoria, l'Albert, et l'Edouard* (Rennes, La Belgique, 1920); and Moeller de Laddersous, *Les grandes lignes*.

Chapter 3. The Process of Social Transformation on Ijwi Island

1. Bishingwe 25/1/72; Luvumba 1/2/72; Kayoga (Muhyahya) 3/2/72; Buzombo 5/2/72; Rubangura 11/2/72; Nzibukiya 1/3/72; Mahenga 9/3/72; Musigi 10/3/72; Mbaraga 28/3/72; Nyenyezi Mabwiiru 15/5/74; and many others. The story is very widely known.

2. Mesokubina, 3/5/72; Bigwana 19/2/73; Kabangala 21/2/73; Gatera Kanega 6/5/74.

3. *Bifunu* grow very slowly and take over 24 hours of slow steaming to cook. The younger population today say they taste bitter. References to *bifunu* are particularly numerous in the traditions of the Bakanga. *Bifunu* are also mentioned in the traditions of Busobe, as will be discussed below.

4. R. Oliver, "The Baganda and the Bakonjo," 31–32; A. Kagwa, *The Kings of Buganda*, ed. M. S. M. Kiwanuka (Nairobi, 1971), 48–52.

5. Biebuyck, "L'organisation politique," 1:301–41.

6. A story is told of why they were driven out from an earlier residence for having "killed" the *mwami* by serving *bifunu* which were not well cooked. Among others: Mesokubina 3/5/72; Nyangurane Nyamulinda 24/5/72.

7. Another name, the Babwehera, has not been included in the discussion here because my interviews contain only 11 references to it and because the general characteristics are similar to those discussed for Nyamuhiva and the Binyalenge. In addition to these three names, there are a few scattered references to other names in the same contexts and some minor variations to the names noted above.

8. The term "Nyamuhiva" is of the form that could be interpreted as the leader of ("possessor of") the hunters—"Muhiva" being derived from the verb *"kuhiva,"* "to hunt." Sometimes the term is rendered as "Bahivi," "the hunters." Similarly sometimes "Cinyalenge," the singular personal form of "Binyalenge," appears in the Lenge traditions. (The prefix "Banya-" or "Binya-" is almost always associated with either a very "old" group as portrayed in the traditions [Binyalenge, Banyakabwa] or a very broad regional identity [Banyarwanda, Banyabungo]. Similarly, "Bene-" is a prefix associated with old groups; it is also used widely in Luba areas in southern Zaire.)

9. These figures are not based on a rigorous statistical sample, although I did interview in all areas of the island. The important point is that the two traditions were clearly predominant in different parts of the island.

10. Two-thirds of the Nyamuhiva references were drawn from such forest areas.

11. In addition, over three-quarters of the references to the Babwehera,

another name associated with this general corpus of traditions, were drawn from villages near the forest areas.

12. Evidence for this is found in Marandura 2/5/74; Zabona (Nkola) 2/5/74; and esp. Bengehya 2/5/74. Murhima's evidence (4/5/74) also implied that he did not know of Nyamuhiva, because those people were a different group; Murhima is a Mwooze. Kilembelembe (sometimes cited as Kiremberembe) is another name associated with this type of tradition, readily identified in Busobe; see Bagereka Balimungu 21/2/73; Kabangala 21/2/73; Mbogo-Mbogo Bazurunguka 21/2/73.

13. These traditions are sketchy but widely spread. An indication of their importance is found in: Ndwanyi Simba 10/3/72; Ndimanyi 21/3/72; Burhola 22/3/72; Kavurha 27/3/72; Mbaraga 28/3/72; Gasarahinga (Bwando) 29/3/72; Sogoro 30/3/72; Ruhingana 16/5/72; Gahanda Shabiniga 26/1/73; Gisayura Mukabyo 2/2/73; Karaza Zagabe 16/2/73; Rubambura (Buruhuka) 16/2/73; Kabangala Kubushano 21/2/73; Mbogo-Mbogo Bazurunguka 21/2/73; Bengehya 2/5/74; Marandura 2/5/74; Ngonyosi 7/5/74. These traditions also tie the Booze to the east, whereas most people assume Balega historical ties to be exclusively with the west.

14. "Kilembelembe" is not recognized as an ancestor in Nkola. Zabona (Nkola, 2/5/74) made a distinction between "Nabusobe" and "Nankola"; Bagereka Balimungu (21/2/73) stated that there were two Nankolas.

15. Kabangala 21/2/73; Mbogo-Mbogo Bazurunguka 21/2/73; Bagereka Balimungu 21/2/73; Bishangi 17/2/73.

16. One Mwooze in Busobe, for example, claimed that the early inhabitants of Busobe were Binyalenge, and others confirmed that (Kabangala 21/2/73). Kabangala denied that he himself was Lenge, but Rutengura (14/2/73) identified him as such.

17. Bagereka 21/2/73; Kabangala 21/2/73.

18. Kabangala 21/2/73.

19. Mbogo-Mbogo Bazurunguka 21/2/73; "kwa" is the Kiswahili preposition meaning "at the place of" or (in this case) "in the land of." The proper Kihavu term would have been *"emwa."* The use of this term stresses the colonial affiliation associated with Kalinda's authority.

20. Though administratively part of Buhavu today, the peninsula of Buzi is thought of on Ijwi as being Hunde, as indeed it was until the Belgian arrival; today Buzi remains the "gateway" to Buhunde from Ijwi. Although scholars today often classify Hunde culture as Interlacustrine (primarily on linguistic grounds), on Ijwi Hunde culture is considered very distinct from others in the Interlacustrine zone (Shi, Rwanda, Rundi). Most Bany'Iju in fact view Buhunde as similar to Tembo and Nyanga cultures, which are, in the terms considered here, forest cultures; see Mweeru 1/2/72 for an example.

21. Of 28 references which relate the Binyalenge to other groups, 14 associated them with Balega, 10 of which were specifically with the Booze; 10 associated them with the Banyakabwa, either through association (e.g., contemporaneity) or direct identity. Because these are regular associations, and consistent over the different times and different regions of my research, they can be seen as variations on a single tradition.

22. Ndayalire 29/4/72.

23. Ndayaza 25/5/74.

24.   Mvano 12/5/72. Rubambiza (Cugi, 25/1/73), Luvumba (1/2/72), Ngwasi (3/3/72), Barhombo (29/1/73), Karaza Zagabe (16/2/73), and Murhima (4/5/74) all provide similar statements.

25.   Kanyama 2/2/72.

26.   Burhola 28/6/72; other examples abound.

27.   Bavugerije 31/1/72.

28.   *"Kabwa"* means "dog." Associating the Banyakabwa with hunting cultures on this basis is almost surely etiological rather than etymological, though dogs are also associated with royal status (as well as with hunting) throughout the area.

29.   Some references to the Binyalenge associate them with Barhwa, who on Ijwi are uniquely forest peoples; others identify them socially with the Bahunde, also considered on Ijwi to be of a forest culture (Mweeru 1/2/72; also Sakari 3/3/72; Ruhamanya 9/8/72). A group of elders (see Ntambuka Sibula 15/3/72) noted: "They were hunters who spoke a language like Kitembo—not Kihavu. Perhaps they were Barhwa; they came about the same time as the Barhwa."

30.   The term "Balega*" will be used here to refer to those Balega who are not members of the Booze, Babambo, or Bashovu subgroups. Frequently others refer to them as Balega b'e Cime, though this also applies to the Bashovu and occasionally is used for all Balega. The Babambo and Booze are distinguished from other Balega by their strong corporate identity, precise historical traditions, and a tendency towards residential localization. These characteristics are shared by the Bashovu, a Lega subgroup in the south, living at Bushovu, and occupationally distinct from others as ironsmiths. In these respects the Babambo, Booze, and Bashovu subgroups are similar to clans of Group III in the classification above. As will be discussed in chapter 7, the Babambo especially, but indirectly also the Booze, are tied to the royal line historically, another characteristic of Group III traditions. Balega* groups ("Balega b'e Cime") form the great majority of Balega on Ijwi.

31.   On recent emigration from Ijwi: Newbury and Newbury, "King and Chief on Ijwi Island."

32.   Since the Balega share historical ties with the western forest areas, the finding that women in Butembo show a significantly lower fertility rate than women in Rwanda is relevant for this analysis. A Belgian medical team, after considerable research in the area, relate low fertility rates to very early marriage ages for females in the forest cultures. There is no indication that this is only a recent pattern, so it is highly unlikely that Balega numerical preponderance on Ijwi has resulted from higher fertility rates associated with cultural attributes.

33.   Despite some passing recognition of Bashovu skills as ironsmiths in the royal rituals of Ijwi, Bashovu participation in the rituals is minimal. See chapter 12 for a more complete discussion of these roles.

34.   For Buganda: Jensen, "Die Erweiterung des Lungerfisch-clans." For Rwanda: de Heusch, *Le Rwanda et la civilisation Interlacustre,* esp. 47–64; and D. Newbury "The Clans of Rwanda." Elsewhere, J. Tosh, *Clan Leaders and Colonial Chiefs in Lango: The Political History of an East African Stateless Society, c. 1890–1939* (Oxford, 1978), 54–57. For a discussion of colonial distortions based on false assumptions of social process in Zaire: Vansina, "Lignage, idéolgie, et histoire"; and Vansina, "Knowledge and Perceptions of the African Past."

35.   The relations between these "western" peoples and the authorities of the Rwandan central court are examined in my " 'Bunyabungo'."

Chapter 4. Rwanda and the Rift

1.   The essential source on the history of Rwanda for this era is A. Kagame, *Inganji Karinga* (Kabgayi, 1959). Overviews of early Rwandan history include A. Kagame, *Histoire du Rwanda* (Leverville, Congo Belge, 1958); Kagame, *Un abrégé,* Vol. 1; Vansina, *L'évolution;* Rennie, "The Precolonial Kingdom of Rwanda." For commentaries on the early traditions, see P. Smith, "La forge de l'intelligence" (*L'homme* 10, 2 [1970], 5–21); P. Smith, "La lance d'une jeune fille" (in *Echanges et communications,* Vol. 2, ed. J. Pouillon and P. Maranda, 1381–408; [La Haye, 1970]); and L. de Heusch, *Rois nés d'un coeur de vache* (Paris, 1982).

2.   Vansina, *L'évolution,* 44–45; de Heusch, *Rois nés,* chap. 2; for a perceptive analysis, see Smith, "La lance d'une jeune fille." Other commentaries on the variations among Rwandan genesis myths include: P. Loupias, "Traditions et légendes des Batutsi sur la création du monde et leur établissement au Rwanda" (*Anthropos 3,* 1 [1908], 1–13); de Lacger, *Ruanda,* 92–95, 162–66; Kagame, *Un abrégé* 1:35–36; Gakaniisha, *Récits historiques,* 61–86; Smith, *Le récit populaire,* 140–47, 284–89.

3.   On Ruganzu, see Pagès, *Un royaume Hamite,* 128–29, 228–345; Kagame, *Un abrégé,* 1:93–109; Vansina, *L'évolution,* 67–68, 86–87; de Lacger, *Ruanda,* 107–8; Gakaniisha, *Récits historiques,* 205–62; de Heusch, *Rois nés,* chaps. 3 and 5; Smith, *Le récit populaire,* 314–19.

4.   Vansina, *L'évolution,* 46–47; de Heusch, *Rois nés,* chap. 4; but cf. d'Hertefelt, *Les clans,* 24.

5.   On Ryangombe, see A. Arnoux, "Le culte de la société sécrète des imandwa au Ruanda" (*Anthropos 7* [1912], 273–95, 529–58, 840–74, *Anthropos 8* [1913], 110–34, 754–74); de Lacger, *Ruanda,* 266–319; I. Berger, *Religion and Resistance. East African Kingdoms in the Precolonial Period* (Tervuren, 1981); de Heusch, *Le Rwanda et la civilisation Interlacustre;* de Heusch, "Mythe et société féodale. Le culte du Kubandwa dans le Rwanda traditionnel" (*Archives de sociologie des religions* 9, 18 [1964], 133–46); C. Vidal, "Anthropologie et histoire: Le cas du Rwanda" (*Cahiers internationaux de sociologie* 43, 2 [1967], 143–57); de Heusch, *Rois nés,* chap. 5; Gakaniisha, *Récits historiques,* 263–70; Smith, *Le récit populaire,* 232–61; Bourgeois, *Banyarwanda et Barundi,* Vol. 3, *Religion et magie* (Bruxelles, 1956), 71–97.

6.   Vansina, *L'évolution,* 70; Kagame (*Les milices,* 61) states that this occurred under Mutara Semugeshi, four reigns before Rwaka/Rujugira; the dynastic names Mutara and Cyilima occupy similar structural positions in the purported "cycle" of Rwandan kings, and it is not uncommon that events of one reign are associated with—or reflected in—the reign of its positional analogue.

7.   A point effectively made by Vansina (*L'évolution,* passim).

8.   On Rwabugiri, see D. Newbury, "Les campagnes de Rwabugiri: Chronologie et bibliographie" (*Cahiers d'études africaines* 14, 1 [1974], 181–92); Kagame, *Un abrégé,* Vol. 2. On his army organizations: Kagame, *Les milices,* passim; C. Newbury, *The Cohesion of Oppression,* chap. 2; Bourgeois, *Banyarwanda et Barundi,* Vol. 1, *Ethnographie.* For Rwabugiri's conquest and occupation of Ijwi Island: D. Newbury, "Rwabuguri and Ijwi."

9. Vansina, *L'évolution,* 70-71; J. Rwabukumba and V. Mudandagizi, "Les formes historiques de la dépendance personnelle dans l'état rwandais," *Cahiers d'études africaines* 14, 1 (1974), 6-25.

10. Reisdorff, "Enquêtes foncières"; C. Newbury, *The Cohesion of Oppression,* chap. 2; Rwabukumba and Mudandagizi, "Les formes historiques." For a general consideration of the importance of land access in precolonial Rwanda: C. Vidal, "Economie de la société féodale rwandaise" (*Cahiers d'études africaines* 14, 1 [1974], 52-74).

11. There are dangers in argumentation of this type, but reasonable conjecture on structural processes arrived at through the analysis of convergent circumstantial evidence is defended in A. M. Hocart, *Kings and Councillors,* ed. R. Needham (Chicago, 1970), 11-29.

12. For conflicting views on Rujugira's reign: Kagame, *Un abrégé,* 1:135-53; and Vansina, *L'évolution,* 51; the sources cited below in note 14 elaborate.

13. On Rwandan army corporations, see especially Kagame, *Les milices;* and Kagame, *Armées bovines.* For a recent reassessment: A. Des Forges, "Court and Corporations in the Development of the Rwandan State" (unpublished manuscript). I am indebted to Dr. Des Forges for making this manuscript available to me and for her insightful comments on many other issues considered in this chapter. Central court moves into areas of western Rwanda are also considered in D. Newbury, " 'Bunyabungo'."

14. Kagame, *La poésie dynastique,* passim; Kagame, *Histoire du Rwanda,* 39-55; Kagame, *Armées bovines,* passim; Kagame, *Les milices,* passim; Kagame, *Un abrégé,* Vol. 1, esp. 135-53; Pagès, *Un royaume Hamite,* esp. 141-226; de Lacger, *Ruanda,* 107-14; Vansina, *L'évolution,* esp. 69-73, 88-94; Rennie, "The Precolonial Kingdom of Rwanda," 11-53. Traditions on the period of Rujugira's reign include the "regency" of his older brother (or usurper), Karemera Rwaka, who is said to have ruled for 16 years but was never officially enthroned: A. Kagame, *La notion de la génération appliquée à la généalogie dynastique et à l'histoire du Rwanda des Xe-XIe siècles à nos jours* (Bruxelles, 1959), 37-39; Kagame, *Les milices,* 81; Kagame, *Un abrégé* 1:130-31. Vansina (*L'évolution,* 51), however, thinks Rwaka was invested as a proper king, but has since been excluded from the official genealogy because he was eventually overthrown by his brother Rujugira. Here we are less concerned with personal identities than with the processes of political and military penetration during the mid-eighteenth century—the period which the court traditions associate with Rujugira's reign. Because there is no distinction made between these two rulers in the official sources and because the exact identification of the reign is irrelevant to the argument, I will use the name Rujugira to denote the period included under the rule of both Rwaka and Rujugira.

15. Vansina, *L'évolution,* 63; R. D. Sigwalt, "Early Rwanda History," esp. 141-42; Rennie, "The Precolonial Kingdom of Rwanda," 21-22, 30.

16. These are most completely detailed, along with their military histories, in Kagame, *Les milices,* 72-125 (but the histories of armies formed in earlier reigns also include information on Rujugira's reign). Kagame (*Un abrégé,* 1:135-53) discusses military history under Rujugira, primarily the Rwandan campaigns against Ndorwa, Gisaka, and Burundi.

17. Kagame, *Les milices,* passim, esp. 72–125; more armies are attributed to Rujugira's reign (11) than to any other single reign, including that of Rwabugiri, the great warrior-king of the late nineteenth century. It is worth noting, as does Des Forges ("Court and Cororations"), that Rujugira's "reign"—which included the period of Rwaka's rule—covered an extended period, and actually overlapped with that of Ndabarasa (Rujugira having named Ndabarasa not only as successor but also as co-regnant during his own lifetime). This extremely long reign may have accounted in part for the number of armies formed under his rule. But only in part: it is not always true that there will be more numerous or more significant innovations under a long reign than under a shorter one. It is impossible to disentangle questions over "origins" and institutionalization, or to assign such processes definitively to one or another reign; what is important is that these processes did focus on the mid-eighteenth century, the time of Rujugira's reign. Indeed, it is likely that in the oral sources Rujugira has become a symbol of processes which originated before him and continued to be consolidated after his rule. But it seems clear, nonetheless, that his reign represented a critical turning point in the reconceptualization and transformation of these corporations. As Des Forges stresses, Rujugira was both usurper and innovator, and the army corporations of his day were marked by these particularities of his rule and character. For the the purposes of understanding Rwandan relations with the western areas, however, it is less important to attribute individual events to specific reigns than to account for the general features which characterized Rwandan social processes and structural transformations during the eighteenth century.

18. These were the "Abatabaga," stationed in Rukoma (Kagame, *Les milices,* 77); the "Ababaga," also from Rukoma (*Les milices,* 79); the "Abatanyagwa" in Budaha, west of the Nyabarongo (*Les milices,* 102); and the "Imbambanyi," a section of the "Abalima," also stationed in Budaha (*Les milices,* 103).

19. Kagame, *Les milices,* passim. Of the 29 armies said to have been recruited before the reign of Yuhi Mazimpaka, 6 have no remembered histories (counting all 3 armies under Ndahiro Cyamatare as one unit, as Kagame does); only 2 army histories are complete; 1 has a hiatus, but nonetheless claims a complete "leadership genealogy" from Kigeri Nyamuheshera, two reigns before Mazimpaka. Eleven of these armies remember a leadership genealogy only from the time of Rujugira, despite their prior formation by at least two reigns; one of these even held the important court function of guardian of the drums. Eight claimed a continuous leadership genealogy only more recent than the time of Rujugira: three from Gahindiro's reign, one each from the reigns of Rwabugiri, Rwogera, Sentabyo, and Ndabarasa, and one of uncertain reign. Kagame (*Les milices,* 17) provides a possible explanation for this. But his explanation applies to family genealogies, not directly to leadership positions of army groups, and therefore it is only marginally relevant. It does not, taken alone, seem to account for all the cases in this general pattern, because army command was not always hereditary, in fact. But court-appointed leadership was such a central feature of the institutional identity of a group at the court that it seems almost a defining characteristic of this continuing identity. Though the figures are not important, the general pattern does seem significant; court-appointed leaders are remembered continuously from Rujugira's reign, but are frequently not remembered before that reign.

20.   The meaning of the term "Hutu" at this time remove is not clear. This social classification has various contextual meanings, and these semantic implications have probably varied over time; historically, one is dealing not only with the evolution of class and ethnic identities in Rwanda, but also with the evolution of the *concept* of class and ethnic identities (C. Newbury, "Ethnicity in Rwanda: The Case of Kinyaga," *Africa* 48, 1 [1978], 17–29). Used in the sense in which it appears in the sources here, the term "Hutu" probably means those not previously under the effective rule of the court, and non-pastoralist (though many "Hutu" in western Rwanda owned cattle, sometimes in important numbers). In this light it is significant that the Hutu armies cited by Kagame do not appear to have been associated with a correspondingly named cattle herd (*"armée bovine"*). This occurred only later, in the time of Rwogera and after (as did regular prestation payments on any large scale) (Kagame, *Les milices,* 77–78, 79–80, and passim).

21.   On *umuheto* functions, see C. Newbury, *The Cohesion of Oppression,* chaps. 3 and 5; and A. Kagame, *Le code des institutions politiques du Rwanda précolonial* (Bruxelles, 1952), chaps. 1 and 2, where Kagame emphasizes the crucial importance of the army organization in providing an administrative framework for pre-colonial Rwanda; see esp. pp. 7–9 and 21, note 2: "Dans la conception traditionelle du Rwanda, l'armée n'est pas uniquement destinée aux combats; elle forme une vaste corporation, à laquelle incombent principalement des dévoirs et des droits d'ordre sociale. Ce serait une grosse erreur que d'entendre par armée chez nous des organisations purement militaires." Also: Kagame, *Les milices,* 9–10; Maquet, *Le système des relations sociales,* 130–46; J. J. Maquet, *The Premise of Inequality in Ruanda: A Study of Political Relations in a Central African Kingdom* (London, 1961), 109–24. For consideration of the transformations of *umuheto* relations (at a later period, in regions outside the central core area of the Rwandan polity): Rwabukumba and Mudandagizi, "Les formes historiques," 6–25, esp. 15–19; C. Newbury, "Deux lignages au Kinyaga," 26–38. More generally, one can refer to C. Vidal, "Le Rwanda des anthropologues ou le fétichisme de la vache" (*Cahiers d'études africaines* 9, 3 [1969], 384–401); J.-F. Saucier, "The Patron-Client Relationship in Traditional and Contemporary Southern Rwanda" (Ph.D. diss., Columbia University, 1974). Kagame (*Les milices,* 37) notes that the court created armies for economic reasons (to provide prestations to the court) from the time of Kigeri Mukobanya (10 reigns before Rujugira). But from the data he provides it appears that this pattern did not become generalized until the time of Rujugira and after.

22.   Kagame, *Armées bovines,* passim.

23.   This is stressed in Kagame, *Les milices,* 8; and Kagame, *Le code des institutions politiques,* 7–9 and chap. 1.

24.   Kagame, *Le code des institutions politiques,* 61–62.

25.   Kagame stresses this in *Le code des institutions politiques,* 24–25, and illustrates it in *La poésie dynastique.* Though this latter work is by no means a complete survey of this genre of literature, and though more poems from later reigns would be remembered and recited, the attribution of poems to different reigns shows a significant pattern. A total of 22 poems are attributed to the five "official" reigns before Rujugira, roughly 4 per reign. Half of those 22 are attributed to Rujugira's predecessor, Mazimpaka (who himself is remembered as a poet of calibre and renown); before

Mazimpaka's reign the average falls to fewer than 3 per reign. Rujugira's reign, however, marks a definite turning point in this tradition of court poetry; from his time, the average leaps to 23 poems per reign. The number within Rujugira's reign itself (30) is significantly above this average and is surpassed only in the last pre-colonial reign. Thus although it is not surprising that more poems are retained from more recent reigns, the pattern of these retentions is still significant, even if only suggestive. The figures are: Ruganzu Ndori—2; Semugeshi—0; Nyamuheshera—3; Gisanura—6; Mazimpaka—11; Rujugira—30; Ndabarasa—4; Sentabyo—21; Gahindiro—12; Rwogera—30; Rwabugiri—41.

26.   The ideological validation of class distinctions and the significance of army organization for the internal development of Rwandan social hierarchy are discussed at greater length in my " 'Bunyabungo'."

27.   L. Delmas, *Généalogies de la noblesse du Ruanda* (Kabgayi, 1950), 67, 93–96; Vansina, *L'évolution,* 70; Rennie, "The Precolonial Kingdom of Rwanda," 38. In *Les milices,* 61–66, Kagame places this under Mutara Semugeshi, several reigns before Rujugira—in fact, the fourth reign in the official "cycle" before Rujugira. It is possible, then, that this is a "cyclic transfer" such as takes place between homonyms in the Rwandan king list in other contexts (Mutara and Cyilima being alternate names in the same position of the cycle of royal names) (D. Newbury, "Cyclic Traditions around Lake Kivu" [unpublished manuscript, 1975]). It is also possible that this refers to the initial entry of the Ryangombe concept to Rwanda rather than to its institutionalization at the court; many traditions portray the person of Ryangombe as a contemporary of Ruganzu, the predecessor of Mutara Semugeshi (de Heusch, *Le Rwanda et la civilisation Interlacustre,* 201–49; I. Berger, "The Kubandwa Religious Complex of Interlacustrine East Africa: An Historical Study, c. 1500–1900" [Ph.D. diss., University of Wisconsin–Madison, 1973], chap. 5, esp. 135–36; Vidal, "Anthropologie et histoire").

28.   Kagame, *Le code des institutions politiques,* 61–62. These armies were especially important in the expansion of the state during the nineteenth century, as shown for Kinyaga in C. Newbury, *The Cohesion of Oppression,* and for the northern regions of Rwanda in Des Forges, "Defeat Is the Only Bad News"; A. Des Forges, " 'The Drum Is Greater Than the Shout': The 1912 Rebellion in Northern Rwanda" (in *Banditry, Rebellion, and Social Protest in Africa,* ed. D. Crummey, 311–33 (London, 1986); and J.-P. Chrétien, "La révolte de Ndungutse (1912). Forces traditionelles et pression coloniale au Rwanda allemand" (*Revue française d'histoire d'outre-mer* 59, 4 [1972], 645–80).

29.   Kagame supports this conclusion in *Le code des institutions politiques,* 55, note 28, where he refers to "l'ère des guerres permanentes sous Yuhi Mazimpaka et son fils Cyilima Rujugira." Kagame also notes that it is from the time of Rujugira that permanent border camps were established for the armies.

30.   Vansina, *"L'évolution,"* 87–89; Kagame (*Les milices,* 89) notes a battle north of Lake Kivu. Rennie, "The Precolonial Kingdom of Rwanda," 31 and 52, Map 5. Rennie concludes that "rather than a firm control it represented at first only the establishment of army positions, royal capitals, or some control over expansionist Tutsi colonisers. Tutsi colonisers pushed northwest into Bugoyi, Bukonya, and Budaha and even far into Rwankeri." But these "colonisers" may not have originally been representatives of the king, as will be noted below.

31.   Kagame, *Les milices,* 72–73, 99. On pages 104–6 Kagame refers to two armies said to have been founded during Rujugira's reign, but the names of these two armies were also the names of two Rundi armies previously defeated by Rujugira. It is possible, therefore, that these were Rundi armies incorporated into the Rwandan army organization.

32.   C. Newbury, *The Cohesion of Oppression,* chap. 2, esp. 63–64. On Ijwi: Rubasha 24/3/72; Sakari 3/3/72; Rubambiza (Mugorhe) 18/3/72; Ngwasi 3/3/72; Pagès, *Un royaume Hamite,* 598, 604; Pauwels ("Le Bushiru," 178–79) notes that the *bami* of both Busozo and Bushiru claim to have come from Gisaka. He dates the establishment of the Bashiru line to the time of Rujugira, but also notes that certain families of Bushiru came from Bunyambiriri. Kagame (*Les milices,* 99, and *Un abrégé,* 1:143) gives an example of an entire army moving into Rwanda from Gisaka.

33.   Kagame, *Les milices,* 104–6; the sources cited in notes 31 and 32 above suggest that this may have been a recurring pattern of recruitment.

34.   Rwandan court traditions assert that Bunyambiriri was incorporated into the Rwandan state during the time of Ruganzu (de Lacger, *Ruanda,* 108; Kagame, *Un abrégé,* 1:104; Pagès, *Un royaume Hamite,* 288–89; Vansina, *L'évolution,* 85; *Historique et chronologie* [Kabgayi, 1956], 71; Reisdorff, "Enquêtes foncières," enquête no. 30). Kagame, *(Histoire du Rwanda)* refers to the annexation of all the areas between the Nile-Zaire Divide and Lake Kivu under Yuhi Gahima, six reigns before Rujugira. But the movement of peoples suggests otherwise, that in fact "control" was minimal, as Kagame suggests also. Their movements indicate that, instead of colonizers, these people were more likely refugees from Rwandan political control, whose movements were a response to political-military events under Ndahiro Cyamatare and Ruganzu Ndori.

In fact, the process of incorporation in these areas was probably very slow and by no means moving inexorably in one direction. The contacts of Bunyambiriri with such areas as Rukoma and Bumbogo (which were incorporated into the Rwandan political network long before the eighteenth century) meant that the inhabitants of the Bunyambiriri area in general had some (probably non-royal) contacts with Rwandan political institutions. But indirect evidence indicates that the area as a whole was not effectively incorporated into the Rwandan polity until the late eighteenth or early nineteenth century. Population movements out of Bunyambiriri, although perhaps caused by drought, could have resulted from land pressure resulting from the decreasing accessibility of land associated with Tutsi infiltration into the region. Pagès suggests that the independence of Suti (in Bunyambiriri)—one of the best known of the formerly independent Hutu polities—was compromised only relatively recently. Although Rwandan sources state that Ruganzu Ndori killed the king of Suti, the kingdom apparently continued (Pagès, *Un royaume Hamite,* 288–89, 441, 599; Kagame, *Un abrégé* 1:104). Ruganzu himself is said to have died from wounds received at the hands of the "montagnards de la région du Rusenyi," just west of Bunyambiriri (Kagame, *Histoire du Rwanda,* 30; Kagame, *Un abrégé,* 1:106), and the king of Bufundu (just south of Bunyambiriri) was conquered only later and with difficulty, by Ruganzu's son (Kagame, *Histoire du Rwanda,* 33; Kagame, *Un abrégé,* 1:109–10). The area was clearly a troubled one from the point of view of the Rwandan court, even after its "conquest" by Ruganzu. In fact, Rwandan sources acknowledge influence from

Burundi in this area until roughly the time of Rujugira (cf. Kagame, *La poésie dynastique*, 42–43, 136–37; Kagame, *Un abrégé*, 1:128–29, 142; Kagame, *Armées bovines*, 32). Thus the indications are that *les montagnards* of this general area (including Bunyambiriri) remained autonomous from Rwandan central court politics into the eighteenth century.

35.   On Bushiru, see Pauwels, "Le Bushiru," 279; for an example of a return movement, a family moving from Bugoyi into Bushiru, see Reisdorff, "Enquêtes foncières," enquête no. 34. On Bugoyi: Pagès, *Un royaume Hamite*, 598: "Les premiers Banyarwanda qui vinrent s'y établir [in Bugoyi] étaient originaires de Suti, village situé dans le Bunyambiriri" (see also 605–6, 644–45). Reisdorff, "Enquêtes foncières," enquête no. 31. For Ijwi, see chapters 6 and 7 below. Many Banyambiriri on Ijwi claim their ancestors came from Nyunyi ya Karonge in Bunyambiriri; all such claims would apply to the mid- or late eighteenth century. For Kinyaga: Reisdorff, "Enquêtes foncières," enquête no. 27; C. Newbury, *The Cohesion of Oppression*, chap. 2. (In addition to those cited, numerous other immigrants to Kinyaga said they came from Bunyambiriri.)

36.   Reisdorff, "Enquêtes foncières," enquête no. 31. Some members of the same family also left Bunyambiriri for Kinyaga; see note 42 below. Other examples of this type of mobility are noted in Reisdorff, "Enquêtes foncières," enquête no. 27; Pauwels, "Le Bushiru," 279; Pagès, *Un royaume Hamite*, 644, "Les Abagango."

37.   This was particularly evident in the interviews carried out in Kinyaga (C. Newbury, *The Cohesion of Oppression*, chap. 2) and on Ijwi: many family traditions cited famine as a cause of departure from Bunyambiriri. Also Pagès, *Un royaume Hamite*, 141–42, 586–92; de Lacger, *Ruanda*, 141; Kagame attributes these famines to Burundi (*Les milices*, 97; *Un abrégé*, 1:141, 143), but these references may also apply to the western mountain areas outside Rwandan court control and an area of significant Rundi influence at this time: see Kagame, *La poésie dynastique*, 42–43, 136–37; Kagame, *Armées bovines*, 32; Kagame, *Un abrégé*, 1:128–29, 142.

38.   *Historique et chronologie*, 12: "Le Territoire de Shangugu fut toujours épargné par les famines qui y provoquèrent une forte immigration d'affamés des autres régions" (noted in a context which suggests that Bunyambiriri is included).

39.   For an example of famine-induced mobility and mobility-induced famine, see B. Lugan, "Causes et effets de la famine 'Rumanura' au Rwanda, 1916–1918" (*Canadian Journal of African Studies* 10, 2 [1976], 347–56). Many people from Ijwi said their families arrived because of famine, though it is possible that this is a metaphorical reference; Ijwi is commonly seen as a place of high agricultural productivity.

40.   Reisdorff ("Enquêtes foncières," enquête no. 23) notes: "De nombreux groupes de pasteurs du Gisaka et du Ndorwa quittèrent au cours du XVIII S. leurs pays regulièrement razzié par le mwami du Rwanda pour passer dans le camp du plus fort. . . . Les pasteurs du Gisaka et du Ndorwa furent souvent envoyés au confins du royaume face à l'Urundi ou au Bunyabungo pour constituer les garnisons frontières et réaliser les premiers peuplements hamites." But it would seem unlikely that the king would intentionally send such groups, regularly, to the border regions. It would seem more likely that most such groups went there on their own, seeking autonomy from the Rwandan state, and only later claimed association with the court, after finding it advantageous to do so in light of later Rwandan expansion into these

very areas. In another example, Reisdorff ("Enquêtes foncières," enquête no. 27) notes a family that left Gisaka for Bunyambiriri; later, in succeeding generations, they continued deeper into the forests along the Nile-Zaire Divide, ending up in Nyantango (just north of Bunyambiriri). Many other families in Bugoyi claim to have come from Ndorwa or Gisaka (Reisdorff, "Enquêtes foncières," enquête no. 31; Pagès, *Un royaume Hamite*, 644–45). This is hardly the behavior one would expect in the case of systematic settlement organized from the court, as some central court sources imply.

41.   De Lacger, *Ruanda*, 111; *Historique et chronologie*, 121–22; Pagès, *Un royaume Hamite*, 142; Rennie, "The Precolonial Kingdom of Rwanda," 31; Vansina, *L'évolution*, 80, 87–88; Kagame (*Les milices*, 89) refers to a battle north of Lake Kivu at the time of Rujugira. The references to "invaders" from the west seem to be a Rwandan court fabrication. In fact, the great majority of inhabitants of Bugoyi were themselves originally from the west. The new groups were therefore simply following a long-established pattern: they were "immigrants" rather than "invaders," but even here the terminology implies that Bugoyi was more separated from the western regions than in fact may have been the case. The fact that the Rwandan sources portray them as invaders speaks more to the expanding Rwandan claims to Bugoyi than to any threat to "Rwandan" territory. Measured in terms of royal appointments and regular prestations required from the armies, Bugoyi was incorporated into Rwanda politically only during the nineteenth century. On the questions of the origin of Bagoyi residents from the west, see Kagame, *La poésie dynastique*, 67, note 103: "Les habitants de notre [*sic*] Bugoyi proviennent des régions congolaises de l'autre côté du Kivu"; Vansina, *L'évolution*, 88; de Lacger, *Ruanda*, 111; Reisdorff, "Enquêtes foncières," enquête no. 31; Pagès, *Un royaume Hamite*, esp. pp. 601, 638: "Les Bagoyi sont presque tous originaires du Nord-Ouest du Lac Kivu"; also pp. 644–45, where he cites over half of the "clans et sous clans Bahutu du Bugoyi" as being unequivocally from the west; pp. 653, 666, where one group returned frequently to Gishari (in Buhunde) to join in a celebration of the ancestors there; also Pagès, "L'histoire des Muets" (in *Un royaume Hamite*, 597–612, esp. 601, 602, note 1), where he notes that the language of Bugoyi has many features similar to that of Buhunde.

42.   Vansina, *L'évolution*, 88; de Lacger, *Ruanda*, 111; *Historique et chronologie*, 121–23; Pagès, *Un royaume Hamite*, 141–43, 598–608; a genealogy of the Abagwabiro from the time of Macumu is found in Pagès, *Un royaume Hamite*, 649; Reisdorff, "Enquêtes foncières," enquête no. 31. Four of the five examples included among other families associated with the Abagwabiro in enquête no. 31 were said to have arrived in Bugoyi during the reign of Rujugira; in fact one referred to Cyilima Rugwe, but this is clearly an anachronism and likely refers to Cyilima Rujugira. The fifth did not identify the king at the time of arrival. Many other examples of this timing are included among other family histories in the same enquête. Although the Abagwabiro are considered by the court to be the vanguard of "Rwandan" conquerors in Bugoyi, they appear to have acted independently of the central court, and to have considered themselves as such. This is especially brought out by Pagès, who provides by far the most complete historical account. He makes the point that although the son of Rujugira established a court presence in Bugoyi under the reign of Rujugira (Pagès, *Un royaume Hamite*, 652), this was but a nominal presence (cf. 608–9, 638, 643). The Abagwabiro maintained their own autonomy in internal matters (607–8), and also

enjoyed close relations as a group with the quasi-independent rainmaker kings at Bunyambiriri (599, 604). Reisdorff also emphasizes that it was only under the reigns of Rwogera and Rwabugiri that the first political prestations were paid to the central court from Bugoyi ("Enquêtes foncières," enquête no. 31, p. 86; also pp. 81, 88 [Rwogera], and pp. 85, 89 [Rwabugiri]). *Historique et chronologie*, 124, notes that until the time of Rwabugiri, command of Bugoyi was under Hutu *"chefs de clans."*

43.   C. Newbury, "Deux lignages au Kinyaga"; C. Newbury, *The Cohesion of Oppression*, chap. 3, 4, 5; Pagès, *Un royaume Hamite*, 606; Vansina, *L'évolution*, 79-80, 88: these alliances were "un indice de prestige dont jouissait le royauté du Rwanda et un signe de la volonté de ses rois d'entreprendre le controle des nouvelles régions à l'occident."

44.   Pauwels, "Le Bushiru," passim (esp. 220-33); de Lacger, *Ruanda*, 75-89; C. Newbury, *The Cohesion of Oppression*, 23-39. Changes in central court politics during the reign of Gahindiro are noted in Vansina, *L'évolution*, 70-71, 79-80.

45.   This is best documented in Meschi, "Evolution des structures foncières"; Rwabukumba and Mudandagizi, "Les formes historiques"; Vidal, "Le Rwanda des anthropologues"; and Vidal, "Economie de la société féodale." All these apply primarily to the areas of central and southern Rwanda. But these findings are paralleled elsewhere, though for a slightly later period, by research in the western regions. C. Newbury, *The Cohesion of Oppression*, esp. chaps. 5, 6; C. Newbury, "Deux lignages au Kinyaga," 26-39; Reisdorff, "Enquêtes foncières," enquêtes no. 31, 33, 37; Pagès, *Un royaume Hamite*, 635-700; Kagame, *Les milices*, 68-69, 159; de Lacger, *Ruanda*, 74. It can therefore be assumed that the processes by which the political elite gained control over land were similar in the west, although in the western regions this may have occurred later and over a shorter time period.

46.   Kagame, *Les milices*, 77-80; on the political incorporation of the western areas, see Reisdorff, "Enquêtes foncières," enquêtes no. 81, 85, 86, 88, 89; C. Newbury, *The Cohesion of Oppression*, chap. 6.

47.   One dimension of this process of social change is illustrated by the growing hegemony of the Rwandan central court in redefining social identities (D. Newbury, "The Clans of Rwanda").

48.   D. Newbury, "Lake Kivu Regional Trade"; and D. Newbury, "Rwabugiri and Ijwi."

49.   Pauwels, "Le pacte de sang au Rwanda."

Chapter 5. Immigrants to Ijwi: Ties across the Lake

1.   The argument presented in the following paragraphs is more fully developed in D. Newbury, "Kings and Clans: A Social History of Ijwi Island (Zaire), c. 1780–1840" (Ph.D. diss., University of Wisconsin–Madison), Appendix 4.

2.   Kadusi 4/6/74; Kadusi was the patriarch of the Banyakabwa (a particularly cohesive group) on Ijwi at the time of the research.

3.   Kabera Bijenje 10/5/72.

4.   On Nyiramavugo: Kagame, *Un abrégé*, 1:210-14; Kagame, *Les milices*, 155-56.

5.   Kabera Bijenje 10/5/72.

6.   Mudahigwa 11/5/72.

7.   Bishimina Mugaru 2/2/73.
8.   These genealogies are analyzed in Appendices 3 and 4 in D. Newbury, "Kings and Clans."
9.   The western areas of Rwanda were often involved in opposition movements to the Rwandan kings, and these movements may in some cases have been associated with succession disputes as well as with resistance to central court expansion. (Both Ndahiro and Ruganzu were killed as a result of western opposition.) Western Rwanda was the home of Sibula, and lakeshore peoples were apparently perceived as distinct from those of Rwandan culture. They are thus anachronistically identified as "Havu" in the Rwandan traditions even before the establishment of Havu (Sibula) kingship in the area (Pagès, *Un royaume Hamite*, 238-511, 260-68, 284-90, 298-317, 328-45; Kagame, *Un abrégé*, 1:87-108; Kagame, *Histoire du Rwanda*, 26-32; Gakaniisha, *Récits historiques Rwanda*, Récits 12, 13, 16. Sibula's ties to Rwanda are considered in Appendix 7 of D. Newbury, "Kings and Clans."
10.   Rwakageyo 9/5/72.
11.   Kagame, *Un abrégé*, 1:182-84, 194-96; Kagame, *Les milices*, 139; Nkongori, "Les Bashakamba (ou l'histoire d'un corps de guerriers au pays du royaume Hamite)," trans. P Schumacher, in *Die Wiener Schule der Völkerkunde*, ed. J. Haekel, A. Hohenwart-Gerlachstein, and A. Slawik, 237-52 (Horn-Wien, 1956).
12.   Kagame, *Les milices*, 94-95; Delmas, *Généalogies*, 61-62, 129.
13.   Nyamuheshera 10/2/72; Makombwa 10/5/72; Rubambiza (Cugi) 25/1/73; Siribo 25/1/73; Nyabiwigule 25/1/73; Gahanda 26/1/73; Bagalo 30/1/73; Binyungu 1/2/73; Bishimina Mugaru 2/2/73; Kabangala 21/2/73; Birongo 12/2/73. In addition to references to Cimbiri, other Banyakabwa refer to an immediate origin in Mwiiru in western Rwanda. These references often claim common ulterior ties with those said to have come to Ijwi from Cimbiri (Bitukuru 9/5/72; Ruhoya 7/3/72; Rukanika [Nkuvu] 27/4/72; Kasi 27/4/72; Gatera Kanega 6/5/74; Nyamwigura Shabuzenzi 8/5/74). This may well be an anachronistic reference, since Mwiiru, a Banyakabwa center still today, is the area in which Nyamuziga, a famous Munyakabwa, sought refuge when expelled by the Basibula. After Nyamuziga fled, many Banyakabwa returned to Ijwi and hence Mwiiru is seen as the "origin" of some Banyakabwa families on Ijwi today. It is possible, therefore, that some Banyakabwa settled at Mwiiru, a secondary dispersal area whence some continued to Ijwi.
14.   A reference to Banyakabwa as Bahunde is found in Bagereka 21/2/73: "Maheshe na Mpama, a Hunde *mwami,* was a Munyakabwa, the son of Ngulumira, the same family as Balimucabo." (On Ijwi, Mpamo, Ngulumira, and Balimucabo are well-known Banyakabwa ancestors, and Maheshe is considered a Hunde name; it is also the name of a spirit frequently called upon by the Bany'Iju and one derived from Buhunde.) Binyungu Lukere 16/2/73 has a similar reference linking Maheshe na Mpamo with the Banyakabwa; also Kalwiira Biseruki 7/3/72. The confirmatory evidence is in the form of marriage ties and contacts between Kirhanga, the area of heavy Banyakabwa settlement in the far north of Ijwi, and Buzi and Buhunde (Bishimina Mugaru 2/2/73; and Gahanda [26/1/73], who states that Balimucabo, one of the earliest of the Banyakabwa on Ijwi, married Nabusarazi). The Basarazi were Bahunde; they were also former dignitaries on Buzi (the formerly Hunde peninsula in the extreme northwestern corner of Lake Kivu) before it was taken over

by the Havu. After their deportation during the early colonial period, several Basarazi came to live on northern Ijwi. Gisayura Mukabyo (2/2/73), the eldest son of the Banyakabwa patriarch Kanywabahizi, also noted that Mpamo, the father of Balimucabo, married a woman from Buhunde. This was confirmed by Kalibwa (3/2/73), who identified her as the "sister" of the Hunde *mwami*. Bayongo Rugombera (15/2/73), Nyamwigura Shabuzeni (8/5/74), and Nyabwiguli (25/1/73) note other Banyakabwa ties with Buzi. The external marriage patterns of the Kabwa will be discussed more fully below.

15.   For example, when asked for other hills in Malambo (northern Ijwi) where Banyakabwa live, one Munyakabwa cited hills in five different kingdoms: Malambo, Karhongo (southern Ijwi), Mpinga, Buzi, Rwanda. In addition he cited blood brothers in Bufumbiro (Rwanda), Goma, Buhunde, Kalehe, Buzi, and many other places (Bishimina Mugaru 2/2/73). Others cited Banyakabwa ties outside Ijwi, and said they travelled there once or twice a year (Nyabwiguli 25/1/73). Bayongo (15/2/73) claimed family ties in Rwanda (Cinunu), Mpinga (Mabula), and Buzi as well as on Ijwi. Others indicated that Banyakabwa ties abroad facilitated their participation in trade—they arrived as "outsiders" but not as "strangers" (Waberagirwa 6/2/73; Bagalo 30/1/73). Both Balimucabo in the north (Gahanda 26/1/73) and Bayebaye in the east (Gatera Kanega 6/5/74) are said to have had wives and children both on Ijwi and on the mainland. The same residential pattern is sometimes found today; there is no reason to assume that close family ties between areas on the mainland and on Ijwi were any less prevalent in the past.

16.   As will be noted for other groups, this phenomenon is not limited to the Banyakabwa. There is no reason to doubt that the patterns best documented for the Banyakabwa also applied to other groups with pre-dynastic (or early dynastic) ties across the lake.

17.   According to different accounts, either Balimucabo (Gahanda 26/1/73) or Mpamo (Kadusi 4/6/74) is said to have married "Nabusarazi," meaning probably the daughter of the leader of the Basarazi. Mpamo also married a "sister" of Kalinda (Kalibwa 3/2/73) and had a bloodpact alliance with Kalinda (Gisayura Mukabyo 27/1/73). ("Kalinda" is the generic name for the kings of Bunyungu, the Hunde kingdom northwest of Lake Kivu. From 1923 Kalinda, and then his son, have been recognized by the colonial (and later post-colonial) authorities as *grand mwami de tout le Buhunde*. Kanywabahizi (see Figure 1) is said to have been a "friend" (i.e., a blood brother) of Kalinda, to have married a daughter of Kalinda (Bishimina Mugaru 2/2/73) as well as a daughter of one of Kalinda's closest associates (Gisayura Mukabyo 2/2/73), and to have married two of his sisters to men from Buzi, one to a Musarazi (Kadusi 4/6/74). Munyuzangabo, Kadusi's brother, also married a woman from Buhunde (and his mother was from Buhunde), and Kadusi married two daughters to men from Buzi (one a Musarazi) and one to Buhunde (Kadusi 4/6/74).

18.   Marriage ties with members of the Havu royal family (both at Mpinga Nord and Mpinga Sud) occurred with Kanywabahizi (Nyabwiguli 25/1/73; Gisayura Mukabyo 27/1/73, 2/2/73) and Kadusi (Kadusi 4/6/74). Some of the most intense ties (including marriage, cattle and bloodpact contracts) appear to have been with members of the royal family who were representatives of the kings, but not kings themselves, north of Kalehe. The striking aspect of the cattle ties of Kanywabahizi, as

reconstructed by his son (Kadusi 4/6/74), is that Kanywabahizi did not give cattle to Rwanda or Buhunde (though he received from both); all cattle were given to men or families living on the western shore of the lake (especially Mpinga Nord and Irhambi) and on Ijwi. Kadusi himself had a wider network with some in Rwanda and at the southern end of the lake. But the major areas of concentration were similar to those of his Banyakabwa predecessors.

19.   Bishimina Mugaru 2/2/73; Mibale 27/1/73; Mudahigwa 11/5/72; Gisayura Mukabyo 27/1/73, 2/2/73; Kadusi 4/6/74; Nyamwigura Shabuzeni 8/5/74.

20.   As with marriage ties there were more cattle ties with Ijwi, especially northern Ijwi, during the colonial period than previously (though the data are unlikely to be complete, and it may be that these more recent external ties are simply better remembered) (Kadusi 4/6/74; Gisayura Mukabyo 2/2/73).

21.   The community of Cugi is 65 percent Banyakabwa today; for the four northern-most villages for which there are statistics, 42 percent of the total population were Bahande, presumably virtually all Banyakabwa; they are the largest clan in all but one of those villages. The principal administrative delegate in this area is a member of the senior descent line of the Banyakabwa. In Figure 1, the names of the different communities of Banyakabwa settlement appear at the bottom. Kirhanga shows the greatest genealogical depth, and clearly serves as the central line from which other lines descend (excepting only Boza, an autonomous community in the extreme southeast of Ijwi).

22.   Aside from Buzigaziga, the most important of these are at Nkuvu (in the south), Muziri (in the north), both the homes of Bayebaye's descendants, and Boza (in the south), settled by the descendants of Bavuneshe. Other early Banyakabwa lived at Nyakalengwa (Buswagiri) and Ntalangwa (Kambi). The exact genealogical relationship of the Kirhanga settlement (especially at Cugi) with the others is unclear, and it is possible that these were two distinct groups despite their claim to common "descent" from Balimucabo and Ngulumira. They each claim ties to quite distinct mainland areas—one at "Mwiiru" in Rusenyi on the western shore; one at Cimbiri in Bugoyi near the northern end of the lake. There is, however, one revealing aspect to the traditions: those who refer to the arrival of Nyamuziga and Bayebaye from Mwiiru often do so in terms of a more recent "return" after having been exiled by the Basibula. Although this time confusion is not uncommon in Ijwi traditions, it is an indication that the Mwiiru community of Banyakabwa was in fact founded from Ijwi (Ruhembe, 2/5/72; Sakari 3/3/72). Most references, even those from Buzigaziga (the former home of Nyamuziga), also acknowledge the pre-eminence of Balimucabo over Nyamuziga, who in turn rebelled from Balimucabo's authority (Musigi 9/3/72; Lwibaye [Boza] 11/5/72; Kabera Bijenje 10/5/72; Lushoka 11/3/72; Gahanda 26/1/73; Kadusi 26/1/73; Burhola 22/3/72; Kigufi 9/5/72: Makombwa 10/5/72; Kakira Ruhamisa 26/5/72).

23.   Many Ijwi sources refer to the kings on Mpembe, explaining that they were deposed or exiled by the Rwanda kings. Among others: Ndeyalire (29/3/72); Bahaza (12/2/72); Nyamienda (17/3/72); Burhola (22/3/72); Makanda (27/3/72); Kabaraka (28/3/72); Ruzigamanzi (29/3/72) (who added that Mugombwa was a rainmaker; "Mugombwa" is often used as a generic term for all Mpembe kings); Mirindi (1/5/72). The Rwandan kings mentioned as having deposed the Mpembe line are

Musinga and Rwabugiri (Nkuruziza 26/5/72; Ndeyalire 29/3/72; Mirindi 1/5/72). Bahaza (12/2/72) commented that they were driven out by "Tutsi-Abarugaruga"; the Abarugaruga were a special armed section created by the Germans to serve under Musinga (Des Forges, "Defeat Is the Only Bad News"). Unfortunately, the data from interviews which I carried out on Mpembe were lost in transit, and other confirmation from the Mpembe area is not yet available. Bwishaza has recently been the focus of an important study by R. Van Walle (see "Aspecten van Staatsvorming in West Rwanda," *Africa-Tervuren* 28, 3 [1982], 64–77).

24.   De Lacger implies that the kings on Mpembe were rainmakers; he notes that the group of Bahinza with powers over rain "n'ont jamais porté ombrage aux rois hamites, qui les ont non seulement maintenus, mais les ont protégés, dans le pensée qu'eux-mêmes et leurs sujets pouvaient y trouver profit. Les plus renommés d'entre eux ont été jusqu'ici ceux de Rubengera dans le Bwishaza et ceux de Suti dans le Bunyambiriri . . ." (de Lacger, *Ruanda*, 85). (See also Pagès, *Un royaume Hamite*, 441, whence de Lacger's passage was borrowed.) The ritual tie-ins between Ijwi and the general area of Bunyambiriri will be considered in chapter 5. Although the Beshaza do not claim to have come from Rubengera (just north of present Kibuye, and a former renowned enclosure of Rwabugiri, the Rwandan king of the late nineteenth century), this does confirm the presence of a polity in the area of Bwishaza, and this reference may indeed properly refer to the Mpembe polity. Pagès (*Un royaume Hamite*, 443) adds: "Les Bahinza [rulers] de la province du Bgishaza [sic] ont eu de tout temps la reputation d'exceller dans l'exercise de ces pouvoirs supranaturels."

25.   The Mpembe ties with Bugoyi were mentioned by Nkuruziza Kabulibuli (26/5/72). On the ties with Bukunzi: Gasarahinga 30/3/72; Nkuruziza 26/5/72; Ndengeyi 2/6/72: "Mugombwa was a friend of Nabukunzi [the ruler of Bukunzi]; he received many cows from Ndagano" (an anachronism; Ndagano was the most famous of the Bukunzi kings, and the name is customarily used to refer to all kings of Bukunzi). All three of these men stated that Rugaba (the last of the Mpembe kings) had married the daughter of Nabukunzi (the ruler of Bukunzi). The statement that Mugombwa (a generic term applying to any Mpembe king) had received cows from Ndagano is interesting because, if it had referred to conventional bridewealth, it would have been expressed as a transfer in the opposite direction; hence it probably represents a non-marital alliance tie. The marriage ties between Bukunzi and Mpembe are confirmed by independent data from Bukunzi, in interviews conducted by Catharine Newbury and Joseph Rwabukumba. Also, Gasarahinga (Bwando, 30/3/72) made the intriguing statement that the *bagingi* on Mpembe came from Bukunzi (a walk of about two days from Mpembe), and that furthermore the grandfather of Rugaba was from Bukunzi. When asked if this meant his maternal grandfather, Gasarahinga clarified this as "the father of Mugombwa." It is possible therefore that the historical ties between Mpembe and Bukunzi were much closer and of longer duration than the short statements above imply. Pagès (*Un royaume Hamite*, 344) gives a genealogy of Bukunzi which includes the name Kabeja, a name which appears in other royal genealogies, including that of Mpembe. Pagès also refers (pp. 296–98, 465) to the ritual marriage of a woman of Bukunzi into the family of ritualists of Bumbogo. This family was responsible for the sorghum and millet prepared for the Rwandan Umuganura ceremony. In a sense this role of the woman from Bukunzi also

parallels that of the Bwishaza wife of the Ijwi king, in the only ritually prescribed royal marriage on Ijwi; this wife was also associated specifically with the preparation of the grain at the Ijwi Muganuro celebration.

26.   E. Ntezimana, "Coutumes et traditions." For Bukunzi's historical ties with the west, see Sigwalt, "The Early History of Bushi," 64–67 (esp. 64, note 16); P. Masson, *Trois siècles chez les Bashi* (Bukavu, 1966), 27–32; Pagès, *Un royaume Hamite,* 332, 434–35; de Lacger, *Ruanda,* 82; Pauwels, "Le Bushiru," 215–16. On the relations of Bukunzi with the central court of Rwanda: Pagès, *Un royaume Hamite,* 332 (Bukunzi was "une vraie souveraineté"), 297 ("Le Bukunzi . . . témoignent une certain indépendance vis-à-vis du prince hamite"), and 298, note 1; d'Hertefelt and Coupez, *La royauté sacrée,* 337–38, 449–50. More recent relations are covered in Des Forges, "Defeat Is the Only Bad News," 297–301; C. Newbury, *The Cohesion of Oppression,* 39–42, 63–66. Ndagano (the name of the last king of Bukunzi, and also the name applied by outsiders to all Bukunzi kings) is known for his rainmaking powers throughout northern Bushi today, and even in the kingdom of Kalonge, far back on the Mitumba Mountains, as well as in the lakeshore areas. Rwanda, too, acknowledged this extraordinary power by sending gifts to the *mwami* of Bukunzi. Pagès (*Un royaume Hamite,* 297) notes that "l'autorité que lui confère l'importance de son role de faiseur de pluie est immense."

27.   For other examples of this interaction: Reisdorff, "Enquêtes foncières," enquête no. 31 (Bunyambiriri-Bugoyi), enquête no. 34 (Bugoyi-Bushiru); Pauwels, "Le Bushiru," 197 (Bushiru-Bunyambiriri); Pagès, *Un royaume Hamite,* 599 (Bunyambiriri-Bugoyi); de Lacger, *Ruanda,* 68, 82, 85, 103, where he notes that Mashira, the king of Nduga, had formed a marriage tie with Buzi, northwest of Lake Kivu. Bukunzi data also indicate that the kings there maintained marriage ties with the royal families of the Shi kingdoms to the west. Examples of this are found in Catharine Newbury's Kinyaga interviews: Ndimubanzi and Gashyamangali 5/2/71; Ntuuro Mashirankinyama, Mukara, Ntibashiimwa 4/2/71; Gahogo 22/5/71.

28.   Ishungu: Buraho 7/8/72; Mulahuko Bigondo 8/8/72; Ndanga 8/8/72. Mabula: Bishimina Bihinga 29/1/73. Buzi: Kamuzinzi (Bwando) 28/3/72; Ndeyalire 29/3/72; Zahura 30/3/72; Malige 18/5/74. Nyamirundi: Rubanga 26/5/72; Rweemera 1/10/70 (the latter interview is part of Catharine Newbury's Kinyaga data). The Beshaza also have a significant presence in Bushi, where they are known as Bashinjahavu; see Sigwalt, "The Early History of Bushi," esp. chap. 7, for a discussion of their ritual and political influence. It is interesting that the people of Kinyaga often cite three levels of social identity; the middle level includes names often used on Ijwi as "clan" names. In this case, the Rwandans claiming origins from Mpembe say they are of the Abasinga "clan" *(ubwooko)* and of the Beshaza "subclan." In the north of Rwanda, this middle level of identity found in Kinyaga forms a more coherent group than the Rwandan clan and carries a term in Kinyarwanda cognate to the Kiny'Iju term *"ishanja,"* used for clan (at various levels of identity) (d'Hertefelt, "Le Rwanda," 41–42; M. d'Hertefelt, "Huwelijk, familie en aanverwantschap bij de Reera," *Zaïre* 13, 2–3 [1959], 115–48, 243–85; and J. M. Freedman, "Principles of Relationship," passim). Another subgroup of the Abasinga found in Kinyaga is known as the Banyambiriri. For a discussion of these factors of identity as they apply to Rwanda, see Appendix 8 of D. Newbury, "Kings and Clans."

29.   Some men from the north claimed that the Beshaza had two additional ritual roles, preparing the bed for the *mwami* and shaving him. But this testimony appeared only in the north of Ijwi; these duties are similar to some of the duties of the Bashaho, considered to be a "sister-clan" to the Beshaza (Bahiga 9/2/73; Mbogo-Mbogo Byongwa 2/5/74; Nzibukira Bayonga 18/5/74). On the relations with the Bashaho see Masuka 2/2/73: "The Bashaho are 'brothers' to the Beshaza." This proximate identity between the two clans is general to Ijwi.

30.   See, for example, Sakari 3/3/72; Gahanga 29/3/72; Gasarahinga (Bwando) 30/3/72.

31.   It appears that several distinct families were involved, and arrived separately from the family of Kigangali and Kigame, who first settled at Bwando (Musahura 17/3/72; Nyamienda 17/3/72; Nyenyezi 18/3/72; Mbanza 23/3/72; Mbaraga 28/3/72; Kabaraka 28/3/72; Ruzigamanzi 29/3/72; Kanigi 12/5/72; Rubangu Kanyarugunda 26/5/72; Nkuruziza 26/5/72; Muyobo Bucakabiri 13/6/72; Rurayi 29/-6/72; Barhombo 29/1/73; Rwango 20/2/73; Nyantaba 20/2/73; Gashoku 27/4/74; Mushayuma Semutwa 3/5/74; Kanega Bishimira 17/5/74; Mutalindwa 17/5/74; Malige 18/5/74; Nzibukira Bayongu 18/5/74; Kanyenju 18/5/74; Misogoro 28/5/74; Kishake 30/5/74). The nature of Beshaza arrival to Ijwi indicates that this emigration from Mpembe probably occurred in reaction to more direct stimuli, perhaps a conquest of the area in the nineteenth century, rather than a response to more subtle cultural-ecological transformations which may have led to the departure of the Banyambiriri, for example.

32.   It is interesting that in the south it was frequently noted that the kings were there before the arrival of some groups, whereas in the north most men denied that the kings preceded them in the area, despite the fact that most families also came through Bwando or arrived after the establishment at Bwando. It thus seems that, in their dispersal from Bwando and after Bwando's establishment, settlement occurred in those precise areas where the kings' authority was minimal. More recent arrival is also indicated in the testimony of Bahaza (12/2/72), who said he knew the history of Mpembe but not the history of Ijwi. (He was one of the few Beshaza in his village of Bugarula, Ijwi Sud.)

33.   Kabaraka 28/3/72; Mahoro 2/5/72; Sanvura 1/5/72; Mukatara Barungu 29/4/72; Bunyerezi 29/4/72; Bahaya 10/2/72; Muyobo 13/6/72; Mafundo 20/3/72; Burhola 22/3/72; Gasarahinga Sanvura 12/5/72; Mushengezi Minani 27/4/74.

34.   Two other important early Beshaza communities in the south, at Nyakibamba and Bulegeyi, were founded by "brothers" of the earliest Bwishaza immigrant at Bwando, and both communities defer to the historical seniority of Bwando. But it is clear that many other Beshaza families arrived independently of the Bwando community. The most important of these are settled at Mugote, Rambo, Buyumbu, and Kagushu.

35.   Mukatara Barungu 29/4/72.

36.   Gashoku 27/4/74.

37.   Gasarahinga Kandiamazi 30/3/72.

38.   Gasarahinga Sanvura 12/5/72.

39.   Ruzigamanzi 29/3/72.

40.   Barhombo 29/1/73; this emphasizes the particularly close familial nature

of these trans-lacustrine ties. It should be noted that since independence the Zairean government has attempted to stop this "smuggling" across the lake, sometimes with very strong measures, including placing troops on the island and confiscating all the canoes. Thus often people would deny participation in this movement in general terms, while speaking freely of it in more precise contexts.

41. Such mobility is also mentioned by Gasarahinga Sanvura (12/5/72), Gatengura (6/6/72), and Kishake (30/5/74). Mpembe today presents the impression of a relatively infertile area, for the most part, characterized by rocky, sandy soil.

42. Biralinzi 13/2/73. On Rumanura see B. Lugan, "Causes et effets."

43. Mushayuma Semutwa 3/5/74.

44. Kizinduka 28/3/72.

45. Ruzigamanzi 29/3/72; it is possible that Rugaba fled to Ijwi once deposed, although if he did so he did not stay. At any rate, this, too, would underscore the very close ties that existed between Ijwi and Mpembe. There is no record of any contact between Rugaba and the Ijwi royal family.

46. Kavurha 27/3/72. It might also be noted that these movements (and the enduring social ties based on them) were to play an important role in the attacks and administration of Rwabugiri, king of Rwanda, on Ijwi during the late nineteenth century: In Bwando, a certain Kizinduka, recently emigrated from Rwanda, was to meet Rwabugiri and to serve as his representative in the area. This policy of co-opting Ijwi residents with close Rwandan ties was used in other areas of Ijwi as well (D. Newbury, "Rwabugiri and Ijwi").

47. Mirindi 1/5/72.

48. On the developing commercial networks around the southern end of Lake Kivu, see D. Newbury, "Lake Kivu Regional Trade," for a consideration of commerce within Rwanda at the end of the nineteenth century, and especially commercial relations with the west, see B. Lugan, "Echanges et routes commerciales au Rwanda, 1880–1914" (*Africa-Tervuren* 22, 2–4 [1976], 33–39).

49. This process of identification with an ethnic group through incorporation into one of its recognized constituent elements seems also to have been an important element in the extension and integration of new areas into an expanding Rwandan cultural context: the incorporative aspect of Rwandan clans is dramatically illustrated by the presence of Hutu, Tutsi, and Twa within each of the major clans of Rwanda. For a further consideration of this point, see D. Newbury, "The Clans of Rwanda."

Chapter 6. Immigrants to Ijwi: Claiming Ritual Status

1. The Balega of Bushovu, often referred to as Bashovu to distinguish them from other Balega, are pre-Basibula emigrants from the west; their cohesive village structure is reinforced on occupational grounds: they are renowned blacksmiths. Most of the non-Balega inhabitants of Bushovu live in the very fringes of the "village," and socially belong to neighboring communities, not the Bushovu community. The same is true of the three non-Ziralo families in Bwiiru.

2. Murihano 9/5/72.

3. Lubaye 9/3/72.

4. Musigi 9/3/72.

5. Mahuba 7/6/72.

6. Kigonya 18/3/72.
7. Mirindi 1/5/72; Mukatara Barungu 29/4/72.
8. Murihano 9/5/72; Rutebuka 7/6/72; Nyamwigama 26/1/72.
9. Nyamwigama 26/1/72; Nyamuhaga 7/2/73; Mahuba 7/6/72; Lugerero 8/2/72 (who adds that the Banyambiriri came from Rwanda "to attack the Basibula [Banyakabwa?]").
10. Nyamwigama 26/1/72.
11. For instance, when asked of the "sons" of Butyangali, Mahenga (9/3/72) included the name "Washingere" in his response. In a fuller genealogy, however, this name came up several generations descendant from Butyangali; yet the form of citation would still accept "Washingere" as a "son" of Butyangali in both genealogies.
12. Musoro 9/3/72: three generations; Lubaye 9/3/72: four; Mahenga 9/3/72: four; Wihorehe 11/5/72: five; Birali 10/6/72: five; Ngirumpatse Christophe 26/6/72: five; Rubenga (Muhungwe) 12/6/72 and 29/6/72: three; Nyamwigama 26/1/72: three; Murihano 9/2/73: four; Gatera (Bulegeyi) 2/5/72: six.
13. Despite the presence of some Banyambiriri at the time the Basibula drove out Nyamuziga, the absence of Banyambiriri traditions relating to the arrival of the Basibula does not affect the argument here. This only attests to the autonomy which prevailed among the different social groups at this time, an autonomy fully reflected in the traditions; for a full discussion of this issue, see D. Newbury, "Kamo and Lubambo: Dual Genesis Traditions on Ijwi Island, Zaire" (*Les Cahiers du CEDAF* [1979, 5]). As noted below, the Basibula quickly withdrew, and these traditions therefore indicate that enduring ties (e.g., royal ritual roles) were not initiated at the time of the Basibula "conquest" of Nyamuziga.
14. Cf. Burume 10/3/72; but the fathers of these two "brothers" are not the same. Hence this is clearly a statement of identity rather than of genealogical descent.
15. Kakomere 6/6/72, 21/6/74. Kigonya (28/6/72) maintained that Ishungwe was the first Banyambiriri center, and that Mutyangali was born there, leaving only later to found Butyangali. This assertion was from the patriarch of a highly motivated, politically ambitious family. In most traditions Mutyangali's importance stems from his role as "founding father" of the Banyambiriri; these traditions unanimously assert that Mutyangali was indeed among the first of the Banyambiriri to arrive from Bunyambiriri on the Nile-Zaire Divide. It seems likely that the claim of Mutyangali's Ijwi birth is more an attempt to assert a status independent of Rwandan ties of any kind, and to assert the historical priority of Ishungwe to Butyangali, than a product of historical tradition alone.
16. For Rwanda: M. d'Hertefelt and A. Coupez, *La royauté sacrée*, chap. 8, 76–94; D. Newbury, "What Role Has Kingship? An Analysis of the *Umuganura* Ritual of Rwanda" (*Africa-Tervuren* 27, 4 [1981], 89–101). Compare these sources with the Ijwi *muganuro* ritual and comparable cases from elsewhere in the region, described in chapter 12, below.
17. Pagès, *Un royaume Hamite*, 441: "Les plus renommés [among the small kingdoms of western Rwanda] ont été ceux de Rubengera dans le Bgishaza [*sic*] et ceux de Suti, dans le Bunyambiriri"; also de Lacger, *Ruanda*, 85.
18. Murihano 9/5/72; among others on Ijwi who claim that the Banyambiriri on the island came from Nyunyi ya Karonge in Bunyambiriri: Murihano (9/5/72);

Musoro (9/3/72); Gashoko (Mugote, 23/3/72); Mukunzi (8/8/72); Nyamulinda (9/8/72); Rwema (12/8/72); Mulwalwa (29/1/73); Kigonya (18/3/72); Gaherwe (20/3/72); Musigi (9/3/72); Bahaza (12/2/72); Lugerero (8/2/72); Bavugerije (31/1/72); Mahuba (7/6/72); Mahenga (15/6/74).

19. Kagame, *Inganji Karinga*, Vol. 1, 32–35.

20. L. Delmas, *Généalogies*, 165. By "double names" he means a drum name (or dynastic name) as well as a personal name. But two names are also a general characteristic of the Bakiga, the people of these mountainous areas; the question thus refers to age, region, and ritual proprieties. Delmas goes on to add that the Abagwabiro of Bugoyi also derive from this line, when, following a conflict within the family, one member fled to Bugoyi, during the reign of Rujugira; this would appear to reinforce the argument presented earlier concerning the contacts between these areas (and the timing of such movement), although the identification of the Abagwabiro as related to the Banyambiriri seems erroneous—as noted earlier, Bunyambiriri seems to have been only one stop for the Abagwabiro on a more extensive itinerary.

21. D'Hertefelt and Coupez, *La royauté sacrée*, 475 ("Myaka"), and text 8, "Inziro y'Umuganura." Compare with the Banyambiriri role noted in chapter 12, below.

22. For further consideration of the Banyambiriri in Rwanda, see D. Newbury, "Kings and Clans," Appendix 5.

23. J.-P. Chrétien ("Les années de l'éleusine, du sorgho, et du haricot dans l'ancien Burundi: Ecologie et idéologie," *African Economic History* 7 [1979], 75–92) considers the role of millet as an early seed grain in Burundi in a way that seems generally applicable to the larger region as a whole. See also R. Portères, "African Cereals," 409–52; and R. Purseglove, "The Origins and Migrations of Crops in Tropical Africa," 291–309; both in *The Origins of African Plant Domestication,* ed. J. Harlan, J. de Wet, and A. Stempler (The Hague, 1976).

24. Another ritual role held by a Munyambiriri, mentioned above, is that of guardian of the royal diadem, the "Ishungwe." This is symbolic of the ritual power associated with the king and the symbols of royalty rather than with popular contributions to Ijwi society (as in the agricultural ritual). But this is a relatively minor ritual role associated primarily with enthronement and thus more independent of the Muganuro ritual; it shows every indication of having been a later addition to ritual functions, poorly integrated into the larger process of ritual performance: the Ishungwe ritualist is not considered by others to be fully integrated into the corporation of ritualists. But one important function of this ritual rule is that it distinguishes the Ishungwe community from other Banyambiriri. Thus, despite common claims to Banyambiriri status the Ishungwe community is in many ways very different in its relation to royalty from that of the Cibishwa (or Butyangali) line of Banyambiriri; the indications are that this is a group in the process of segmenting off from the larger group. This case, therefore, would appear to confirm the wider argument advanced here, that social functions serve to distinguish between emergent identity groups.

25. In this sense "to reign" means to act in a ritually prescribed manner; this would include the *mwami's* functions at enthronement or Muganuro, or other ritual occasions. In a sense then this sentence could be read: "The *mwami* cannot be enthroned without us."

26. Balagire 7/2/72.

27. See, for example, A. R. Radcliffe-Brown, "On Joking Relationships" (*Africa* 13, 3 [1940]: 195–210); also Freedman, "Joking, Affinity," for a theoretical discussion of such relationships.

28. Freedman, "Principles of Relationship"; also de Heusch, *Le Rwanda et la civilisation Interlacustre,* passim.

29. M. d'Hertefelt, personal communication; on the global figures see d'Hertefelt, *Les clans,* table 2.

30. Delmas, *Généalogies,* 165.

31. On *ubuse* relations in Rwanda: A. Kagame, *Les organisations socio-familiales de l'ancien Rwanda* (Bruxelles, 1954), 209–13; d'Hertefelt, "Le Rwanda," 42; d'Hertefelt and Coupez, *La royauté sacrée,* 310; cf. Freedman, "Principles of Relationships," passim.

32. Cf. d'Hertefelt, "Le Rwanda," 42; Freedman, "Principles of Relationship," chap. 3.

33. A parallel case, in Gisaka (southeastern Rwanda), is illustrated in a fascinating discussion found in L. de Heusch, *Le Rwanda et la civilisation Interlacustre,* 47, 57. There, totemic identities and traditions of exogamy retained the memory of former clan distinctions, distinctions which were subsequently blurred in shifts by which formerly autonomous units were joined within larger over-arching identities. The Ijwi case (discussed in chapter 3), the Renge case in Rwanda (which probably represents many independent regionally distinct cases), and the eighteenth-century transformations in clan identities in western Rwanda (discussed in my "Clans of Rwanda") all present comparable—if not precisely similar—examples of such a transformation as de Heusch discusses for Gisaka. But because these were such long-term, slowly evolving processes, and because they were closely tied to changing political identities, the precise mechanisms of such transformations (the "event history") are rarely retained in oral sources. Once the process was completed, both the former situation and, especially, the unfolding of the process itself were almost entirely effaced from memory within the political unit concerned; that is why understanding such forms of social change inevitably requires comparative data which transcend social boundaries. A comparative approach is necessary because these cultural conceptions rarely leave traces of former modes of thought within the society involved. That is one reason it has proved so difficult to come to grips with this type of problem of structural change; other reasons are discussed in the Conclusion, below.

Chapter 7. Immigrants to Ijwi: Creating Ritual Status

1. Of the 62 married men of the village, 59 were Baziralo (95 percent); the non-Baziralo were socially considered members of neighboring villages, living on the very periphery of Bwiiru, and forgotten even by the capita in recording the people of the hill with me.

2. Strong corporate sentiment was expressed, among others, by Mungazi (6/3/72); Ciruza (6/3/72); Malekera (Bwiiru, 6/3/72); Mugala (6/3/72); Nyamuhuku (16/5/72); Binyene (26/5/72); Muyorha (29/5/72).

3. On the basis of the figures available, 37 percent of all Baziralo on Ijwi lived in Bwiiru, the highest localization percentage of any clan. Almost 70 percent lived in just three major centers (Bwiiru, Bwando, Kisheke), all in the eastern highlands.

4. This is the more striking since references to Nyamuziga and the Banya-kabwa are widely known in the area. If this can be interpreted as an indication that the Baziralo arrived after the battle between Nyamuziga and Mwendanga, then it also indicates that the Baziralo arrived after the Basibula.

5. Ciruza 6/3/72; Mungazi 6/3/72, 28/6/72; Muyorha 29/5/72; Mahusi 26/6/72; Makala 7/5/74.

6. Cf. Mahenga 15/6/74.

7. A. Kagame, "Le code ésotérique de la dynastie du Rwanda ancien," *Zaïre* 1, 4 (1947), 363–86, esp. 365–72; d'Hertefelt, "Le Rwanda," 71–72.

8. D'Hertefelt and Coupez, *La royauté sacrée*, 480 (note on "Nyabirungu"). This source stresses the roles of the ritualist as a *"roi rituel."* Kagame, however, appears to take issue on this point: in "Le code ésoterique" (pp. 368–69) he states categorically: "This dignitary does not enjoy the privileges of royal status." The same source also ties this ritualist (through another army) to the drum "Ndamutsa." This is the name of the second drum on Ijwi, also guarded by the Beeru.

9. Bacigumanya 9/5/74.

10. Kagame, *Inganji Karinga,* section V, #5–7, 30, 34; Kagame, *Les milices,* 23–24; Kagame, *Un abrégé,* 1:39.

11. Kagame, *Les Milices,* 24; d'Hertefelt and Coupez, *La royauté sacrée,* 465–66 (note on "Karaza"), 480 (note on "Nyabirungu").

12. Mungazi 28/6/72; also one of the praise poems from Bwiiru included a reference to Nyabutega: Nyakahomo Ntalengwa 8/3/72. In this he also refers to "Shakwe"; according to de Lacger (*Ruanda,* 84) "Shakwe" is also the praise name for some of the rulers of the small polities of western Rwanda before the Nyiginya conquest.

13. Mahusi 26/6/72.

14. Rwesi (Mpene) 25/1/72, 23/6/72.

15. Kagame, *Les milices,* 20–21.

16. J. Hiernaux, "Note sur un ancien population du Ruanda-Urundi: Les Renge," *Zaïre* 10, 4 (1956), 351–60; Kagame, *Inganji Karinga,* Vol. 2, #10–12; Kagame, *Un abrégé,* 1:27–28, 30, 39–40, 43; Kagame, *Les milices,* 23–26.

17. Kagame, *Inganji Karinga,* Vol. 2, #10–12; Kagame, *Un abrégé,* 1:39–40; Kagame, *Les milices,* 23–24; Hiernaux, "Les Renge;" Pagès, *Un royaume Hamite,* 543–54. J. K. Rennie also provides interesting comparative data which further associates the Abarenge with early drum rituals ("The Precolonial Kingdom of Rwanda," 18 and note 37).

18. Cf. the sources noted in note 17 with Delmas, *Généalogies,* 161–62; Pagès, *Un royaume Hamite,* 543–58; and esp. d'Hertefelt, *Les clans,* 24, note 12.

19. Kagame, *Inganji Karinga,* Vol. 2, #5, 10; Kagame, *Un abrégé,* 1:27 (where the Renge are identified as "Hamites"); but cf. Hiernaux, "Les Renge," 353, 355; C. Gakaniisha, *Récits historiques,* 143–49.

20. Muyorha 29/5/72:

AUTHOR: Why are you called a Mushamvu?
RESPONDENT: Because we make the drums. But our clan is Balega. . . . All those who make the drums in Bushi, Rwanda, Irhambi, are called Bashamvu, but their clan is Balega. . . . The Baziralo and the Balega . . . they are one clan.

294 Notes to Pages 132–34

21. Nangarama 30/4/74.

22. Bacigumanya 9/5/74.

23. The term "Barenge" (or cognates) is widely found southwest of Lake Kivu as well (Biebuyck, *Lega Culture*, 7, 68–71). The ruling dynasty of Buvira is known as the Balenge (J. M. F. Depelchin, "From Precapitalism to Imperialism: A History of Social and Economic Formations in Eastern Zaire (Uvira Zone, c. 1800–1965)" [Ph.D. diss., Stanford University, 1974], chap. 2 [esp. 44–48] and 100–106; Sigwalt, "The Early History of Bushi," 112). Finally the term "Alenga" is associated with an ancient form of kingship in the area southwest of the lake (Biebuyck, *Lega Culture*, 24, 67–70; Mulyumba wa Mumba Itongwa, "Aperçu sur la structure politique des Balega-Basile," *Les Cahiers du CEDAF* [1978, 1] 19–20, 28–30, 36–37, and passim; Sigwalt, "The Early History of Bushi," chap. 5). As will be shown in chapter 8 below, there are many historical linkages of Havu royal traditions with areas south of Lake Kivu. It is also worth noting that on Ijwi (and elsewhere) the prefix "Banya-" ("Binya-") is frequently associated with very old groups (or archaic groups no longer represented), in place of the more common "Ba-" prefix for personal plurals: Banyakabwa, Binyalenge, Munyakalinga, Nyamuhiva (instead of the more expected "Muhiva"), Nyabutege (in Rwanda), for titular head of the Abatege ritual group.

24. Delmas, *Généalogies*, 28–29; Kagame, *Inganji Karinga*, section II, #10; section V, #30; Kagame, *Les milices*, 23–26. For a discussion of different versions of the social interpretations of the Abarenge-Abasinga, see d'Hertefelt, *Les clans*, 77, note 12; Smith, "La forge de l'intelligence," 5–21; de Heusch, *Rois nés*, chaps. 2, 3, 4. For a more detailed summary of the sources, see Appendix 7 of D. Newbury, "Kings and Clans."

25. Kagame, *Inganji Karinga*, section II, #9–13; section V, #30.

26. For a further consideration of these transformations see D. Newbury, "The Clans of Rwanda."

27. Delmas, *Généalogies*, 28–29.

28. This account is based on Kagame, *Inganji Karinga*, section VII, #61–68; Kagame, *Les milices*, 24; Kagame, *Un abrégé*, 1:89–91; Delmas, *Généalogies*, 29; J. Vansina, *L'évolution*, 85–86. But the western sources provide a vital perspective from which to assess and analyze these elaborate Rwandan traditions; see Appendix 7 of D. Newbury, "Kings and Clans," for further consideration of these sources.

29. Because of the incomplete nature of the Sibula accounts in the Havu traditions, this account will draw on the Rwandan traditions; see Appendix 7 of D. Newbury, "Kings and Clans," for a consideration of the Rwandan traditions relating to Sibula. The Havu have only the vaguest echo of Sibula in their traditions—in legends associated with the Bahande clan, in traditions explaining the derivation of the royal line from the Shi line, and in the dynastic name itself. This last is in fact a source of some confusion, since most Havu traditions, drawing on the parallels of the two kings, confuse Sibula Nyebunga (associated with the Rwandan drum histories) with his Havu homonym of the late nineteenth century. (One Havu tradition from the mainland notes that Sibula fought in Rwanda at a river called Kabagala [Mazinganoko, Ruhinda, Ngurube, et al., 10/11/72]).

30. Kagame, *Un abrégé*, 1:72–81; Kagame, *Inganji Karinga*, section VII, #26–27, 39–40.

31. *Butega* were a type of bracelet-anklets made of raphia, and were popular trade items in the nineteenth century (D. Newbury, "Lake Kivu Regional Trade").

32. The succession disputes of this time are discussed in Kagame, *Inganji Karinga*, section VII, #41–68; Kagame, *Histoire du Rwanda*, 26–29; Kagame, *Un abrégé*, 1:86–87; Delmas, *Généalogies*, 49; Vansina, *L'évolution*, 67, 85–86; Rennie, "The Precolonial Kingdom of Rwanda," 27–28.

33. Kagame, *Un abrégé*, 1:90. No explanation is given of who these "numerous warriors" were: there is no indication of either a dense population at this time or of centralized authority in Buhavu; in fact the data argue against both. This phrase is likely to be a *post facto* elaboration to explain Ndahiro's defeat.

34. Kagame, *Inganji Karinga*, section VII, #61–68; Kagame, *Un abrégé*, 1:89–91; Kagame, *Les milices*, 24, note 1; Delmas, *Généalogies*, 29; Pagès, *Un royaume Hamite*, 238–51; see also Appendix 7 of D. Newbury, "Kings and Clans."

35. "Drum" is the term used on Ijwi to refer to "reign," or "dynasty," as well as "throne" in this generalized sense. The term apparently has a similar semantic field in Rwanda; see Kagame, *Un abrégé*, 1:39.

36. Delmas, *Généalogies*, 29; Kagame, *Inganji Karinga*, section VII, #68; Kagame, *Les milices*, 24, note 1.

37. D. Newbury, "Les campagnes de Rwabugiri"; and D. Newbury, "Rwabugiri and Ijwi."

38. Some precedent did exist for this. According to Kagame (*La poésie dynastique*, 39–40), Ruganzu Ndori (the "son" of and successor to Cyamatare) also attacked Ijwi and "detached" the island from "Bunyabungo," making it part of Rwanda. (Kagame usually uses "Bunyabungo" to refer to Bushi. There is no indication in any source that Ijwi was ever a part of Bushi. This reference, then, illustrates the confusion so frequently apparent in Kagame's references to western areas.) One of the dynastic poems (no. 170, p. 91) does mention Ruganzu "à la recherche du Rwoga fait prisonnier." (Rwoga was the name of the royal drum.) If this applies to the attacks against Ijwi, it would have provided a justification for these attacks. If indeed these poems date from the distant past, it is curious that this episode seems to have been unknown to Rwabugiri, and that he did not use the poem as justification for his attacks. The fact that the poem includes reference to "Rwoga fait prisonnier" and that Kagame elsewhere says that this history was unknown until the time of Rwabugiri indicates the possibility that the poem is of recent derivation, at least in its present form. Furthermore, if Ruganzu did incorporate Ijwi into Rwanda, it is interesting that the sources state only that Nyabutege's descendants returned to Rwanda (Kagame, *Un abrégé*, 1:103; Kagame, *Les milices*, 24), but they do not indicate that Ruganzu located him on Ijwi and brought him back, as one might expect if the search for the drum (and rituals) truly had been his goal, as Poem 170 suggests, and if Ijwi had been incorporated into Rwanda. But Rwabugiri is said to have done exactly this, later on. This therefore likely provides an example of confusing the heroic deeds of two great warrior kings; Kagame notes that Ruganzu and Kigeli (Rwabugiri's drum name) were "dynastic homonyms" (Kagame, *Le code des institutions politiques*, 59–60, note 34). (For other examples of this confusion, see D. Newbury, "Cyclic Traditions.") Nor is this possibility beyond the time span for detail, as frequently encountered in other Rwandan traditions; in other words, the omission of the drum loss at the time of

Sibula is not a result of a structural characteristic of Rwandan narrative. The argument presented here, that the tradition represents a case of *post facto* reconstruction, a type of non-literate "feedback," does not rest on negative evidence alone. I am not denying that the Ijwi drums were imported directly from Rwanda simply because the traditions which assert this are historically unreliable or implausible. Instead, I am arguing that historical understanding must be based on more than oral accounts alone—especially when those oral accounts drawn exclusively from the court milieu. On the basis of ethnographic and historical evidence independent of that milieu, this chapter offers an alternate interpretation and reconstruction.

39.   Kagame, *La poésie dynastique,* 39–40; Kagame, *Un abrégé,* 1:104; Vansina, *L'évolution,* 87. In some sources, Kagame asserts that Terengoma, the Rwandan ritualist seized by Sibula, escaped back to Rwanda (Kagame, *Les milices,* 24; Kagame, *Un abrégé,* 1:103). But this is contradicted in Kagame, *Inganji Karinga,* section VII, #68. It would also seriously question the supposed "absence" of these traditions in Rwanda, and raise a question of why these traditions became known only under Rwabugiri 300 years after Cyamatare's death, according to Kagame's own reasoning (cf. Kagame, *La notion,* passim).

40.   These attacks are the more suspect because there is no local evidence that Sibula ever resided on the island, because there was no functioning "kingdom" on Ijwi at the time (at least not in the sense that Kagame assumes), and because Ruganzu is considered a dynastic homonym to Kigeri Rwabugiri, who did attack Ijwi and who also attacked a Havu mainland king named Sibula. Kagame, *Le code des institutions politiques,* 59–60, note 34: "Les deux noms [Ruganzu and Kigeri] sont dynastiquement homonyms." Traditions associated with one king are frequently transposed to be associated with his homonyms, in Rwandan traditions as with those of other areas; see D. Newbury, "Cyclic Traditions."

41.   D'Hertefelt and Coupez, *La royauté sacrée,* 77–93; Delmas, *Généalogies,* 107; Kagame, *Inganji Karinga,* section V, #31.

42.   Delmas, *Généalogies,* 107.

43.   Mainland interviews: Shamvu 20/11/72; Nabwibize 15/11/73.

44.   Kagame, *Inganji Karinga,* section V, #31; Kagame, *Les milices,* 27; Kagame, *Un abrégé,* 1:41–42. The Abatsoobe were the most important of the Rwandan ritualists (d'Hertefelt and Coupez, *La royauté sacrée,* 493; Kagame, *Inganji Karinga,* section V, #31; Kagame, *Les milices,* 26–27). They lived in the Bumbogo-Rukoma region, and may have been incorporated into the Rwandan ritual functions from a previous independent status (Vansina, *L'évolution,* 46–47; Sigwalt, "Early Rwanda History," 141–42; and de Heusch, *Rois nés,* chap. 4); but for a critique of this interpretation see d'Hertefelt, *Les clans,* 24.

45.   They probably arrived during the reign of Kabego, the second of the Ijwi Basibula kings (Rwesi [Mpene] 23/6/72). They also show continuing ties with Mpinga today; the daughter of one current family there was sent to live with relatives in Mpinga, for example, in hopes of marrying there, because bridewealth was higher on the western mainland than on Ijwi. This pattern of women marrying west is also apparent between western Rwanda and Ijwi (cf. Kakomere 21/6/74).

46.   Rwesi (Mpene) 25/1/72, 23/6/72. These genealogies differ slightly, but in both "Nyabutega" is located five generations ascendant from the respondent. He also

notes that Nyabutega came from Rwanda to "Irhambi" (Buhavu). Mahusi (26/6/72) also refers to Nyabutega in his genealogy; he is the only Mwiiru (from Bwiiru) to do so, but for many years he has lived at Buhumba, near the western Baziralo on Mpene. Although Munyakalinga, the lineage head of the Baziralo at Bwiiru, confirmed that the Beeru were sometimes known as the Abateege (Mungazi 28/6/72), he did not, nor did anyone else now living on Bwiiru, include Nyabutega in his genealogy.

47.   Mainland interview: Shamvu 20/11/72; he is referred to in Kalehe as Munyakalinga.

48.   Muyorha 29/5/72; Makala 8/5/74; Bacigumanya 9/5/74.

49.   Kagame, *Inganji Karinga,* section V, #30. We are told only that Nyamuhindula, "qui avait transformée un arbre en un tambour," was the son of Rubunga, who originally informed Gihanga (the first Umunyiginya "king") of the Abarenge (Abasinga) esoteric code and drum rituals.

50.   Ntabandagaro 4/2/72: "Mwendanga came with Kalinga [the royal drum]; the Beeru came after, at the time of Kabego"; also Lubaye 9/3/72; Binyene 26/5/72; Rwesi (Mpene) 23/6/72. But dating is hampered by telescoping in the traditions relating to the two Havu kings known as Sibula. The most recent was a contemporary of Kabego; like his predecessor, he fought against a Rwandan military king (Rwabugiri), and died in Rwanda.

51.   Mungazi 28/6/72: "Lugyaka [the first Muziralo at Bwiiru] did not bring a drum with him. The *mwami* only met him and asked him to 'make' a drum." Mungazi is the head of Bwiiru, and a very strong figure; he was probably in his mid- or late forties at the time of the interviews. When Mungazi refers to the *mwami's* asking "Lugyaka" to make a drum, the pronoun "him" in this context, apparently referring to "Lugyaka," could also refer to descendants of Lugyaka as well as to Lugyaka himself. Sources from outside of Bwiiru refer to Mutemura as the first Muziralo. Since Lugyaka is accepted almost universally as the founder of Bwiiru and ancestor of Mutemura, it is possible that this reference refers to the first Muziralo "ritualist"—the role that most characterizes the Baziralo today—rather than the first Muziralo settler (Mahusi 26/6/72; Makala 8/5/74).

52.   Rwesi (Mpene, 23/6/72), a member of the western Ziralo lineage, and a son of Ruwhiza, stated that Rwamakaza, a descendant of Shamvu and Nyabutega, left Irhambi for Ijwi at the time of Kabego on Ijwi and of Sibula at Irhambi. He died with Kabego, killed by Rwabugiri. It appears that after Rwabugiri's occupation of Ijwi the drum rituals went to Mutemura's line; see also Ntambuka Barhahakana 13/9/74. If the drum rituals originally arrived on Ijwi with this line, as the tenuous evidence suggests, and were then transferred to the eastern Baziralo at Bwiiru, then the arrival of Rwamkaza during Kabego's reign would conform to other evidence which indicates that the Beeru acquired their status as drum ritualists only relatively recently.

53.   Mayange (18/6/74) asserted that the name of one of the drums of Mwendanga was "Ngongomulyango" and that Mwendanga did not have the Kalinga when he came to Ijwi. This was confirmed by Ndongozi (20/6/74), a Muziralo from Mpene and a son of Ruwhiza, who said that "Kalinga" (i.e., the present royal drum) was brought to Ijwi by his "grandfather" at the time of Kabego. In this context the conceptual connections of the term "drum" with the concepts of "reign" or "dynasty,"

or even royalty in the abstract, becomes significant, because other evidence also indicates that Kabego may have been the first king really to "reign"—in the full ritual sense—on Ijwi.

54. The royal rituals of Mpinga (Kalehe) have not been celebrated since the early 1940s, when Muhigirwa Bahole, a Catholic, acceded to the drums (1943) with the strong support of the Catholic church interceding with the administration on his behalf. Nonetheless, interviews conducted there with the families of the former ritualists provided hints of the former Mpinga system.

55. Although the drum concepts in Buhavu and Rwanda may have both derived from pre-Banyiginya ritual forms, Rwandan traditions also imply that the earliest Rwandan drums and other rituals associated with royalty were originally obtained from pre-Banyiginya forms in western Rwanda and from areas west of the Rusizi, as well as from the north of present Rwanda—in other words, from peoples who, as we have seen above, were similar in culture and perhaps social-historical descent to contemporary Havu-Ijwi populations; see Kagame, *Inganji Karinga*, section V, #5–7, 30; Kagame, *Un abrégé*, 1: 39–43, esp. 42: "L'empire de Gihanga, à l'examen des traditions recueillies, débordait largement les limites du Rwanda actuel. Le Code ésoterique nous montre sa résidence au Bunyabungo, sur la rive Zairoise sud-occidentale du lac Kivu. C'est dans les environs de cette résidence que la Cour du Rwanda se procurait des objets requis dans la célébration des Prémices, parce que Gihanga aurait pris les mêmes objets en cet endroit précis." Appendix 6 in D. Newbury, "Kings and Clans," discusses Rwandan sources on the drum rituals in greater detail.

56. From the available accounts, the drums do not seem to have played a central role in the definition of kingship in Bushi (Colle, *Monographie*, 257–67; Sosne, "Kinship and Contract in Bushi," Appendices 2 and 3. In Buhaya (Kabare, the senior Shi kingdom) the drum, named Beremera, is not among the "sacred regalia" considered by Colle (*Monographie*, 260), and according to his account plays only a minor role in the enthronement (p. 263). In Ngweshe, only the skin said to have covered the first drum is conserved (Colle, *Monographie*, 263). Furthermore, the drum ritualists do not appear among the principal *bagingi* associated with the First Fruits ceremony, Mubande. In Bushi in general, the ritual authorities seem to derive their prestige much more from the groups they represent than as ritual functionaries of the court, as on Ijwi. In keeping with this, there is greater corporate identity with *bugingi* in Bushi than on Ijwi. There, ritual power and prestige adheres much more to an individual *mugingi*, the Bashaho and Baziralo being the only exceptions, and even in their cases the corporate identity with *bugingi* is less marked than in Bushi.

Chapter 8. The Antecedents of Basibula Royalty

1. This character of political life in the area is reflected in the quality (if not always directly in the content) of traditions from the area. Referring to the precolonial period, they note that the power of the *mwami* in the area was "more symbolic than real," and the effective power of the *mwami* applied only to villages near the court; authorities more distant offered their nominal allegiance to the *mwami* but did not feel under his control. And the sources further imply high personal mobility and frequently shifting allegiance in this area, what Bishikwabo refers to as *"des autonomies*

internes" (Bishikwabo C., "L'origine des chefferies de l'ouest de la Rusizi: Bufulero, Buvira et Burundi au XIX–XXe siècle," *Culture et société: Revue de civilisation burundaise* 4 [1981], 107–21, esp. 109–10, 116). G. Weis (*Le pays d'Uvira* [Bruxelles, 1959], 144) and Moeller de Laddersous (*Les grandes lignes,* 137) also refer to such institutional fluidity. Further fieldwork may help illuminate the complex histories of the eighteenth and nineteenth centuries in this Tanganyika-Kivu corridor. But for the moment we are left only with the rich but more indirect sources drawn from Burundi, Bushi, and Rwanda.

2.   Oral data from Busoozo, one of the small polities in southwestern Rwanda, which remained independent of the Rwandan central court until 1926, confirm the intensity of personal and historical ties with Burundi (Ntezimana, "Coutumes et traditions").

3.   The Shi sources on Sibula (Nsibula) are found in Colle, *Monographie;* Moeller de Laddersous, *Les grandes lignes;* and P. Masson, *Trois siècles;* and most fully in Ciribagula, "Histoire des rois du Buhaya" (unpublished manuscript, Bukavu; I am indebted to the Missionaries d'Afrique at CELA in Bukavu, and to R. Sigwalt for consultation of this source). The Rwandan sources are slightly different from the Shi traditions, tying Sibula to devastating wars against the Rwandan kings. It is possible that these traditions of Sibula were earlier than the Shi traditions, because Sigwalt mentions that the Nyebunga tradition in the Shi sources may be a recent addition ("The Early History of Bushi," 118, note 2). At any rate because of their obvious functional uses and the contradictions within them, they can clearly not be taken literally. For a further discussion of the Rwandan Sibula traditions, see Appendix 7 in D. Newbury, "Kings and Clans."

4.   Ntambuka Barhahakana 28/12/70, 20/4/72; Mugenzi 28/12/70; Mulyumba wa Mamba, "Aperçu sur la structure politique," 36. The importance of Lwindi in the development of kingship in this region is evident in Sigwalt, "The Early History of Bushi," chap. 5; also Moeller de Laddersous, *Les grandes lignes;* Cuypers, "Les Bantous Interlacustres"; Colle, *Monographie,* 220; Masson, *Trois siècles,* 14.

5.   Sigwalt, "The Early History of Bushi," 137; Bishikwabo, "L'origine des chefferies"; Moeller de Laddersous, *Les grandes lignes,* 136.

6.   On many occasions people on Ijwi mentioned that it was easier for them to understand Mazibaziba (the language of Kaziba) than Mahaya (the language of the central Shi kingdom).

7.   Sigwalt, "The Early History of Bushi," 122, 136; Bishikwabo C., "Histoire d'un état Shi en Afrique des Grand Lacs: Kaziba au Zaïre (c. 1850–1940)" (Ph.D. diss., Université de Louvain-la Neuve, 1982), 235–37. Ijwi rituals are discussed in chapter 12, below.

8.   For a more complete discussion, with fuller references, see chapter 12.

9.   The Ijwi forms are more egalitarian still than the Rundi forms, perhaps because they are less directly tied to the political structure. On Burundi: A. A. Trouwborst, "Le Burundi," in *Les anciens royaumes de la zone Interlacustre méridionale,* ed. M. d'Hertefelt, A. A. Trouwborst, and J. Scherer, 113–69 (Tervuren, 1962), esp. 151–52; A. Trouwborst, "L'organisation politique en tant que système d'échanges au Burundi," *Anthropologica,* n.s. 3, 1 (1961), 65–81; A. Trouwborst, "L'organisation politique et l'accord de clientèle au Burundi," *Anthropologica,* n.s. 4, 1 (1962), 9–43;

Mworoha, *Peuples et rois de l'Afrique des lacs,* 187–90; E. Simons, "Coutumes et institutions des Barundi," *Bulletin des juridictions indigènes et du droit coutumier congolais* 12, 10 (1944), 208–13. On Buha: J. J. Tawney, "Ugabire: A Feudal Custom amongst the Waha," *Tanzania Notes and Records* 17 (1944), 6–9. On Rwanda: Maquet, *Le système des relations sociales,* chap. 6; Kagame, *Les organisations socio-familiales,* 266–94; Vidal, "Le Rwanda des anthropologues"; C. Newbury, *The Cohesion of Oppression,* passim; Saucier, "The Patron-Client Relationship"; P. Gravel, "The Transfer of Cows in Gisaka (Rwanda): A Mechanism for Recording Social Relationships," *American Anthropologist* 69, 3 (1967), 322–31.

10.   One of the spirits celebrated in northwestern Burundi—an area of considerable historical interaction with southern Lake Kivu—is named Rubambo, said to represent the spirit of diviners. In the same area of Burundi, diviners are said sometimes to use a calabash doll in practicing their art; this doll is named Nyabukobwa (a cognate to Nkobwa, the name of Lubambo's daughter) (Trouwborst, "Le Burundi," 157–59; E. Simons, "Coutumes et institutions," 153–57; B. Zuure, *Croyances et pratiques religieuses des Barundi* [Bruxelles, 1929], 50, 103–8, 114; J. Vansina, *La légende du passé* [Tervuren, 1972], 74, 79, 98, 100 [where Rubambo is said to have "made a king"—not unlike the situation in Kinyaga, as will be discussed below]).

11.   In addition to the names Ntare and Rubambo, another name prominent in Ijwi dynastic traditions has parallels in areas south of the lake. According to Ijwi traditions, Kabwiika was the father of Mwendanga, Ijwi's first king. Kabwiika also is a name prominent in the dynastic tradition from Bufuliiro, as a king who ruled in the late eighteenth or early nineteenth century (Depelchin, "From Precapitalism to Imperialism," 50; H. Meyer, *Les Barundi: Une étude ethnologique en Afrique orientale* [ed. and annotated by J.-P. Chrétien] [Paris, 1984], 243–44, note 44).

12.   Sigwalt, "The Early History of Bushi," 66–67, 123; Masson, *Trois siècles,* 28–32 (where he refers to Mushaka, a hill near Bukunzi); Colle, *Monographie,* 221–22; Pagès, *Un royaume Hamite,* 344 (also 294–98); M. Pauwels, "Le Bushiru," 230, 215–16, note 20.

13.   Rwandan influence may have been instrumental in the schism which occurred between Buhaya and Ngweshe, today the two largest Shi states (Sigwalt, "The Early History of Bushi," chap. 3; Masson, *Trois siècles,* 28–30). Rwanda traditions refer to much earlier contact when the Rwandan kings are said to have fled to "Bunyabungo" at the time of the "Banyoro" invasions during the reigns of Mukobanya and Mutabazi in the sixteenth century (Kagame, *Un abrégé,* 1:77–79; Kagame, *Inganji Karinga,* Vol. 2, section VII, #27; Vansina, *L'évolution,* 84–85). Rwanda traditions also refer to a joint Rundi-Rwanda attack against the area west of the Rusizi in the time of Mibambwe (Kagame, *Inganji Karinga,* Vol. 2, section VII, #39).

14.   Kagame, *Armées bovines,* 32; Vansina, *La légende du passé,* 201.

15.   Kagame, *Les milices,* 97–100, 106, 108; Kagame, *La poésie dynastique,* 42–43; Kagame, *Armées bovines,* 32; Vansina, *La légende du passé,* 203. The Rundi traditions are silent on this count (Vansina, *La légende du passé,* 204).

16.   There are numerous references to Bushi in the Rundi traditions in general (Vansina, *La légende du passé,* 48, 60, 80, 81, 104, 140, 141, 158, 162, 175, 198, 206;

J. Gorju et al., *Face au royaume hamite du Ruanda: Le royaume frère de l'Urundi* [Bruxelles, 1938], 36).

17.   On the Rusizi Valley, for example, a colonial territorial administrator noted in 1933 that it was about 1800 (under Ntare II) when the kings of Burundi sought to introduce their own subjects into the area (cited in Bishikwabo, "L'origine des chefferies," 110).

18.   Vansina, *La légende du passé*, 206, citing R. Kandt, *Caput Nili* (Berlin, 1921), 320–29. In fact, the situation referred to here may have preceded the reign of Ntare II, and therefore may not have resulted directly from it.

19.   For a fascinating discussion of the elaborate literary development of the Rundi traditions on Twarereye: Vansina, *La légende du passé*, 145–55; and on Kilima: Vansina, *La légende du passé*, 32–50, 206, 216; E. Simons, "Coutumes et institutions," 144–45.

20.   That the sources are strangely silent on this area would indicate that it was not then a part of the Burundi state. In the nineteenth century, in fact, the Rusizi Corridor was continually a cradle of revolt against the Rundi kings—a "marcher area" in the conflicts between Burundi and its two neighbors to the north, Bushi and Rwanda. Although Rundi sources refer to Kilima as Shi, this is more likely an epithet of opprobrium than an ethnographic fact. Though he may well have drawn on Shi alliances for the political and material resources with which to carry on his revolt, he was probably from the Rusizi Valley area itself. There is no knowledge of him in the Shi areas; consequently if he were Shi he was not likely to have been of the Shi political hierarchy, nor would he have easily mobilized support in the Rusizi Corridor. (Kilima himself claimed to be the legitimate heir to Rundi kingship, born while his mother had fled to Bushi; this is a common cliché on the part of pretenders to power throughout the region.) But he also retained excellent relations both with Swahili coastal traders on Lake Tanganyika and (initially, at least) with Europeans. From Vansina's account Kilima seems to have been part of a long tradition of successful resistance to outside control by leaders from the Rusizi Valley (Vansina, *La légende du passé*, 216). He was finally captured and deported by the Germans, who sought to reinforce and stabilize central court authority under Mwezi Gisabo. On Kilima: Vansina, *La légende du passé*, 206–16; Mworoha, *Peuples et rois de l'Afrique des lacs*, 292–93, 309–10; Gorju et al., *Face au royaume hamite*, 36; E. Mworoha et al. (eds.), *Histoire du Burundi* (Paris, 1987), 148; Meyer, *Les Barundi*, 210, 216, 218, 243–44, and plate 17; Louis, *Ruanda-Urundi*, 117–21, 132; L. Ndoricimpa, "Du roi fondateur au roi rebelle: Le récit du rebelle dans les traditions orales du Burundi," in *L'arbre-mémoire: Traditions orales du Burundi*, ed. L. Ndoricimpa and C. Guillet (Paris, 1984), 56–57; the latter cites an unpublished thesis that I have not been able to consult: V. Shingereje, "L'anti-roi Kilima ou l'échec d'une tentative dynastique du Burundi" (Mémoire de Licence, Université du Burundi, 1982). For an interesting study of succession/secession conflicts in Burundi (in which Kilima is discussed on p. 273), see R. Botte, "La guerre interne au Burundi," in *Guerres des lignages et guerres d'états en Afrique*," ed. J. Bazin and E. Terray (Paris 1982). The same author has contributed two other valuable articles on internal political confrontation in Burundi: R. Botte, "De quoi vivait l'état?" *Cahiers d'études africaines* 22, 3–4 (1982), 277–325; and

R. Botte, "Processus de formation d'une classe sociale dans une société africaine précapitaliste," *Cahiers d'études africaines* 14, 4 (1974), 605–26.

21.   Louis, *Ruanda-Urundi*, 132.

22.   Despite a vast literature on the Shi, there is as yet no comprehensive analytic pre-colonial history of the Shi as a whole, and much of the literature to date on pre-colonial Shi history simply repeats the colonial historical imagery and stereotypes. Nonetheless Bishikwabo provides a short introduction ("Le Bushi au XIXe siècle: Un peuple, sept royaumes," *Revue français d'histoire d'outre-mer* 67, 1–2 [1980], 89–98). Standard sources on the pre-colonial period include Colle, *Monographie;* Cuypers, "Les Bantous Interlacustres"; Masson, *Trois siècles;* Moeller de Laddersous, *Les grandes lignes;* most others derive from these. (Earlier historical assumptions and stereotypes pertaining to the region, which all these works share, are considered in D. Newbury, "Bushi and the Historians," 31–51.) A thoughtful analysis of the early traditions of origin is provided in Sigwalt, "The Early History of Bushi." Early published sources on the Bashi include: P. Colle, "L'organisation politique des Bashi," *Congo* 2, 2 (1921), 657–84; P. Colle, "Les clans au pays Bashi," *Congo* 3, 1 (1922), 337–52; and P. Colle, "Au pays Bashi," *Congo* 6, 1 (1925), 399–404. Colle's work is brought together in his *Monographie.* There is a wealth of material included in the numerous Travaux de fin d'Etudes and Mémoires de Licence at the Institut Supérieur Pédagogique in Bukavu, and at the Université de Lubumbashi. A wide-ranging study of Kaziba, one of the small "southern tier" Shi states, is found in Bishikwabo, "Histoire d'un état Shi." Of particular interest for the region as a whole is Mugaruka bin Mubibi, "Histoire clanique et évolution des états dans la région sud-ouest du Lac Kivu (des origines à 1900)" (Ph. D. diss., Université de Lubumbashi, 1986). Colonial and post-colonial Bushi is considered in Bashizi C., "Paysannat et salariat agricole rural au Bushi, 1920–1960" (Ph. D. diss., Université de Lubumbashi, 1981); and E. D. Sosne, "Colonial Peasantization and Contemporary Underdevelopment: A View from a Kivu village" (in *Zaire: The Political Economy of Underdevelopment,* ed. G. Gran, 189–210. ([New York, 1979]). A catalogue of works mentioning Bushi is found in Bashizi C., "Histoire du Kivu: Sources écrites et perspectives d'avenir" (*Likundoli* 4, 2 [1976], 65–113).

23.   An example of refuge east of the lake is Bukunzi, a small kingdom in the highlands east of the Rusizi River, now in Rwanda. It remained independent of the Rwandan central court until conquered in a joint Belgian-Rwandan campaign in 1926; see Masson, *Trois siècles,* 27–32; Ntezimana, "Coutumes et traditions"; and Ntezimana, "L'arrivée des Européens au Kinyaga." On the colonial conquest of Bukunzi: Smith, *Le récit populaire,* 320–25 ("Fin d'un roitelet," narrated by A. Bapfakulera); C. Newbury, *The Cohesion of Oppression,* 65–66, 258–59 (n. 42).

24.   An excellent analysis of the early origin of kingship in the area, focussing on the Banyamwocha dynasty of central Bushi, is found in Sigwalt, "The Early History of Bushi." Sigwalt accepts Shi traditions on Havu origins, and does not consider Havu traditions. A more plausible hypothesis, as suggested by Bishikwabo ("L'origine des chefferies") is that the political currents on which the Basibula drew were parallel to those on which the Banyamwocha drew, rather than later derivations from the Banyamwocha. This hypothesis is supported by oral sources and cultural indications from both the Havu areas and those areas along the southern tier of

present Bushi. Without going into the details here, the Basibula antecedents seem in many ways more closely tied, historically and culturally, to the Kaziba, Luhwinja, and Burhinyi populations than to the Bahaya-Ngweshe traditions. The common Shi sources that portray the Havu dynastic line as subordinate to the Shi royal line, of a form found frequently throughout the region, appear more as ideological statements than sound historical accounts.

25.   The campaigns of Rwabugiri, the warrior-king of Rwanda during the last third of the nineteenth century, probably reinforced Shi political preoccupations with the area; earlier in the nineteenth century Shi moves to benefit from the increasing commercial intensity on the Tanganyika-Kivu Corridor concentrated on the area south of Lake Kivu. For a general overview of the mainland areas considered here, see Kirhero N. "Evolution politique des localités de Lugendo et Ishungu (1920–1964)" (Mémoire de Licence, ISP–Bukavu, 1977). On Luhihi under Shi administration: Miderho L., "Ciringwe et l'essor de Luhihi (1927–1976)" (Travail de Fin d'Etudes, ISP–Bukavu, 1980).

26.   It is a curious feature of these "traditions of genesis" of Ijwi royalty that they are known by members of only two clans; with but a few exceptions, the details are virually absent among other groups, even among the Basibula themselves. The two clans to retain coherent traditions of this period are today very small clans on Ijwi, and politically relatively unimportant. Furthermore, the traditions recounted by members of these two clans are entirely independent of each other, and (except for one personnage) non-intersecting; the characters recalled, the events recounted, even the styles of recitation themselves, differ markedly between the two historical accounts. The details of such traditions, the differences between them, and an explanation for this intriguing pattern of differences are analyzed at length in my "Kamo and Lubambo." On the concept of "traditions of genesis," see J. Vansina, "Traditions of Genesis," *Journal of African History* 15, 2 (1974), 317–22.

Chapter 9. The Arrival of the Basibula Dynasty on Ijwi

1.   On the recent history of the Basibula line at Mpinga (Kalehe), see Ngongo B., "Contribution à l'histoire politique du Buhavu: Le Mpinga sous les derniers Basibula" (Travail de Fin d'Etudes, ISP–Bukavu, 1985). Some traditions (cf. Moeller de Laddersous, *Les grandes lignes,* 126–31) and official (government) sources state that, in addition to the Ijwi line, another segment of the royal family left to establish themselves in Kalonge. This kingdom is located in the foothills of the Mt. Kahuzi massif, straddling the open areas of highland pasture and forested areas of the western slopes of the Mitumba Mountains. Today the kingdom of Kalonge is composed of two distinct population segments: one, living on the plateau, is formed of essentially Shi-speaking people; the other, living in the forested sectors to the west of the plateau, is essentially Tembo in language and culture (and it is identified as such by other Tembo). There is no hint in the Havu sources independent of the official written sources of this historical link to the Basibula line—or even in the traditions of Kalonge. (I carried out research in Kalonge in August and September of 1972.)

2.   Ciringwe 16/1/75.

3.   For examples of these texts, see D. Newbury, "Kings and Clans," Appendices 13 and 14. This episode is very widely recounted, primarily among members of

the Babambo clan, both on Ijwi and on the mainland. These traditions, and those on which the following analysis is based, are more fully discussed in my "Kamo and Lubambo."

4. Ciringwe 16/1/75; on the dating proposed here, see D. Newbury, "Kings and Clans," Appendix 10.

5. As a result of these alliance ties, Lubambo is considered in some traditions today as a representative of Gahindiro (the king of Rwanda) to Kinyaga. (Although today a part of Rwanda, Kinyaga lay outside the direct authority of the Rwandan central court during the early nineteenth century, at the time of Gahindiro.) The weight of considerable evidence throughout Kinyaga, however, indicates that it is unlikely that Lubambo served in any official political capacity. Consequently assertions of this nature appear to result from reading more recent historical patterns of clientship into early alliance patterns which were of a totally different character. Some Ijwi traditions assert the same: that Mwendanga arrived on Ijwi with Gahindiro's support. But there is no substance to support the generalization, which therefore seems a product of later perceptions rather than testimony of a historical alliance.

6. The sources, of course, omit the fact that Mwendanga was eventually to claim his own throne. Given the tendencies of these traditions to be selective and given the lack of interaction between Ijwi and the mainland Havu kingdom, it is surprising that the traditions do not portray this military victory as legitimizing his rule. In fact, all sources claim that the Ijwi line is the junior Basibula line; the question of Mwendanga's royal status prior to his arrival on Ijwi is left ambivalent.

7. Two examples of these traditions—unrepresentative of the greater body of Ijwi traditions because of their length and coherence—are provided in D. Newbury, "Kings and Clans," Appendices 11 and 12.

8. The conflict between Mwendanga and the Babambo is portrayed in a cliché: that one party broke the "knee" of the other (cf. Gahamire 26/2/74; mainland interview: Musengo 21/4/75, for one example). This cliché also appears in other contexts of conflict with the royal family (Runiga 15/5/72; Nyamuheshera 17/5/72; Gahamire Mondo 18/6/74; Gahenzi Rubabura 12/6/72; Garuhinga 9/6/72).

9. The claim to royal heritage is a fiction on two counts: Kabwiika was not himself enthroned king, nor was Mwendanga a legitimate son of this pretender.

10. In the Ijwi succession struggle, as in the earlier mainland conflict against Kamerogosa, the Babambo were to support a contender who, like Mwendanga himself, was born to a Mubambo woman and who lived in an area of their influence. They were thus again involved as maternal uncles and principal political supporters of one of the contenders, Vuningoma, who was otherwise ill-placed in strategic terms, much as Mwendanga had been earlier. And, once again, the Babambo were implicated (all too eagerly in some traditions) with the death of a king: Mwendanga died while visiting his son Vuningoma, the Babambo candidate for the throne. (For further discussion of this episode, see pp. 185–87 below and my "Kamo and Lubambo," 30–31.)

11. This point is discussed more fully in my unpublished manuscript "Cyclic Traditions."

12. In this case all Babambo became "maternal uncles" to the Ijwi king, even in later generations, where the kinship determinants may be at variance with this

designation. This social identification of the Babambo is retained on Ijwi even today. Here, as sometimes elsewhere in politically important roles on Ijwi, the institutions of "perpetual kinship" are apparent, reflecting the much more highly developed and widespread nature of these institutions among the Shi neighbors of the Havu to the southwest (E. D. Sosne, "Kinship and Contract in Bushi," passim).

13.   The traditions which retain Mwendanga's alliance patterns with specific clans are totally distinct from each other: a tradition relating to one alliance group never contains a reference to another. Even the royal traditions themselves do not synthesize alliance patterns as a whole. This characteristic of the traditions, and the associated feature of differences in form, are discussed at length in D. Newbury, "Kamo and Lubambo."

14.   This tradition—or rather the fragmentary bits and pieces which together make up the traditions—is marvellously rich in metaphor and cultural allusion. The references to the "sack," to mobility, to cords and ropes, to certain forms of occult power, all evoke themes common in the forest cultures west of the lake. When Kamo arrives at a homestead, he asks for bananas, and places them in the sack (as food for Mwendanga) with the exhortation: *"Bihago*—that it may eat!" (or more colloquially, "Let's give this bag something to eat!"). *"Bihago"* is the term for a type of sack made of special forest vines, but Bihago was also the dynastic name of one of the early Basibula kings—and therefore an ancestor of Mwendanga. Since individuals often take on the names of their forebears in this area (where positional succession is frequent), this statement could also refer to "Mwendanga—let him eat!" But there are other subtle allusions contained in this exhortation as well. The word for "to eat" is also a cognate of that for "to rule." Food consumption and political authority are overlapping concepts, so the terms can also be understood as "Mwendanga (Bihago)—may he reign!" These elements (and many others) of a highly complex set of traditions are discussed in greater detail in my "Kamo and Lubambo."

15.   The Baloho alliance assumed particular significance during the early years of Basibula establishment on Ijwi. It therefore will be discussed at greater length in chapter 10 below. For a fuller discussion of the traditions on these points, see D. Newbury, "Kamo and Lubambo," esp. chap. 3.

16.   The conclusion that this is primarily ideological is reinforced by several factors. There seems to have been no Babambo settlement on Ijwi prior to Mwendanga. After their close alliance on the mainland, there seems to have been no reason to have sent Mwendanga away from the areas of Babambo strength, when on Ijwi they seem to have been more dependent on him than he on them. Finally, the subsequent role and inability on the part of the Babambo to establish their influence on Ijwi make it unlikely that they would have originally sent him there. It is more likely that they accompanied him; the tradition then probably reflects an attempt by the Babambo to retain the central role and initiative in this early history.

17.   Musigi 9/3/72; Makombwa 11/3/72; Ruvugwa Paul 28/3/72; Rukanika (Nkuvu) 27/4/72; Kasi 27/4/72; Bitukuru 9/5/72; Kigufi 9/5/72; Makombwa 10/5/72; Kabera Bijenje 10/5/72; Muhamagala 26/5/72; Bakengamwami 24/6/72; Buraho 7/8/72; Rubambiza (Cugi) 25/1/73; Gahanda 26/1/73; Kadusi 26/1/73; Gatera Kanega 6/5/74; cf. also D. Newbury, "Kings and Clans," Appendices 4, 13, 14, 15.

18.   For a discussion of Banyakabwa origins, see chapter 4 above; also D. New-

bury, "Kings and Clans," Appendices 3–4. Some sources claim Balimucabo "summoned" Mwendanga from Bujombo to aid him against Nyamuziga, but these references seem to stem from the fact that ultimately it was Nyamuziga who was "deposed" and driven out; there is no evidence for an alliance of Mwendanga with Balimucabo (Buswagiri 5/6/72; Kabera Bijenje 10/5/72; Buraho 7/8/72; Musigi 9/3/72). Most others recall that it was Nyamuziga who sought Mwendanga's support against Balimucabo, his elder brother in the north (Makombwa 11/3/72, 10/5/72; Rukanika [Nkuvu] 27/4/72; Bitukuru 9/5/72; Gahanda 26/1/73; Kadusi 26/1/73; Kasi 27/4/72; Rubambiza [Cugi] 25/1/73; Gatera Kanega 6/5/74).

19. Surprisingly, this is absent from other Banyakabwa traditions; it is a regional tradition found only on the southwestern peninsulas of Ijwi. On Kambi separating from Nyamuziga: Muhamagala 26/5/72; Bakengamwami 24/6/72; Kalibanya Bishovu 22/6/72.

20. Muhamagala 26/5/72; Kalibanya Bishovu 22/6/72. This was common in interviews carried out in Mwiiru in April 1975.

21. This variant is widespread among Banyakabwa; for an example, see D. Newbury, "Kings and Clans," Appendix 13.

22. The nature of the traditions seem to imply that Nyamuziga had formerly held some sort of power; it was he whom Mwendanga drove out, and therefore "replaced." If Mwendanga is seen as immediately establishing a full kingship, it is tempting to portray similar powers in Nyamuziga's hands—tempting, but invalid. There is not a single indication either that Mwendanga established a fully functioning kingship or that Nyamuziga held political power over others. Even were the former true, it would not imply the latter—though the latter assumption seems to derive from the former. That is, the recent institution of kingship on Ijwi is projected back into an indefinite past, thus avoiding the need for any explanation of social process.

23. In some traditions the use of deceit, by ignoring the responsibilities of the bloodpact, emphasizes the royal aspect of Mwendanga's power (his ability to flout social convention without repercussions). This is best brought out in Rwakageyo (Buzigaziga) 11/3/72, 9/5/72; and Bitukuru 9/5/72.

24. I have discussed this problem at greater length, with reference to differing perceptions by separate parties of a single episode of Ijwi's past, in "Kamo and Lubambo." This case, of course, presents a particular paradox for historians: to understand the perceptions one needs to understand the history that molded such perceptions, but to understand the history, one has to rely on traditions which are themselves products of those perceptions.

25. This is a consistent feature of later succession struggles, discussed in chapter 10. The single exception to this generalization was Mwendanga himself, who may have initially obtained little internal support on Ijwi. But he apparently arrived on the island at a time when enough people—perhaps some themselves recent immigrants—were willing to identify with his goals to allow him in effect to create his own "internal" basis of support on Ijwi.

26. Beyond the normative protestations of "eternal friendship" associated with the bloodpact were often goals of a more individualist nature, sometimes exactly contradictory to the nature of the symbolic gesture (as here), sometimes less directly apparent. People today say that ties of blood-brotherhood are more binding on an

individual than are kinship ties, precisely because they are contracted consciously and willingly. Breaking a bloodpact oath leads to death, say the Bany'Iju, whereas breaking a kinship taboo can be atoned for by certain socially prescribed mechanisms. At the same time, it is a contract entered into for some calculated gain, economic, social, or psychic; it is not something ascribed by birth. Traders, for example, see bloodpact ties as necessary to deposit trade merchandise at the homes of their "friends" in the certain knowledge that these goods will not be pilfered. Several cases were cited to me by traders who had continually lost merchandise where they lodged until they contracted a bloodpact, whereupon the losses ceased. Thus bloodpact ties can be motivated by defensive criteria as well as aggressive calculations, as with Mwendanga who profited at the direct expense of his blood-brother. But Mwendanga's behavior is also associated with the aura of kingship:

AUTHOR: Why did Mwendanga expel his friend [e.g., his blood-brother, Nyamuziga]? RESPONDENT: Because a Musibula doesn't have friends; he never makes bloodpacts; he does bad [things] to his friends. (Bitukuru 9/5/72)

27.   Rwakageyo (Buzigaziga) 9/5/72; he was a descendant of Nyamuziga.
28.   Makombwa (11/3/72, 10/5/72) claims that Nyamuziga had royal drums. Most others deny this. The particular ritual attributes of Nyamuziga's putative royal status are nowhere stated. Such pretensions are based on two assertions: that the Banyakabwa and Basibula are both segments of an older and more inclusive clan identification, the Bahande; and that Nyamuziga is part of a continuous succession of noteworthy pre-eminent individuals on Ijwi, and thus shares the status of later kings. The importance of drums in legitimizing the use of power can be seen by the way in which the language defined illegitimate power or status: both the colonial chiefs and such historical figures as Nyamuziga and Nyamuhiva are frequently described as "kings without drums" (i.e., rulers without legitimate claims to kingship).
29.   Not only did no one (not even his Banyakabwa brothers) flee with Nyamuziga, but also there is no recollection that Mwendanga took similar actions against other groups or individuals on the island at the time. This implies that other groups were neither directly involved with the dispute nor directly associated with Nyamuziga, despite their presence on the island (and their proximity to Buzigaziga). The internal quarrels of the Banyakabwa were therefore of a segmentary nature; they focussed on internal differentiation within the Banyakabwa social network. In their struggles with each other, there is no indication, aside from the few references to Kambi's tie with Mwendanga, that the Banyakabwa sought alliances with other groups. This quality of Banyakabwa social organization is also illustrated in their relations with the Binyalenge, discussed in chapter 3.

Chapter 10. The Social Alliances of the Basibula on Ijwi

1.   Ciringwe 16/1/75.
2.   There are many references to Mwendanga's strong tie to Bujombo; this is common knowledge on Ijwi. Among others: Rwankuba 8/3/72; Runiga 15/5/72; Zaluka Michel 15/5/72; Nyangurane Nyamulinda 24/5/72; Ndengeyi 2/6/72; Rusingiza 10/6/72; Mushayuma Ngubuguru 9/8/72; Mayange 18/6/74; Kabulo 14/6/72; Rukanika (Nkuvu) 27/4/72 provides a typical account:

Mwendanga came from Irhambi [in this context, meaning the western lakeshore in general]. He left Irhambi at Bujombo and occupied Lugendo, Ishungu, Kishoke, Birava. [All these are along the western shoreline of the southern pedicule of the lake.] He expelled Nyamuziga and took over Ijwi and all the islands. . . . Kabwiika was in "Bushi" [an anachronism]; Mwendanga was still very young. Mwendanga stayed there till he grew up. He occupied all the villages in Bushi. Then he occupied all the islands as well. He died on Ishungu.

3.   The oldest genealogies are from Lubuye, a community high up on the forested shoulders of the central massif of Ijwi (called Nyamusize). The Bashaho there form a compact group (genealogically and residentially) whose location and genealogy point to long residence; more recent groups of such compact residence have located near the shores of the island. Furthermore, traditions from elsewhere—north as well as south—indicate that Lubuye formed an early diffusion center for the Bashaho moving into other areas (especially Cassi, Bushake, Musama, and, more recently, Nyakalengwa) (Makombwa 10/5/72; Gasarahinga Bishovu 17/5/72; Tegera 30/5/72; Kajibwami Bijenji 29/1/73.) A second old community is that at Mushovu, between Kihumba and Kimomo. This is more important in terms of an identity center; some Bashaho refer to Mushovu as the center for ancestral propitiation for all Bashoho on Ijwi. But this claim to common corporate identity may indeed have resulted from more recent history—proximity to the kings, central locations, more intense contacts with other clans (Makombwa 10/5/72; Ntayira 15/5/72; Runiga 15/5/72). Bitukuru (9/5/72): "Ngulamagala was a Mushovu; then he went to Kihumba. From there he found this place [Bushake] and that pleased him. So he came here and built here. But he had lived at Mushovu before coming here." It is clear from multiple sources that both Lubuye and Mushovu (as well as its offshoots, Kihumba and Bushake) were well established before the royal family arrived.

4.   Bavugerije 31/1/72; Rwakageyo (Buzigaziga) 11/3/72; Bitukuru 9/5/72; Makombwa 10/5/72.

5.   Runiga 15/5/72.

6.   Mayange 25/5/72.

7.   Ntati 27/5/72.

8.   Makombwa 11/3/72. This is a typical statement of this feeling, expressed frequently. Other strong statements to this effect are found in Bavugerije 1/2/72; Zahura 30/3/72; Ntayira 15/5/72; Gasarahinga 17/5/72.

9.   Among early royal enclosures, Cimenwe is contiguous to Bushake, Humule is in the Bashaho "heartland" area (Mushovu-Kihumba), and Rukambura is near Lubuye, another village with a large Bashaho contingent.

10.   Camarage, a son of Mwendanga, came to Mulyamo (the home of Mushaho) with Mushaho; this was after other Bashaho were already there (Ntati 27/5/72). Gangaboga was also a son of Mwendanga, at Gashara (Mushingi 25/5/72). Cimanuka (son of Mwendanga) lived at Karhongo, near Mushovu (Nyamwegama 23/6/72). Ciriba (son of Mwendanga) was also at Karhongo, but he may have arrived later (Budaho Maheshe 15/5/72).

11.   The Bashaho are heavily congregated in the southern portion of Ijwi. In the east, they are present in only a few villages—and there they are very strong (e.g., Mugote, Bushake). But (except for Bushake, an autonomous settlement with its own

identity) these are contiguous to the major Bashaho center in the Kimomo-Karhongo-Lubuye area. Elsewhere in the south (in Mpene and Nyakalengwa localities), Bashaho are present in all but 1 of the villages and have over 20 members in 11 of the 26 villages (excluding neighboring islands). Claims to western origins are common but not universal. Bashaho in the north often claim historical ties to Rwanda and Buhunde. Even those in the south claim Rwandan ties, some specifically to Ndorwa, where the former ruling dynasty was of the Bashambo clan, a collateral clan to the Bashaho on Ijwi. Centers where Rwandan claims were particularly strong among the Bashaho were Bwando and Lushindi; some individuals note ties to both areas (east and west of the lake) postulating a migration to explain these divergent identities (Makombwa 10/5/72; Nyamulisa 31/5/72). But the overwhelming historical identity of the Bashaho today is with the western mainland. Those who claim that the Bashaho were direct supporters of the king include Bavugerije (31/1/72), Rwakageyo, the elder Banyakabwa spokesman at Buzigaziga (11/3/72), Bitukuru (9/5/72), and Tegera (30/5/72).

12. Bavugerije 1/2/72; Makombwa 11/3/72; Zahura 30/3/72; Gasarahinga 17/5/72. Ntayira (15/5/72): "When a *mwami* wants to be enthroned, Mushaho sits on the throne before the *mwami* does. . . . Bashaho are always by his side." There are many others who made similar statements; see also chapter 2 above. Correlate clans in Bushi (Bashinjahavu) and Rwanda (Beega) do not have the same close identity with the king (Colle, *Monographie*, 226–63; d'Hertefelt and Coupez, *La royauté sacrée*, passim). In Buhunde too, the Bashaho are seen as opposed to the king (or distinct from him) (Biebuyck, "L'organisation politique," 2).

13. In Bushi Nyiganda was not so closely identified with the king; he also could not sit on the stool—that was the prerogative of another ritualist named Mushaho. Mushaho's roles on Ijwi thus appear to cumulate various roles which are separated elsewhere. Ijwi ritual patterns are discussed in chapter 12.

14. There are two separate "traditions of genesis" on Ijwi. Baloho traditions claim Basibula origins west of Lake Kivu, linking Mwendanga's historical roots to the forest culture. The Babambo traditions claim origins east of Lake Kivu, tying Mwendanga to the Rwandan context. The traditions thus emphasize the the differing royal claims on Ijwi, mediating between the two dominant cultural traditions, east and west, which intermingle on Ijwi. I consider this detail in "Kamo and Lubambo."

15. Rubambiza (Mugorhe) 18/3/72; Rugo 14/6/74.

16. These are likely anachronistic references to later Kinyaga locales; alternatively (or additionally) these people stopped in "Bushi," where they introduced the people there to cows and the use of milk as a food (Rubambiza [Mugorhe] 18/3/72).

17. Ntambuka Barhahakana 26/4/72; Malekera (Bulegeyi) 1/5/72; Magendo 3/5/72; Rugo 14/6/74; Ngwasi 12/10/74; Rubambiza (Mugorhe) 18/3/72, 17/6/74, 22/6/74, 23/6/74, 26/6/74.

18. The present *mwami* noted that, after Kabwiika's death, Kamo served as a "regent" for Mwendanga (Ntambuka Barhahakana 21/4/72). For a full consideration of the "sack" theme in these traditions, see D. Newbury, "Kamo and Lubambo."

19. Ngwasi 25/6/74, 12/10/74; Rubambiza (Mugorhe) 18/3/72, 17/6/74.

20. Rubambiza (Mugorhe) 22/6/74. See Appendix 15 of D. Newbury, "Kings and Clans," for other accounts of this.

21. Among the ancestors of a man on Ijwi, the paternal grandmother often holds an outstanding position; on Mwakabugubugu: Ntambuka Barhahakana 21/5/72, 21/1/73.

22. These ties were especially brought out in the traditions pertaining to Baloho ties with Mwendanga prior to his arrival on Ijwi, discussed more fully in D. Newbury, "Kamo and Lubambo." Some traditions portray the Baloho as having even greater mystical power than Mwendanga. They imply that the Basibula alliance with the Baloho was associated with the supernatural power of kingship in contrast with the physical power of kingship, more associated with Mwendanga's alliance to the Babambo.

23. Nyamuheshera 17/5/72. The fact that the children of Nculo and Mwendanga shared common maternal uncles served to strengthen the ties between them. Later on, the kings themselves were to become maternal uncles of the Baloho (e.g., Shankulu).

24. Rubambiza (Mugorhe) 18/3/72, 20/3/75; Nyamuheshera 10/2/72; Mikabule 18/5/74.

25. Malekera (Bulegeyi) 1/5/72; Magendo 2/5/72; Ngwasi 5/5/72, 25/6/74.

26. Gisayura Lujongo 26/6/72.

27. Nyamuheshera 10/2/72; Kalibanya Bishovu 22/6/74. The effect of this was to provide the Baloho with a certain renown in this area, since Nculo's daughter went to live on Ishungu. There she gave birth to a royal son who also lived there throughout his adult life. Meanwhile Camukenge's brother-in-law (his wife's full brother) lived on an Ijwi peninsula not far from Ishungu. Consequently, in these areas the Baloho are known as royal in-laws rather than as Mwendanga's allies.

28. Rubambiza (Mugorhe) 20/3/75.

29. Rubambiza (Mugorhe) 20/3/75; Kalibanya Bishovu 22/6/74; Ruhamanya 9/8/72; and Bwayo 9/8/72.

30. Nyamuheshera 10/2/72.

31. Rubambiza (Mugorhe) 20/3/75. The family ties sometimes get confused here because another Rusine is said to be a "son" (or, alternatively, ancestor) of Kamo (Rubambiza [Mugorhe] 18/3/72; Malekera [Bulegeyi] 1/5/72). Still another "daughter of Rusine," this time from the western mainland, was a wife of Mwendanga's grandson Ndogosa, who reigned during the early years of this century.

32. Zahiga Paulo 14/6/74. The exception was Bisangwa, a son of Mwendanga; his family was later expelled from Ijwi as traitors, by Kabego, thus confirming the rebellious reputation of this area, from the court perspective. It is noteworthy that Kabego did not marry a Muloho woman, nor did any of his sons; the one Musibula to reside in the area of Baloho strength was expelled as a traitor. This was a period of the consolidation of the Basibula royalty—and clearly a time of tension with the eastern areas (as reflected also in the struggle over ritual power within the Ziralo clan of drum ritualists). This then would confirm at least the spirit of the Baloho claim that they formerly held "royal status" in the east. Whether they formerly held the insignia of royalty in any literal sense is uncertain. But that this was an area of weak Basibula authority is confirmed by much circumstantial evidence of this sort. Baloho relations to Basibula royalty apparently passed from alliance (under Mwendanga), to antagonism (under Kabego), to association (under Ndogosa).

33.   In citing the *"barhunyi"*—the court favorites—of Mwami Ndogosa, Bany'Iju invariably cite Camukenge (Bitaha) first and Cibagasha, son of Bigaba, next. Shankulu was more renowned as a warrior than as a *murhunyi*, or councillor; his exploits include battles in Bushi and Ndorwa with Rwabugiri during the time of Rwabugiri's occupation of Ijwi. It was he, also, who travelled to Ngweshe to seek Ndogosa (then in exile) and bring him back to Ijwi after Rwabugiri's death. But otherwise his personal career was more independent of the royal court than was that of Camukenge (Malekera [Bulegeyi] 1/5/72; Magendo 2/5/72; Magaju 3/5/72; Rugo 14/6/74). During the colonial period, when the Belgians sought to deport the *mwami* Ndogosa, it was Camukenge who served as Ndogosa's representative. When he refused to divulge the whereabouts of his patron, he was, so the traditions relate in great detail, buried alive by the Belgians. His death is an eloquent testimony to the hardship endured under colonial rule, and on Ijwi it has become symbolic of both colonial brutality and Ijwi resistance and suffering.

34.   Ngwasi 12/10/74.

35.   At the time of the research, the Baloho formed roughly 1 percent of the total Ijwi population; but they held about 5 percent of the positions as *barhambo*. (In the past, there were clearly many fewer capita positions; the effect of this would have been to increase further the percentage of Baloho *barhambo*—and thus also the discrepancy between that figure and their population figures.)

36.   Rubambiza (Mugorhe) 20/3/75; Rugo 14/6/74, 20/3/75.

37.   Rubambiza (Mugorhe) 17/6/74, 26/6/74, 20/3/75; Rugo 14/6/74; Appendix 16 of D. Newbury, "Kings and Clans."

38.   Rubambiza (Mugorhe) 23/6/74.

Chapter 11. External Alliances and the Establishment of Royalty on Ijwi

1.   I have outlined the broad trends of changing commerical patterns in "Lake Kivu Regional Trade." Other exceptions to this generalization include: Lugan, "Echanges et routes commerciales"; A. Nyagahene, "Les activités économiques et commerciales du Kinyaga dans la séconde partie du XIXe siècle" (Mémoire de License, UNR–Butare, 1979); Birhakaheka N. and Kirhero N., "Nyangezi dans ses relations commerciales avec le Rwanda, le Burundi, et le Bufulero (fin XIXe siècle— début XXe siècle)" (*Etudes rwandaises* 14, 1 [1981], 36–51); Bishikwabo, "Histoire d'un état Shi"; Depelchin, "From Precapitalism to Imperialism." Studies which relate to the economic substructures of Rwanda include: Reisdorff, "Enquêtes foncières"; Meschi, "Evolution des structures foncières"; Vidal, "Economie de la société féodale"; P. Leurquin, *Le niveau de vie des populations rurales du Ruanda-Urundi* (Louvain, 1960). (The list is obviously not exhaustive.)

2.   I have considered the external dimensions of these alliance patterns in greater detail in "Rwabugiri and Ijwi."

3.   This is considered in greater detail in D. Newbury, "Lake Kivu Regional Trade."

4.   For an example of this tradition: D. Newbury, "Kings and Clans," Appendix 12.

5.   It is noteworthy that in Ijwi traditions relations of force deal almost exclusively with conflicts within the royal family, usually during succession disputes; these

were, of course, times when relations of force and "institutionalized chaos" only served to reinforce the ideological underpinnings of royal power—with the kingship serving as the fount of "peace and stability," or "law and order," depending on the idioms of any given political order.

6.   This narrative is not intended to serve as a comprehensive overview of Ijwi political history. Instead this historical survey of succession struggles on the island is intended only to illustrate the essential nature of alliance patterns affecting the royal family, and the importance of local factors on which Ijwi royalty was based. The next chapter illustrates another dimension of this reality. For a general survey of royal history, see Murhebwa L. K., "Histoire politique d'Idjwi sous les Basibula: Essai de périodisation" (Travail de Fin d'Etudes, ISP–Bukavu, 1976).

7.   This succession dispute is examined in more detail, but from a slightly different perspective, in D. Newbury, "Kamo and Lubambo."

8.   On the ritual consolidation of kingship on Ijwi, see chapters 7 and 12.

9.   On Ijwi's relations to these areas see Bushige B. and Munganga B., "Relations socio-éconmiques entre Idjwi et ses régions périphériques" (Travail de Fin d'Etudes, ISP–Bukavu, 1987).

10.   The Ijwi sources on this are extremely numerous and are linked to a variety of other episodes unfolding simultaneously as part of Ijwi's wider royal history. Aside from the internal succession dispute and Nkundiye's alliance with Rwabugiri, this was a period of rapid social change on Ijwi, induced in part by the impact of Rwandan cultural norms introduced to Ijwi during the Rwandan occupation, which lasted a full generation. In addition, these events are linked to the eventual division of Kabego's unified domain into northern and southern portions of the island, a political division to achieve its most clear-cut distinction during colonial rule, with the "conquest" or domination (under colonial auspices) of the south by the northern segment of the royal family. For more extensive consideration, see D. Newbury, "Rwabugiri and Ijwi"; and Newbury and Newbury, "King and Chief on Ijwi Island."

11.   Malugire 31/1/72; Kayirara 24/5/72; Ndayalire 29/4/72; Nyangurane Nyamulinda 24/5/72; Bazungu 25/5/72; Kakira Ruhamisa 26/5/72; Gahangaza 9/6/72; Runesha 24/6/72; Buraho 7/8/72; Mushayuma Ngubuguru 9/8/72; Kacuka Kaboye 9/8/72; Gahanda 26/1/73; Gashoku 29/4/74; Barhonga 23/5/74; Ngwasi 25/6/74.

12.   For an elaboration of this incident, see D. Newbury, "Rwabugiri and Ijwi."

13.   D. Newbury, "Les campagnes de Rwabugiri," provides a more complete discussion of Rwabugiri's campaigns and Ijwi's place within them. The sequence of Rwabugiri's specific attacks on Ijwi (and the methods, goals, and events behind them) are considered in D. Newbury, "Rwabugiri and Ijwi."

14.   The account presented here provides only a skeletal summary of the complex events involved with Nkundiye's struggle to succeed Kabego. In particular, because I seek to situate these events within the larger argument on the relation of external resources to internal legitimacy in defining kingship on Ijwi, this account does not consider in any detail the internal struggles and the significance of these divisions on the island. The principal struggle was that between Nkundiye and Tabaro, the son of Balikage, himself the son of Mwendanga. Balikage had been Mwendanga's representative in the north of Ijwi, and Tabaro acceded to that role on

Balikage's death. Like Nkundiye, Tabaro had also aided Rwabugiri's attacks and he was named as Rwabugiri's administrator in the north. Nkundiye's execution of Tabaro, nominally resulting from a dispute concerning administrative authority over several hills in the south, was therefore an act of *lèse-majesté* against Rwabugiri, even while in the internal Ijwi context it was an assertion of the earlier pre-eminence of the king in the south over the delegate in the north. In a further twist of fate, Nkundiye was later betrayed to Rwabugiri by his own son, Katobera, just as Kabego had been betrayed by his son Nkundiye; Katobera sought the protection of Rwabugiri (as originally had Nkundiye) and was eventually killed by the Rwandan king—a fate parallel to that of his father. D. Newbury, "Rwabugiri and Ijwi," discusses this entire episode from a different perspective and in much greater detail.

15.   This was "the land of Munganga," the region of Lwindi, and the ultimate cradle-land of kingship norms for the area; see Sigwalt, "The Early History of Bushi"; and Yogolelo Tambwe ya Kasimba, "Essai d'interprétation du cliché de Kangere dans la région des Grands Lacs africains," *Journal of African History*, 31, 3 (1990), 353–72.

16.   Greater detail on this complex incident is found in D. Newbury, "Rwabugiri and Ijwi."

17.   The events and patterns of this turbulent period of early colonial rule on Ijwi between the wars are considered in greater detail in Newbury and Newbury, "King and Chief on Ijwi Island."

18.   For a general consideration of the policy of deportation (or internal exile) so frequently used by the Belgian administration to try to "bring to heel" local authorities in the region, see Bashizi T. Z., "De la relégation dans l'ancien territoire de Kalehe (1920–1964)" (Mémoire de Licence, ISP–Bukavu, 1982).

19.   The reasoning for this dating is found in D. Newbury, "Kings and Clans," Appendix 10; and D. Newbury, "Kamo and Lubambo," chap. 1, note 18.

Chapter 12. Kings and Clans: The Muganuro Ceremony

1.   R. Packard *(Chiefship and Cosmology)* argues that ecological well-being and agricultural production are the basis of continued rule among the Nande. Even though this relationship is expressed as the king's control over nature, the relationship is more truly seen as a question of nature's effect on the continuation of a given reign. I concur with that assessment.

2.   The information presented here on the Ijwi Muganuro is based on personal observation. My wife, Catharine, and I attended Muganuro in 1972, and she did so again in 1973; these were the last two times that the Muganuro ritual was held as a public ceremony. What follows is a description of the ceremony as we saw it; it is thus written in the past tense, for these were events unfolding, not ideal descriptions. Interviews were subsequently carried out with the principal *bagingi* on many occasions; to avoid undue complexity in the presentation, these are not individually cited. For clarity, some of the detailed data on the ceremony have also been omitted. For a fuller account, see chapter 9 of my Ph.D. dissertation, "Kings and Clans."

3.   The regalia would be arranged in an identical manner throughout the later ceremony of Muganuro, but later they would separate the *mwami* (and the Bashaho ritualists) from the other *bagingi* and the drums.

4.   For a diagram of the royal enclosure where Muganuro took place, see Appendix 18 in D. Newbury, "Kings and Clans." The entrances to Kagondo and Kambere faced south by west, oriented to Bujombo, whence Mwendanga left for Ijwi. I do not know if this is a significant fact to the participants, but the 1982 enthronement proceedings (which replicated the Muganuro ceremony in virtually every detail), though undertaken at a different locale (Rambo), were carried out before a Kambere with the same orientation. For a comparable case where orientation was important, see D. W. Cohen, *Womunafu's Bunafu. A Study of Authority in a Nineteenth Century Community* (Princeton, 1977).

5.   The hide of the sacrificed bull was later to be made into a royal drum; this material transformation from bull's hide to royal drum strengthened the ritual identification of the bull with the drum and hence with kingship, as discussed in the following section. It is possible that Mushaho was actually taking the place of the *mwami* in this instance, rather than simply ritually representing him through analogy. The *mwami*, about 70 years old at the time, faced a demanding two-day schedule. Kuper gives an example of this substitution in similar circumstances in the Swazi ritual (H. Kuper, "A Royal Ritual in a Changing Political Context," *Cahiers d'études africaines* 12, 4 [1972], 607, fn. 1, iii).

6.   The nominal Mukwizanyundo means, roughly, "one who announces (or diffuses) the hammer [*nyundo*—the symbol of royal power]." But this is a nickname, not a title; his given name was Balihana.

7.   Mushovu (pl. Bashovu) is the classificatory name of an inhabitant of the village of Bushovu. The term is generally equated with being a Mulega; Bushovu is over 85 percent Balega, and non-Balega are located on the village's periphery.

8.   Cirunga (10/3/73, 19/6/74) noted that Mirimba drew water to "cool" Nyarushara (i.e., to contain or harness Nyarushara's ritual power) during forging. But he seems to have confused Mirimba's role with that of another *mugingi*, Gahamire Ntahira. Mirimba himself (18/5/72) said that it is his family that must symbolically "forge" a new *nyarushara* with each reign. He must be present to pour a libation of one-day-old beer *(kibabi)* on the metal, and must also strike the first blow with the *nyundo*, the smith's hammer. He also said that the first member of his family to serve as *mugingi* for the iron regalia did so under the reign of Kabego.

9.   This might be reinforced as a carryover from the mainland, where Nyiganda, the "ancestor" of the ritualist Bashaho on Ijwi, is also a ritual smith for Bushi. But in general the Bashaho in Bushi (known as Bashinjahavu) are not particularly well-known for their smithing.

10.   The independence of the ritualists from the court was well illustrated when in 1973 Kakomere delayed his arrival for the Muganuro, which could not proceed without the *bulo,* the central feature of the ritual. Some said he did so because he had not received enough beer from the court for his services; others said simply that the *bagingi* are always like that with the king—"they are not his children." At any rate the court personnel were quite exercised over this "blackmail," and sent him more beer. Munyakalinga showed the same independence of thought vis-à-vis the *mwami*—and other officials—on many occasions.

11.   Yet another Munyambiriri important to the royal rituals is Mugako. He is the formal *mukumbi* to the *mwami,* a role reflecting perhaps the (formalized) tension

between the king and the two other Banyambiriri roles. These roles (of both Kako-meres) deal with plants and their transformation into food—food of a particularly potent nature in the context of the Muganuro ritual.

12. Gahamire 11/3/73, 28/11/73, 18/6/74, 4/10/74, 28/10/74. The term *"ba-gingi"* is not always clearly defined: who is a *mugingi* and how are they named/recognized? Gahamire claimed to be a *mugingi;* others (including the king) denied it. It would seem more that he was an aspirant to the title. At any rate, he was assiduous in his pursuit of the recognition, present at all rituals of the court, with his *mubande,* for which he was renowned on Ijwi. He also made a great issue of his knowledge of herbs and soils that constitute the *mubande,* travelling to the mainland as well as widely on Ijwi for elements. (Notwithstanding our fairly close relationship, however, he was not very forthcoming on the exact locales visited and materials included.)

13. Mushengezi Gahengezi Munyama (Nzuki) 2/6/72; Bagalo 30/1/73. Na-bwibiize (Mainland interview, Tshofu) (15/11/72) described a similar ceremony (with the fish) performed in the Havu kingdom on the mainland at the enthronement of a new king. Fishing with an *omugera* is also mentioned by Antoine de Ligne (*Africa: L'évolution d'un continent,* 102).

14. Beidelman sees a similar process in the Swazi Incwala ritual, where rituals (and kingdoms) are "dangerous" because they combine different elements, each of which has its own "logical" existence. Indeed, the ritual helps define the logic of the classification (T. O. Beidelman, "Swazi Royal Ritual," *Africa* 36, 4 (1966), 373–405, esp. 389–90).

15. The classic work on sacrifice is H. Hubert and M. Mauss, *Sacrifice: Its Nature and Function* (Chicago, 1964).

16. There are in fact two Banyakalinga in the ceremony: one presents Nda-mutsa, the other presents Cihumuliza. But outside the Muganuro ceremony the term "Munyakalinga" is used only for Mungazi today. The other, Nyamuhuku Munya-kalinga, a Muziralo now living at Kimomo, is simply referred to as a Mwiiru. Similarly there are two men named Mushaho; both are descendants of a former Mushaho, the present ritualist's grandfather. Finally, there are two ritualists named Kakomere within the Banyambiriri clan; each performs a different ritual function.

17. This is partly the case in *bukumbi* rites (rites which require members of joking clan relations), but the effect is diluted because a given *mukumbi* is selected from one of two or more possible clans.

18. It is possible that, in the ceremony I witnessed, Mushaho actually did take the position normally reserved for the king; see note 5 above. The iron regalia are also important in one other aspect of the ritual. The night before the ceremony, the king sleeps with his ritual wife while the Nyarushara is placed under his head—just as the regalia were aligned with and at the head of the bull and the drums (during the public ceremonies) in other aspects of Muganuro. This is also an important element to the Rwandan Umuganura ceremony; see my "What Role Has Kingship?"

19. I have argued this in greater detail for the analogous Umuganura ceremony in Rwanda in "What Role Has Kingship?" The same argument—for the same reasons—applies in the case of the role of the king in the Ijwi Muganuro ceremony discussed here. The fact that this is also true for a different king in the enthronement ceremonies proves that this role of the *mwami* was a ritually prescribed stance (as in

the Rwandan ritual), not a personality trait of the individual king in question. The Rwandan rituals of kingship, including the Umuganura ritual, are considered more fully in Smith "La forge de l'intelligence"; Smith, "La lance d'une jeune fille"; and de Heusch, *Rois nés.*

20.   At least he is not "divine" in the sense in which the term "divine kingship" has come to be used in Western political terminology. There the Divine King derives his powers from and bases his claims to legitimacy on a divine source, one autonomous of and often opposed to the society over which he rules. In "What Role Has Kingship?" I have argued a conception of the Rwandan kingship similar to that proposed here for Ijwi; independently, J.-P. Chrétien (in "La royauté capture les rois," addendum to P. Ndayishinguje, L'intronisation d'un mwami, 61–70 [Nanterre, 1977]) has proposed a similar concept for Burundi, based on an analysis of the Rundi rituals of enthronement.

However, the concept of sacral kingship spelled out here is not universal. In Swaziland, for example, the king is leader of the military regiments, and in historical terms, kingship there essentially derived from this military role. The *ncwala* ceremonies in Swaziland emphasize the role of the king as a powerful force in itself and he as leader of the regiments; Kuper's analyses of this elaborate ritual emphasize the role of the king as leader of the regiments over the roles of the representatives of the various participating clans and ethnic groups. (On the Swazi royal rituals, see H. Kuper, *An African Aristocracy* [London, 1947], chap. 13; H. Kuper, "A Royal Ritual in a Changing Political Context"; M. Gluckman, "Rituals of Rebellion in South East Africa" [1954], reprinted in M. Gluckman, *Order and Rebellion in Tribal Africa* [London, 1963], 110–37; T. O. Beidelman, "Swazi Royal Ritual.")

In another comparative case, E. E. Evans-Pritchard also emphasizes the importance of the opposition of the constituent parts in the concepts of kingship among the Shilluk. In this case the primary division is that between the northern and southern sectors of the Shilluk kingdom: "The participation of the two halves of Shillukland in *the making of a king* is further emphasized in the intense opposition between them expressed in the drama of investiture, which at the same time enacts the conquest and settlement of the country by Nyikanga [the mystical embodiment of kingship, represented as the first king]" ("The Divine Kingship of the Shilluk" [1948], reprinted in E. E. Evans-Pritchard, *Essays in Social Anthropology* [London, 1962], 68; emphasis added). Although this analysis approaches that of Gluckman, Evans-Pritchard avoids the vague psycho-biological dimension which forms an integral part of Gluckman's functional analysis.

21.   This is convincingly argued in the case of the Bashu by R. Packard (*Chiefship and Cosmology*). But there, political centralization followed ritual centralization; on Ijwi, ritual centralization, or the domination of the ritually expressed conception of Ijwi kingship, helped impede political centralization over the short run, by promoting the role and identity of clan units.

22.   Indeed one might conclude that political centralization was only embryonic and never fully realized in administrative terms before colonial rule: the court held no unequivocal power over land, there was no standing army, and material tribute remained a personal and rather haphazard affair.

23.   Other factors were also important in this trend towards increasing distance

of the court from the population. One factor was simply the size of Bushi, both in extent and in population. Another was the concentration of private European plantations in Bushi, the significant scale of land alienation, and the consequent creation of a significant rural proletariat there. Still a third factor was the imposing presence of the Catholic church in the area, allowing some people institutional as well as economic and ideological autonomy from the indigenous political structures. The ages of the two principal kings in Bushi were also relevant. At the time of independence, one (in Buhaya) was very old and only marginally involved in the affairs of his kingdom, the other (in Ngweshe) was rather young and fully involved in the politics of the Zairean state—to his detriment, since (after having risen to become a member of the elite Conseil Executif of the party) he was later arrested and brutally tortured by government agents. Still another factor can be seen as the continuation of colonial history: Bushi had been conquered militarily only after a prolonged resistance. The senior kingdom (Buhaya) had been administered for the last 20 years of colonial rule by a colonially appointed chief, a man drawn from the junior (and historically the secessionist) kingdom, against which Buhaya had fought many times; after having been slapped in the face in public by a colonial official, the *mwami* of Buhaya had gone into voluntary exile in Kinshasa, returning only after independence. Though a member of the royal family, the new administrator, backed by colonial power, was seen as a traitor, if not also a usurper, by the population. All those factors contributed to the increasing sense of estrangement of the population from the court in Bushi.

24.   Mirenge 25/5/74; also Zabona (Nkola) 2/5/74. This pattern is similar to the social role of *bajinji* in Bushi.

25.   It is possible that this difference results from the fact that for two generations Malambo has been under the administrative rule of colonially imposed "chiefs," not themselves *bami*. The functions of *bugingi* (and the conception of *bugingi*) in the north of the island may therefore be seen more as providing autonomy from the court than as assuring service to the king. However, there are also indications that the concept of *bagingi* as autonomous of royal power was formerly also shared in the south. Therefore this conceptualization of *bugingi* may well be representative of an earlier general pattern rather than either a product of enduring regional differences or a product of "functional atrophy" under colonial rule in the north (except in the sense that the concept of *bugingi* in the north did not evolve in the same manner as that in the south). In this more general (and older?) pattern, there may have been more prestige attached to the trappings of ritual sovereignty retained by the *bagingi* than to personal service, as in the case of the prototype model proposed in chapter 2. Many ritualists in Buhunde, Bushi, and Rwanda retain the trappings of ritual sovereignty, to which their political subservience to the king and ties to the court are only secondary. Still, the concept of *bugingi* on Ijwi today is clearly tied to that of kingship; Nankola (in the north), for example, is said to have become a *mugingi* only after the *mwami* came (during the reign of Kabego, the second Basibula king on Ijwi, and the son of Mwendanga) (Bengehya 2/5/74). Marandura (2/5/74) also noted that Nankola became a *mugingi* only under Kabego. He added that although Nankola does not now perform any ritual functions as *mugingi,* he will continue to be a *mugingi* as long as there is a *mwami* on Ijwi. Similarly, Mushayuma Semutwa (3/5/74) said that the *mwami* could not go onto the land of Nkola because it was considered "like a

bwami. . . . Nankola is like a *mwami,* a *mwami* in his own domain *(mwami emwage)".* Others noted the same status.

26.   The conjunction of early (pre-Basibula) Bashaho arrival and the arrival of Mushaho with Mwendanga is illustrated by Ntayira (15/5/72), but is present in many other testimonies:

> RESPONDENT: . . . The Bashaho are from Lwindi; when they heard Mwendanga was here they came here.
> AUTHOR: Did they come with Mwendanga?
> RESPONDENT: The Bashaho came before Mwendanga. They lived [then] in Mushovu [Cimomo], and then in Bushake and Kihumba [two old Bashaho centers].
> AUTHOR: Who was the first Mushaho to come?
> RESPONDENT: Gahindo. [This refers to the *mugingi* named Mushaho; Gahindo is his ancestor. But he was not a particularly "early" arrival on Ijwi, according to his descendants today.] When Gahindo came he met Mwendanga already here, as well as the Banyambiriri, Bahande, and all other clans, including the Bashaho.
> . . . The Bashaho are everywhere, in all the countries; but I have never heard that they were *bami.* When a *mwami* is enthroned there must always be a Mushaho next to him. . . .
> . . . Mushaho was chosen by the *mwami,* as we all are together [the Bashaho]. When a *mwami* is sitting in public, the Bashaho dance for him; when the *mwami* wants to be enthroned, Gahindo sits in the chair before the *mwami* sits in it. [This was also a belief common on Ijwi; the Banyambiriri are also sometimes said to have this role.]

27.   Colle, *Monographie,* 263, 226: "Nyiganda a pour titre 'Mushaho' et il est gardien du marteau *Walengera.* . . . Il participe toujours à l'intronisation de Kabare et de Ngweshe. Le titre du Mushoho lui vient du fait qu'en étant chef du clan Bega, il est aussi du clan Bashoho, subdivision du clan Bega." Among those on Ijwi who spoke of Bashaho identity with Nyiganda: Ntambuka Nsibula (28/12/70); Bishingwe (25/-1/72); Ndayalire (29/4/72, 13/5/72); Mayange (25/5/72, 18/6/74); Musafiri Yalumire (6/6/72).

28.   The same verb *("kuyima")* is used for "to be enthroned" and "to reign" (in a ritual context), that is, "to participate in the royal rituals of the kingdom." Thus this statement can be read: "When he celebrated Muganuro. . . ." From this it can also be inferred that every time the *mwami* celebrates Muganuro, he is "enthroned."

29.   Mayange 25/5/72. Mayange was a member of the Bashaho clan, genealogi-cally more closely related to Cirunga and Mukwizanyundo than to Mushaho.

30.   Cirunga 15/2/72.

31.   Mirimba 18/5/72. (This testimony differs from Cirunga's portrayal of Mirimba's role, which he confuses with that of Gahamire Ntahire [Cirunga 19/6/74].) Mirimba added that the Bashaho are not smiths themselves today. But among the *bagingi,* they hold the senior status positions. The fact that Mukwiza-nyundo, the only effective practicing smith among the Bashaho ritualists today, is from a family which traces its ancestry to Bwando (another old smithing center) and does not claim any ties to Nyiganda in Bushi may indicate that some Bashaho families were indeed smiths on Ijwi before the Basibula arrival, and were later incorporated into the Bashaho smithing rituals, as part of the process of clan consolidation. The

ideological ties to the Bashinjahavu (and to Nyiganda—the ritual blacksmith in Bushi) enhance Bashaho claims to ritual smithing status on Ijwi.

32. Segmentation within the families of the *bagingi* is common and is probably tied to the strong sense of group cohesion produced by the function of *bugingi* itself. All three principal families of *bugingi* status on Ijwi show this tendency. In addition to the Baziralo, there are two ritualists among the Banyambiriri, both with the name Kakomere, indicating that their ritual identities did not originate from specific and different functions. The Bashaho, too, illustrate this tendency. There are two men named Mushaho on Ijwi, each claiming *bugingi* status, though only one performs functions at the court. Both are descendants of Gahindo, the first Mushaho to hold that specific status of *bugingi* on Ijwi.

33. Rwesi (Mpene) 23/6/72. This was corroborated by Rwesi's half-brother, Ndongozi (20/6/74), and by the *mwami* Ntambuka Barhahakana (11/9/74).

34. Mukwizanyundo 19/6/74.

35. Rulinda 17/4/72, 22/6/72, 23/6/72. Before that time (i.e., during the reign of Kabego) the bull had been kept by the family of Nyakahavu from Muhungwe (Nyakalengwa).

36. Mushengezi Gahengezi Munyama 2/6/72.

37. By far the most comprehensive source on the Rwandan Umuganura is the official ritual code, the Ubwiru, collected by A. Kagame and published by d'Hertefelt and Coupez (*La royauté sacrée*, see esp. 76–94). Other sources on the Rwandan Umuganura include: Bourgeois, *Banyarwanda et Barundi*, Vol. 1, *Ethnographie*, 418–28; Pagès, *Un royaume Hamite*, 498–503; Delmas, *Les généalogies*, 107; and Kagame, "Le code ésotérique."

38. In another work, I have examined the Rwandan Umuganura ritual at this level of analysis in greater detail than can be considered here; see my "What Role Has Kingship?"

39. Accounts of Umuganuro in Burundi include Trouwborst, "Le Burundi," 122, 125, 144–45, 151; J. Rugomana, "Inkuru y'Umuganuro uko wagira kera" (trans. and annotated by F. M. Rodegem as "La fête des prémices au Burundi") (*Africana Linguistica* 5 [1971], 207–54); Mworoha, *Peuples et rois de l'Afrique des lacs*, 150–52, 161, 162, 253–62; Simons, "Coutumes et institutions," 248–54; A. Gille, "Notes sur l'organisation des Barundi" (*Bulletin des jurisdictions indigènes et du droit coutumier congolais* 5, 3 [1937], 75–81); A. Gille, "L'*Umuganuro* ou la fête du sorgho en Urundi" (*Bulletin des juridictions indigènes et du droit coutumier congolais* 14, 11 [1946], 368–71); Zuure, *Croyances et Pratiques*, 24–28, 48, 129–86; J. M. M. Van der Burght, *Un grand peuple de l'Afrique équatoriale: Eléments d'une monographie sur l'Urundi* (Bois-le-Duc, 1903); G. Smets, "L'*Umuganuro* (fête du sorgho) chez les Barundi" (in *Compte-rendu de la deuxième session*, Congrès International des Sciences Anthropologiques et Ethnologiques, 273–74 [Copenhague, 1939]; Bourgeois, *Banyarwanda et Barundi*, Vol. 1, *Ethnographie*, 428–30; Gorju et al., *Face au royaume Hamite*, 42–50; and J. Gahama, "La disparition du Muganuro" (*L'arbre-mémoire: Traditions orales du Burundi*, ed. L. Ndoricimpa et al., 169–95 [Paris/Bujumbura, 1984]); and A. Ndikuriyo, "Contrats de betail, contrats de clientèle, et pouvoir politique dans le Butuutsi du XIXe siècle;" *Etudes d'histoire africaine* 7 (1975), 59–76, esp. 60–66.

40.   It is difficult to assess the social and structural meaning of Umuganuro in Burundi, because all the accounts available focus primarily on the king. However, as elsewhere, the actions carrying the greatest structural significance are frequently those not associated with the person of the king, and in consequence are frequently slighted or omitted entirely in observer accounts. Chrétien proposes a general conceptualization of kingship as shown in the Burundi enthronement ritual similar to that which I argue here for Umuganura in Rwanda and Muganuro on Ijwi. But I suggest carrying the analysis one step further: just as "kingship captures the kings," so too society encapsulates kingship. See J.-P. Chrétien, "La royauté capture les rois."

41.   G. Smets, "Funérailles et sépultures des *bami* et *bagabekazi* de l'Urundi," IRCB, *Bulletin des séances* 12, 2 (1941), 210–34; J.-P. Chrétien and E. Mworoha, "Les tombeaux des bami du Burundi: Un aspect de la monarchie sacrée en Afrique orientale," *Cahiers d'études africaines* 10, 1 (1970), 40–79; Mworoha, *Peuples et rois de l'Afrique des lacs,* 152–55, 282–84. The Biru are also referred to as Banyange in Burundi. This terminology helps elucidate the use of white cattle egret feathers by the *bagingi* on Ijwi during Muganuro. Cattle egrets *(enyanga)* frequently accompany cattle grazing; this "function" of guarding the cattle is analogous to the *bagingi* "guarding" the *mwami*—the "Rusanga" of the kingdom. The pure white feathers of this bird are an added emphasis to the ritual role of the *bagingi*. Nakalangane is the Ijwi *mugingi* responsible for bringing the *enyanga* feathers to Muganuro (Mushaho 18/6/74). For an overview of the court milieu of Burundi during the late nineteenth century, see E. Mworoha, "La cour du roi Mwezi Gisabo (1852–1908) du Burundi à la fin du XIXe siècle," *Etudes d'histoire africaine* 7 (1975), 39–58.

42.   For a discussion of these plants in the history and rituals of Burundi, see J.-P. Chrétien, "Le sorgho dans l'agriculture, la culture, et l'histoire du Burundi" (*Journal des africanistes* 52, 1–2 [1982], 145–62); and Chrétien, "Les années."

43.   Mworoha, *Peuples et rois de l'Afrique des lacs,* 254, note 6; Chrétien, "Les années"; Chrétien "Le sorgho dans l'agriculture, la culture, et l'histoire"; C. Kayondi, "Muranga, colline de Burundi: Etude géographique," *Cahiers d'outre-mer* 25, 2 (1972), 164–204.

44.   J. M. J. de Wet, "Domestication of African Cereals," *African Economic History* 3 (1977), 15–33, esp. 20, 22; R. Portères, "Berceaux agricoles primaires sur le continent africain," "*Journal of African History* 3, 2 (1962), 195–210; Purseglove, "The Origins and Migrations of Crops in Tropical Africa," 291–309, and Portères, "African Cereals," 409–52 (where he claims that *Eleusine* millet was first cultivated in India, but still was very old in East Africa); C. Ehret, "Patterns of Bantu and Central Sudanic Settlement in Central and Southern Africa, c. 1000 BC–500 AD," *Transafrican Journal of History* 3, 2 (1973), 1–21, where he identifies the *-lo* radical (of *bulo*) as a very old widespread lexical root.

45.   Mworoha, *Peuples et rois de l'Afrique des lacs,* 255, and Chrétien, "Le sorgho dans l'agriculture, la culture, et l'histoire" (for Burundi); Pagès, *Un royaume Hamite,* 499–500 (for Rwanda).

46.   Kabangala 21/2/73. Pre-Abanyiginya polities in Rwanda are also said to have shared a similar conceptual universe as expressed in these rituals (de Lacger, *Ruanda,* 83–85). Van Walle notes the presence of a local First Fruits ceremony,

independent of the Rwandan state structures, within individual lineages on the western lakeshore regions of Rwanda (Van Walle, "Aspecten van Staatsvorming in West Rwanda," 68).

47. For a masterful analysis by which origin traditions are shown to reveal not only the "origin" of present-day states or dynasties but the development of the concept of kingship as well, see R. Sigwalt, "The Early History of Bushi," esp. chap. 5. On Kaziba: Bishikawabo, "Histoire d'un état Shi."

48. Sigwalt, "The Early History of Bushi," 135–36; among the Basile, just to the south of the Shi states (whence Sigwalt traces the dominant historical currents influencing the development of royalty in Bushi) there is also a special mixture of animal and vegetable elements used in a royal context (Mulyumba wa Mamba, "Aperçu sur la structure politique," 42). Numerous other parallels exist in the ideology, symbolism, and regalia between this area and the Kivu lacustrine kingdoms; compare Mulyumba with Sigwalt, "Early History of Bushi," for example. There is also among the Basile an annual ceremony reinforcing the sacral powers of the *mwami*, which includes various types of foods (Mulyumba wa Mamba, "Aperçu sur la structure politique," 47–48). On Kaziba, see Bishikwabo, "Histoire d'un état Shi," 235–37. For an overview of the broader ritual context of Bushi, see Dikonda wa Lumanyisha, "Les rites chez les Bashi et les Bahavu" (Ph. D. diss., Université Libre de Bruxelles, 1971).

49. This ceremony has not been performed in Bushi since the early 1950s; therefore the documentation on this point is, at best, incomplete. But descriptions of this ceremony are found in Sosne, "Kinship and Contract in Bushi," Appendix 3, "La cérémonie du Mubande" (1971), by A. Lwanwa, 312–17); Colle, *Monographie,* 259, 261, 264–66; Mworoha, *Peuples et rois de l'Afrique des lacs,* 260; and Sigwalt, "The Early History of Bushi," 135–36.

50. Sigwalt, "The Early History of Bushi," 135–36.

51. Colle, *Monographie,* 264.

52. Colle, *Monographie,* 259.

53. Masson, *Trois siècles,* chap. 1; Colle, *Monographie,* 219–20; and esp. Sigwalt, "The Early History of Bushi."

Conclusion

1. J. C. Mitchell, *The Kalela Dance. Aspects of Social Relationships among Urban Africans in Northern Rhodesia* (Manchester, 1956). See also A. Epstein, *Politics in an Urban African Community* (Manchester, 1973), for the urban background to this study. For a critique of Mitchell's work, see, *inter alia,* B. Magubane, "A Critical Look at Indices Used in the Study of Social Change in Colonial Africa," *Current Anthropology* 12, 4–5 (1971) 419–30. Another study which considers a phenomenon similar to the Kalela dance, but over a broader area and greater time depth than Mitchell's study, is T. O. Ranger, *Dance and Society in Eastern Africa* (Berkeley, 1975). Although I agree with many of the criticisms of Mitchell's work, here I focus on one particular aspect of the essay which I find particularly insightful (despite the now outdated phraseology).

2. Mitchell, *The Kalela Dance,* 29.

3. Mitchell, *The Kalela Dance,* 30.

4. F. Barth, ed., *Ethnic Groups and Boundaries* (London, 1969), Introduction.

5. Barth, *Ethnic Groups and Boundaries*, 15.

6. A. W. Southall, "The Illusion of Tribe," in *The Passing of Tribal Man in Africa*, ed. P. C. W. Gutkind, 28–51. (Leiden, 1970). Many of the contributions in J.-L. Amselle and E. M'Bokolo (*Au coeur de l'ethnie* [Paris, 1985]) adopt a similar approach.

7. M. C. Young, *Politics in the Congo* (Princeton, 1965), 232–73; these concepts are also developed in chap. 2 of C. Anderson, F. von der Mehden, and M. C. Young, *Issues in Political Development* (Englewood Cliffs, 1967); M. C. Young, *The Politics of Cultural Pluralism* (Madison, 1978); and Young, "Nationalism, Ethnicity, and Class in Africa." Wyatt MacGaffey's work illustrates the administrative dimension of this process in *Custom and Government in the Lower Congo* (Berkeley, 1970); for an analogous process at work in the legal realm, see W. MacGaffey, "The Policy of National Integration in Zaire" (*Journal of Modern African Studies* 20, 1 [1982], 87–105).

8. L. Vail makes the same point for southern Africa in his introduction to *The Creation of Tribalism*. I agree with him that it is an error to interpret enduring ethnic identity as some form of "collective irrationality." But I demur from his assertion that ethnic consciousness is exclusively an ideological construct of the twentieth century. Vail is correct to expose the crass and shallow manipulation of Western assumptions by present political powers, and the incorporation of concepts of unchanging "tribal" culture within the politics of colonialism as the fictive basis of apartheid. The empirical evidence drawn on by Vail does indeed show ethnicity—as it exists today—to be a modern concept. But the fact that ethnic consciousness occurs in a modern context (and therefore is a "modern phenomenon") does not *ipso facto* mean that it did not also occur in an earlier context; the processes which led to ethnic consciousness have seldom been explored for earlier periods. Equally, the fact that group identities were formed in the past does not mean that those specific ethnic constructions formed under colonial rule are not "new." In both content and in function they may indeed be new; but in terms of social process, such occurrences are not unique to the modern period. The social processes by which ethnic identities have been constructed outside of the colonial context simply have not been investigated very thoroughly—with the most useful analytic tools and with an appropriate contextual understanding.

9. J. L. Comaroff ("Of Totemism and Ethnicity," 306) makes a parallel argument, that although current ethnic classifications are recent creations, ethnic identity is not exclusive to modern Africa: "The marking of contrasting identities—of the opposition of self and other, we and they—is 'primordial' in the same sense that classification is a necessary condition of social existence. But the way in which social classification is realized in specific forms of collective identity, ethnicity no less than any other, is always a matter to be decided by the material and cultural exigencies of history." To be sure, in this article Comoroff distinguishes between ethnic groups and clans (which he refers to as totemic groups). Nonetheless, at least in the Ijwi case, the processes he associates with the formation of a specific ethnic identity are equally applicable to the emergence of specific clan identities.

10. T. Bender, *Community and Social Change in America* (Baltimore, 1978), 87. At a broader level, many of the analytic approaches found in Bender's work—and in many of the other works cited here—are also drawn on in the study of nationalism; see, for example, E. J. Hobsbawm, *Nations and Nationalism since 1780* (Cambridge: Cambridge University Press, 1990).

11. Bender, *Community and Social Change,* 43.

12. M. Bloch has developed this line of reasoning most fully in "Symbols, Song, Dance and Features of Articulation: Is Religion an Extreme Form of Traditional Authority?" (*Archives européennes de sociologie* 15, 1 [1974], 55–81). This and all of Bloch's articles mentioned here are reprinted in his *Ritual, History, and Power: Selected Papers in Anthropology* (London, 1989).

13. This argument is elaborated in M. Bloch, "The Past and the Present in the Present" (*Man,* n.s. 12 [1977], 278–92). For a collection of essays, many of which touch on this point—and many of which also share the principal assumptions guiding this work: D. Cannadine and S. Price, eds., *Rituals of Royalty* (Cambridge, 1987); in this collection, the article by M. Bloch, "The Ritual of the Royal Bath in Madagascar," 271–97, is particularly apposite.

14. Bloch, "Symbols, Song, Dance," passim.

15. Bloch, "Symbols, Song, Dance," 67. Neglecting this point is one of the reasons the debate on clans in Rwanda (and neighboring areas) appears so inconclusive. See de Heusch, *Le Rwanda et la civilisation Interlacustre;* Vidal, "Le Rwanda des anthropologues"; Mworoha, *Peuples et rois de l'Afrique des lacs;* Mugaruka, "Histoire clanique"; Mushanga, "The Clan System." D'Hertefelt, *Les clans,* provides an excellent summary of the debate for Rwanda; for an interesting commentary on d'Hertefelt's study, see D. W. Cohen, "Precolonial History," 467–72.

16. Hocart, *Kings and Councillors.*

17. Hocart, *Kings and Councillors,* 69. As mentioned above, I go further: the ritual defines them as different even while it establishes their "equivalence."

18. E. P. Thompson, *The Making of the English Working Class* (Harmondsworth, 1968), 9–10, 12.

19. Thompson, *English Working Class,* 939, cited from his own previous work, "The Peculiarities of the English" (*The Socialist Register 1965*).

Glossary of Place Names

Bubale. The region on the eastern slopes of the Mitumba Mountains, west of Lake Kivu, bounded by the Buzi peninsula on the north and the Mabula peninsula to the south.

Bugoyi. The region northeast of Lake Kivu. Now Bugoyi is part of Rwanda (roughly equivalent to the prefecture of Gisenyi), but formerly this area had only an ambiguous relation to the state system of Rwanda. The people of this region have historically had ties with Buhunde (and other areas to the west), which were at least as intensive as those with Rwanda. (Maps 1, 4, 6, 7)

Buhaya. One of the largest and most powerful states of Bushi, located on the fertile plateau southwest of Lake Kivu; the royal line of Buhaya is considered the senior line among all Shi states. (Maps 11, 14)

Buhavu. The region west of Lake Kivu, ruled by kings of the Basibula family. The central area is Mpinga, but Buhavu today also includes Mabula, Bubale, and Buzi, as well as Ibinja and other islands. Most colonial maps also include Ijwi as part of Buhavu. (Maps 1, 4, 6, 11, 14)

Buhunde. The region to the northwest of Lake Kivu. The people of Buhunde have close historical ties with the people of Bugoyi to the east, those of Bunyanga and Butembo to the west, and Buhavu and Ijwi to the south. (Maps 1, 4, 6, 7)

Bukunzi. A small kingdom southeast of Lake Kivu, on the Nile-Zaire Divide. Independent of the Rwandan state until conquered with colonial assistance in 1925, Bukunzi's historical ties were with Bushi, west of the Rusizi River. Now it is a part of the Cyangugu Prefecture of Rwanda. The *mwami* of Bukunzi was held in great esteem throughout the area for his purported rainmaking skills. (Map 6)

Bunyabungo. A term, sometimes applied in a derogatory sense, given to the peoples west of Lake Kivu by people east of the lake. Sometimes it refers specifically to Bushi, at other times it has a more general application to all peoples west of the lake. (Map 7)

Bunyambiriri. A region located on the Nile-Zaire Divide. Formerly independent, but now part of the Rwandan state, located at the conjunction of the present prefectures of Cyangugu, Kibuye, and Gikongoro. Many groups on Ijwi claim historical ties with Bunyambiriri. (Maps 4, 6, 7)

Bunyungu. A Hunde kingdom on the lakeshore northwest of Lake Kivu, just north of the Buzi peninsula. (Map 4)

Burhinyi.   One of the smaller states along the "southern tier" of Bushi, southwest of Lake Kivu. High in the mountains, the people of Burhinyi maintained many ties with the cultures west of the Mitumba Mountains. (Maps 11, 14)

Bushi.   The area southwest of Lake Kivu. Today one of the most densely populated areas of the region, this area includes eight formerly independent kingdoms, of which the two largest were Buhaya and Ngweshe. Other states of Bushi include Ninja, Kaziba, Luhwinja, Burhinyi, Katana, and Nyangezi. (Maps 1, 4, 6, 11, 14)

Busozo (Busoozo).   An independent kingdom located in the high forest on the Nile-Zaire Divide; after colonial conquest in 1926, it was incorporated into the Rwandan state, as part of Kinyaga. Now it forms part of the Cyangugu Prefecture of Rwanda. (Maps 4, 6)

Butembo.   A collective term for the region west of the Mitumba Mountains directly west of Lake Kivu. The region was formerly characterized by many small independent polities. Under colonial demarcations these included Bufumandu, Ziralo, Mubugu, Buloho, Kalima, and Walowa-Loanda; in addition there are Tembo populations in Mpinga, Ninja, and Kalonge. As used in this text, the term should not be confused with the important commercial town of the same name in North Kivu. (Maps 1, 4, 6, 11, 14)

Buzi.   A large peninsula on the northwestern shore of Lake Kivu. Formerly a part of Buhunde, Buzi was conquered early in this century by the Havu kings. Many families in the north of Ijwi retain important social and commercial ties with the people on Buzi. (Maps 1, 4)

Bwiiru.   The hill/village where the Ijwi royal drums are kept when not in ritual performance. (Map 9, 10)

Cishoke.   The mainland area on the western shore of Lake Kivu just southwest of the Ishungu peninsula. The prominent hills of Nyabihunge and Bujombo, considered to be the mainland home of the Ijwi Basibula dynasty, are located in Cishoke. (Map 13)

Irhambi.   The mainland region directly west of Ijwi, south of Mpinga. Although formerly ruled by Havu kings, in the late nineteenth century Irhambi was conquered by the kings of Buhaya, and subsequently came to form part of Bushi. Over time this region has become a quasi-independent kingdom known as Katana. (Maps 12, 13)

Ishungu.   A peninsula on the southwestern shore of Lake Kivu, and one of the mainland areas closest to Ijwi. Until early in this century, Ishungu was part of the domain of the Ijwi kings; today the people there still retain close ties with Ijwi. (Maps 12, 13)

Katana.   The name of the political unit (also a commercial center) in Irhambi, west of Lake Kivu. Descendants of the royal line of Buhaya, the kings of Katana now have a quasi-independent ritual status. (Map 13)

Kaziba.   One of the small states of the "southern tier" of Bushi. Located in the highlands just west of the Rusizi River, Kaziba has had a long history of intense commercial (and cultural) relations with Kinyaga and Rwanda to the east, Bufuliiro, Buvira, and Burundi to the south, and Ngweshe and Buhaya to the north. (Maps 11, 14)

Kinyaga.   The region south of Lake Kivu and east of the Rusizi River; now a part of the Cyangugu Prefecture of Rwanda. (Maps 1, 6, 7, 12)

Luhihi.   The broad plain along the southwestern shore of Lake Kivu, north of Cishoke and south of Irhambi. Today part of Bushi, historically Luhihi was associated with the mainland home of the Havu kings. (Map 13)

Lwindi.   The high mountainous region southwest of Lake Kivu. Culturally and historically, Lwindi is considered a crossroads between Lega and Bembe west of the Mitumba Mountains and the Shi east of the mountains. Associated politically with Bunyindu, this region is considered central to the early development of kingship west of Lake Kivu. (Maps 11, 14)

Mabula.   A prominent peninsula about halfway up the western shore of Lake Kivu. Part of the domain of the mainland Havu kings. (Map 13)

Mpinga.   The central region of the mainland Havu kings, located along the west-central shores of Lake Kivu. (Maps 1, 12, 13)

Ngweshe.   One of the largest and most powerful of the Shi states, located on the broad, fertile plateau southwest of Lake Kivu. The royal family of Ngweshe descends from the royal line of Buhaya. During the eighteenth and nineteenth centuries, this region had close ties to Bukunzi and Rwanda east of the Rusizi River. (Maps 11, 14)

Nyamirundi.   A large peninsula on the southern shore of Lake Kivu, and the closest mainland area to Ijwi. Formerly Nyamirundi formed part of Kinyaga; now it is part of the Cyangugu Prefecture of Rwanda. (Maps 12, 13)

Glossary of Terms

bami. Plural of *mwami.*

bagingi/bajinji. Plural of *mugingi/mujinji.*

bakapita. Plural of *mukapita.*

bakumbi. Plural of *mukumbi.*

banotabule (sing. *munotabule*). A colonial term used to denote administrative authorities (derived from the French *"notable"*). The semantic field of *banotabule* overlaps with that of *barhambo* in some contexts, but generally is used only in more formal contexts.

barhambo. Plural of *murhambo.*

barhunyi. Plural of *murhunyi.*

Barhwa (sing. Murhwa). A social group, culturally identified with the Bambuti forest peoples (often referred to in popular parlance as pygmies). Referred to as Batwa in Bushi, Rwanda, Burundi.

barhwali. Plural of *murhwali.*

bombo. Plural of *mumbo.*

bugabire. A complex form of cattle transfer, forming an enduring alliance between two men, an alliance which defined the exchange of milk, meat, hides of the cattle transferred, and the return of every third (or fourth) offspring to the original donor. The details of the arrangement took many different forms; its exact features varied from place to place and over time. *Bugabire* was only one of numerous forms of cattle transfer on Ijwi; the term also sometimes referred to temporary land transfer. Most instances of *bugabire* on Ijwi in the past did not carry the hierarchial clientship dimensions characteristic of many forms of cattle clientship in Rwanda; more recently, with the control of cattle on the island increasingly confined to the rich and powerful, *bugabire* on Ijwi has become more hierarchical in nature, requiring other responsibilities of the recipient to the donor.

bukumbi. A joking relationship which allows pleasantries, insults, and liberties with another, and which carries certain mutual ritual responsibilities. Partners in a *kumbi* relationship are determined by clan membership; members of any given clan share *kumbi* relations with members of other, specifically identified clans. In some parts of the island (especially in southwestern Ijwi), similar relations exist between certain degrees of cross-cousins. The relationship is usually, but not always, reciprocal.

bulo.   Millet; a very old seed crop in the region, and an important food item in the Muganuro ritual.

butega.   A collective term referring to bracelets or anklets made of fiber from forest plants; there were many different varieties of *butega,* distinguished by size, type of fiber, and weave. In the past, *butega* were significant commodities in the Lake Kivu commercial networks.

bwami.   Either (a) the location of the royal court on Ijwi, or (b) an abstract noun referring to the qualitative characteristics of kingship, especially to its spiritual and ritual dimensions.

capita (also *mukapita,* pl. *bakapita*).   The administrative head of a village, appointed by the royal court. This is a colonial term (or its derivative), to refer to a position whose occupant is primarily responsible for conveying administrative demands to the population and facilitating such administrative tasks as census-taking, tax collection, police patrols. But usually the village capita is an influential person, able to represent the interests of the village members at the court, and often important in resolving local conflicts or as a formal witness to contracts between village members.

cihango.   A blood pact; a voluntary friendship tie between two men, formalized by the exchange of blood in a prescribed ceremony. Specific responsibilities accompany blood pact ties. Blood pacts were especially important in the formation of commercial networks, so that a person involved in trade could depend on his blood-brother's family for food, lodging, and a secure place to store trade goods. Breaking the trust formed within a blood pact relationship brought severe repercussions—even more severe than those incurred for lack of respect for family solidarity, since a blood pact relationship was a voluntary commitment, freely chosen by the participants.

Cihumuliza.   One of the royal drums on Ijwi.

cikumi (pl. *bikumi*).   Especially in Nyanga and Tembo cultures, a *cikumi* was a female pawn, often transferred from one lineage to another as a young girl in exchange for the temporary use of a field, hunting domain, or fishing rights. In other cases a *cikumi* might serve as an alliance mechanism between lineages, or to ensure later payment of a juridical fine. Though usually unmarried, a *cikumi* could produce children claimed by the host lineage; such children would retain their identity to the host lineage even when the *cikumi* returned to her natal lineage.

eralire.   One of the plants used to form the *olusiro* in the royal rituals (and in other ritual and symbolic contexts) on Ijwi.

imigera.   Plural of *omugera.*

Interlacustrine cultures.   A collection of similar cultures stretching from Lake Albert, the Victoria Nile, and Lake Victoria in the north and east, to Lake Edward and the Mitumba Mountains (west of Lake Kivu) in the west, and to Burundi and Buha (in Tanzania, just south of Burundi) in the south. Though a region of many cultural variations, Interlacustrine Africa was characterized by highly centralized and powerful state structures, a marked degree of social differentiation within individual state structures, and mixed economies based on cattle-keeping and seed agriculture. While there were many smaller polities in the region, the largest and best known of the Interlacustrine states included Bunyoro, Buganda, Nkore, Karagwe, Rwanda, and Burundi.

ishanja (pl. *mashanja*). A term for a corporate identity, based on a descent ideology; on Ijwi, roughly translated by the term "clan."

ishungwe. The royal diadem worn by the *mwami* and certain *bagingi* in ritual occasions on Ijwi; it contains several cowrie shells (three in the case of the *mwami*, two in the cases of *bagingi*).

Kalinga. The name of the principal royal drum on Ijwi.

kurherakera. To commemorate one's ancestors through formal ritual procedures.

Mpembe. A ritual trumpet carved from an elephant tusk; used in the Muganuro and enthronement ceremonies on Ijwi.

mubake. The person embodying ritual authority and social focus for the small political communities among the Tembo and Nyanga cultures. In some respects a *mubake* shared status analogous to that of a *mwami* in the Interlacustrine societies, though a *mubake* controlled only minimal political resources and exercised little direct power of command over others.

mubande. On Ijwi: a substance formed of earth, herbs, and other substances of a ritually prescribed nature and provenience. Often used in healing rites, *mubande* is most prominently used in royal rituals such as the Muganuro and the enthronement rites. In Bushi, this term refers to a ritual ceremony roughly analogous to Muganuro on Ijwi. Among the Nyanga, *mubande* refers to certain ritual ceremonies of kingship, to the corporation of males responsible for organizing such rituals, and to certain quartz crystals invested with important ritual status.

Muganuro. The First Fruits ceremony, the most important of the annual royal rituals on Ijwi; performed at the time of the sorghum harvest (February–March). In its basic structure, and in many of its details, it repeats the rituals of enthronement, and thus symbolizes the annual renewal of the kingdom. Held at a time of public celebration (since no one is supposed to partake of sorghum from the recent harvest until after the performance of Muganuro), it is one of the most important symbolic expressions of popular participation in kingship, and of the subordination of the king to the corporate power of the *bagingi*. Muganuro thus represents both the historical continuity and the social dimensions of kingship.

mugingi (pl. *bagingi*). A member of the corporation of royal ritualists on Ijwi; a person responsible for preserving royal regalia or performing royal ritual. The position is usually hereditary, and often those holding this title carry high status and considerable influence; they are able, for example, to take issue with the king in public, and often do, something no one else would conceive of doing. Their formal title is often treated as their name, both as term of address and term of reference (e.g., Mushaho or Munyakalinga). In some cases they represent corporate interests (e.g., of a clan group) subordinated to an overarching kingship; in other cases the position is more individual in nature. This analysis treats them as occupying an ambiguous position in the social structure, mediating between the king and the population in some respects, but at the same time very much products of kingship. In a sense their social power is greater than that of the king, since as a corporation they represent kingship in its abstract formal essence; through their ritual performance, collectively they create the king. But their social roots are in different population groups. The *bagingi* act as a corporate unit only in ritually defined formal contexts; outside that context they often have no greater power than any other individual.

mujinji (pl. *bajinji*).   Shi form of the Ijwi term *"mugingi,"* ritualist.

mukapita (pl. *bakapita*).   Local form of the colonial term "capita," village headman.

mukumbi (pl. *bakumbi*).   A joking partner; see *bukumbi.*

mumbo (pl. *bombo*).   In the Nyanga and Tembo political communities, the classficatory sister of the *mubake;* the woman responsible for producing the heir to the *mubake* status. In some respects, the *mumbo* is more essential to the effective political functioning and continuity of the unit than the *mubake* himself.

murhambo (pl. *barhambo*).   An appointee of the court within the administrative network of the kingdom. This category of official can include *bakapita* (village headmen), but in common parlance the term is usually applied to regional authorities (acting over 10–15 *bakapita*) rather than to village-level authorities.

murhunyi (pl. *barhunyi*).   A formally recognized court favorite, an advisor to the king. *Barhunyi* were often influential as advocates or judges in legal cases, as pathways for commoners seeking access to the king, and as advisors to the king on social issues.

murhwali (pl. *barhwali*).   A direct descendant (usually a son) of a king, exercising political authority (often important in minor court cases).

Musao.   Among the Tembo, Nyanga, and Hunde cultures, Musao is an important ritualist; analogous to the Havu ritual position of Mushaho, in many respects the ritualist position most closely associated with the *mwami.*

mwami (pl. *bami*).   The sovereign of an independent (or formerly independent) polity. But the position was crucially defined not by political power alone. Instead, a *mwami* is the essential personage in the correct performance of royal rituals, and thus pre-eminently the symbol of the ritual autonomy and ritual wholeness of any given political unit. During the colonial period in this part of Zaire (then the Belgian Congo) the head of a political unit who lacked such ritual legitimacy was designated by the term *"sultani";* currently there is less distinction given to local level ritual authority of this political position.

Ndamutsa.   One of the royal drums of the Ijwi kingdom.

ngaligali.   A formally recognized "friend" of the king, with free and open access to the court. Unlike *barhunyi, ngaligali* live away from the court, in the hills, but are autonomous of normal administrative channels of the kingdom. They often serve as advisors to the king on local matters and provide the king with an independent source of information on the conduct of the *bakapita,* the village administrative heads.

ngisha.   A ritual whistle made of antelope horn, thought to carry powerful effect when directed against individuals.

Ngobosa.   A long, delicate, pronged wooden element used in the royal rituals to ward off evil.

nsanga.   A collective term for the ritual animals, the bull and the ram; see Rusanga entry.

Nyarushara.   A ritual iron implement shaped like a *fleur-de-lis.*

okunyw'omubande.   An important royal ritual in the Shi states of Buhaya and Ngweshe, performed at the time of the sorghum harvest.

okurhy'omwaka.   A family ritual in Burundi, and a local-level agricultural ritual in Bushi, carried out at the time of millet harvest (about April).

olushasha.   A plant used on Ijwi in the Muganuro ceremony as part of the *olusiro* and in other ritual contexts.

olusiro.   A bouquet of ritually prescribed plants, used in the Ijwi Muganuro ceremony to introduce the ritual, as if to separate the domain of ritual performance from the domain of everyday activities. The *olusiro* bouquet contains the local plants of *omugohwa, olushasha,* and *eralire.*

omugera (pl. *imigera*).   A long, thin, iron spear, used for spearing fish; also used in the Muganuro and enthronement rituals on Ijwi.

omugohwa.   A plant used in the *olusiro* and in many other ritual contexts on Ijwi.

Rusanga.   The name of the ritual bull or ritual ram on Ijwi.

sultani.   A colonial term for the highest local-level administrative authority in a locale. During colonial rule a *sultani* was considered equivalent to a *mwami,* but without the legitimacy derived from the ritual authority of kingship.

Umuganura.   The First Fruits ceremony in Rwanda; one of the most important and complex of the royal rituals of the state, various elements of this ritual occur at intervals throughout the year and include many of the most important of the royal ritualists.

Umuganuro.   An important royal ritual in Burundi, carried out annually at the time of the distribution of the sorhum seeds to the population; it included other agricultural plants as well.

Walengere.   An iron bar about 15 inches long, part of the royal regalia on Ijwi.

List of Ijwi Oral Sources

The following is a selected list of persons formally interviewed in the course of this work. They are listed by name, village, and date(s) of interview(s). English language notes of these interviews, and French translations of those portions taped, are in my possession, and are available for consultation by other scholars.

Babisha Burhula (Bunyakiri, Ijwi Nord) 13/2/73.
Bacigumanya Burahano (Bukinanyana, Ijwi Nord) 9/5/74.
Bacondo (Kisheke, Ijwi Nord) 28/5/74.
Badafabasheka Gahehwa (Kisheke, Ijwi Nord) 30/5/74.
Baderha Rwisheshenga Gahamire (Kimomo, Ijwi Sud) 15/5/72.
Bagalo Lwa Kalyo Gahero (Buyumbu, Ijwi Nord) 30/1/73.
Bàgereka Balimungo (Busobe, Ijwi Nord) 21/2/73.
Bagula (Kishenyi, Ijwi Nord) 2/2/73.
Bahale (Edouard) (Lushindi, Ijwi Sud) 9/6/72.
Bahanamwenda (Muhyahya, Ijwi Sud) 15/2/72.
Bahashaluvumba (Cassi, Ijwi Sud) 31/1/72.
Bahaya Mbisa (Cisiiza, Ijwi Sud) 10/2/72.
Bahaza (Bugarula, Ijwi Sud) 12/2/72.
Bahiga Kalimba (Karhonda, Ijwi Nord) 9/2/73.
Bahimba (Rambo, Ijwi Sud) 21/4/72.
Bahinuza Lukwebo (Cisiiza, Ijwi Sud) 9/2/72.
Bahisi Nyabahama (Buhumba, Ijwi Sud) 26/6/72.
Bakenga Rutara (Kishumbu, Ijwi Nord) 19/2/73.
Bakengamwami (Kasihe, Ijwi Sud) 24/6/72.
Balagire (Muhyahya, Ijwi Sud) 7/2/72.
Balagire Yafali (Cibanda, Ijwi Nord) 25/5/74.
Balike (Mpene, Ijwi Sud) 26/1/72.
Balike Nyabalinda (Burhonga, Ijwi Nord) 15/2/73.
Banweju (Rambo, Ijwi Sud) 14/1/72.
Barhezake (Josephu) (Cassi, Ijwi Sud) 31/1/72.
Barhobahana (Mugote, Ijwi Sud) 22/3/72.
Barhombo Luhuma (Buyumbu, Ijwi Nord) 29/1/73.
Barhonga (Kagushu, Ijwi Nord) 23/5/74.

Barhungu (Karhongo, Ijwi Sud) 27/6/72.
Barhungu Luvuga (Cisiiza, Ijwi Sud) 10/2/72.
Barume Mushoboze (Muziri, Ijwi Nord) 30/4/74.
Barungu (Ngula, Ijwi Nord) 16/5/74.
Baruti Bugo (Bukinanyana, Ijwi Nord) 7/5/74; 8/5/74.
Basaza (Lweza, Ijwi Nord) 21/5/74.
Bashana (Kihumba, Ijwi Nord) 3/2/73.
Bashwira (Nkuvu, Ijwi Sud) 27/4/72.
Batindi (Mugote, Ijwi Sud) 24/3/72.
Bature Orekene (Lubuye, Ijwi Sud) 22/3/72.
Bavugerije (Cassi, Ijwi Sud) 31/1/72; 1/2/72.
Bayongo Rugombera (Burhonga, Ijwi Nord) 15/2/73.
Bazungu Hakizumwami (Gashara, Ijwi Sud) 24/5/72; 25/5/72.
Bendera (Buruhuka, Ijwi Nord) 16/2/73.
Bendera Bagaluza (Mboho) (Buruhuka, Ijwi Nord) 16/2/73.
Bengehya (Nkola, Ijwi Nord) 2/5/74; 4/5/74.
Bengehya Karhanga (Jerome) (Busobe, Ijwi Nord) 21/2/73.
Bibuguvugu Bulungu (Lugendo) 10/8/72.
Bifuko Balambo (Bunyakiri, Ijwi Nord) 12/2/73.
Bigwana Munyama (Kishumbu, Ijwi Nord) 19/2/73.
Bihage (Buhoro, Ijwi Sud) 12/2/72.
Bihango (Buhoro, Ijwi Sud) 11/2/72.
Bihinga Nyamurangwa (Bugarula, Ijwi Nord) 27/4/74.
Bihombe (Kashiraboba, Ijwi Nord) 13/5/74.
Bijaci Mulira (Lugendo) 19/8/72.
Bikenyere Rwamigabo (Cimalamungo, Ijwi Nord) 31/1/73.
Bikere (Lubuye, Ijwi Sud) 21/3/72.
Bikoma (Mugote, Ijwi Sud) 20/3/72.
Bingwana (Kishumbu, Ijwi Nord) 19/2/73.
Binombe Shabuli (Gashiraboba, Ijwi Nord) 13/5/74.
Binyene (Michel) (Ntalangwa, Ijwi Sud) 26/5/72.
Binyungu Lukere (Buruhuka, Ijwi Nord) 16/2/73.
Binyungu Mbenga (Kishenyi, Ijwi Nord) 1/2/73.
Birali (Mubale, Ijwi Sud) 10/6/72.
Biralinzi Miruhu (Bunyakiri, Ijwi Nord) 13/2/73.
Birizene (Kashiraboba, Ijwi Nord) 13/5/74.
Birongo Mutamzamba (Bunyakiri, Ijwi Nord) 12/2/73.
Birusha Shangabugaragu (Bunyama, Ijwi Sud) 29/5/72; 3/6/72.
Bishangi Ntulu (Buruhuka, Ijwi Nord) 17/2/73.
Bishimina Bihinga (Buyumbu, Ijwi Nord) 29/1/73.
Bishimina Mugaru (Kishenyi, Ijwi Nord) 2/2/73.
Bishingwe (Mpene, Ijwi Sud) 25/1/72.
Bishugi Batimuka (Kilala, Ijwi Sud) 2/6/72.
Bitukuru (Buzigaziga, Ijwi Sud) 9/5/72.
Budaho Maheshe (Kimomo, Ijwi Sud) 15/5/72.
Budaho Rutengura (Ntalangwa, Ijwi Sud) 26/5/72.
Bugabanda Ruhogo (Ishungu) 7/8/72.

Bugabo Ndahushuli (Bukenge, Ijwi Nord) 30/4/74.
Bugale Ntalyoma (Bunyakiri, Ijwi Nord) 12/2/73.
Bulambagiri Birhi Musangani (Mulamba, Ijwi Sud) 1/6/72.
Bulemu Bulungu (Muhungwe, Ijwi Sud) 12/6/72.
Bulingeni Mushayuma (Bunyakiri, Ijwi Nord) 13/2/73.
Bundi (Muhyahya, Ijwi Sud) 4/2/72.
Bunyerezi (Nyakibamba, Ijwi Sud) 19/4/72; 29/4/72.
Buraho Ndako (Ishungu) 7/8/72.
Burasa (Ntalangwa, Ijwi Sud) 27/5/72.
Burharha Mahebera (Ntalangwa, Ijwi Sud) 27/5/72.
Burhola (Mugote, Ijwi Sud) 22/3/72; 28/6/72.
Burumanga (Lweza, Ijwi Nord) 22/5/74.
Burumanga Mikamba (Lweza, Ijwi Nord) 22/5/74.
Burume (Butyangale, Ijwi Sud) 10/3/72.
Bushanula (Mpene, Ijwi Sud) 29/1/72; 23/6/72.
Buswagiri Munyazangabo (Mubale, Ijwi Sud) 5/6/72.
Buzigaziga Nyamugoka (Bushake, Ijwi Sud) 11/3/72; 13/3/72.
Buzombo (Muhyahya, Ijwi Sud) 5/2/72.
Bwayo Bamporice (Ishungu) 9/8/72.
Bwehe (Zacharia) (Mazina, Ijwi Sud) 13/6/72.
Bweshe (Mazina, Ijwi Sud) 13/6/72.
Bwiiza (Buzibu, Ijwi Sud) 27/1/72.
Byacanda Cusha (Bunyakiri, Ijwi Nord) 13/2/73.
Byakazi Sumari (Buhumba, Ijwi Sud) 26/6/72.
Byarubara (Bukole, Ijwi Nord) 8/2/73.
Camboko Luvebya (Buruhuka, Ijwi Nord) 16/2/73.
Camiraye Kabanda (Gashiraboba, Ijwi Nord) 10/5/74.
Campanda (Buholo-Karhongo, Ijwi Sud) 16/2/72.
Cangacanga (Nkuvu, Ijwi Sud) 27/4/72.
Cantwali (Buruhuka, Ijwi Nord) 17/2/73.
Cibwami (Bukere, Ijwi Sud) 7/3/72.
Cihonzi (Bugarula, Ijwi Sud) 8/2/72.
Cingamugera (Bugarula, Ijwi Sud) 8/2/72.
Cirasi (Mugote, Ijwi Sud) 24/3/72.
Ciringwe (Luhihi) 16/1/75.
Cirunga (Muhyahya, Ijwi Sud) 15/2/72; 10/3/73; 19/6/74; 8/10/74.
Ciruza (Bwiiru, Ijwi Sud) 6/3/72.
Fafa Munyazangabo (Bulegeyi, Ijwi Sud) 2/5/72.
Fungulo Mushobekwa (Nyakibamba, Ijwi Sud) 29/4/72.
Gacuka (Buholo, Ijwi Sud) 11/2/72.
Gacuka Mumbagwa (Ngula, Ijwi Nord) 16/5/74.
Gafuko Rubanguka (Mubale, Ijwi Sud) 8/6/72.
Gahalalo Lushombo Mukoba (Buyumbu, Ijwi Nord) 30/1/73.
Gahalalo Mudosa (Mubale, Ijwi Sud) 8/6/72.
Gahamire Mondo (Kasihe, Ijwi Sud) 11/3/73; 28/11/73; 26/2/74; 18/6/74; 3/10/74;
    4/10/74; 28/10/74.
Gahanda Shabiniga (Cugi, Ijwi Nord) 26/1/73.

Gahanga (Bwando, Ijwi Sud) 29/3/72.
Gahangamira (Buruhuka, Ijwi Nord) 17/2/73.
Gahangaza (Lushindi, Ijwi Sud) 9/6/72.
Gahenga Zurhwagarwa (Cimenwe, Ijwi Sud) 8/5/72.
Gahenzi Kaboye (Rambo, Ijwi Sud) 29/6/72.
Gahenzi Rubabura (Muhungwe, Ijwi Sud) 12/6/72.
Gaherwe (Mugote, Ijwi Sud) 20/3/72.
Gahire Gwagitale (Kihumba, Ijwi Nord) 27/1/73.
Gakezi (Busobe, Ijwi Nord) 21/2/73.
Gakubwa Milagalaga (Bunyakiri, Ijwi Nord) 13/2/73.
Gakwaya (Evariste) (Bugarula, Ijwi Nord) 3/5/74.
Ganukula Kazibi (Burhonga, Ijwi Nord) 15/2/73.
Garhungu (Bukere-Bwando, Ijwi Sud) 7/3/72.
Garhwana Sanzibi (Mulamba, Ijwi Nord) 14/2/73.
Garuhinga (Lushindi, Ijwi Sud) 9/6/72.
Garuka Shawanja (Rambo, Ijwi Sud) 29/6/72.
Gasarahinga Bishovu (Karhongo, Ijwi Sud) 17/5/72.
Gasarahinga Kandiamazi (Bwando, Ijwi Sud) 29/3/72; 30/3/72.
Gasarahinga Sanvura (Kigera, Ijwi Sud) 12/5/72; 13/5/72.
Gaseserwa (Bukere, Ijwi Sud) 23/3/72.
Gashabo Basengi (Buholo, Ijwi Sud) 8/2/72.
Gashagaza (Kishumbu, Ijwi Nord) 19/2/73; 7/3/73.
Gashaku (Bugarula, Ijwi Nord) 29/4/74.
Gashamangali (Kimomo, Ijwi Sud) 15/5/72.
Gashina Gasanani (Muziri, Ijwi Nord) 6/5/74.
Gashoko (Mugote, Ijwi Sud) 23/3/72.
Gashoko (Bukole, Ijwi Nord) 6/2/73.
Gashoku Shangako (Bugarula, Ijwi Nord) 27/4/74; 29/4/74.
Gasholi (Musama, Ijwi Sud) n.d.
Gashondi Nyamurangwa (Muhyahya, Ijwi Sud) 3/2/72.
Gashugurho Muhimbo (Buyumbu, Ijwi Nord) 30/1/73.
Gashugushu (Bukere, Ijwi Sud) 7/3/72.
Gasirahinga Gashovu (Cisiiza, Ijwi Sud) 9/2/72.
Gatengura Mahebera (Lemera, Ijwi Sud) 6/6/72.
Gatera (Bulegeyi, Ijwi Sud) 2/5/72.
Gatera (Mubale, Ijwi Sud) 10/6/72.
Gatera Kanega (Muziri, Ijwi Nord) 6/5/74; 9/5/74.
Gatera Nyakabinga (Mubale, Ijwi Sud) 10/6/72.
Gatumwa (Mpene-Bwiiru, Ijwi Sud) 24/1/72.
Gatumwa (Mubale, Ijwi Sud) 10/6/72.
Giduhu Mandevu (Albert) (Kishenyi, Ijwi Nord) 2/2/73.
Gihimbi (Kilala, Ijwi Sud) 2/6/72.
Gihire Ntabogulwa (Bulehe, Ijwi Nord) 31/1/73.
Gisangani Rwango (Cugi, Ijwi Nord) 25/1/73.
Gisayura Lujongo (Buhumba, Ijwi Sud) 26/6/72.
Gisayura Mukabyo (Kishenyi, Ijwi Nord) 27/1/73; 2/2/73.

Gushoko Nzibukira (Bukole, Ijwi Nord) 6/2/73.
Habimana (Bugarula, Ijwi Sud) 8/2/72.
Habimana (Bulehe, Ijwi Nord) 31/1/73.
Hakiza Pierre (Bukinanyana, Ijwi Nord) 8/5/74.
Hakizumwami Siringi (Bukinanyana, Ijwi Nord) 9/5/74.
Hisunga (Mulamba, Ijwi Sud) 1/6/72.
Kabale Samagwa (Mpene, Ijwi Sud) 22/6/72.
Kabangala Kubushano (Busobe, Ijwi Nord) 21/2/73.
Kabango (Bushovu, Ijwi Sud) 3/5/72; 4/5/72; 8/5/72.
Kabango Lukere (Lemera-Bwina, Ijwi Sud) 7/6/72.
Kabaraka (Bwando, Ijwi Sud) 28/3/72.
Kabeme (Mugote, Ijwi Sud) 24/3/72.
Kabera Bijenje (Bushake, Ijwi Sud) 10/5/72.
Kabera Tembo (Gashara, Ijwi Sud) 26/6/72.
Kabirambare (Bwando, Ijwi Sud) 27/3/72.
Kabolo (Karama, Ijwi Sud) 14/6/72.
Kabona (Nkola, Ijwi Sud) 2/5/74.
Kaboye (Muhyahya, Ijwi Sud) 5/2/72.
Kaboyi Nyamugunjeka (Kishumbu, Ijwi Nord) 19/2/73.
Kabugo Nyakurwa Cerungwe (Lugendo) 11/8/72.
Kabulo Karhego (Karama, Ijwi Sud) 14/6/72.
Kacuka (Ngula, Ijwi Nord) 16/5/74.
Kacuka Kaboye (Ishungu) 9/8/72.
Kadogo Rhwantunda (Kasihe, Ijwi Sud) 24/6/72.
Kadole (Buholo, Ijwi Sud) 11/2/72.
Kadorho (Michel) (Kimomo, Ijwi Sud) 27/6/72.
Kadusi (Kihumba, Ijwi Nord) 26/1/73; 4/6/74.
Kagoye Bironone Muhindu (Bukenge, Ijwi Nord) 29/4/74.
Kahanga (Bwando, Ijwi Sud) 29/3/72.
Kahangamubo (Buruhuka, Ijwi Nord) 17/2/73.
Kahara Lushayire (Karama, Ijwi Sud) 14/6/72.
Kahenzi (Muhungwe, Ijwi Sud) 12/6/72.
Kahonera (Bukere, Ijwi Sud) 8/3/72.
Kajebika Kasinde (Kihumba, Ijwi Nord) 3/2/73.
Kajibwami Bijenji (Buyumbu, Ijwi Nord) 29/1/73.
Kajibwami Nyamukubugu (Lemera, Ijwi Sud) 7/6/72.
Kakira Ruhamisa (Ntalangwa, Ijwi Sud) 26/5/72.
Kakira Shamuhuza (Mpene, Ijwi Sud) 19/6/74.
Kakola Mahugo (Kinji, Ijwi Nord) 3/5/74.
Kakomere (Cibishwa, Ijwi Sud) 19/2/72; 16/5/72; 6/6/72; 21/6/74.
Kalambagira (Lubuye, Ijwi Sud) 21/3/72.
Kalekuzi (Muhungwe, Ijwi Sud) 12/6/72.
Kalibanya (Muziri) 8/5/74.
Kalibanya Bishovu (Mpene, Ijwi Sud) 22/6/72; 22/6/74.
Kalibwa (Gihumba, Ijwi Nord) 3/2/73.
Kalire (Gashara, Ijwi Sud) 24/5/72; 29/5/72.

Kalugurha Kanyamukenge (Ishungu) 9/8/72.
Kalwiira Biseruki (Bukere, Ijwi Sud) 7/3/72.
Kalwiira Shabesho (Bulehe, Ijwi Nord) 31/1/73.
Kalwiira Shabozo (Mubale, Ijwi Sud) 5/6/72; 8/6/72; 10/6/72.
Kalwiira Shulirhu (Kishenyi, Ijwi Nord) 1/2/73.
Kamaka (Mpene, Ijwi Sud) 22/6/72; 23/6/72.
Kamana Mirenga (Cibanda, Ijwi Nord) 25/5/74.
Kamenju (Kagushu, Ijwi Nord) 18/5/74.
Kampayane (Bugarula, Ijwi Nord) 2/6/74.
Kamuzinzi (Bwando, Ijwi Sud) 28/3/72.
Kamuzinzi (Rambo, Ijwi Sud) 29/6/72.
Kanega Bishimira (Kagushu, Ijwi Nord) 17/5/74.
Kanega Migayo (Gashiraboba, Ijwi Nord) 14/5/74.
Kanigi (Kigera, Ijwi Sud) 12/5/72.
Kantwali Rhweshamenyu (Buruhuka, Ijwi Nord) 17/2/73.
Kanyabashi Bitahinda (Cimalamungu, Ijwi Nord) 31/1/73.
Kanyagala Marcel (Mulamba, Ijwi Sud) 1/6/72.
Kanyama (Cikumbo-Cassi, Ijwi Sud) 2/2/72.
Kanyenju Kahise (Kagushu, Ijwi Nord) 18/5/74.
Kanywesi (Ngula, Ijwi Nord) 16/5/74.
Karaza Ntibanyorwa (Bukenge, Ijwi Nord) 1/5/74.
Karaza Zagabe (Buruhuka, Ijwi Nord) 16/2/73.
Kariyonga (Karama, Ijwi Sud) 14/6/72.
Kashengera (Buzibu, Ijwi Sud) 27/1/72.
Kasi (Nkuvu, Ijwi Sud) 27/4/72.
Kasigwa (Mpene, Ijwi Sud) 21/1/72; 24/1/72; 25/1/72.
Kasisi (Bunyama, Ijwi Sud) 29/5/72.
Kasisi Cilimwami (Bushake, Ijwi Sud) 28/4/72.
Katwanyi Cigorombo (Ishungu) 9/8/72.
Kavuku Buruteri (Buhumba, Ijwi Sud) 26/6/72.
Kavurha (Bwando, Ijwi Sud) 27/3/72.
Kayirara Lwisimanga (Gashara, Ijwi Sud) 24/5/72.
Kayoga (Muhyahya, Ijwi Sud) 3/2/72.
Kayoga (Bukenge, Ijwi Nord) 29/4/74.
Kaziga (Emmanuel) (Ishungu) 12/8/72.
Kazungu (Bunyakiri, Ijwi Nord) 13/2/73.
Kigonya (Mugote, Ijwi Sud) 18/3/72; 20/3/72; 28/6/72.
Kigufi Midende (Bushake, Ijwi Sud) 9/5/72.
Kihonza Shabuli (Mugote, Ijwi Sud) 23/3/72.
Kilaliira (Kilala, Ijwi Sud) 8/6/72.
Kilimushi Nyambwe (Bulegeyi, Ijwi Sud) 1/5/72.
Kilumira Gafumbu (Kishenyi, Ijwi Nord) 1/2/73.
Kinyabuguma Balike (Bunyakiri, Ijwi Nord) 12/2/73.
Kirhalira Mwerekandi (Kimomo, Ijwi Sud) 16/5/72.
Kirhandaliri (Mafula, Ijwi Nord) 27/5/74.
Kishake Minyeri (Kisheke, Ijwi Nord) 30/5/74.

Kishera Mazimwa (Bukenge, Ijwi Nord) 30/4/74; 30/5/74.
Kishikanyi (Lushindi, Ijwi Sud) 9/6/72.
Kivunyira (Bwando, Ijwi Sud) 28/3/72.
Kizinduka (Bwando, Ijwi Sud) 28/3/72.
Kulimushi (Bulegeyi, Ijwi Sud) 1/5/72.
Kuma Kimpale (Kisheke, Ijwi Nord) n.d.
Kushiga Baliko (Muhungwe, Ijwi Sud) 12/6/72.
Kuzanwa Matabaro (Buyumbu, Ijwi Nord) 29/1/73.
Lubaye (Butyangali, Ijwi Sud) 9/3/72.
Lubombo Ndeyaliza (Mulamba, Ijwi Sud) 1/6/72.
Ludunge Baluhire (Buhumba, Ijwi Sud) 26/6/72.
Ludwaye (Boza, Ijwi Sud) 11/5/72.
Luganwa Kabonjo (Mugote, Ijwi Sud) 22/3/72.
Lugerero (Bugarula, Ijwi Sud) 8/2/72.
Lukera (Buruhuka, Ijwi Nord) 16/2/83.
Lukwebo Bahinyiza (Karhongo, Ijwi Sud) 27/6/72.
Lushoka (Bushake, Ijwi Sud) 11/3/72; 28/4/72; 8/5/72; 9/5/72.
Luvuga Sangabo (Boza, Ijwi Sud) 11/5/72.
Luvumba Bahafa (Cassi, Ijwi Sud) 1/2/72.
Lwahimba Fakage (Buhoro II, Ijwi Sud) 1/3/72.
Lwibaye (Boza, Ijwi Sud) 11/5/72.
Lwibaye (Mugote, Ijwi Sud) 22/3/72.
Lwibaye Njembeka (Cimenwe, Ijwi Sud) 8/5/72.
Lwoyaga Ntabasima (Karama, Ijwi Sud) 14/6/72.
Madali (Kagushu, Ijwi Nord) 16/5/74; 27/5/74.
Madali (Muhyahya, Ijwi Sud) 4/2/72.
Madihano Mwandagaliro (Cibanda, Ijwi Nord) 23/5/74.
Mafundo (Mugote-Kishovu, Ijwi Sud) 20/3/72; 21/3/72.
Magaju Kavumba (Bulegeyi, Ijwi Sud) 21/4/72; 3/5/72.
Magamba Ndihaliza (Bukere, Ijwi Sud) 7/3/72.
Magambo Kabasuru (Muganzu, Ijwi Nord) 9/2/73.
Magendo (Bulegeyi, Ijwi Sud) 2/5/72; 3/5/72.
Magongo (Kishenyi, Ijwi Nord) 1/2/73; 19/4/73.
Mahebera (Kashiraboba, Ijwi Nord) 11/5/74.
Mahenga (Butyangali, Ijwi Sud) 9/3/72; 15/6/74.
Mahoko Lwahisha Murerebwa (Mafula, Ijwi Nord) 27/5/74.
Mahomba (Kishumbu, Ijwi Nord) 19/2/73.
Mahoro (Bulegeyi, Ijwi Sud) 2/5/72; 3/5/72.
Mahuba Gahimano Kanyarubara (Lemera, Ijwi Sud) 7/6/72.
Mahusi (Gérard) (Buhumba, Ijwi Sud) 26/6/72.
Majuku Rwisamanga (Muziri, Ijwi Nord) 6/5/74.
Makala Rusinyangerero (Bukinanyana, Ijwi Nord) 7/5/74; 8/5/74.
Makanda (Bwando, Ijwi Sud) 27/3/72.
Makangura (Bushovu, Ijwi Sud) 4/5/72.
Makombwa Ruganguka (Bushake, Ijwi Sud) 11/3/72; 10/5/72; 12/5/72.
Malekera (Bulegeyi, Ijwi Sud) 21/4/72; 1/5/72; 21/5/72.

Malekera (Bwiiru, Ijwi Sud) 6/3/72.
Malekera (Lweza, Ijwi Nord) 22/5/74.
Malekera Bosa (Kishenyi, Ijwi Nord) 1/2/73.
Malige (Kagushu, Ijwi Nord) 18/5/74; 27/5/74.
Malugire (Cassi, Ijwi Sud) 31/1/72.
Maluhuko (Kashiraboba, Ijwi Nord) 13/5/74.
Mamboleo (Cibanda, Ijwi Nord) 25/5/74.
Maneke (Bugarula, Ijwi Sud) 8/2/72.
Mantama Mulikuza (Kihumba, Ijwi Nord) 26/1/73.
Marafande Gasahane (Gashara, Ijwi Sud) 24/5/72.
Marandura Madihano (Nkola, Ijwi Nord) 2/4/74; 2/5/74.
Marhandanya (Kashiraboba, Ijwi Nord) 15/5/74.
Masasa Rubimbura (Mulamba, Ijwi Nord) 14/2/73.
Masuka Gahwarha (Kishenyi, Ijwi Nord) 2/2/73.
Masumbuka Bitate (Nkola, Ijwi Nord) 11/5/74.
Matabaro (Lushindi, Ijwi Sud) 9/6/72.
Matagana (Buholo, Ijwi Sud) 11/2/72.
Mayange Kahamire (Gashara, Ijwi Sud) 25/5/72; 10/3/73; 27/11/73; 18/6/74; 4/11/74.
Mbanza (Mugote, Ijwi Sud) 23/3/72.
Mbaraga (Bwando, Ijwi Sud) 28/3/72; 21/3/75.
Mbogo-Mbogo Bayongwa (Nkola, Ijwi Nord) 2/5/74.
Mbogo-Mbogo Bazurunguka (Busobe, Ijwi Nord) 21/2/73.
Mbogobogo Miderho (Bugarula, Ijwi Nord) 26/4/74.
Mesokubina Rhukuburha (Bushovu, Ijwi Sud) 3/5/72.
Mibale Musomokwere (Buzamuka, Ijwi Nord) 27/1/73.
Migayo Shamahanga (Bunyakiri, Ijwi Nord) 12/2/73.
Mikabule Hakizumwami (Kagushu, Ijwi Nord) 18/5/74.
Miravumba (Rambo, Ijwi Sud) 29/6/72.
Mirenge (Kibanda, Ijwi Nord) 25/5/74.
Mirimba Lukwebo (Karhongo, Ijwi Sud) 18/5/72.
Mirindi (Bulegeyi, Ijwi Sud) 1/5/72.
Miringa Habyesi (Bukenge, Ijwi Nord) 30/4/74.
Misogoro Ntangale (Kisheke, Ijwi Nord) 28/5/74.
Mpalala (Mpene, Ijwi Sud) 18/6/74.
Mpanzi Mushayuma (Gashara, Ijwi Sud) 25/5/72.
Mparara (Mpene, Ijwi Sud) 26/1/72; 29/1/72.
Mpinja Yambayamba (Muganzu, Ijwi Nord) 9/2/73.
Mubwira (Lushindi, Ijwi Sud) 9/5/72.
Mucyura (Pascal) (Bulegeyi, Ijwi Sud) 1/2/72.
Mudahama (Buzibu, Ijwi Sud) 27/1/72.
Mudahigwa (Boza, Ijwi Sud) 11/5/72.
Muduha Ngotanyi (Jean) (Mulamba, Ijwi Sud) 1/6/72.
Mugala (Bwiiru, Ijwi Sud) 6/3/72.
Mugenzi (Nyakalengwa, Ijwi Sud; Bukenge, Ijwi Nord) 28/12/70; 18/12/72;

18/2/73; 11/9/73; 12/9/73; 26/4/74; 1/5/74; 4/5/74; 11/5/74; 15/5/74; 1/6/74; 3/6/74; 4/6/74; 5/6/74; 6/6/74; 2/1/75.

Mugombwa (Bushake, Ijwi Sud) 10/5/72.

Mugotanye Nankola (Nkola, Ijwi Nord) 2/5/74.

Muguruntege (Bukole, Ijwi Nord) 6/2/73.

Muhamagala Bujuli (Ntalangwa, Ijwi Sud) 26/5/72.

Muhamiriza (Hurhu, Ijwi Nord) 26/1/73.

Muhomba Kuburhano (Kishumbu, Ijwi Nord) 19/2/73.

Muhozi (Buholo II, Ijwi Sud) 2/3/72.

Mujarubamba Rubadoka Muzeru (Bunyama, Ijwi Sud) 3/6/72.

Mukanira Kaje (Buhagwa, Ijwi Sud) 31/5/72.

Mukatara (Bulegeyi, Ijwi Sud) 21/4/72; 12/5/72.

Mukatara Barungu (Nyakibamba, Ijwi Sud) 29/4/72; 21/5/72.

Mukera (Boza, Ijwi Sud) 11/5/72.

Mukulu Rhurhabona (Muhyahya, Ijwi Sud) 3/2/72.

Mukunzi Gahyuhyu (Ishungu) 8/8/72.

Mukwizanyundo (Muhyahya, Ijwi Sud) 3/2/72; 19/6/74; 8/10/74.

Mulahuko Bigondo (Ishungu) 8/8/72.

Mulahuko Shanzigi (Gashiraboba, Ijwi Nord) 13/5/74.

Mulengera Ruteeka (François) (Buhagwa, Ijwi Sud) 30/5/72.

Mulengezi (Kihumba, Ijwi Sud) 13/5/72.

Mulengezi (Kimomo, Ijwi Sud) 18/5/72.

Mulengezi (Lweza, Ijwi Nord) 21/5/74.

Mulengezi Kaboye (Cinji, Ijwi Nord) 30/4/74.

Mulinzi (Cibanda, Ijwi Nord) 25/5/74.

Mulwalwa Bagayamukwe (Buyumbu, Ijwi Nord) 29/1/73.

Mulyango Rugurukira (Mafula, Ijwi Nord) 27/5/74.

Munazi (Karhongo, Ijwi Sud) 10/2/72.

Munda (Bulegeyi, Ijwi Sud) 1/5/72; 3/5/72; 8/5/72; 21/6/74.

Mungazi Mutemura (Munyakalinga) (Bwiiru, Ijwi Sud) 6/3/72; 28/6/72; 10/3/73.

Munyampara Kiyorha (Bweshu, Ijwi Nord) 19/2/73.

Munyankiko (Karhongo, Ijwi Sud) 9/2/72; 18/5/72.

Munyantole (Lweza, Ijwi Nord) 21/5/74.

Munyi (Muhungwe, Ijwi Sud) 12/6/72.

Murhegera Kabaye (Ishungu) 11/8/72.

Murhima Kabangu (Nkola, Ijwi Nord) 4/5/74.

Murhonyi Shabwisho (Buhagwa, Ijwi Sud) 30/5/72.

Murhungane (Kamole, Ijwi Nord) 7/2/73.

Murihano Kamanzi (Ngwarha) (Bushake, Ijwi Sud) 9/5/72.

Murogoya (Bulegeyi, Ijwi Sud) 3/5/72.

Murungu (Bukinanyana, Ijwi Nord) 9/5/74.

Musafiri Kitambara (Karhongo, Ijwi Sud) 17/5/72.

Musafiri Yalumire (Lemera, Ijwi Sud) 6/6/72.

Musahura (Mugote, Ijwi Sud) 17/3/72.

Musaka Muhimuzi (Rambo, Ijwi Sud) 20/6/72.

Musanganya Ntawamake (Cugi, Ijwi Nord) 25/1/73.
Musebwa Nyantega (Buholo, Ijwi Sud) 11/2/72.
Musemakweli (Nkola, Ijwi Nord) 4/5/74.
Musemakweli (Kishumbu, Ijwi Nord) 19/2/73.
Musemakweli Malibarha (Gashiraboba, Ijwi Nord) 11/5/74.
Mushaho (Mulyamo, Ijwi Sud) 15/2/72; 9/3/73; 13/10/73; 18/6/74.
Mushaka (Rambo, Ijwi Sud) 29/6/72.
Mushayuma (Muhyahya, Ijwi Sud) 5/2/72.
Mushayuma Ngubuguru (Ishungu) 9/8/72.
Mushayuma Semutwa (Kinji, Ijwi Nord) 3/5/74.
Mushega (Cimenwe, Ijwi Sud) 8/5/72.
Mushengezi Gahengezi Munyama (Nzuki) (Kilala, Ijwi Sud) 2/6/72.
Mushengezi Minani (Bugarula, Ijwi Nord) 27/4/74.
Mushingi (Gashara, Ijwi Sud) 25/5/72.
Mushingi Hungwe (Kisheke, Ijwi Nord) 31/5/74.
Mushingi Kizingazinga (Muziri, Ijwi Nord) 9/5/74.
Mushoko (Mafula, Ijwi Nord) 27/5/74.
Musigi (Butyangali, Ijwi Sud) 9/3/72; 10/3/72.
Musoro (Butyangali, Ijwi Sud) 9/3/72.
Musoro Bwangarama Kaboye (Mulamba, Ijwi Sud) 1/6/72.
Musumbuku (Mazina, Ijwi Sud) 13/6/72.
Mutalindwa (Kagushu, Ijwi Nord) 17/5/74.
Mutamba (Mazina, Ijwi Sud) 13/6/72.
Mutanyerera (Boza, Ijwi Sud) 11/5/72.
Mutarambirwa (Nkola, Ijwi Nord) 4/5/74.
Muterangusho (Kirhabo, Ijwi Nord) 12/9/73.
Muyoba Cigame (Karhondo, Ijwi Nord) 10/2/73.
Muyobo (Mazina, Ijwi Sud) 13/6/72.
Muyorha Nvuyengore (Bunyama, Ijwi Sud) 29/5/72.
Mvano (Joseph) (Kigera, Ijwi Sud) 12/5/72.
Mwagamba (Mulamba, Ijwi Sud) 1/6/72.
Mwandulo Muhigirwa (Bukole, Ijwi Nord) 6/2/73.
Mwanganyo Miderho (Buhagwa, Ijwi Sud) 31/5/72.
Mwarugamba (Mpene) 20/6/74.
Mweeru (Cassi, Ijwi Sud) 31/1/72; 1/2/72.
Mwihuzi (Mugote, Ijwi Sud) 23/3/72.
Myavu (Kilala, Ijwi Sud) 2/6/72.
Nadorho (Michel) (Muganzu, Ijwi Nord) 9/2/73.
Namutembe Mahuko (Mulamba, Ijwi Nord) 14/2/73.
Nandugu (Bukinanyana, Ijwi Nord) 7/5/74.
Nangarama (Bugarula, Ijwi Nord) 30/4/74.
Ndahaliza (Mafula, Ijwi Nord) 27/5/74.
Ndahaliza Budaho (Lugendo) 10/8/72.
Ndaku Masegeta (Ishungu) 9/8/72.
Ndanga Mihanda (Ishungu) 8/8/72.
Ndayalire (Kihumba, Ijwi Sud) 28/4/72; 29/4/72; 13/5/72.

Ndayaza Gifakwenda (Cibanda, Ijwi Nord) 25/5/74.
Ndengeyi Ntama (Kilala, Ijwi Sud) 2/6/72.
Ndengeyinka (Bukere, Ijwi Sud) 23/3/72; 14/6/74.
Ndeyalire (Bwando, Ijwi Sud) 29/3/72.
Ndimanyi (Lubuye, Ijwi Sud) 21/3/72.
Ndokabirya Makuza Lushombo (Ngula, Ijwi Nord) 15/5/74.
Ndongozi (Mpene, Ijwi Sud) 20/6/74.
Ndwanyi (Noel) (Bukere, Ijwi Sud) 13/6/74; 14/6/74.
Ndwanyi Simba (Bwando, Ijwi Sud) 29/2/72; 10/3/72.
Ngaboyeka Kalwiira (Bulehe, Ijwi Nord) 31/1/73.
Ngereza (André) (Bukere, Ijwi Sud) 24/3/72.
Ngirumpatse (Christophe) (Buhumba, Ijwi Sud) 26/6/72.
Ngirumpatse Ntamuhanga (Mpene, Ijwi Sud) 23/6/72.
Ngonyosi Rutegamabuko (Bukinanyana, Ijwi Nord) 7/5/74.
Ngonyoze Ndababonye (Mubale, Ijwi Sud) 5/6/72.
Ngonyozi Bifuko (Bukinyanyana, Ijwi Nord) 10/5/74.
Ngotanyi Minani (Ngula, Ijwi Nord) 15/5/74.
Ngwarha (Bushake, Ijwi Sud) 9/5/72.
Ngwarha Birongo (Kishenyi, Ijwi Nord) 27/1/73.
Ngwasi (Musama, Ijwi Sud) 3/3/72; 4/3/72; 25/3/72; 5/5/72; 25/6/74; 12/10/74.
Ngwasi Sevumba (Mazina, Ijwi Sud) 13/6/72.
Ngwije (Thomas) (Nkonde, Ijwi Sud) 22/6/72; 29/6/72.
Nkotanyi (Ngula, Ijwi Nord) 15/5/74.
Nkuruziza Kabulibuli (Ntalangwa, Ijwi Sud) 26/5/72; 27/5/72.
Nkwali (Ntalengwa, Ijwi Sud) 27/5/72.
Ntabandagaro (Muhyahya, Ijwi Sud) 4/2/72.
Ntabugulwakise (Bukenge, Ijwi Nord) 1/5/74.
Ntahonde Nyerezi (Kinji, Ijwi Nord) 3/5/74.
Ntakebuka (Bukinanyana, Ijwi Nord) 8/5/74.
Ntamati (Bukole, Ijwi Nord) 6/2/73.
Ntambuka Barhahakana (Rambo, Ijwi Sud) 28/12/70; 11/1/72; 13/1/72; 20/4/72;
    21/4/72; 26/4/72; 21/5/72; 21/1/73; 9/3/73; 19/3/73; 21/3/73; 11/9/74; 13/9/74;
    19/3/75.
Ntambuka (Benoit) (Ntalangwa, Ijwi Sud) 26/6/72.
Ntambuka Nsibula (Karama, Ijwi Sud) 28/12/70; 14/3/72; 15/3/72; 16/3/72;
    14/9/72.
Ntamire (Kamole, Ijwi Nord) 7/2/73.
Ntamuhanga (Mpene, Ijwi Sud) 23/6/72.
Ntamusige (Buzibu, Ijwi Sud) 15/4/72.
Ntamusige (Mazina, Ijwi Sud) 13/6/72.
Ntamusige (Nkonde, Ruhundu, Ijwi Sud) 22/6/72.
Ntamusige Bihumire (Cibanda, Ijwi Nord) 25/5/74.
Ntamusige Bingwana (Mubale, Ijwi Sud) 8/6/72.
Ntasongero Muhindo (Lushindi, Ijwi Sud) 9/6/72.
Ntati Shebikoma (Ntalangwa, Ijwi Sud) 27/5/72.
Ntayira (Kimomo, Ijwi Sud) 15/5/72.

Ntayire Cifuno (Kisheke, Ijwi Nord) 28/5/74.
Ntundanyi Kagulu (Kamole, Ijwi Nord) 7/2/73.
Ntwarane (Bushovu, Ijwi Sud) 8/5/72.
Nyabwiguli (Cugi, Ijwi Nord) 25/1/73.
Nyaburungu (Kilala, Ijwi Sud) 8/6/72.
Nyakabingo Mabangara (Kihumba, Ijwi Nord) 3/2/73.
Nyakahama Bazamuka (Buruhuka, Ijwi Nord) 16/2/73.
Nyakahomo Ntalengwa (Bwiiru, Ijwi Sud) 8/3/72.
Nyamienda (Mugote, Ijwi Sud) 17/3/72; 25/3/72.
Nyamigorha (Nkuvu, Ijwi Sud) 27/4/72; 28/4/72.
Nyamirali Ruvuma (Muziri, Ijwi Nord) 6/5/74.
Nyamorha Ntambara (Kimomo, Ijwi Sud) 15/5/72.
Nyamuga Mulengero (Bugarula, Ijwi Nord) 1/12/72.
Nyamuhaga (Kamole, Ijwi Nord) 7/2/73.
Nyamuhamba Gahamire (Bukinanyana, Ijwi Nord) 8/5/74.
Nyamuhara Ndahaliza (Lushindi, Ijwi Sud) 9/6/72.
Nyamuheshera (Karhongo, Ijwi Sud) 10/2/72; 17/5/72; 18/5/72; 27/5/72; 27/6/72.
Nyamuhuku Munyakalinga (Kimomo, Ijwi Sud) 16/5/72.
Nyamulinda Musole Munyali (Ishungu) 9/8/72.
Nyamulisa Bihangi (Buhagwa, Ijwi Sud) 31/5/72.
Nyamushara (Mazina, Ijwi Sud) 13/6/72.
Nyamwegama Minana (Mpene, Ijwi Sud) 26/1/72; 23/6/72.
Nyamwigura (Bulehe, Ijwi Nord) 31/1/73.
Nyamwigura (Nkuvu, Ijwi Sud) 27/4/72.
Nyamwigura Shabuzeni (Muziri, Ijwi Nord) 8/5/74.
Nyandekwa Mbavu Bafokulera (Nyakibamba, Ijwi Sud) 29/4/72.
Nyangurane (Lweza, Ijwi Nord) 22/5/74.
Nyangurane Nyamulinda (Gashara, Ijwi Sud) 24/5/72.
Nyantaba Zahura (Bweshu, Ijwi Nord) 20/2/73.
Nyenyezi (Bushovu, Ijwi Sud) 4/5/72; 8/5/72.
Nyenyezi (Karhongo, Ijwi Sud) 9/2/72; 17/2/72; 18/3/72; 17/5/72; 21/1/73; 2/1/75.
Nyenyezi Mabwiiru (Ngula, Ijwi Nord) 15/5/74.
Nyirinkinde Vinerandi (Boza, Ijwi Sud) 1/5/72.
Nzibukira (Bukere, Ijwi Sud) 8/3/72.
Nzibukira Bayongu (Kagushu, Ijwi Nord) 18/5/74.
Nzibukiya (Buholo II, Ijwi Sud) 1/3/72.
Nzigi (Rambo, Ijwi Sud) 29/6/72.
Placide (Bwando, Ijwi Sud) 28/3/72.
Rienzi Buhuzu (Bukole, Ijwi Nord) 8/2/73.
Rubagincura (Nkuvu, Ijwi Sud) 28/4/72.
Rubaka Bikura Kalyoko (Muganzu, Ijwi Nord) 9/2/73.
Rubambiza (Mugorhe, Ijwi Sud) 18/3/72; 17/6/74; 22/6/74; 23/6/74; 24/6/74;
    26/6/74; 20/3/75.
Rubambiza Birega (Burhonga, Ijwi Nord) 15/2/73.
Rubambiza Muhindu (Cugi, Ijwi Nord) 25/1/73.
Rubambura (Buruhuka, Ijwi Nord) 16/2/73.

Rubambura (Cinji, Ijwi Nord) 3/5/74.
Rubambura Kaboye (Gashiraboba, Ijwi Nord) 13/5/74; 15/5/74.
Rubangu Kanyarugunda (Ntalangwa, Ijwi Sud) 26/5/72.
Rubanganjura (Nkuvu, Ijwi Sud) 28/4/72.
Rubanguka (Bulegeyi, Ijwi Sud) 2/5/72.
Rubangura (Buholo, Ijwi Sud) 11/2/72.
Rubara (Musama, Ijwi Sud) 3/3/72.
Rubasha (Mugorhe, Ijwi Sud) 24/3/72.
Rubenga (Buholo II, Ijwi Sud) 2/3/72.
Rubenga (Karhongo, Ijwi Sud) 17/2/72; 18/5/72.
Rubenga (Muhungwe, Ijwi Sud) 12/6/72; 29/6/72.
Rubenga Mulembi (Bushovu, Ijwi Sud) 4/5/72.
Rubenga Rukundumwami (Karhongo, Ijwi Sud) 18/5/72.
Rubibi Mungereza (Bunyama, Ijwi Sud) 29/5/72; 3/6/72.
Rubihya (Bukinanyana, Ijwi Nord) 9/5/74.
Rubimbura Ntawabo (Kinji, Ijwi Nord) 3/5/74.
Ruboneza (Mubale, Ijwi Sud) 10/6/72.
Rucoca (Bweshu, Ijwi Nord) 20/2/73.
Rugali Rwahunga (Ntalangwa, Ijwi Sud) 26/5/72.
Rugalika Musaka (Ishungu) 7/8/72.
Rugo (Mugorhe, Ijwi Sud) 14/6/74; 17/6/74; 22/6/74; 20/3/75.
Rugwira Mugondobondo (Buhumba, Ijwi Sud) 26/6/72.
Ruhamanya Bitate (Ishungu) 8/8/72; 9/8/72.
Ruhangamugabo (Buruhuka, Ijwi Nord) 17/2/73.
Ruhangara (Mugorhe, Ijwi Sud) 20/3/72.
Ruhembe (Nkuvu, Ijwi Sud) 27/4/72; 2/5/72.
Ruhingana (Kimomo, Ijwi Sud) 16/5/72.
Ruhingana Bayanga (Burhonga, Ijwi Nord) 15/2/73.
Ruhingana Gahusi (Bunyama, Ijwi Sud) 3/6/72.
Ruhinganya Binobinji (Kimomo, Ijwi Sud) 16/5/72.
Ruhinganya Mbuga (Bwando, Ijwi Sud) 28/3/72.
Ruhirika Sekanabanga (Karama, Ijwi Sud) 14/6/72.
Ruhoya (Bukere, Ijwi Sud) 7/3/72; 8/3/72.
Ruhoyi Kerhakubwa (Buhumba, Ijwi Sud) 26/6/72.
Ruhoza Muhanya (Bulegeyi, Ijwi Sud) 1/2/72.
Ruhumuza Busoro (Butyangali, Ijwi Sud) 8/3/72.
Ruhwika (Kamole, Ijwi Nord) 7/2/73.
Rukanika (Lweza, Ijwi Nord) 21/5/74; 1/6/74; 11/6/74.
Rukanika (Nkuvu, Ijwi Sud) 27/4/72; 28/4/72.
Rukomera (Lubuye, Ijwi Sud) 21/3/72.
Rulinda (Mpene, Ijwi Sud) 17/4/72; 22/6/72; 23/6/72.
Runesha Minani (Kasihe, Ijwi Sud) 24/6/72.
Runiga (Kimomo, Ijwi Sud) 15/5/72.
Rurayi Kikere (Rambo, Ijwi Sud) 29/6/72.
Rusaku Byahingane (Bukenga, Ijwi Nord) 26/4/74.
Rushara Gashamangali (Mulamba, Ijwi Nord) 14/2/73.

Rusingiza (Lushindi, Ijwi Sud) 10/6/72; 19/6/72.
Rusumbantwali (Bweshu, Ijwi Nord) 20/2/73; 29/2/73.
Rusumbantwali Bayongwa (Karhongo, Ijwi Sud) 27/6/72.
Rutaguranura Senabandi (Mulamba, Ijwi Sud) 1/6/72.
Rutebuka Gahunga (Lemera, Ijwi Sud) 7/6/72.
Rutengura Shamazi (Mulamba, Ijwi Nord) 14/2/73.
Ruvugwa Nyakaboko (Mubale, Ijwi Sud) 5/6/72.
Ruvugwa Paul (Bwando, Ijwi Sud) 27/3/72; 28/3/72.
Ruyenzi (Bukole, Ijwi Nord) 8/2/73.
Ruyenzi Bunyagara (Nkola, Ijwi Nord) 30/4/74.
Ruyenzi Manihaburwa (Bunyakiri, Ijwi Nord) 12/2/73.
Ruzigamanzi (Bwando, Ijwi Sud) 29/3/72.
Ruzigamanzi Seebundo (Bunyama, Ijwi Sud) 30/5/72.
Ruzihimo Burhano (Bukinanyana, Ijwi Nord) 10/5/74.
Ruzihiro (Bukinanyana, Ijwi Nord) 10/5/74.
Ruziraboba (Karama, Ijwi Sud) 15/6/72.
Rwabaduka Semutwa (Kisheke, Ijwi Nord) 30/5/74.
Rwagaya (Karama, Ijwi Sud) 14/6/72.
Rwakageyo (Buzigaziga, Ijwi Sud) 11/3/72; 13/3/72; 9/5/72.
Rwakegeyo (Kisheke, Ijwi Nord) 31/5/74.
Rwambaguma Nkungirwa (Kishenyi, Ijwi Nord) 2/2/73.
Rwango (Bweshu, Ijwi Nord) 20/2/73.
Rwangoko Maragane Lukwebo (Bugarula, Ijwi Nord) 27/4/74.
Rwankuba (Bukere, Ijwi Sud) 8/3/72.
Rwantunda (Bwando, Ijwi Sud) 30/3/72.
Rwema Cikuta (Ishungu) 12/8/72.
Rwesi (Bwando, Ijwi Sud) 30/3/72.
Rwesi (Mpene, Ijwi Sud) 14/1/72; 25/1/72; 18/4/72; 23/6/72; 20/6/74.
Rwesi Hakizumwami (Muziri, Ijwi Nord) 6/5/74.
Rwesingisa Mideso (Buzibu, Ijwi Sud) 28/1/72.
Rwisamanga Kampanda (Ishungu) 7/8/72.
Sagatwa (Cassi, Ijwi Sud) 1/2/72.
Sakari (Musama, Ijwi Sud) 3/3/72.
Sangara Sinzahera (Mpene, Ijwi Sud) 24/1/72.
Sanvura (Bulegeyi, Ijwi Sud) 1/5/72.
Sebisaho Ndayelire (Bukinanyana, Ijwi Nord) 7/5/74.
Semandwa Mumbara (Ngula, Ijwi Nord) 16/5/74.
Semanyeshi Bwirahira Mushengo (Buhagwa, Ijwi Sud) 31/5/72.
Shabahalika (Musama, Ijwi Sud) 3/3/72.
Shabuli (Buzibu, Ijwi Sud) 28/1/72.
Shamavu Garhangali (Gashiraboba, Ijwi Nord) 14/5/74; 16/5/74.
Shamavu Sezikeye (Muganzu, Ijwi Nord) 9/2/73.
Shanzige Ntamusige (Bukole, Ijwi Nord) 8/2/73.
Shebidoka (Bukere, Ijwi Sud) 7/3/72.
Shimbo (Cassi, Ijwi Sud) 1/2/72.
Shumbiika (Mpene-Bwiiru, Ijwi Sud) 24/1/72.

Simuni Nkashi (Buhagwa, Ijwi Sud) 31/5/72.
Sirazi Bulungu (Bulehe, Ijwi Nord) 31/1/73.
Siribo Gashamura (Cugi, Ijwi Nord) 25/1/73.
Sogoro (Bwando, Ijwi Sud) 30/3/72.
Taracise Timbiri Ruvudukana (Mubale, Ijwi Sud) 5/6/72.
Tegera Rwamagira (Buhagwa, Ijwi Sud) 30/5/72.
Vandire Habimana (Buyumbu, Ijwi Nord) 30/1/73.
Vuye-Kurhe (Jean) (Muhyahya, Ijwi Sud) 4/2/72.
Waberagirwa Ntamati (Bukole, Ijwi Nord) 6/2/73.
Warhubwene Rhutarhushu (Cassi, Ijwi Sud) 31/1/72.
Wihorehe Semikiro (Boza, Ijwi Sud) 11/5/72.
Yamba Yamba (Bukole, Ijwi Nord) 6/2/73.
Zabika Kabengerezo (Buruhuka, Ijwi Nord) 17/2/73.
Zabona (Bwiiru, Ijwi Sud) 6/3/72.
Zabona (Nkola, Ijwi Nord) 12/9/73; 20/9/73; 2/5/74.
Zahiga Kabego (Paulo) (Bukere, Ijwi Sud) 14/6/74; 12/10/74.
Zahinda (Bugarula, Ijwi Nord) 14/5/74.
Zahura (Bwando, Ijwi Sud) 30/3/72.
Zaluka (Butyangali, Ijwi Sud) 9/2/72.
Zaluka (Michel) (Kimomo, Ijwi Sud) 15/5/72.
Zirazi Mayabera (Buholo, Ijwi Sud) 8/2/72.

Bibliography

The following abbreviations are used in this bibliography:

ARSC: Académie Royale des Sciences Coloniales.
ARSOM: Académie Royale des Sciences d'Outre-Mer.
CEDAF: Centre d'Etude et de Documentation Africaines.
CELA: Centre d'Etude des Langues Africaines (Bukavu, Zaire).
IRCB: Institut Royal Colonial Belge.
IRSAC: Institut de Recherches Scientifiques en Afrique Centrale.
ISP: Institut Supérieur Pédagogique (Université Nationale du Zaire).
MRAC: Musée Royal de l'Afrique Centrale.
UNR: Université Nationale du Rwanda.

Alnaes, K. "Nyamayongi's Song: An Analysis of a Konzo Circumcision Song." *Africa* 37, 4 (1967): 453–65.

Amselle, J.-L., and E. M'Bokolo, eds. *Au coeur de l'ethnie.* Paris: Editions la Découverte, 1985.

Anderson, C., F. von der Mehden, and M. C. Young. *Issues in Political Development.* Englewood Cliffs: Prentice-Hall, 1967.

Arnoux, A. "Le culte de la société sécrète des imandwa au Ruanda." *Anthropos* 7 (1912): 273–95, 529–58, 840–74; 8 (1913): 110–34, 754–74.

Barns, T. A. *Across the Great Craterland to the Congo.* London: Benn, 1923.

Barth, F., ed. *Ethnic Groups and Boundaries.* London: Allen and Unwin, 1969.

Bashizi, C. "Histoire du Kivu: Sources écrites et perspectives d'avenir." *Likundoli* 4, 2 (1976): 65–113.

Bashizi, C. "Paysannat et salariat agricole rural au Bushi, 1920–1960." Ph.D. diss., Université de Lubumbashi, 1981.

Bashizi, T. Z. "De la relégation dans l'ancien territoire de Kalehe (1920–1964)." Mémoire de License, ISP–Bukavu, 1982.

Bayange Mudahigwa. "L'évolution du régime foncier coutumier et le problème des terres dans la Zone d'Idjwi sous les Basibula." Mémoire de Licence, ISP–Bukavu, 1984.

Beattie, J. "Nyoro Kinship." *Africa* 27, 4 (1957): 317–39.

Beattie, J. "Nyoro Marriage and Affinity." *Africa* 28, 1 (1958): 1–22.

Beattie, J. "Rituals of Nyoro Kingship." *Africa* 29, 2 (1959): 134–44.

Beidelman, T. O. "Swazi Royal Ritual." *Africa* 36, 4 (1966): 373–405.

Bender, T. *Community and Social Change in America*. Baltimore: Johns Hopkins University Press, 1978.

Berger, I. "The Kubandwa Religious Complex of Interlacustrine East Africa: An Historical Study, c. 1500–1900. Ph.D. diss., University of Wisconsin–Madison, 1973.

Berger, I. *Religion and Resistance. East African Kingdoms in the Precolonial Period*. Tervuren: MRAC, 1981.

Biebuyck, D. "Les divisions du jour et de la nuit chez les Nyanga." *Aequatoria* 21, 4 (1958): 134–38.

Biebuyck, D. *Hero and Chief: Epic Literature from the Banyanga (Zaire Republic)*. Berkeley: University of California Press, 1978.

Biebuyck, D. *De Hond bij de Nyanga: Ritueel en sociologie*. Bruxelles: ARSOM, 1956.

Biebuyck, D. *Lega Culture: Art, Initiation and Moral Philosophy among a Central African People*. Berkeley: University of California Press, 1973.

Biebuyck, D. "La Monnaie Musanga des Balega." *Zaïre* 7, 7 (1953): 675–86.

Biebuyck, D. "De Mumbo-instelling bij de Banyanga (Kivu)." *Kongo-Overzee* 21, 5 (1955): 441–48.

Biebuyck, D. "On the Concept of Tribe." *Civilisations* 16, 4 (1966): 500–515.

Biebuyck, D. "L'organisation politique des Banyanga: La chefferie Ihana," *Kongo-Overzee*, Part 1 in 22, 4–5 (1956): 301–41; Part 2 in 23, 1–2 (1957): 58–98.

Biebuyck, D. *Rights in Land and Its Resources among the Nyanga*. Brussels: ARSOM, 1966.

Biebuyck, D. "Six Nyanga Texts." In *A Selection of African Prose*, Vol. 1, ed. W. H. Whitely, 55–61. Oxford: Clarendon Press, 1964.

Biebuyck, D. "La société Kumu face au Kitawala." *Zaïre* 11, 1 (1957): 7–40.

Biebuyck, D., and Mateene Kahombo. *Une anthologie de la littérature orale des Nyanga*. Bruxelles: ARSOM, 1970.

Biebuyck, D., and Mateene Kahombo. *The Mwindo Epic from the Banyanga*, recited by Candi Rureke. Berkeley: University of California Press, 1969.

Biraro Wakumona. "Evolution des formations médicales à Idjwi, 1928–81." Travail de Fin d'Etudes, ISP–Bukavu, 1982.

Birdsall, R. *Berkshire County: A Cultural History*. New Haven: Yale University Press, 1959.

Birhakaheka Njiga and Kirhero Nsibula. "Nyangezi dans ces relations commerciales avec le Rwanda, le Burundi, et le Bufulero (fin XIXe siècle—début XXe siècle)." *Etudes rwandaises* 14, 1 (1981): 36–51.

Bishikwabo Chubaka. "Le Bushi au XIXe siècle: Un peuple, sept royaumes." *Revue française d'histoire d'outre-mer* 47, 1–2 (1980): 89–98.

Bishikwabo Chubaka. "Histoire d'un état Shi en Afrique des Grands Lacs: Kaziba au Zaïre (c. 1850–1940)." Ph.D. diss., Université de Louvain-la Neuve, 1982.

Bishikwabo Chubaka. "Mythes d'origine et croyances religieuses: Bases d'une communauté de royauté Interlacustre dans l'est du Kivu." In *La civilisation ancienne des peuples des Grands Lacs*, ed. L. Ndoricimpa et al., 64–80. Paris: Karthala, 1981.

Bishikwabo Chubaka. "Notes sur l'origine de l'institution du bwami et fondements du pouvoir politique au Kivu oriental." *Les Cahiers du CEDAF* (1979, 8).

Bishikwabo Chubaka. "L'origine des chefferies de l'ouest de la Ruzizi: Bufulero, Buvira et Burundi au XIX–XXe siècle." *Culture et société: Revue de civilisation burundaise* 4 (1981): 107–21.

Bishikwabo Chubaka and D. Newbury. "Recent Research in the Area of Lake Kivu: Rwanda and Zaire." *History in Africa* 7 (1980): 23–45.

Bloch, M. *From Blessing to Violence: History and Ideology in the Circumcision Ritual of the Merina of Madagascar.* Cambridge: Cambridge University Press, 1986.

Bloch, M. "The Past and the Present in the Present." *Man*, n.s. 12 (1977): 278–92.

Bloch, M. *Ritual, History and Power: Selected Papers in Anthropology.* London: Athlone Press for the London School of Economics, 1989.

Bloch, M. "The Ritual of the Royal Bath in Madagascar." In *Rituals of Royalty*, ed. D. Cannadine and S. Price, 271–97. Cambridge: Cambridge University Press, 1987.

Bloch, M. "Symbols, Song, Dance and Features of Articulation: Is Religion an Extreme Form of Traditional Authority?" *Archives européennes de sociologie* 15, 1 (1974): 55–81.

Botte, R. "De quoi vivait l'état?" *Cahiers d'études africaines* 22, 3–4 (1982): 277–325.

Botte, R. "La guerre interne au Burundi." In *Guerres des lignages et guerres d'états en Afrique*, ed. J. Bazin and E. Terray, 271–317. Paris: Editions des Archives Contemporaines, 1982.

Botte, R. "Processus de formation d'une classe sociale dans une société africaine précapitaliste." *Cahiers d'études africaines* 14, 4 (1974): 605–26.

Botte, R. "Rwanda and Burundi, 1889–1930: Chronology of a Slow Assassination." *International Journal of African Historical Studies* 18 (1985): no. 1, 53–91; no. 2, 289–314.

Bourgeois, R. *Banyarwanda et Barundi.* Vol. 1. *Ethnographie.* Bruxelles: ARSC, 1957.

Bourgeois, R. *Banyarwanda et Barundi.* Vol. 3. *Religion et magie.* Bruxelles: ARSC, 1956.

Bourgeois, R. "Le pacte du sang au Bushi (cihango ou kunywana)." *Bulletin des juridictions indigènes et du droit coutumier congolais* 27, 2 (1959): 33–36.

Bourgeois, R. "Le pacte du sang au Rwanda." *Bulletin des juridictions indigènes et du droit coutumier congolais* 25, 2 (1957): 39–42.

Boyer, P., and S. Nissenbaum. *Salem Possessed: The Social Origins of Witchcraft.* Cambridge: Harvard University Press, 1974.

Bucyalimwe Mararo. "Land Conflict in Masisi, Eastern Zaïre: The Impact and Aftermath of Belgian Colonial Policy, 1920–1989." Ph.D. diss., Indiana University, 1990.

Bucyalimwe Mararo. "Une rationalisation? Les migrations rwandaises au Kivu, Zaïre." In *Ambiguité de l'innovation: Sociétés rurales et technologies en Afrique centrale et occidentale au XXe siècle*, ed. B. Jewsiewicki and J.-P. Chrétien, 39–54. Québec: Safi Press, 1984.

Bushige Barume and Munganga Byabuze. "Relations socio-économiques entre Idjwi et ses régions périphériques." Travail de Fin d'Etudes, ISP–Bukavu, 1987.

Cannadine, D., and S. Price, eds. *Rituals of Royalty.* Cambridge: Cambridge University Press, 1987.

CELA. "Histoire des Bahunde." Unpublished typescript. White Fathers, Bukavu, n.d.

CELA. "Histoire des Havu." Unpublished typescript. White Fathers, Bukavu, n.d. (1961?).

Chrétien, J.-P. "Les années de l'éleusine, du sorgho, et du haricot dans l'ancien Burundi: Ecologie et idéologie." *African Economic History* 7 (1979): 75–92.

Chrétien, J.-P. "Le Buha à la fin du XIXe siècle: Un peuple, six royaumes." *Etudes d'histoire africaine* 7 (1975): 9–38.

Chrétien, J.-P. "Echanges et hiérarchies dans les royaumes des Grands Lacs de l'est africain." *Annales: économies, sociétés, civilisations* 29, 6 (1974): 1327–37.

Chrétien, J.-P. "La révolte de Ndungutse (1912). Forces traditionnelles et pression coloniale au Rwanda allemand." *Revue française d'histoire d'outre-mer* 59, 4 (1972): 645–80.

Chrétien, J.-P. "La royauté capture les rois." Addendum to P. Ndayishinguje, *L'intronisation d'un mwami*, 61–70. Nanterre: Laboratoire d'ethnologie et de sociologie comparative, 1977.

Chrétien, J.-P. "Le sorgho dans l'agriculture, la culture, et l'histoire du Burundi." *Journal des africanistes* 52, 1–2 (1982): 145–62.

Chrétien, J.-P., and E. Mworoha. "Mwezi Gisabo et le maintien d'une fragile indépendance au Burundi." In *Les africains*, Vol. 2, ed. C. A. Julien, 251–76. Paris: Editions J. A., 1977.

Chrétien, J.-P. and E. Mworoha. "Les tombeaux des bami du Burundi: Un aspect de la monarchie sacrée en Afrique orientale." *Cahiers d'études africaines* 10, 1 (1970): 40–79.

Ciribagula, A. "Histoire des rois du Buhaya" [Ecicisi c'Obwami e Buhaya]. Unpublished typescript. CELA, Bukavu.

Codere, H. *The Biography of an African Society: Rwanda 1900–1960.* Tervuren: MRAC, 1973.

Codere, H. "Power in Ruanda," *Anthropologica* (Canada), n.s. 4, 1 (1962): 45–85.

Cohen, D. W. "Precolonial History as the History of 'Society'." *African Studies Review* 17, 2 (1974): 467–72.

Cohen, D. W. *Womunafu's Bunafu. A Study of Authority in a Nineteenth Century Community.* Princeton: Princeton University Press, 1977.

Cohen, R. "Oedipus Rex and Regina." *Africa* 47, 1 (1977): 11–31.

Colle, P. "Au pays Bashi." *Congo* 6, 1 (1925): 399–404.

Colle, P. "Les clans au pays des Bashi." *Congo* 3, 1 (1922): 337–52.

Colle, P. *Monographie des Bashi.* 2nd ed. Bukavu: CELA, 1971; originally published 1937.

Colle, P. "L'organisation politique des Bashi." *Congo* 2, 2 (1921): 657–84.

Comaroff, J. *Body of Power, Spirit of Resistance: The Culture and History of a South African People.* Chicago: University of Chicago Press, 1985.

Comaroff, J. L. "Of Totemism and Ethnicity." *Ethnos* 52, 3–4 (1987): 301–22.

Corti, B. *Les mois du sorgho.* Bruxelles: Charles Dessart, 1955.

Cuypers, J. B. *L'alimentation chez les Shi.* Tervuren: MRAC, 1970.

Cuypers, J. B. "Les Bantous Interlacustres du Kivu." In *Introduction à l'ethnographie du Congo*, by J. Vansina, 201–11. Kinshasa: Editions Universitaires du Congo, 1965.

Cuypers, J. B. "Les relations sociales et les attitudes entre Shi (Bantu) et Rhwa (pygmées) à l'ouest du Lac Kivu." In *Proceedings of the East African Institute of Social Research Conference*. Kampala: East African Institute of Social Research, 1963.

d'Arianoff, A. *Histoire des Bagesera, souverains de Gisaka*. Bruxelles: IRCB, 1952.

Davis, N. Z. *Society and Culture in Early Modern France*. Palo Alto: Stanford University Press, 1975.

de Heusch, L. *Ecrits sur la royauté sacrée*. Bruxelles: Editions de l'Université de Bruxelles, 1987.

de Heusch, L. *Essais sur le symbolisme de l'inceste royale en Afrique*. Bruxelles: Université Libre de Bruxelles, 1958.

de Heusch, L. "Mythe et société féodale. Le culte du Kubandwa dans le Rwanda traditionnel." *Archives de sociologie des religions* 9, 18 (1964): 133–46.

de Heusch, L. *Rois nés d'un coeur de vache*. Paris: Gallimard, 1982.

de Heusch, L. *Le Rwanda et la civilisation Interlacustre*. Bruxelles: Université Libre de Bruxelles, 1966.

de Lacger, L. *Ruanda*. 2nd ed. Kabgayi, Rwanda: Imprimérie de Kabgayi, 1961; originally published 1939.

de Ligne, A. *Africa: L'évolution d'un continent vue des volcans du Kivu*. Bruxelles: Librairie générale, 1961.

Delmas, L. *Généalogies de la noblesse du Ruanda*. Kabgayi, Rwanda: Vicariat apostolique du Ruanda, 1950.

de Mahieu, W. "Cosmologie et structuration de l'espace chez les Komo." *Africa* 45 (1975): 123–38, 236–57.

de Mahieu, W. "A l'intersection du temps et de l'espace dans l'histoire des idéologies: L'exemple Kumu." *Cultures et développement* 40 (1979): 415–37.

de Mahieu, W. *Structures et symboles*. Londres: International African Institute, 1980.

de Mahieu, W. "Le temps dans la culture Komo." *Africa* 43, 1 (1973): 2–17.

Depelchin, J. M. F. "From Precapitalism to Imperialism: A History of Social and Economic Formations in Eastern Zaire (Uvira Zone, c. 1800–1965)." Ph.D. diss., Stanford University, 1974.

Des Forges, A. "Court and Corporations in the Development of the Rwandan State." Unpublished manuscript.

Des Forges, A. "Defeat Is the Only Bad News: Rwanda under Musinga, 1896–1931." Ph.D. diss., Yale University, 1972.

Des Forges, A. " 'The Drum Is Greater Than the Shout': The 1912 Rebellion in Northern Rwanda." In *Banditry, Rebellion, and Social Protest in Africa*, ed. D. Crummey, 311–33. London: James Currey, 1986.

de Wet, J. M. J. "Domestication of African Cereals." *African Economic History* 3 (1977): 15–33.

d'Hertefelt, M. *Les Clans du Rwanda ancien. Eléments d'ethno-sociologie et d'ethno-histoire*. Tervuren: MRAC, 1971.

d'Hertefelt, M. "Huwelijk, familie en aanverwantschap bij de Reera (Noordwestelijk Rwaanda)." *Zaïre* 13 (1959): no. 2, 115–48; no. 3, 243–85.

d'Hertefelt, M. "Le Rwanda." In *Les anciens royaumes de la zone interlacustre méridionale*, ed. M. d'Hertefelt, A. A. Trouwborst, and J. H. Scherer, 9–112. Tervuren: MRAC, 1962.

d'Hertefelt, M. "The Rwanda of Rwanda." In *The Peoples of Africa*, ed. J. M. Gibbs, 403–40. New York: Holt, Rinehart, and Winston, 1965.

d'Hertefelt, M., and A. Coupez, eds. *La royauté sacrée de l'ancien Rwanda*. Tervuren: MRAC, 1964.

d'Hertefelt, M., A. A. Trouwborst, J. H. Scherer, eds. *Les anciens royaumes de la zone interlacustre méridionale*. Tervuren: MRAC, 1962.

Dikonda wa Lumanyisha. "Les rites chez les Bashi et les Bahavu." Ph.D. diss., Université Libre de Bruxelles, 1971.

Durkheim, E., and M. Mauss. *Primitive Classification*. Chicago: University of Chicago Press, 1963.

Edel, M. *The Chiga of Southwestern Uganda*. London: International African Institute, 1957.

Ehret, C. "Patterns of Bantu and Central Sudanic Settlement in Central and Southern Africa, c. 1000 BC–500 AD." *Transafrican Journal of History* 3, 2 (1973): 1–21.

Epstein, A. *Politics in an Urban African Community*. Manchester: Manchester University Press for the Institute of African Studies, University of Zambia, 1973; originally published 1958.

Evans-Pritchard, E. E. "The Divine Kingship of the Shilluk." In his *Essays in Social Anthropology*, 66–86. London: Faber and Faber, 1962; originally published 1948.

Fallers, M. C. *The Eastern Lacustrine Bantu*. London: International African Institute, 1960.

Fox-Genovese, E., and E. Genovese. "The Political Crisis of Social History: Class Struggle as Subject and Object." In their *Fruits of Merchant Capital: Slavery and Bourgeois Property in the Rise and Expansion of Capitalism*, 179–212. Oxford: Oxford University Press, 1983.

Freedman, J. M. "Joking, Affinity, and the Exchange of Ritual Services among the Kiga of Northern Rwanda: An Essay in Joking Relationship Theory." *Man*, n.s. 12, 1 (1977): 154–65.

Freedman, J. M. *Nyabingi: The Social History of an African Deity*. Tervuren: MRAC, 1984.

Freedman, J. M. "Principles of Relationship in Rwandan Kiga Society." Ph.D. diss., Princeton University, 1974.

Freedman, J. M. "Three Muraris, Three Gahayas, and the Four Phases of Nyabingi." In *Chronology, Migration, and Drought in Interlacustrine Africa*, ed. J. B. Webster, 175–87. New York: Africana, 1979.

Gahama, J. *Le Burundi sous administration belge*. Paris: Karthala, 1983.

Gahama, J. "La disparition du Muganuro." In *L'arbre-mémoire: Traditions orales du Burundi*, ed. L. Ndoricimpa et al., 169–95. Paris: Karthala, 1984.

Gakaniisha, C. *Récits historiques Rwanda*, ed. A. Coupez and T. Kamanzi. Tervuren: MRAC, 1962.

Gérard, J. "La grande initiation chez les Bakumu du nord-est et les populations avoisinantes." *Zaïre* 10, 1 (1956): 87–94.

Gille, A. "Notes sur l'organisation des Barundi." *Bulletin des juridictions indigènes et du droit coutumier congolais* 5, 3 (1937): 75–81.

Gille, A. "L'*Umuganuro* ou la fête du sorgho en Urundi." *Bulletin des juridictions indigènes et du droit coutumier congolais* 14, 11 (1946): 368–71.

Gluckman, M. "Rituals of Rebellion in South East Africa." In his *Order and Rebellion in Tribal Africa*, 110–37. London: Cohen and West, 1963; originally published 1954.

Gorju, J. *Entre le Victoria, l'Albert, et l'Edouard*. Rennes, La Belgique: Procure des Pères Blancs, 1920.

Gorju, J., et al. *Face au royaume Hamite du Rwanda: Le royaume frère de l'Urundi*. Bruxelles: Bibliothèque Congo, 1938.

Gravel, P. "The Transfer of Cows in Gisaka (Rwanda): A Mechanism for Recording Social Relationships." *American Anthropologist* 69, 3 (1967): 322–31.

Gross, R. A. *The Minutemen and Their World*. New York: Hill and Wang, 1976.

Hartwig, G. *The Art of Survival in East Africa: The Kerebe and Long Distance Trade*. New York: Africana, 1976.

Hiernaux, J. "Note sur un ancien population du Ruanda-Urundi: Les Renge." *Zaïre* 10, 4 (1956): 351–60.

Hiernaux, J., and E. Maquet. "Cultures préhistoriques de l'âge des métaux au Ruanda-Urundi et au Kivu (Congo belge). Première partie." ARSC, *Bulletin des séances* 2, 6 (1957): 1126–49.

Hiernaux, J., and E. Maquet. *Cultures préhistoriques de l'âge des métaux au Ruanda-Urundi et au Kivu (Congo belge), IIe partie; suivi de: Deux sites archéologiques à briques en territoire Walikale (Kivu)*. Bruxelles: ARSOM, 1960.

Hiernaux, J., and E. Maquet. "Un haut fourneau préhistorique au Buhunde (Kivu, Congo Belge)." *Zaïre* 8, 6 (1954): 615–19.

Historique et chronologie du Rwanda. Kabgayi: Vicariat apostolique du Ruanda [1956].

"History and Theory: An Editorial." *History Workshop Journal* 6 (1978): 1–6.

Hobsbawm, E. J. *Nations and Nationalism since 1780*. Cambridge: Cambridge University Press, 1990.

Hocart, A. M. *Kings and Councillors*, ed. R. Needham. Chicago: University of Chicago Press, 1970; originally published 1936.

Hubert, H., and M. Mauss. *Sacrifice: Its Nature and Function*. Chicago: University of Chicago Press, 1964.

Iluba Kisungi wa Bule. "Evolution des structures agraires chez les Basile: Zone de Mwenga." *Antennes: Bulletin du CERUKI* (Bukavu, Zaire) 2, 2 (1974): 165–215.

Jensen, J. "Die Erweiterung des Lungerfisch-clans in Buganda (Uganda) durch den Anschlush von Bayuma-Gruppen." *Sociologus* 19, 2 (1962): 153–66.

Johanssen, E. *Ruanda: Kleine Anfange-grosse Aufgaben der evangelischen Mission im Zwischenseengebiet Deutsch-Ostafrikas*. Bethel bei Bielefeld: Verlagshandlung der Anstalt Bethel, 1912.

Judt, T. "A Clown in Regal Purple: Social History and the Historians." *History Workshop Journal* 7 (1979): 66–94.

Kagame, A. *Un abrégé de l'ethno-histoire du Rwanda*. Vol. 1. Butare: Editions universitaires du Rwanda, 1972.

Kagame, A. *Un abrégé de l'histoire du Rwanda de 1853 à 1972*. Vol. 2. Butare: Editions universitaires du Rwanda, 1975.

Kagame, A. "Le code ésotérique de la dynastie du Rwanda ancien." *Zaïre* 1, 4 (1947): 363–86.

Kagame, A. *Le code des institutions politiques du Rwanda précolonial*. Bruxelles: IRCB, 1952.

Kagame, A. *L'histoire des armées bovines dans l'ancien Rwanda*. Bruxelles: ARSOM, 1961.

Kagame, A. *Histoire du Rwanda*. Leverville, Congo Belge: Bibliothèque de l'étoile, 1958.

Kagame, A. *Inganji Karinga*, 2 vols. 2nd ed., Kabgayi, Rwanda: n.p., 1959. 1st ed., Butare, n.p., Vol. 1: 1943, Vol. 2: 1947.

Kagame, A. *Les milices du Rwanda précolonial*. Bruxelles: ARSOM, 1963.

Kagame, A. *La notion de génération appliquée à la généalogie dynastique et à l'histoire du Rwanda dès Xe–XIe siècles à nos jours*. Bruxelles: ARSC, 1959.

Kagame, A. *Les organisations socio-familiales de l'ancien Rwanda*. Bruxelles: ARSC, 1954.

Kagame, A. *La poésie dynastique au Rwanda*. Bruxelles: IRCB, 1951.

Kagame, A. "La structure des quinze clans du Rwanda." *Annali Lateranensi* 18 (1955): 103–17.

Kagwa, A. *The Kings of Buganda*, ed. M. S. M. Kiwanuka. Nairobi: East African Publishing House, 1971; originally published 1901.

Kajiga, G. "Marriage coutumier des Bahunde et Bahavu." Unpublished typescript, Mission St. Joseph, Bobandana, Zaire, 1956.

Kalinda Kibanja. "Essai de biographie du Mwami Kalinda Muteso (André) de la chefferie Buhunde, 1904–1976." Travail de Fin d'Etudes, ISP–Bukavu, 1982.

Kandt, R. *Caput Nili*. Berlin: Dietrich Reimer, 1921.

Karugire, S. R. *A History of the Kingdom of Nkore in Western Uganda to 1896*. Oxford: Clarendon, 1971.

Kashamura, A. *Famille, sexualité, et culture*. Paris: Payot, 1973.

Kayondi, C. "Murunga, colline de Burundi: Etude géographique." *Cahiers d'outre-mer* 25, 2 (1972): 164–204.

Kenny, M. G. "The Relation of Oral History to Social Structure in South Nyanza, Kenya." *Africa* 47, 3 (1977): 276–88.

Kirhero N. "Evolution politique des localités de Lugendo et Ishungu (1920–1964)." Mémoire de Licence, ISP–Bukavu, 1977.

Kirk, G. S. *Myth: Its Meaning and Functions*. Berkeley: University of California Press, 1970.

Kiwanuka, M. S. M. *A History of Buganda. From the Foundation to 1900*. London: Longman, 1971.

Kuper, H. *An African Aristocracy*. London: Oxford University Press for the International African Institute, 1947.

Kuper, H. "A Royal Ritual in a Changing Political Context." *Cahiers d'études africaines* 12, 4 (1972): 593–615.

Le Roy Ladurie, E. *Carnival in Romans*. New York: Penguin, 1981.

Le Roy Ladurie, E. *Montaillou*. New York: Vintage, 1979.

Lévi-Strauss, C. *Totemism*. Boston: Beacon Press, 1963; originally published 1962.

Leurquin, P. *Le niveau de vie des populations rurales du Ruanda-Urundi*. Louvain: Nauwelaerts for the Institut de Recherche Economique et Sociale, 1960.

Lockridge, K. A. *A New England Town: The First Hundred Years*. New York: Norton, 1970.

Louis, W. R. *Ruanda-Urundi, 1884–1919*. Oxford: Clarendon, 1963.

Loupias, P. "Traditions et légendes des Batutsi sur la création du monde et leur établissement au Rwanda." *Anthropos* 3, 1 (1908): 1–13.

Lugan, B. "Causes et effets de la famine 'Rumanura' au Rwanda, 1916–1918." *Canadian Journal of African Studies* 10, 2 (1976): 347–56.

Lugan, B. "Echanges et routes commerciales au Rwanda, 1880–1914." *Africa-Tervuren* 22, 2–4 (1976): 33–39.

MacGaffey, W. *Custom and Government in the Lower Congo.* Berkeley: University of California Press, 1970.

MacGaffey, W. "The Policy of National Integration in Zaire." *Journal of Modern African Studies* 20, 1 (1982), 87–105.

Magubane, B. "A Critical Look at Indices Used in the Study of Social Change in Africa." *Current Anthropology* 12, 4–5 (1971): 419–30.

Maquet, J. J. *The Premise of Inequality in Ruanda: A Study of Political Relations in a Central African Kingdom.* London: Oxford University Press for the International African Institute, 1961.

Maquet, J. J. "Rwanda Castes." In *Social Stratification in Africa,* ed. A. Tuden and L. Plotnicov, 93–124. New York: Free Press, 1970.

Maquet, J. J. *Le système des relations sociales dans le Ruanda ancien.* Tervuren: MRAC, 1954.

Masson, P. *Trois siècles chez les Bashi.* 2nd ed. Bukavu: La Presse Congolaise, 1966; originally published, Tervuren: MRAC, 1962.

Mastaki Lwissonga. "Bananier et société à Idjwi." Travail de Fin d'Etudes, ISP–Bukavu, 1982.

Mauss, M. *The Gift.* London: Cohen and West, 1954; originally published 1923–1924.

Meeussen, A. E. "De Talen van Maniema." *Kongo-Overzee* 19, 6 (1953): 385–91.

Meschi, L. "Evolution des structures foncières au Rwanda: Le cas d'un lignage Hutu." *Cahiers d'études africaines* 14, 1 (1974): 39–52.

Meyer, H. *Les Barundi: Une étude ethnologique en Afrique orientale,* ed. and annotated by J.-P. Chrétien. Paris: Société Française d'Histoire d'Outre-Mer, 1984.

Miderho L. "Ciringwi et l'essor de Luhihi (1927–1976)." Travail de Fin d'Etudes, ISP–Bukavu, 1980.

Mitchell, J. C. *The Kalela Dance. Aspects of Social Relationships among Urban Africans in Northern Rhodesia.* Manchester: Manchester University Press for the Rhodes Livingstone Institute, 1956.

Moeller de Laddersous, A. *Les grandes lignes des migrations des Bantous de la Province Orientale au Congo Belge.* Bruxelles: IRCB, 1936.

"Le Mpandi ou le Mubande chez les Banyanga et les Bahunde." Typescript, Mission St. Joseph, Bobandana, Zaire, n.d.

Mugaruka bin Mubibi. "Histoire clanique et évolution des états dans la région sud-ouest du Lac Kivu (dès origines à 1900)." Ph.D. diss., Université de Lubumbashi, 1986.

Muhinyuzi Muhirwa. "L'impact socio-économique de la Société LINEA–Idjwi sur la population d'Idjwi (1927–1973)." Travail de Fin d'Etudes, ISP–Bukavu, 1980.

Muhinyuzi Muhirwa. "Le rôle de la pirogue à Idjwi." Mémoire de Licence, ISP–Bukavu, 1982.

Mulyumba wa Mamba, I. "Aperçu sur la structure politique des Balega-Basile." *Les Cahiers du CEDAF* (1978, 1).

Murhebwa, L. "Histoire politique d'Idjwi sous les Basibula: Essai de périodisation." Travail de Fin d'Etudes, ISP–Bukavu, 1976.

Mushanga, M. T. "The Clan System among the Banyankore." *Uganda Journal* 34, 1 (1970): 29–33.

Mworoha, E. "La cour du roi Mwezi Gisabo (1852–1908) du Burundi à la fin du XIXe siècle." *Etudes d'histoire africaine* 7 (1975): 39–58.

Mworoha, E. *Peuples et rois de l'Afrique des lacs.* Dakar, Sénégal: Les Nouvelles Editions Africaines, 1977.

Mworoha, E., et al. *Histoire du Burundi.* Paris: Hatier, 1987.

Nahimana, F. "Les bami ou roitelets Hutu du corridor Nyabarongo-Mukungwa avec ses régions limitrophes." *Etudes rwandaises* 12, numéro spécial (1979): 1–25.

Nahimana, F. "Les principautés Hutu du Rwanda septentrional." In *La civilisation ancienne des peuples des Grands Lacs,* ed. L. Ndoricimpa, 115–37. Paris: Karthala, 1984.

Ndayishinguje, P. *L'intronisation d'un Mwami.* Nanterre: Laboratoire d'Ethnologie et de Sociologie Comparative, 1977.

Ndikuriyo, A. "Contrats de bétail, contrats de clientèle, et pouvoir politique dans le Butuutsi du XIXe siècle." *Etudes d'histoire africaine* 7 (1975): 59–76.

Ndoricimpa, L. "Du roi fondateur au roi rebelle: Le récit du rebelle dans les traditions orales du Burundi." In *L'arbre-mémoire: Traditions orales du Burundi,* ed. L. Ndoricimpa and C. Guillet, 53–93. Paris: Karthala, 1984.

Nenquin, J. *Contribution to the Study of the Prehistoric Cultures of Rwanda and Burundi.* Tervuren: MRAC, 1967.

Newbury, C. *The Cohesion of Oppression: Clientship and Ethnicity in Rwanda, 1860–1960.* New York: Columbia University Press, 1988.

Newbury, C. "Deux lignages au Kinyaga." *Cahiers d'études africaines* 14, 1 (1974): 26–39.

Newbury, C. "Ethnicity in Rwanda: The Case of Kinyaga." *Africa* 48, 1 (1978): 17–29.

Newbury, D. " 'Bunyabungo': The Western Frontier in Rwanda, c. 1750–1850." In *The African Frontier: The Reproduction of Traditional African Societies,* ed. I. Kopytoff, 162–92. Bloomington: University of Indiana Press, 1986.

Newbury, D. "Bushi and the Historians: Historiographical Themes in Eastern Kivu." *History in Africa* 5 (1978): 131–51.

Newbury, D. "Les campagnes de Rwabugiri: Chronologie et bibliographie." *Cahiers d'études africaines* 14, 1 (1974): 181–92.

Newbury, D. "The Clans of Rwanda: An Historical Hypothesis." *Africa* 50, 4 (1980): 389–403.

Newbury, D. "Cyclic Traditions around Lake Kivu." Paper presented at Research Colloquium, IRSAC, Lwiro, 1975.

Newbury, D. "From Frontier to Boundary: Some Historical Roots of Peasant Strategies of Survival in Zaire." In *The Crisis in Zaire: Myths and Realities,* ed. Nzongola Ntalaja, 87–99. Trenton: Third World Press, 1986.

Newbury, D. "Kamo and Lubambo: Dual Genesis Traditions on Ijwi Island, Zaire." *Les Cahiers du CEDAF* (1979, 5).

Newbury, D. "Kings and Clans: A Social History of Ijwi Island (Zaire), c. 1780–1840." Ph.D. diss., University of Wisconsin–Madison, 1979.

Newbury, D. "Lake Kivu Regional Trade in the Nineteenth Century." *Journal des africanistes* 50, 2 (1980): 6–30.

Newbury, D. "Rwabugiri and Ijwi." *Etudes d'histoire africaine* 7 (1975): 155–75.

Newbury, D. "Sibula, Ruganzu, and Rwanda: A Reconsideration of Rwandan Chronology." Unpublished manuscript.

Newbury, D. "What Role Has Kingship? An Analysis of the *Umuganura* Ritual of Rwanda." *Africa-Tervuren* 27, 4 (1981): 89–101.

Newbury, D., and C. Newbury. "King and Chief on Ijwi Island, Zaire." *International Journal of African Historical Studies* 15, 2 (1982): 221–46.

Ngongo Bisimwa, "Contribution à l'histoire politique du Buhavu: Le Mpinga sous les derniers Basibula." Travail de Fin d'Etudes, ISP–Bukavu, 1985.

Nkongori, L. "Les Bashakamba (ou l'histoire d'un corps de guerriers au pays du royaume Hamite)," trans. P. Schumacher. In *Die Wiener Schule der Völkerkunde*, ed. J. Haekel, A. Hohenwart-Gerlachstein, and A. Slawik, 237–52. Horn-Wien: Verlag Ferdinand Berger, 1956.

Ntezimana, E. "L'arrivée des Européens au Kinyaga et la fin des royaumes Hutu du Bukunzi et du Busozo." *Etudes rwandaises* 13, 3 (1980): 1–29.

Ntezimana, E. "Coutumes et traditions des royaumes Hutu du Bukunzi et du Busozo." *Etudes rwandaises* 13, 2 (1980): 15–39.

Nyagahene, A. "Les activités économiques et commerciales du Kinyaga dans la séconde partie du XIXe siècle." Mémoire de Licence, UNR–Butare, 1979.

Oberg, K. "Kinship Organisation of the Banyankore." *Africa* 11 (1938): 129–38.

Oliver, R. "The Baganda and the Bakonjo." *Uganda Journal* 18, 1 (1954): 31–33.

Packard, R. M. *Chiefship and Cosmology: An Historical Study of Political Competition.* Bloomington: University of Indiana Press, 1981.

Packard, R. M. "The Politics of Ritual Control among the Bashu of Eastern Zaïre during the Nineteenth Century." Ph.D. diss., University of Wisconsin–Madison, 1976.

Pagès, A. *Au Ruanda. Sur les bords du Lac Kivu, Congo belge. Un royaume Hamite au centre de l'Afrique.* Bruxelles: IRCB, 1933.

Pauwels, M. "Le Bushiru et son *muhinza* ou roitelet Hutu." *Annali Lateranensi* 31 (1967): 205–322.

Pauwels, M. "Le pacte du sang au Rwanda." *Annali Lateranensi* 22 (1958): 9–40.

Portères, R. "African Cereals." In *The Origins of African Plant Domestication*, ed. J. Harlan, J. de Wet, and A. Stempler, 409–52. The Hague: Mouton, 1976.

Portères, R. "Berceaux agricoles primaires sur le continent africain." *Journal of African History* 3, 2 (1962): 195–210.

Purseglove, J. W. "The Origins and Migrations of Crops in Tropical Africa." In *The Origins of African Plant Domestication,* ed. J. Harlan, J. de Wet, and A. Stempler, 291–309. The Hague: Mouton, 1976.

Radcliffe-Brown, A. R. "A Further Note on Joking Relationships." *Africa* 19, 2 (1949): 133–40.

Radcliffe-Brown, A. R. "On Joking Relationships." *Africa* 13, 3 (1940): 195–210.

Ranger, T. O. *Dance and Society in Eastern Africa.* Berkeley: University of California Press, 1975.

Reisdorff, I. "Enquêtes foncières au Rwanda." Unpublished manuscript. Butare: Institut national de recherche scientifique, 1952.

Rennie, J. K. "The Precolonial Kingdom of Rwanda: A Reinterpretation." *Trans-african Journal of History* 2, 2 (1972): 11–53.

Roscoe, J. *The Banyankore.* Cambridge: Cambridge University Press, 1923.

Rugomana, J. "Inkuru y'Umuganuro uko wagira kera." Trans. F. M. Rodegem as "La fête des prémices au Burundi." *Africana Linguistica* 5 (1971): 207–54.

Rwabukumba, J., and V. Mudandagizi. "Les formes historiques de la dépendance personnelle dans l'état rwandais." *Cahiers d'études africaines* 14, 1 (1974): 6–25.

Sahlins, M. *Historical Metaphors and Mythical Realities: Structure in the Early History of the Sandwich Islands.* Ann Arbor: University of Michigan Press, 1981.

Sahlins, M. *Islands of History.* Chicago: University of Chicago Press, 1985.

Sahlins, M. "Other Times, Other Customs: The Anthropology of History." *American Anthropologist* 85, 3 (1983): 517–43.

Saucier, J.-F. "The Patron-Client Relationship in Traditional and Contemporary Southern Rwanda." Ph.D. diss., Columbia University, 1974.

Schlee, C. *Identities on the Move: Clanship and Pastoralism in Northern Kenya.* Manchester: Manchester University Press for the International African Institute, 1989.

Schlee, C. "Interethnic Clan Identities among Cushitic-speaking Pastoralists." *Africa* 55, 1 (1985): 17–38.

Schmidt, P. R. "A New Look at the Interpretations of the Early Iron Age of East Africa." *History in Africa* 2 (1975): 127–37.

Shackell, R. S. "Mweso—The Board Game." *Uganda Journal* 2, 1 (1934): 14–26.

Shingereje, V. "L'anti-roi Kilima ou l'échec d'une tentative dynastique du Burundi." Mémoire de Licence, Université du Burundi, 1982.

Sigwalt, Richard D. "The Early History of Bushi: An Essay in the Historical Use of Genesis Traditions." Ph.D. diss., University of Wisconsin–Madison, 1975.

Sigwalt, Richard D. "Early Rwanda History: The Contribution of Comparative Ethnograpy." *History in Africa* 2 (1975): 137–46.

Sigwalt, Richard D., and E. Sosne. "A Note on the Luzi of Bushi." *Etudes d'histoire africaine* 7 (1975): 137–41.

Simons, E. "Coutumes et institutions des Barundi." *Bulletin de juridictions indigènes et du droit coutumier congolais* 12 (1944): no. 7, 137–60; no. 8, 163–79; no. 9, 181–204; no. 10, 205–27; no. 11, 237–65; no. 12, 269–82.

Simoons, F. *Eat Not This Flesh.* Madison: University of Wisconsin Press, 1963.

Smets, G. "Funérailles et sépultures des *bami* et *bagabekazi* de l'Urundi." IRCB, *Bulletin des séances* 12, 2 (1941): 210–34.

Smets, G. "The Structure of the Barundi Society." *Man* 46, 6 (1946): 12–16.

Smets, G. "L'*Umuganuro* (fête du sorgho) chez les Barundi." In *Compte rendu de la deuxième session: Copenhague 1938,* Congrès International des Sciences Anthropologiques et Ethnologiques, 273–74. Copenhague: 1939.

Smith, P. "La forge de l'intelligence." *L'homme* 10, 2 (1970): 5–21.

Smith, P. "La lance d'une jeune fille. Mythe et poésie au Rwanda." In *Echanges et communications: Mélanges offerts à Claude Lévi-Strauss à l'occasion de son 60e anniversaire,* Vol 2, ed. J. Pouillon and P. Maranda, 1381–1408. La Haye: Mouton, 1970.

Smith, P. *Le récit populaire au Rwanda.* Paris: Armand Colin, 1975.

Sosne, E. D. "Kinship and Contract in Bushi: A Study in Village-Level Politics." Ph.D. diss., University of Wisconsin–Madison, 1974.

Sosne, E. D. "Colonial Peasantization and Contemporary Underdevelopment: A View from a Kivu Village." In *Zaire: The Political Economy of Underdevelopment,* ed. G. Gran, 189–210. New York: Praeger, 1979.

Southall, A. W. "The Illusion of Tribe." In *The Passing of Tribal Man in Africa,* ed. P. C. W. Gutkind, 28–51. Leiden: Brill, 1970.

Taussig, M. *The Devil and Commodity Fetishism in South America.* Chapel Hill: University of North Carolina Press, 1980.

Tawney, J. J. "Ugabire: A Feudal Custom amongst the Waha," *Tanzania Notes and Records* 17 (1944), 6–9.

Taylor, B. K. *The Western Lacustrine Bantu.* London: International African Institute, 1962.

Thompson, E. P. *The Making of the English Working Class.* Harmondsworth: Penguin, 1968; originally published 1963.

Tosh, J. *Clan Leaders and Colonial Chiefs in Lango: The Political History of an East African Stateless Society, c. 1890–1939.* Oxford: Clarendon, 1978.

Townshend, P. "Les jeux de Mankala au Zaïre, au Rwanda et au Burundi." *Les Cahiers du CEDAF* (1977, 3).

Traube, E. *Cosmology and Social Life: Ritual Exchange among the Mambai of East Timor.* Chicago: University of Chicago Press, 1986.

Tripe, W. B. "The Death and Replacement of a Divine King in Uha." *Man* 39, 21 (1939): 22–25.

Tripe, W. B. "The Installation *(kusamwa)* of the Chief of Uha." *Man* 35, 54, (1935): 53–56.

Trouwborst, A. A. "Le Burundi." In *Les anciens royaumes de la zone interlacustre méridionale,* ed. M. d'Hertefelt, A. A. Trouwborst, and J. H. Scherer, 113–69. Tervuren: MRAC, 1962.

Trouwborst, A. A. "La mobilité de l'individu en fonction de l'organisation politique des Barundi." *Zaïre* 13, 8 (1959): 787–800.

Trouwborst, A. A. "L'organisation politique en tant que système d'échanges au Burundi." *Anthropologica,* n.s. 3, 1 (1961): 65–81.

Trouwborst, A. A. "L'organisation politique et l'accord de clientèle au Burundi." *Anthropologica,* n.s. 4, 1 (1962): 9–43.

Turnbull, C. *The Forest People.* Garden City: Doubleday for the American Museum of Natural History, 1962.

Turnbull, C. *Wayward Servants: The Two Worlds of the African Pygmies.* Garden City: Natural History Press, 1965.

Vail, L., ed. *The Creation of Tribalism in Southern Africa.* London: James Currey, 1989.

Van Bulck, S. J. *Les recherches linguistiques au Congo Belge.* Bruxelles: Librarie Falk, G. van Campehout, 1948.

Van der Burgt, J. M. M. *Un grand peuple de l'Afrique équatoriale: Eléments d'une mono-*

graphie sur l'Urundi. Bois-le-Duc, Nederland: Société l'Illustration catholique, 1903.

Van Geluwe, H. *Les Bira et les peuplades limitrophes.* Tervuren: MRAC, 1957.

Van Grunderbeek, M. C., and E. R. U. Doutrelepont. "L'âge du fer ancien au Rwanda et au Burundi: Archéologie et environnement." *Journal des africanistes* 52, 1–2 (1982): 5–58.

Van Noten, F. L. "The Early Iron Age in the Interlacustrine Region: The Diffusion of Iron Technology." *Azania* 14 (1979): 61–80.

Van Noten, F. L. "Excavations at Matupi Cave." *Antiquity* 51 (1977): 35–40.

Van Noten, F. L. *Histoire archéologique du Rwanda.* Tervuren: MRAC, 1983.

Van Noten, F. L. *Les tombes du roi Cyirima Rujugira et de la reine-mère Nyirayuhi Kanjogera: Description archéologique.* Tervuren: MRAC, 1972.

Van Noten, F. L., ed. *The Archeology of Central Africa.* Graz, Austria: Akademische Druck-und-Verlagsanstalt, 1982.

Vansina, J. "Deep-Down Time: Political Tradition in Central Africa." *History in Africa* 16 (1989): 341–62.

Vansina, J. *L'évolution du royaume Rwanda dès origines à 1900.* Bruxelles: ARSOM, 1962.

Vansina, J. "L'homme, les forêts et le passé en Afrique." *Annales: économies, sociétés, civilisations* 6 (1985): 1307–34.

Vansina, J. "L'influence du mode de compréhension historique d'une civilisation sur ses traditions d'origine: L'exemple Kuba." *Bulletin ARSOM,* n.s. 19 (1973): 220–40.

Vansina, J. "Introduction," in *Les anciens royaumes de la zone Interlacustre méridionale,* ed. M. d'Hertefelt, A. Trouwborst, and J. Scherer, 3–7. Tervuren: MRAC, 1962.

Vansina, J. *Introduction à l'ethnographie du Congo.* Kinshasa: Editions Universitaires du Congo, 1966.

Vansina, J. "Knowledge and Perceptions of the African Past" In *African Historiographies,* ed. B. Jewsiewecki and D. Newbury, 28–42. Beverly Hills: Sage, 1986.

Vansina, J. *La légende du passé: Traditions orales du Burundi.* Tervuren: MRAC, 1972.

Vansina, J. "Lignage, idéologie, et histoire en Afrique équatoriale." *Enquêtes et documents de l'histoire africaine* 4 (1980): 133–56.

Vansina, J. "Note sur la chronologie du Burundi ancien." *Bulletin de l'Académie royale des sciences d'Outre-Mer* 38 (1967): 429–44.

Vansina, J. "Notes sur l'histoire du Burundi." *Aequatoria* 14, 1 (1961): 1–10.

Vansina, J. "Once upon a Time: Oral Traditions as History in Africa." *Daedalus* 100, 2 (1971): 442–68.

Vansina, J. *Oral Tradition.* Chicago: Aldine, 1965; first published as *De la tradition orale,* Tervuren: MRAC, 1961.

Vansina, J. *Paths in the Rainforests: Toward a History of Political Tradition in Equatorial Africa.* Madison: University of Wisconsin Press, 1990.

Vansina, J. "The Peoples of the Forest," in *History of Central Africa,* Vol. 1, ed. D. Birmingham and P. Martin, 75–118. London: Longman, 1983.

Vansina, J. "The Power of Systematic Doubt in Historical Inquiry." *History in Africa* 1 (1974): 109–27.

Vansina, J. "Towards a History of Lost Corners of the World." *Economic History Review* 35, 2 (1982): 165–78.

Vansina, J. "Traditions of Genesis." *Journal of African History* 15, 2 (1974): 317–22.

Vansina, J. "The Use of Ethnographic Data as Sources for History." In *Emergent Themes in African History,* ed. T. O. Ranger, 97–124. London: Heinemann, 1968.

Vansina, J. "The Use of Oral Tradition in African Culture History." In *Reconstructing African Culture History,* ed. C. Gabel and N. R. Bennett, 57–82. Boston: Boston University Press, 1967.

Vansina, J. "The Use of Process Models in African History." In *The Historian in Tropical Africa,* ed. J. Vansina, R. Mauny, and L. V. Thomas. London: Oxford University Press for the International African Institute, 1964.

Van Walle, R. "Aspecten van Staatsvorming in West Rwanda." *Africa-Tervuren* 28, 3 (1982): 64–77.

Verdonck (FungaFunga). "District du Kivu, Territoire du Buhavu: Décès du Mwami Rushombo: Intronisation du Mwami Bahole." *Congo* 1, 3 (1928): 294–309.

Viaene, L. "Coup d'oeil sur la littérature orale des Bahunde." *Kongo-Overzee* 21, 3–4 (1955): 212–40.

Viaene, L. "Coup d'oeil sur la vie intellectuelle des Bahunde." *Kongo-Overzee* 22, 4–5 (1956): 360–83.

Viaene, L. "Essai de monographie des Bahavu." Unpublished manuscript, CELA, Bukavu, n.d. (1961?).

Viaene, L. "L'organisation politique des Bahunde." *Kongo-Overzee* 18 (1952): Part 1 in no. 1, 8–34; Part 2 in no. 2–3, 111–21.

Viaene, L. "La religion des Bahunde (Kivu)." *Kongo-Overzee* 18, 5 (1952): 388–425.

Viaene, L. "La vie domestique des Bahunde (Nord-Est du Kivu)." *Kongo-Overzee* 12, 2 (1951): 111–56.

Vidal, C. "Anthropologie et histoire: Le cas du Rwanda." *Cahiers internationaux de sociologie* 43, 2 (1967): 143–57.

Vidal, C. "Economie de la société féodale rwandaise." *Cahiers d'études africaines* 14, 1 (1974): 52–74.

Vidal, C. "Le Rwanda des anthropologues ou le fétichisme de la vache." *Cahiers d'études africaines* 9, 3 (1969): 384–401.

Vis, H. L. "Situation nutritionalle dans le Bushi et le Buhavu (notes préliminaires)." *Chronique de l'IRSAC* 2, 1 (1967).

Vis, H. L., et al. "La situation nutritionnelle au Bushi et au Buhavu: Etude de la consommation alimentaire." Mimeo, IRSAC, Zaire.

Weis, G. *Le pays d'Uvira.* Bruxelles: ARSOM, 1959.

Winter, E. "The Aboriginal Political Structure of Bwamba." In *Tribes Without Rulers,* ed. J. Middleton and D. Tait, 136–66. London: Routledge and Kegan Paul, 1958.

Winter, E. *Beyond the Mountains of the Moon: The Lives of Four Africans.* Urbana: University of Illinois Press, 1959.

Winter, E. *Bwamba Economy.* Kampala: East African Institute of Social Research, 1955.

Wolf, Eric. *Europe and the People Without History.* Berkeley: University of California Press, 1982.

Yogolelo Tambwe ya Kasimba. "Essai d'interprétation du cliché de Kangere dans la région des Grands Lacs africains. *Journal of African History,* 31, 3 (1990), 353–72.

Yogolelo Tambwe ya Kasimba. "Introduction à l'histoire des Lega: Problèmes et Méthode." *Les Cahiers du CEDAF* (1975, 5).

Young, M. C. "Nationalism, Ethnicity, and Class in Africa: A Retrospective." *Cahiers d'études africaines* 26, 4 (1986): 421–95.

Young, M. C. *Politics in the Congo.* Princeton: Princeton University Press, 1965.

Young, M. C. *The Politics of Cultural Pluralism.* Madison: University of Wisconsin Press, 1978.

Zuure, B. *Croyances et pratiques religieuses des Barundi.* Bruxelles: Bibliothèque Congo, 1929.

Index